More Praise for the second edition of
Discipline Survival Guide for the Secondary Teacher

"In my first year as a New York City Public School teacher, I utilized Thompson's helpful thoughts on how to be a more effective educator. Her common-sense advice for teachers is a breath of fresh air. Applied consistently, the principles in this book will help every teacher perfect their craft by addressing the most important factor in teaching: classroom discipline. If you are looking for real tools that you can use to make the most of your and your students' time, this book is for you!"

—*Adam Kofod,* classroom teacher, Petaluma, CA

"After a tough power struggle with a student in my classroom, Julia Thompson helped me calmly implement different methods based on student behavior to cool the situation, rather than have it escalate beyond repair. Her book provides a series of different strategies to engage in with students, since in many cases the first strategy used may not work. Thompson also teaches us to find the positive in students. When I let students and their parents know about the positive aspects of their work and behavior—instead of just problems—it creates a better working relationship."

—*Michele Sambiase,* secondary teacher, Fairfax County Public Schools, VA

"Julia G. Thompson has packed so much valuable information about student discipline into her new book that it could stand alone as the only resource a teacher needs."

—*Jill Hare,* editor, TheApple.com

Praise for *The First-Year Teacher's Survival Guide*

"Julia Thompson earns an A+ for her practical and comprehensive *First-Year Teacher's Survival Guide.* This veteran educator skillfully provides effective classroom-tested strategies to guide the new teacher through the possible problems and potentially stressful situations often encountered during that memorable first year of teaching. . . . *The First-Year Teacher's Survival Guide* should be required reading for all new teachers!"

—*Jack Umstatter,* veteran teacher of thirty-five years
and educational consultant, Islip, New York

"I can't think of anything this guide doesn't have! . . . Thompson's *The First-Year Teacher's Survival Guide* will prove to be an invaluable tool for new teachers. Seasoned teachers will love it for its new and innovative ideas. I would have one available for each teacher on opening day!"

—*Gloria Smith,* early childhood staff developer,
District 7, Bronx, New York

"This book is like having a personal mentor to guide new teachers through the demanding process of becoming educators. Experienced teachers will also find fresh insight that can transform effective instruction from instinctive to intentional."

—*Elisabeth H. Fuller,* coordinator of grants, budget, and resources,
Isle of Wight County Schools, Virginia

Jossey-Bass Teacher

Jossey-Bass Teacher provides educators with practical knowledge and tools to create a positive and lifelong impact on student learning. We offer classroom-tested and research-based teaching resources for a variety of grade levels and subject areas. Whether you are an aspiring, new, or veteran teacher, we want to help you make every teaching day your best.

From ready-to-use classroom activities to the latest teaching framework, our value-packed books provide insightful, practical, and comprehensive materials on the topics that matter most to K–12 teachers. We hope to become your trusted source for the best ideas from the most experienced and respected experts in the field.

Discipline Survival Guide for the Secondary Teacher

Secondary Teacher

SECOND EDITION

JULIA G. THOMPSON

JOSSEY-BASS
A Wiley Imprint
www.josseybass.com

Published by Jossey-Bass
A Wiley Imprint
989 Market Street, San Francisco, CA 94103-1741—www.josseybass.com

Jossey-Bass books and products are available through most bookstores. To contact Jossey-Bass directly call our Customer Care Department within the U.S. at 800-956-7739, outside the U.S. at 317-572-3986, or fax 317-572-4002.

Jossey-Bass also publishes its books in a variety of electronic formats. Some content that appears in print may not be available in electronic books.

Library of Congress Cataloging-in-Publication Data

Thompson, Julia G.
    Discipline survival guide for the secondary teacher / Julia G. Thompson.—2nd ed.
        p. cm.—(J-b ed: survival guides; 161)
    Includes index.
    ISBN 978-0-470-54743-4 (pbk.)
        1. Classroom management.   2. Education, Secondary.   3. Teacher effectiveness.   4. Teacher-student relationships.   I. Title.
    LB3013.T56 2010
    373.1102′4—dc22
                                                                            2010013835

Printed in the United States of America
SECOND EDITION
PB Printing   10 9 8 7 6 5 4 3 2 1

About This Book

If you teach, you will have discipline problems. In fact, discipline problems in today's secondary classrooms are so prevalent and disruptive that in survey after survey teachers report that their frustrations with discipline issues are the most unpleasant part of their profession. The failure to manage a classroom successfully is often the reason that even the most dedicated teachers leave education for a less stressful career.

If you are a teacher who has faced challenging and discouraging discipline problems, the second edition of *Discipline Survival Guide for the Secondary Teacher* has been written specifically for you. You will find valuable, classroom-tested advice on how to adopt a comprehensive approach to discipline as you work to create a positive classroom environment. You will learn how to help your students become self-disciplined, goal-oriented, successful learners as you hone your skills and enhance your charisma as a classroom leader.

Each section of *Discipline Survival Guide for the Secondary Teacher* offers a variety of sound ideas and teaching tools designed to enable you to apply the most up-to-date theories and research about crucial topics such as student motivation, classroom management systems, teacher-student relationships, effective instructional techniques, student safety, and the importance of high expectations. This book also provides workable suggestions about how to prevent discipline issues from disrupting the learning climate in your classroom. As you work through each section, you will also find reproducible activities for your students, forms to help you efficiently organize your school day, and opportunities to reflect on your strengths as an educator. The realistic support and invaluable guidance within each section will enable you to create an orderly, positive, productive classroom where all of your students can learn and succeed.

About the Author

Best-selling author Julia G. Thompson has been a public school teacher for more than thirty years. She has taught a wide variety of subjects, including English, reading, special education, math, geography, home economics, physical education, and employment skills. Her students have ranged from reluctant seventh graders to gifted college students. Thompson currently teaches in Fairfax County, Virginia, and she is an active speaker and consultant. Author of *The First-Year Teacher's Survival Guide* and *The First-Year Teacher's Checklist*, she also publishes a Web site that offers tips for teachers on a variety of subjects. As a classroom expert, Thompson also provides discipline advice as "Dear Julia" at TheApple (www.theapple.monster.com) and at TeacherAdvice@Twitter.com. To learn more, go to www.juliagthompson.com.

Acknowledgments

I am especially grateful to my editor, Marjorie McAneny, for her insight, guidance, and patient support during the preparation of this book.

Special thanks to the teachers who take time to write e-mails that share their struggles and triumphs as they strive to help their students reach for a bright future. Their unshakable belief in the power of an education serves as inspiration for us all.

CONTENTS

Section Seven: Create and Maintain a Partnership with Students' Families   149

Section Eight: Establish a Cooperative Classroom Climate   167

Section Nine: Maintain Order with Effective Instruction   197

Section Ten: Promote Achievement and Learning   243

For Phil, with gratitude, admiration, and love

Introduction

A great deal has changed in secondary classrooms since *Discipline Survival Kit for the Secondary Teacher* was first published. In the intervening years our classrooms have expanded to include an increasingly diverse population as immigrants from across the world send their children to schools unprepared for a large influx of nonnative speakers. The troubling decrease in the literacy rate continues to cause concern as educators strive to help students whose inadequate reading and critical thinking skills result in record poor standardized test scores and low graduation rates. The global economic downturn has also had a detrimental effect on schools as funds for much-needed improvements, training, and equipment have all but vanished in many districts. In perhaps the most heartbreaking turn of events, incidents of horrific school violence have instilled an unprecedented sense of fear in teachers and students alike. And not surprisingly, in recent years the teacher shortage has become more and more severe as educators opt for less-challenging careers.

In spite of the troubles that our profession has weathered since the first publication of *Discipline Survival Kit for the Secondary Teacher*, there have also been many noteworthy positive changes. Dedicated researchers have teamed with classroom teachers to develop instructional strategies that focus on reaching the needs of all learners. Ongoing research has taught us a great deal about how to apply the knowledge that we now have about how the human brain functions and how we can help our students learn. Even with a lack of funds, teachers still involve themselves in professional development activities. With professional reading, online courses, study groups, online forums, and independent studies, we strive to learn as much as we can from our colleagues and other experts in our profession. The rapid growth of personal technological resources has made it easier for us to access information easily. With just a few keystrokes, we can discuss classroom issues with teachers in other parts of the world, find innovative lesson plans, research the best way to decorate our classrooms, and even share stress-relieving laughter over humorous classroom incidents. Finally, the Internet has become an indispensable classroom tool as more and more students have access to computers.

Even though a great deal has changed for secondary teachers both for better and worse in the last few years, much has remained the same. Many teachers across our country are coping beautifully with the recent, anxiety-provoking changes in education. These teachers manage their students' difficult behavior with skill and grace. Their students are successful, and they themselves find a great deal of personal satisfaction in the positive learning environment that they have established in their classrooms.

The dreams that they had when they chose education as a career are everyday realities. These secondary teachers have found successful ways to help their students become self-motivated and self-disciplined.

The *Discipline Survival Guide for the Secondary Teacher* provides a useful desktop reference filled with essential techniques and strategies necessary to manage the wide range of problems and responsibilities related to discipline in the secondary classroom. It serves as a practical guide to solving many of the behavior management problems that secondary teachers encounter each day. The timely, school-tested solutions in the *Discipline Survival Guide for the Secondary Teacher* help you develop a classroom climate where cooperative students can focus on positive behaviors rather than negative ones. Experienced and novice teachers alike will find strategies, activities, tips, and tools that provide solutions to many of the frustrating problems involved in managing student behavior.

Specifically, the goals of this Guide are to

- Allow you to be in control of your class
- Help you create the kind of motivational environment where mannerly conduct and successful learning are the order of the day
- Use the technological resources available to you and your students
- Provide some solutions for the problems caused by the rapid changes brought about by technology
- Use instructional strategies appropriate for all learners
- Help you develop your classroom leadership skills
- Provide you with up-to-date solutions to some of the most common discipline problems that are unique to secondary classrooms
- Save you time with an array of easy-to-use charts, forms, checklists, and reproducible materials
- Help you guide students toward more successful collaborative relationships with you and with each other
- Help you create a productive learning environment where you and your students can feel a sense of safety and belonging
- Enable you to reduce disruptions and effectively manage student behavior
- Help you motivate your students to take the initiative for their own learning
- Increase your confidence in your ability to find the satisfaction that a career in education can bring

Within the Guide are a broad range of topics designed to help teachers move beyond controlling a crowd of unruly adolescents to teaching a group of self-disciplined students who love learning. The information in each section helps you meet the challenges that your students bring to school each day. For example:

Section One: Accept responsibility for creating the positive discipline climate that you want for your students.

Section Two: Begin the process of designing your personal discipline plan using the most effective discipline practices available to you.

Section Three: Develop your full potential as a classroom leader.

Section Four: Use three key elements to establish a positive classroom environment.

Section Five: Begin the process of moving your students toward becoming self-disciplined learners.

Section Six: Develop and implement effective classroom management systems.

Section Seven: Establish a productive relationship with the families of your students.

Section Eight: Cultivate a classroom climate where students work in harmony with each other and with you.

Section Nine: Design and deliver effective instruction that encourages students to stay on-task for the duration of the class.

Section Ten: Use a variety of motivational techniques to help students achieve.

Section Eleven: Prevent discipline problems with a variety of strategies.

Section Twelve: React appropriately once misbehavior has occurred in your classroom.

Busy secondary teachers can use this resource in many ways. You can browse through it section by section, gathering ideas to fit your own classroom situation. You could use the table of contents to find advice quickly in a particular section that addresses a concern you have at the moment. Or you can use this Guide to analyze the discipline problems happening in your classroom. The most effective use of the information in these pages, however, would be to enable you to create the kind of positive classroom environment where the teacher is in control and where students are engaged in the enjoyable process of becoming lifelong learners.

SECTION ONE

Successful Discipline
Rests with You

✓ **In this section you will learn**

- How to accept responsibility for establishing a positive discipline climate
- How to select effective discipline strategies
- How to allow students to make appropriate choices
- How to anticipate student behavior patterns
- How to use proactive attitudes to help students be successful

YOU CAN MAKE A DIFFERENCE

This is a book about classroom discipline. This is not a book about lesson plans or grading papers or writing objectives on the board each day. It's not about taking attendance or delivering lectures or even about designing fair test questions.

Instead, it is about an issue far more puzzling and complex than any of these. It's about being sent to the principal and sassing the teacher and passing notes in class. It's also about teen substance abuse and bullies and students who bring weapons to school.

These problems have plagued teachers for as long as students have been coming to school. If you have discipline problems during the school year, take heart. Everyone who teaches does. *Everyone*.

We long for a positive discipline climate in our classes. Everything runs smoothly when that happens. We teach well. Our students learn what we want them to learn. The school day is a joyful, satisfying experience. When the climate is a negative one, however, even our best lesson plans are useless. We can't teach because our students are too disruptive to pay attention. We do not enjoy these frustrating days. We endure them. Our students do, too.

With this in mind, it's understandable that the word *discipline* usually has an unpleasant connotation for most of us. Our hearts sink at the thought of coping with discipline issues. We tend to think of *discipline* in the same way we think of the word *misbehavior*: discipline referral, disciplinary detention, or being sent to the office for disciplinary action.

Discipline in this book is not a negative. Quite the opposite is true. In this book the word *discipline* means the systematic and positive training you provide for your students to help them develop self-control. It is the means by which we have orderly classrooms and high-achieving students.

Fortunately, the discipline dilemma that all teachers face has solutions. We can take control of our classes. We can have a positive learning environment in our classrooms.

This book offers a wide variety of ways to create a peaceful and productive classroom. It's about how to manage the students in your class with sensitivity and dignity so that there is harmony in your classroom instead of strife.

This book is also about the most important factor in the discipline dilemma: the teacher. Never doubt that you make a difference in the lives of your students. In many ways teachers are the most idealistic people in our communities. While other adults see a group of teens loitering on the sidewalk just wasting time, we teachers don't seem to notice the silly clothing and too-cool hairstyles. Instead, we see the future.

We see what others cannot: potential doctors, teachers, accountants, lawyers, soldiers . . . our colleagues-in-waiting. Perhaps it is this gift that makes us struggle in the face of so many obstacles to help our students become the people we know they can be.

ACCEPT RESPONSIBILITY

Establishing a positive classroom discipline environment is a complex undertaking. It can cover issues as insignificant as dealing with a lost pencil or a talkative student to more serious ones such as incomplete assignments, cheating, and weapons at school. Creating a positive classroom discipline climate is a challenging task that demands that students operate within carefully constructed boundaries while, at the same time, developing into independent and self-disciplined learners.

The difficult and complex nature of classroom discipline issues is the result of several significant factors. Classroom discipline practices vary widely from region to region, district to district, and even from teacher to teacher. Discipline practices are also affected by the ages, abilities, personalities, maturity levels, backgrounds, and interests of the students they govern.

To further complicate matters, a classroom discipline climate is an ever-shifting environment where the naturally occurring daily changes that happen as students learn and mature influence discipline practices.

Because of the fluid nature of classroom discipline, no magic bullet exists. There is not a perfect solution that will work in every classroom all the time. Instead, teachers today must do what sensible teachers everywhere have always done: craft discipline plans uniquely designed to create a comfortable, businesslike, and safe learning climate where their students can achieve academic success.

The responsibility for a successful discipline climate rests with the classroom teacher. Although too many of us blame our students, their families, the school board, or even society for the discipline problems we encounter, the ultimate responsibility for creating a productive classroom is ours.

If we are the ones who are responsible for the discipline climate in our classrooms, then we are the ones who can make positive and effective choices to help our students. When we assume responsibility for the discipline climate in our classes, then we also gain the power to make positive changes.

Luckily for those teachers who accept this responsibility, the skills necessary to create a positive discipline climate can be learned. If we want to provide an atmosphere for achievement where we engage our students in actively acquiring knowledge through cooperation and motivated hard work, then we must realize that we are the keys to their success. Students will respond positively to our personalities, our energy, our enthusiasm, and our charisma.

Accepting this responsibility does not mean that a career in education becomes any easier; we still face unique problems. We have little or no chance for advancement and many of us are poorly paid. We are seldom recognized publicly for our hard work. Parents and principals may be grateful, but they don't knock on our classroom doors every day to tell us what a good job we are doing.

Teachers who decide to develop positive relationships with their students, who decide to use alternatives to punishments and threats, who decide to cope with the problems that we all share become successful teachers who are free to make positive changes because they have accepted responsibility for their actions.

YOU ARE NOT ALONE

Take comfort in the thought that you are not alone with your discipline problems. We *all* experience them, even those teachers who seem to have well-disciplined classes. Successful teachers *do* have discipline problems just like the rest of us, but they have found ways to minimize their negative impact.

Many of our discipline problems, surprisingly enough, are not directly caused by our students. Here is a list of some of the many factors that can have a negative impact on your classroom performance:

- Overcrowded classes
- Too little productive time with students
- Students with overwhelming family problems
- Ineffective local discipline policies
- Overworked and unsympathetic administrators
- Parents or guardians who do not support school personnel and policies
- Parents or guardians who are unreachable or difficult to contact
- Buildings that need repairs and better maintenance
- Colleagues whose problems with classroom management spill over into our classes
- Uncertainty over the right action to take when problems occur
- Outdated textbooks, equipment, and other materials
- Teacher distress and burnout

In addition to the negative factors that can affect classrooms, many positive factors can also help you create the classroom that you would like for your students. Here is a list of those influences that have a positive bearing on your classroom performance:

- Economic status, race, and gender are no longer the barriers to education that they once were.
- School districts continue to develop a variety of programs designed to meet the unique needs of every student. We no longer offer a one-size-fits-all version of education.

- Today we know more than ever about which teaching methods are effective in helping our students learn. Research-based learning strategies and differentiated instruction are just two of the positive methods that are changing how we teach.

- Many private businesses and foundations recognize the need for assistance in public education and are generous in their support.

- Teachers are better prepared than ever to assume their professional responsibilities. Professional development opportunities abound both locally and on the Internet. New teachers have become one of our best resources.

- Technology makes it easier for us to be better teachers. We can reach out to students and their families in a variety of ways, learn new information, access lesson plan ideas from thousands of other teachers, and keep abreast with the latest news and trends in our field with just a few keystrokes.

WHY PUNISHMENT AND OTHER INEFFECTIVE DISCIPLINE TECHNIQUES DO NOT WORK

Teachers who want to create a well-disciplined class realize they cannot do this by using outdated practices. It is only natural that we tend to model our teaching styles on the experiences we had in school. We want to re-create for our students the positive experiences that we enjoyed. We want to inspire them as we were inspired. We want to shape their lives as school shaped ours.

But in our attempts to do this, we sometimes re-create the negative experiences that we had in school as well. Punishment is used far too often in public schools today. It is, in fact, the most often-used discipline practice in secondary schools across our nation.

Punishment is a historical tradition in child rearing. We have been taught that if we "spare the rod," we will "spoil the child," even though research has shown time and time again that spanking has an adverse effect on almost every child. Yet very few adults can say they were never spanked when they were children.

Another reason that punishment is used in schools is that both parents and children expect it. Teachers who decide never to resort to punishment may seem to be too nice or too weak to be effective classroom leaders.

The problem is that punishment often does work—in the short run. If you want to establish brief control of a class, setting an example by punishing one pupil will quickly cause the others to sit up and take notice that you mean business. Many of us can recall embarrassing moments at the hands of an insensitive teacher. Most of us can also clearly remember an unfair incident in a class long after we have forgotten the weighty content of the course.

Many adults look back with nostalgic fondness on particular teachers who were very strict. These tough teachers held their students to very high standards of conduct and taught their subject matter thoroughly and well. Class reunions abound with fond stories about these respected teachers. More careful consideration, however, indicates that those tough teachers are revered only if they were caring, knowledgeable, and fair as well as strict.

If the modeling that we attempt for our students includes crowd control mainly through punishment and the fear of punishment, then it is not likely that we will be successful in creating the kind of positive classroom environment that we want. Rising dropout rates and the increase in the numbers of at-risk students are only two indications that we need to move away from discipline practices that are mainly punitive to take a more humane approach to our students.

WHAT YOU SHOULD KNOW ABOUT ADOLESCENTS

The turbulent adolescent years are marked by erratic growth and unpredictable changes. The turmoil of these years produces students who need understanding, reasonable, and compassionate teachers. Although making broad generalizations about any group is a risky business, many secondary students share some relevant character traits. These traits can have a significant impact on the success or failure of classroom discipline policies.

In the following list, you will find a few of these shared adolescent character traits, together with the chief challenge each one poses for the classroom teacher. This will be followed by three brief suggestions for making sure that each character trait can have a positive effect on your classroom.

Peer Pressure Is Intense for Teens

It is no surprise to teachers that teens are greatly influenced by their peers. Adolescents turn to their peers for support and guidance. Unfortunately, the guidance they receive is not always beneficial.

The Challenge

To give students the positive values that will enable them to resist negative peer pressure.

How Teachers Can Help

▶ Create positive identities for all of your students by including team-building exercises in collaborative work so that students can learn to work together in a positive way for a common goal.

▶ Create positive peer pressure by allowing students to participate in the creation of class rules, policies, and procedures. Involving students in this process will encourage them to work together to enforce them.

▶ Bring in brief articles for class discussions about positive values that would benefit your students. Use them to discuss the choices they make about almost every aspect of their lives and the positive and negative outcomes of those choices. You can extend the impact of these discussions by displaying these articles on a bulletin board. They will serve as visual reminders of the values you want your students to develop.

A Teenager's Emotional Energy Is High

The world of adolescence is a technicolored one. Emotions and experiences that are familiar to most adults are brand-new for your students. This makes teens easily impressionable, sensitive, moody, and excitable.

The Challenge

To channel this intensity into productive outlets.

▶ Build in class activities that allow students to be active and involved. Role-playing, panel discussions, and games are positive ways to begin.

▶ Use the time that might be wasted at the end of class for a forum to discuss teens' current concerns. Even a brief discussion can give your students some options other than the unacceptable responses they might make to events in their lives.

▶ Adjust your own attitude. Learn to view adolescents as joyful and vigorous rather than annoying. Laugh with them. Use that mixture of relief and nostalgia that you feel when you recall your own teen years as a guide to understanding your students.

Having Fun Is Very Important to Secondary Students

The competition that many educators feel with the entertainment value of popular culture, the Internet, the music industry, and television is real. Many students, used to attractive and fast-paced entertainment, grow restless when they are expected to concentrate for a long time.

The Challenge

To engage our students' attention fully for an entire class period.

How Teachers Can Help

▶ Divide lesson plans into ten-minute blocks of time and include several shorter activities in a lesson.

▶ Use a variety of activities to make class interesting for yourself and for your students. Don't be afraid to be creative and a little off-the-wall in your approach.

▶ Include music, art, and other areas of popular culture in your lessons. Have students fill out questionnaires to find out their interests. (See Section Eight for student interest inventories.)

Secondary Students Don't Always Use Time Wisely

Students in the secondary grades are very busy people. They have after-school jobs, active social lives, and a dizzying round of family, sports, and community activities. Even though they may fill their days with numerous activities, many teens tend to choose activities that offer short-term gains rather than long-lasting benefits.

The Challenge

To guide students in making wise use of their time.

► Watch out for the signs of trouble—sleepiness, inattention, or poor performance in class—and talk with the student. If the problem persists, contact the student's parents or guardians for help.

► Work with your students to help them set both long-term and short-term goals for themselves. Help them determine what activities need to take priority if they are to reach their goals.

► Focus on time-management techniques to help students stay on track. Show your students how to use a daily planner, a syllabus, and a personal calendar.

Adolescents Want Their Schooling to Have a Practical Purpose

Secondary students are intensely pragmatic about the work they are assigned in school. Vague assurances that "You will need this when you get to college" just do not provide the relevance that many students need to do their best work.

The Challenge

To make students understand why they need to learn the material in a lesson.

How Teachers Can Help

► Follow sound educational theory and design lessons around a clearly stated objective. Use this to motivate your students to want to learn the material. Make sure that you yourself know how and why they will need this information. Just because it is part of your district's curriculum is not a convincing reason.

► Include as many real-world applications for the knowledge and skills that you teach as you can. Build in the connections to past learning and to what the students have learned in other classes.

► At the end of class, ask students to brainstorm ways that they can use the material in the day's lesson before the next class meeting.

Adolescents Do Not Want Absolute Freedom

Secondary students need and want guidance from caring adults. They need positive role models who will show them how to build constructive relationships with others and how to manage the sometimes troubled course of their lives.

The Challenge

To provide support and guidance for a large group of needy young people.

▶ Be a positive role model. Studies have shown that positive and helpful teachers tend to create positive and helpful students. Modeling stable behavior is a good way to begin.

▶ Set reasonable limits on the behaviors you will and will not tolerate. When your students test those limits, you have an opportunity to teach them—by your example—how to set limits for themselves.

▶ Be accessible for your students. Plan time after school when you can meet with students or sponsor a school organization. Above all, be a friendly adult who cares about their concerns.

Insecurity Is a Far-Reaching Problem

Even the toughest adolescents are not always as sure of themselves as they would like us to think. Their confidence is a thin shell that is easily cracked by failure or the fear of failure.

The Challenge

To make students feel more confident about their ability to succeed in school.

How Teachers Can Help

▶ Involve all of your students in your lessons. Many students have learned the fine art of being invisible in a classroom. Be sensitive to their fears and shyness, but get students engaged in positive activities where they can succeed.

▶ Be positive with your students. Focus on their good points. Make sure you let them know about the good things they do. Students have no reason to try harder if a cranky teacher is going to criticize them needlessly.

▶ Begin a unit of study with activities that are easier to complete successfully than the ones later in the unit. When students see they can accomplish the work, they tend to try harder to complete assignments.

Mistakes Usually Arise from Inexperience

Contrary to what we may believe on a day when nothing is going right, our students do not get out of bed with the intention of failing our class and upsetting as many people as possible in the process. Students miscalculate the amount of time that it will take to complete a project, or they say the wrong thing to the wrong person at the wrong time. These errors and countless others like them are made by young people who are trying to figure out the complicated business of living.

The Challenge

To reduce the negative effects of the mistakes that students make.

► Spend time each day showing students how to do their assignments. Many of them need to practice such skills as breaking down a long-term project into manageable sections, previewing a reading passage, or following directions.

► Teach your students that mistakes are part of living. We all make them. Be quick to apologize when you make yours. You will set a good example if you do.

► Be patient. Try not to overreact. Consider whether the error was intentional or accidental. There is a big difference, for example, between a swear word whispered to another student in the back of the room and one shouted at you.

Teens Need to Be Treated as Worthwhile People

Our students want the same things other humans want: to be taken seriously. Handling discipline problems in as dignified a manner as possible will show your students that you value and respect them.

The Challenge

To foster mutual respect through courtesy.

How Teachers Can Help

► Refuse to fall into the trap of backing a misbehaving student into an emotional corner. Do not become confrontational if you want to treat your students with respect.

► Never belittle a student's hairstyle, manner of dress, way of speaking, ideas, beliefs, aspirations, or any other personal quality. There is a big difference between correcting a student's error in a professional manner and making fun of that student.

► Listen to your students. One of the best ways to connect with your students is to allow them to talk to you, a caring adult.

HOW MUCH AUTONOMY SHOULD YOU ALLOW?

One of the most puzzling challenges confronting teachers in secondary schools is how to determine just the right amount of autonomy to allow students. While many teens are mature enough to independently manage their social and academic responsibilities, almost every class has students who require more support, encouragement, redirection, and intervention than others.

There are many factors to consider when making decisions about just how much freedom to allow students. Two of the most obvious ones are the age and general maturity level of the students in a particular class. For example, twelfth graders should be capable of more independence than younger students.

Another aspect to consider is the length of time that you have known your students. At the beginning of a school term, it is wise to be conservative in your approach. As you get to know your students, then you can confidently allow them an appropriate mix of freedom and supervision. Don't be afraid to set firm limits at the start of the year and then relax them as your students prove themselves capable of handling more freedom.

As you consider the question of student independence in your class, keep in mind that it is very important that your students perceive you as being fair to all students. Be able to demonstrate that the freedom you provide for one student or group of students is available to all of the students in your class.

The amount of autonomy to grant your students is also influenced by your teaching situation. Those instructors who teach physical education, laboratory sciences, or similar courses with a high potential for injury must consider the question of student autonomy in a very different light from those teachers who are in a less active classroom where it is easier to keep students safe. It is essential that you closely supervise students in situations where they

- ▶ May get hurt
- ▶ May harm someone else
- ▶ Could steal or cheat
- ▶ May engage in seriously disruptive behaviors
- ▶ Could be significantly off-task and unproductive

Finally, you must be completely comfortable with your decisions about student autonomy. Don't be cajoled into granting permission for activities that students may enjoy, but that would not be ones that you would enjoy having a supervisor watch. It is far easier to relax a strict rule than to try to regain control of an unruly class.

THE BEHAVIORS YOU CAN EXPECT FROM YOUR STUDENTS

As a secondary teacher you will find that no two school days are alike. Constant change is perhaps the chief characteristic of secondary students in general. You will find that the young people who arrive on the first day of class will by the last day not only have learned the course material, but also will have matured physically and emotionally as well.

Between those two days, however, you can expect several general behaviors from your students. Anticipating these behaviors will allow you to plan how you will react to them in a positive way.

- ▶ Because there can be a mixture of ages and maturity levels in the typical secondary classroom, you can expect to see behaviors that reflect this range. Some of your students will appear older than their years, and their behavior will reflect this maturity. Still others will strike you as immature and impulsive.
  - Get to know your students as well as you can as quickly as you can. Learning about them as individuals will help you cope successfully with their needs.
  - Offer a variety of learning activities to appeal to as many students as possible. Provide plenty of opportunities for enrichment and remediation so that all students can master the material.
  - Teach and require courtesy. Help all students move to become self-disciplined about their work and their behavior.

▶ In each class, some of your students will want to be invisible and others will vie for attention or even notoriety as class clown.

- Make sure all students know how to do their work well. Anxious students who are prepared for class will find it easier to behave appropriately and not act out in an attempt to disguise their insecurity.

- Call on all students equitably and respectfully. Giving students an opportunity to jot down their thoughts before they are required to make an oral response will make class discussions much less stressful and more productive for all students.

- Ignore as many negative behaviors as you can and promote as many positive ones as possible. Keep students focused on what is acceptable and what is not to mitigate both types of behaviors.

▶ Some students will seek power and control in positive ways and others will seek it at any cost. Finding ways to harness this desire without engaging in a power struggle is one of teaching's greatest challenges.

- Resist the urge to make a sarcastic remark to quell students who want to be noticed. Not only will you lose the sympathy of the targeted student's classmates, but you will lose their respect also.

- Make sure that you present yourself as the clear leader of the class. When students sense that you are uncertain or faltering, they may attempt to take advantage of your weakness.

- Provide opportunities for those who want to be noticed to gain attention for positive, cooperative behaviors instead of oppositional ones.

▶ Almost every student will engage in a constant and almost reflexive testing of the boundaries set by the adults in their lives. This may manifest itself in restlessness, distraction, defiance, and off-task behavior.

- Make sure that the rules, policies, and procedures for your class are not only clear, but that your students are aware of them.

- Build in plenty of choices for students. Helping them learn to make wise choices will not only make the routines of your classroom run smoothly, but will also benefit all of your students in the future.

- Stress the positive consequences that can happen when students cooperate with you and work within the confines of the school environment.

▶ Secondary students have a strong desire to have their voice heard. They will seek opportunities to express themselves in a variety of positive and negative ways.

- When a student speaks to you, stop and give that person your full attention.

- Encourage students to express themselves in a positive way. Provide opportunities for interaction such as class discussions, mock trials, student publications, and other collaborative projects whenever feasible.

- Allow students a voice in classroom decision making. Solicit their opinions about various topics such as due dates, classroom chores, or the establishment of common rules.

▶ Secondary students enjoy helping others less fortunate than themselves. Their developing sense of altruism can enrich almost any lesson.

- Encourage students to participate in some of the many online charities such www.freerice .com, the popular site that provides food for the UN World Food Program. (See Section Ten for more information about charitable online opportunities.)

- Post articles that highlight teen community service activities. Local newspapers are good sources for information and articles about community service activities for your students.

- Design a class project that involves your students in an activity that benefits their school or community.

▶ Students are acutely sensitive to actions that they deem as unfair. They are quick to protest the slightest hint of inequity—real or imagined.

- Although it is one of the biggest challenges that all teachers face, make a point of being as consistent as you can in making decisions that can affect an entire class.

- Be sure that all of your rules and policies are reasonable and easy to enforce.

- Whenever you can, be as flexible as you can. For example, students often regard as extremely unfair those teachers who refuse to round up a grade when the fraction is at least half a point. If you can make it a policy to always round up, then your students will probably not challenge you on that topic.

PROACTIVE ATTITUDES THAT CAN HELP YOU CREATE A POSITIVE DISCIPLINE CLIMATE

According to conventional wisdom, it isn't the problems we face that determine our successes or failures. It is our attitude about our problems that ultimately determines whether our teaching is a success or a failure. Since discipline problems are inevitable, you will benefit from accepting them as challenges and not as stumbling blocks to success.

One of the most important factors in determining the success or failure of the discipline climate in a classroom is the collection of attitudes the teacher brings to work each day. Those upbeat and confident teachers who come to work convinced that their students can succeed are inspiring to us all. Their successful attitudes may be invisible, but they are absolutely vital in the creation of a positive discipline climate in their classrooms.

Being an optimistic person doesn't mean that serious problems don't exist. A positive attitude just means you are working on a solution in a productive and efficient manner. Problems move you forward when you choose to work to solve them. When you experience discipline problems, don't be discouraged; they will stimulate you to use your creativity and talents to create a well-disciplined classroom. Spend your energy on the larger problems first. Choose to deal with those problems that will give you the greatest benefit right away.

Small attitude changes can also create substantial patterns of success. For example, many teachers claim that at least one of their classes is terrible. However, when they stop to look at the situation clearly, they do not have a terrible class. What they have is a class with many well-behaved students in it and just a few who are not.

Fortunately for all teachers, many useful resources are available for those who want to have a well-run classroom where students are engaged in self-directed activities. To learn more about how to create a productive classroom, turn to these sources:

▶ Parents, guardians, and families of your students

▶ Your students' current teachers

- ▶ Your students' past teachers
- ▶ Coaches and other extracurricular activities sponsors
- ▶ Your students themselves
- ▶ School records
- ▶ Standardized tests
- ▶ Internet sources
  - You Can Handle Them All (www.disciplinehelp.com). Here you will find suggestions for successfully managing more than one hundred common discipline problems.
  - National Education Association (www.nea.org). At the NEA's Web site, use the "Tools and Ideas" tab to access helpful resources about successful classroom management.
  - American Federation of Teachers (www.aft.org). At the AFT's Web site, use *discipline* as a search term to find hundreds of useful suggestions.

We all know that in creating a productive classroom atmosphere, we must do more than teach academic content. We need to take a positive approach to our students and to our teaching responsibilities if we want to make a difference in our students' lives. You can take several significant actions to communicate to your students your positive attitudes about their potential for success.

Have Confidence in Yourself

You must have confidence in your own ability to reach your students. If you are to be successful in overcoming the barriers to a positive discipline climate, you must communicate your belief that your students can grow and change for the better. Few students will try to succeed without a confident teacher who believes in them.

Show Your Students That You Care About Them

Communicate your positive attitudes to your students to show them you care about their success or failure in your class. To do this you must develop a personal relationship with each one. You do this when you show you are interested in their opinions and concerned about their welfare.

Plan Lessons That Are Challenging But Attainable

Let your students know you have confidence in their power to succeed by designing lessons where success is attainable. When you plan a unit of study, begin with information that students can relate to previous learning so that they immediately feel confident about what they already know. As the unit progresses, the work should gradually become more difficult so that those students who may have been reluctant to try at first are willing to take a chance and do the challenging work necessary for successful mastery.

Conduct Yourself Professionally

Present yourself to your students and to your colleagues as a professional educator. That means doing all of the things good teachers do: maintain order, be very organized, teach innovative lessons, and provide your students with the kind of adult role model that they need.

Accept Responsibility

Take responsibility for your attitude about the discipline problems in your classroom. Let go of the negative thoughts you have about your students and about the past experiences you have had with them. Concentrate on the positive steps you can take to help your students become self-disciplined.

At the end of every section of this Guide, you will find a brief table of some of the positive choices relating to the topics in that section. In this section's "Making Positive Choices," you will find the first of these choices that can transform the school day for you and your students.

Making Positive Choices

Instead of . . .	Try to . . .
▶ Blaming others for the failures of your students	▶ Accept responsibility for what happens in your classroom
▶ Bemoaning the ill effects of peer pressure	▶ Help students learn to work together as a team
▶ Forcing students to work quietly too often	▶ Provide safe outlets for energy, emotions, and enthusiasm though active learning strategies
▶ Delivering long-winded lectures	▶ Break class into ten- to fifteen-minute intervals of activity
▶ Wondering why you should be forced to entertain your students	▶ Create lively, appealing lessons that engage student interest and ignite curiosity
▶ Saying, "You're going to need to know this someday"	▶ Involve students in activities with real-world applications
▶ Overreacting when a student misbehaves	▶ Pause and reflect on the cause before reacting
▶ Becoming confrontational with a misbehaving student	▶ Make arrangements to work together to find a solution
▶ Giving students too much freedom	▶ Consider the age, maturity, and personalities of your students as well as safety issues
▶ Feeling annoyed at the exaggerated emotions of your students	▶ View your students as joyful, lively, and on their way to a bright future

QUESTIONS FOR REFLECTION

Use the information in this section to guide you as you think about these questions. They are designed to encourage you to think more deeply about the issues in the text or to discuss those issues with colleagues.

▶ Do you agree with the author's assertion that every teacher has discipline problems? What implications does your belief have for your teaching practices?

▶ Although all teachers may face similar discipline dilemmas, not all teachers have serious discipline issues in their classrooms. Recall a teacher in your past who never seemed to experience serious discipline issues. What techniques did that teacher use that you could implement in your class? What are some positive and negative factors that affect the discipline climate in your classroom?

▶ If, as the author believes, adolescents do not want absolute freedom, how can teachers provide their students with structure and boundaries as well as freedom and choices?

SECTION TWO

Adopt a Comprehensive Approach for a Successful Discipline Climate

In this section you will learn

- How to create a personalized discipline plan

- How to establish a productive classroom environment

- How to avoid the most common discipline mistakes

- How to put your high expectations for student success to work

- How to communicate your high expectations to your students

BEGIN THE PROCESS WITH A BROAD VIEW

It is impossible to create a productive discipline climate when you have a simplistic view of the issues involved in the undertaking. The complexity of this formidable task demands that teachers assume broad-minded attitudes and use a variety of methods to promote as many positive behaviors as possible. Your discipline plan should encompass the general requirements of the scope of your responsibilities as well as the daily procedural details that will satisfy the academic, behavioral, and social needs of your students throughout the school term.

As you begin the process of making the decisions that will shape the discipline climate in your classroom, you should consider several critical factors as you work to create the type of discipline environment where your students can be successful learners and where you can be an effective teacher. When you adopt a comprehensive approach to the creation of a discipline plan that will work for your students, allow your thinking to be shaped by

- ► The expectations for a successful discipline climate established by your school district
- ► The methods you choose to move your students to be self-disciplined
- ► The strategies you select to learn about and connect with your students and their families
- ► The instructional practices that work best for your students
- ► The physical environment of your classroom and the time available for instruction
- ► Your personal classroom leadership skills

THE CHARACTERISTICS OF A WELL-MANAGED TWENTY-FIRST-CENTURY CLASSROOM

Should teachers still worry about students who chew gum? What should we do about those students whose cell phones ring in class? How should we react when we hear students using offensive language?

As secondary teachers, we wonder what to do about these and the countless other adolescent behaviors that we witness each school day. Are these the issues that should concern us or should we focus exclusively on the more serious problems confronting our students? After all, dealing with gum and cell phones seems rather silly when weapons at school are a real concern for many teachers.

Many educators are unsure of how to define a class that is well-disciplined because today's discipline issues are neither simple nor self-evident. For example, we may want our students to be engaged in active learning, but those classroom activities can appear chaotic and noisy. We also struggle with thorny new issues such as cyberbullies, sexting, and online cheating.

Even though we may not always be in agreement about the exact definition of a well-disciplined classroom, most educators certainly know when things are not going well. Misconduct referral notices are remarkably uniform in the types of behaviors that teachers and administrators do not find acceptable. A quick survey of these reveals just a few of the serious misbehaviors that we do not want our students to engage in:

- ► Violence
- ► Disrespect for authority
- ► Failure to complete work
- ► Bullying
- ► Dishonesty
- ► Tardiness
- ► Truancy

No sensible teacher wants to deal with these behaviors and their unpleasant aftermath because we know that they signal significant disruptions in the learning process and in the success of all of the students in our care.

Since we know what a disorderly classroom is, what then are the characteristics of an orderly classroom? Although there are as many hallmarks of a well-disciplined class as there are teachers and classes, a few of the most significant ones fall under the following broad categories.

The Physical Environment Is Invitational

In a well-disciplined classroom, the room itself is appealing. Many of us teach in cramped and over-crowded rooms without enough basic materials and certainly not expensive equipment such as interactive whiteboards and LCD projectors. Despite these restrictions, effective secondary teachers can manage to create an environment where students focus on learning. We can arrange desks to encourage collaboration as well as independent work, minimize traffic-flow problems, and make sure materials are readily available. We can use the walls to stimulate student engagement with displays of student work.

Students Understand the Rules and Procedures They Are Expected to Follow

The teacher has obviously given much thought to planning and establishing a well-organized learning climate. Class rules, procedures, and notices of upcoming activities are posted in convenient places to help students stay on track. Encouraging mottoes remind students of their goals and responsibilities. Students follow class routines for daily chores without nagging. In a well-disciplined class, students understand what they are expected to achieve each day and how they are to go about it.

Students Are Actively Engaged in the Pursuit of Knowledge

There is movement and laughter and noise. Active learning generates a much higher noise level than the silent classrooms of the past. Students are up and out of their seats while engaged in a variety of interesting activities that encourage thought and discovery. They do more talking than the teacher does on most days. A well-disciplined class is a place where no student sleeps or sits idly waiting for dismissal.

There Is a Persistent Tone of Mutual Respect

Teachers and students treat each other with obvious respect. This is evident in such nonverbal interactions as body language and tone of voice as well as in what students and teachers say to each other. Students speak with confidence because they feel their opinions are valued. Students in a well-disciplined class also respect their classmates. They have been taught to appreciate each other's unique contributions to the class as well as appropriate ways to resolve conflicts. There is a general sense of togetherness and steadfast courtesy.

Students Take Responsibility for Their Learning

In a well-disciplined class, teachers may lead students, but they do not coerce them into good behavior through threats of dire punishment. Instead, teachers encourage students to understand the importance of choosing good behavior and its lasting rewards over the short-term thrills of bad behavior. In an orderly class, self-directed students not only encourage each other, but they also work with their teacher to achieve academic and behavioral goals that they themselves have helped establish. Successful teachers employ a variety of strategies to promote responsible decision making and create self-reliant students.

FIVE COMMONSENSE STEPS TO A PRODUCTIVE CLASSROOM ENVIRONMENT

Although the establishment of a productive classroom environment is a difficult and complicated task, it certainly is not an impossible one. Below you will find five commonsense actions that will make this task manageable.

Step 1

Become thoroughly familiar with the content of the courses you teach. If you don't know the material you are supposed to cover, then your instruction will lack authority. Secondary students are quick to spot teachers who do not have a good command of content, and they are justified in having no patience with such teachers.

Step 2

Quickly get to know your students. When you are familiar with your students, you will be better able to establish the kind of rapport with them that you need in order to be a better teacher. Successful teachers have a sound working knowledge of adolescent behavior in general and of their own students in particular.

Step 3

Don't rely on punishment to control your classes. Instead, learn as much as you can about the various disciplinary practices that are available to you. Knowing the actions that can prevent or minimize potential discipline problems will help you establish a productive, positive classroom environment.

Step 4

Present yourself to your students and to your colleagues as a professional educator. That means doing all of the things excellent teachers do: maintain order, organize your time and materials, teach innovative lessons, and inspire students by being the adult role model they need.

Step 5

Assume responsibility for your attitude about the discipline problems in your classroom. Concentrate on the positive steps you can take to help your students become self-disciplined. Learn to monitor and manage your own stress level so that you can be the effective educator your students need.

THE MOST COMMON DISCIPLINE MISTAKES THAT SECONDARY TEACHERS MAKE

Although all teachers bring their personal strengths and weaknesses to school each day, those who are aware of the common mistakes that even the most well-intentioned teachers make are more likely to avoid them.

▶ **Giving students "free time" at the end of an assignment, a class, or even at the end of the year sends the message that class time is not important.** At the end of a class or an assignment, try a structured review of information or allow students to select from a variety of brief, engaging activities. At the end of the year, plan independent projects, activities that review material, instruction for enrichment, or teach some of the topics that you and your students were not able to cover earlier.

▶ **Not listening to students sets an unpleasant tone and can leave you vulnerable to charges of unfairness.** While you don't want to be perceived as a pushover, you do want to create opportunities for students to provide feedback on various issues such as class activities and instructional methods. Teachers should be especially careful to listen to students before taking action when a problem has occurred.

▶ **Allowing students to sleep because "they are not bothering anyone else" not only sends the message that class time is not important, but also that some students are so annoying that you don't want to cope with them.** Although it may take time, patience, and effort, be persistent in working with students who are so disruptive or overwhelmed that they engage in this behavior.

▶ **Not being prepared for class is an easy mistake for busy teachers to make.** Make a point of planning instruction with an overview of the term, unit plans, and daily plans. Demonstrating that you are well-organized and confident will preempt the potential for off-task behavior.

▶ **Being inconsistent is one of the easiest mistakes for teachers to make.** In trying to reach every student, we sometimes overlook behaviors that are not in the best interests of our students. One way to avoid this mistake is to have clearly defined policies and procedures in place so that students are aware of what they need to do to be successful.

▶ **Allowing students to be disrespectful to you or their classmates occurs most often when the disrespect is subtle or disguised as a student's clumsy attempt to be funny.** However, it is better and far easier to stop this behavior when you first notice it. Be politely calm and firm when discussing this with misbehaving students. Set clear limits on what is acceptable behavior and what is not.

▶ **Not being fair is a mistake that occurs most often when teachers put the needs of one student above the needs of the entire class.** Students are quick to notice and protest when they believe that they are not being treated fairly. Although it is impossible to be fair to all students all the time, it is important for class morale for students to perceive you as treating everyone as fairly as possible.

▶ **Giving up on students is all too easy to do when they meet your efforts to motivate them to perform well with resistance or even disrespect.** The outcome is usually an escalation of the unpleasant atmosphere in a class. When faced with this temptation, many teachers brainstorm a list of possible resolutions and work through them until they find a workable solution. Often it may take a variety of approaches to reach every student.

▶ **Putting misbehaving students in the hall for more than just a few minutes is a mistake that can have serious consequences if the student leaves the area or other students interfere with your student.** Be careful to ask a student to wait in the hall only briefly when you want to speak privately.

▶ **Ignoring school rules, procedures, or policies can happen when individual teachers do not accept or are too busy to enforce them.** If you refuse to honor an established schoolwide guideline, this makes it easier for students to continue to test boundaries. If you disagree with a school rule, procedure, or policy, work with your supervisors to change it, but honor it until the change is made.

▶ **Not having a transparent classroom is a mistake that is all too easy for busy teachers to make.** It is not always convenient to stop the flow of our planning time and focus on contacting parents and guardians through e-mails, notes, classroom Web sites, or phone calls to keep them apprised of upcoming events, assignments, issues, or grades. When we neglect this important aspect of our responsibilities, however, misunderstandings between home and school can intensify. Be proactive in reaching out to parents and keeping the channels of communication open.

▶ **Failing to provide enough models and examples for students to have a clear understanding of what they need to do to be successful occurs frequently when teachers underestimate the amount of guidance that students need at the start of an assignment.** The result is the frustration of students becoming disruptive as they lose interest in their work.

▶ **Allowing subtle bullying and cliques tends to make a teacher complicit in this type of misbehavior.** Because most secondary students are aware of the serious repercussions of overt bullying, this behavior is usually a hidden problem in a class. Be on the alert for any mumbled insults or even comments made in jest.

▶ **Neglecting to build in relevance can create situations where students are not interested in doing their work because they see no purpose for it.** Make sure your students know why the material is important and how they will benefit from learning it.

▶ **Ignoring the importance of teaching literacy skills can occur when teachers want to believe that older students already have acquired the reading skills they need to comprehend instructional material.** Instead of making this assumption, make a quick assessment of your students' literacy skills at the start of the term and differentiate your instruction based on the results of that assessment.

▶ **Assuming that someone else has taught your students how to study is an easy mistake to make, especially with mature students.** Because every discipline has its own requirements, students need help in learning the best ways to master your course content. Spend time each day showing students how to prepare their assignments, memorize information, practice skills, and stay organized.

▶ **Not having appropriate procedures, policies, and rules in place can create a chaotic classroom atmosphere.** Plan, create, teach, and review the procedures, policies, and rules that fit the needs of your students. The time that you spend doing this at the start of the school term will result in a more efficiently run class for the rest of the year.

▶ **Losing your temper can happen when you are frustrated, exhausted, or not prepared.** When teachers react in anger instead of solving a problem, not only do they lose valuable instructional time, but they also diminish their reputations as caring, self-disciplined adults. Make it a point that you will remain calm in front of your students.

- **Neglecting to monitor student behavior throughout the class period is a sure way to increase off-task behavior.** Make a point of staying attuned to your students' behavior from the beginning until the end of class.

- **Adopting a sarcastic or impatient tone does nothing to enhance your stature as a role model.** Take time to deliberately consider the effect of your words before you speak if you want to develop a positive relationship with your students.

- **Not giving students enough voice and responsibility in class decisions can result in frustrated students who test the rules or who choose not to work.** When you ask their opinions in small and large decisions, seek feedback, or assign classroom chores, you preempt many conflicts.

- **Forgetting that you are a role model can lead to a loss of respect.** Students have a fairly clear idea of the behaviors they want from the adults in their lives. Make a point of being the adult you would want your students to grow into.

- **Not being enthusiastic about your students and your class will create a corresponding loss of enthusiasm in your students.** Your enthusiasm is infectious. Consider it one of your best tools to motivate your students to be at their best.

- **Ignoring your students' learning styles will frustrate them as they attempt to complete their assignments.** You will make it easier for all of your students to stay engaged and working when you design instruction that appeals to their learning preferences as often as you can.

- **Allowing misbehavior to escalate by not contacting parents or guardians early is an easy mistake for teachers to make.** We are often so busy teaching that by the time we have a spare moment to call a student's home, it seems easier to ignore the behavior. Unfortunately, this does not often produce positive results. Try setting aside a specific time each day to contact parents or guardians either by phone or with a quick e-mail if possible.

EFFECTIVE MANAGEMENT AND DISCIPLINE PRACTICES

If punitive measures are not effective ways to manage a class, then what works in today's twenty-first-century classroom? In order to take a balanced, comprehensive approach to creating a positive classroom discipline climate, you should make wise choices based on the options available to you. Here are the best practices that can serve as a guide:

- Remember that you are a professional educator and allow the principles of professionalism to be your guide as you navigate your school days. When you adopt a consistently professional attitude, your students will see you as a role model.

- Even though it is the most obvious, one frequently overlooked way to establish an orderly and productive classroom discipline climate is to design and deliver instruction that is so engaging that students will choose to do their work rather than be tempted to misbehave. Instruction that is intrinsically interesting because students find it useful and challenging will prevent almost every potential discipline problem. Be prepared for class with dynamic lessons. Most of your classroom discipline battles will be fought successfully when you do this.

- In recent years the increased emphasis on the importance of classroom rules, routines, and procedures has made secondary teachers aware of the important role these play in establishing and maintaining an orderly classroom. Many teachers find it worthwhile to spend time at the start of a term making sure that students are completely aware of the behaviors necessary to make their classroom run smoothly.

▶ Another approach to building an orderly classroom is to establish both positive and negative consequences for behaviors. Positive consequences such as tangible rewards or good grades can be very effective for some students. Negative consequences such as detentions or phone calls home can also have a beneficial effect in deterring students from misbehavior. In either case, the consequences should be appropriate for the behavior.

▶ At first glance, establishing a caring relationship with your students may not appear to be a way to create a positive discipline climate, but when students feel that their well-being is important to a teacher, then the tendency to misbehave is tempered by a desire to cooperate.

▶ In addition to a positive relationship with their teacher, those students who have a positive relationship with their classmates, who feel they are members of a group of like-minded individuals, who feel they are part of something larger than themselves, will value that connection and behave better to maintain it.

▶ The positive peer pressure engendered by feeling that they contribute to the good of the group and would be missed if they were not part of it is a powerful way to motivate students to behave well. Many teachers use peer pressure to encourage good behavior by setting common class goals and then working with students to achieve them.

▶ Teachers who have learned to pace instruction in accordance with their students' needs and keep students busily engaged in learning will find that they have far fewer negative incidents than those teachers who allow bored students enough down time to misbehave instead of engage in productive learning.

▶ Teachers who focus their students' efforts with carefully planned goals create a sense of purpose for the work they ask of their students. With a clear sense of direction, most students will tend to stay on task longer than those students who do not know how they will benefit or why they have to complete an assignment. Having clearly defined goals creates a purposeful and businesslike atmosphere in a class.

▶ Set up your classroom space in such a way that your students can work productively. Sometimes a simple issue such as desks that are not the right size for students can cause problems for those students who are easily distracted.

▶ Experienced teachers know that they cannot manage the various personalities in each class without help from other caring adults. They rely on advice, insight, and support from students' parents or guardians and other school personnel such as guidance counselors, coaches, and previous teachers to reach every student.

▶ Another effective approach to avoiding discipline problems is to be as proactive as possible in preventing or at least minimizing them. Actively working to avoid potential problems in classroom activities, with student motivation, and in interpersonal relationships will make it easier for you to have a positive and productive class.

▶ Every teacher has to cope with at least some disruptions to the planned flow of instruction and classroom activities. Although many of these disruptions can be avoided, savvy teachers find ways to lessen their impact on a class. Even something as simple as waiting to determine the reason for a student's tardiness so as not to interfere with the other students' learning can contribute to a positive classroom environment.

Teacher Self-Assessment

HOW WELL-DISCIPLINED IS YOUR CLASS?

If you are not sure if your classroom is as well-disciplined as you think it could be, use this list to compare what happens in your class with just a few of the many things that happen in a well-disciplined class.

Put a "+" in the space beside the good behaviors that you can feel confident that your class already practices. If you need to work on a less-than-successful characteristic, put a "−" in that space. While no class is perfect, a well-disciplined class will earn far more positive marks than negative ones.

_____ When you're not there, students stick with class routines.

_____ Your students help each other. You can count on them to help you, too.

_____ Your students talk more than you do, but their conversation is mainly about their class work. Their energy is focused on the assignment.

_____ No one shouts or nags. Everyone remembers to be polite.

_____ Students do not condone their classmates' bad behavior.

_____ Students take pride in their work. Work areas are left tidy at the end of class.

_____ The noise level is often high, but it's the noise of enthusiasm.

_____ Community issues are part of the class.

_____ Everyone is involved. Everyone is valued. Diversity is not just tolerated, but celebrated.

_____ Students have long-term and short-term goals for their lives and work with you to achieve them.

_____ The work is challenging, but students can be successful.

_____ You don't need to call students to order. They start working as soon as they enter the room.

_____ The needs of individual students are recognized in the mixture of activities designed to promote learning as well as in the variety of discipline strategies used in the class.

_____ Students perceive you as a firm and friendly teacher who treats them with fairness.

_____ You have a plan for preventing discipline problems and for dealing with those that do occur.

Teacher Worksheet

DEVELOP YOUR CLASSROOM DISCIPLINE PLAN

As you begin to make plans to create the productive discipline climate that will work best for your students, you should consider many different factors. Use the questions below as a guide as you begin the systematic planning that will help you shape a plan that will work well for your students.

1. What are the expectations for a successful discipline climate in my school? How can I include these expectations in a plan that will meet the needs of my students?

   _____

   _____

   _____

2. How can I encourage my students to become self-disciplined?

   _____

   _____

   _____

3. What types of behaviors do I find positive and productive? How can I communicate my beliefs to my students?

   _____

   _____

   _____

4. Why types of behaviors do I find intolerable? How can I communicate my beliefs to my students?

   _____

   _____

   _____

5. Why do my students misbehave? What can I do to learn more about this? How can I use this knowledge to help my students improve their academic and social behaviors?

   _____

   _____

   _____

6. Which student misbehaviors can I plan to safely ignore?

_____

_____

_____

7. How much autonomy am I comfortable offering my students?

_____

_____

_____

8. What do I know about my students' needs, preferred learning styles, and interests? How can I use this knowledge to help my students improve their academic and social behaviors?

_____

_____

_____

9. Which instructional practices tend to promote productive behavior in my class? Which ones cause students to become off-task or disruptive?

_____

_____

10. What are the problems with the physical layout of my classroom that contribute to off-task behavior? What can I do to remedy them?

_____

_____

_____

11. How can I make sure that I communicate effectively with my students and their families?

_____

_____

_____

12. Which aspects of my classroom leadership are productive? Which ones should I improve?

_____

_____

_____

(Continued)

Teacher Worksheet *(Continued)*

DEVELOP YOUR CLASSROOM DISCIPLINE PLAN

13. How can I use routines, procedures, and policies to establish a smoothly running classroom?

_____

_____

_____

14. What can I do to prevent or minimize disruptions caused by misbehavior?

_____

_____

_____

15. Whom can I turn to when I have questions or experience difficulties with student behavior?

_____

_____

_____

Teacher Self-Assessment

THINK IT THROUGH: HOW WOULD YOU RATE YOUR NEW DISCIPLINE PLAN?

After you have undertaken the systematic approach necessary for the creation of a sound classroom discipline plan, you should set aside enough time for reflection. Because of the complex nature of the task, crafting a sound discipline plan will take time and planning. To guide your reflection, you should ask yourself the following questions about your new discipline plan. Rate your response on a three-point scale with three being the highest score you can earn.

1   2   3   Is my plan based on the unique requirements of my students?

1   2   3   Does my plan take a balanced and comprehensive approach to the issue?

1   2   3   Does my plan help my students develop the self-management skills necessary for them to become self-disciplined learners?

1   2   3   Is the emphasis in my plan on the prevention of problems rather than on dealing with misbehavior?

1   2   3   Does my plan take a problem-solving approach when misbehavior does occur?

PUT YOUR HIGH EXPECTATIONS TO WORK

When you walk through the halls of almost any secondary school, you will observe students engaged in a variety of activities. In some classrooms, students are allowed to sleep or to chat with their friends because they have finished their work for the day, while in others you will find active students rushing to finish their assignments before the class ends.

What creates this difference in classroom activity? Why do some students become self-disciplined learners early in their school careers, while others never achieve more than just enough to get by? Why is one classroom a place where students have nothing better to do than rest (and be disruptive), while in others students have so much to do that they have to hurry to complete their assignments before the class is over?

The chief difference in these classes is not in the students nor is it in the subject matter. Instead, one of the biggest differences between teachers whose students perform well and those whose students perform poorly lies in the expectations that teachers have for their students. In many classrooms students do not reach their academic or behavioral potential because their teachers are satisfied with poor performance.

When teachers begin with the basic belief that their students are capable of doing meaningful work of high quality, they set the stage for a productive classroom environment. This is the first step in an important cycle of belief and behavior that permeates successful classrooms, promoting self-disciplined behavior in the students fortunate enough to be in those classes. Here's how this cycle works.

Teachers Believe Their Students Are Capable of the Successful Mastery of the Material They Plan to Teach

Common sense indicates that if teachers don't believe students are going to do well on an assignment, then they are not going to deliver the well-structured lessons that students need to learn. These teachers are also not going to provide the supportive learning environment that will motivate students to succeed.

Teachers Communicate Their Expectations to Students

We communicate our expectations for success to our students through a number of ways. The most important one is, of course, providing them with challenging work to do. When students have enough meaningful and challenging work, then they are going to achieve at a higher performance level than those students whose teachers do not communicate their expectations for success.

Our Expectations Indicate to Our Students That We Are Confident in Their Ability to Do Well

When we show our students that we have confidence in their ability to do the work we have planned for them, then we send a clear message to them that they are capable learners. Many students are crippled by a lack of confidence in their ability to do well in school. Some give up early and turn into at-risk students. Far too many others struggle on halfheartedly, never really learning or achieving very much. Still others, though, have teachers who convince them that they are good students who are capable of worthwhile efforts. These students are successful.

If Students Are Confident in Their Ability to Succeed, They Will Try Harder

Once students perceive that we regard them as capable and are willing to help them do their work, then they will soon assimilate this belief for themselves. Research and common sense both show that students who believe they can achieve at high performance levels will find it easier to keep on trying until they become successful.

Your Students' Success Will Create More Success

When students start achieving at higher levels, the success cycle created by expectations begins again because teachers continue to expect students to be capable learners once more. Although it is easier to teach students who are ready for a challenge, the cycle of successful high expectations for both academic and behavioral success must begin with the teacher. When we give students the opportunities to succeed that will motivate them to try even harder, we are creating the kind of positive classroom climate that will help them all continue to move toward being self-directed learners (see Figure 2.1).

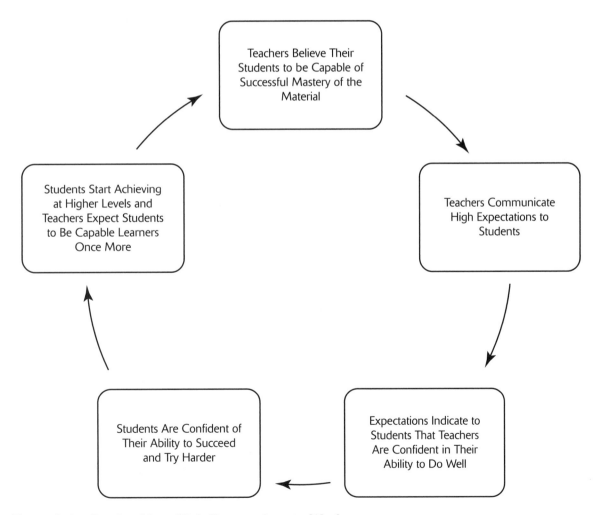

Figure 2.1. Putting Your High Expectations to Work

▶ Encourage your students to succeed by taking a "can-do" approach. Communicate to them that the work you are asking them to do is worthy of their efforts and you expect them to do a good job on it.

▶ Be careful to reward only responsible behavior and good work or efforts toward both behavioral and academic success.

▶ Make sure students have enough work to do that is interesting, challenging, and achievable.

▶ Show students how to succeed. Be specific in the criteria for success. Give them plenty of samples, models, and examples as well as sufficient practice.

▶ Do not allow students to refuse to participate in class by sleeping or just not working. Call on every student every day.

▶ Provide a time-management structure for students so that they know when they must hand in work to you. Use planners such as a syllabus, checklist, or reminders on the board to help students stay on track.

▶ Give useful feedback as promptly as you can. Be specific about what students need to do to continue their success.

▶ Offer plenty of extra help to students who may be struggling with their work. You do not have to stay after school every day in order to do this, but you should make some time available to help students who need an extra little push.

▶ Teach students to visualize their goals for assignments before they begin. This allows them to plan what they need to do to complete their work to a satisfactory standard.

▶ Refuse to accept work that is messy or inaccurate. You do not have to be unpleasant about this, but students who try to turn in poorly rendered work should be stopped. One way to handle this is to have students redo their work and turn it in the next day.

In this section's "Making Positive Choices," you will find choices about adopting a comprehensive approach to discipline that can transform the school day for you and your students.

Making Positive Choices

Instead of . . .	Try to . . .
▶ Neglecting the importance of a tidy, inviting, and businesslike work area	▶ Use the décor and layout of your classroom to enhance instruction
▶ Working though your state's curriculum requirements by rote	▶ Plan innovative instruction that shows students the importance of working with focus and purpose
▶ Assuming control of your class	▶ Work with students to share responsibility for establishing a positive and productive classroom environment
▶ Not always being as prepared as you should be	▶ Make sure that you are completely familiar with the content of the course
▶ Using outdated discipline methods	▶ Brainstorm a list of the methods that will work best for your students and set to work applying them fairly and consistently
▶ Allowing students to goof off or sleep instead of working	▶ Employ a variety of interventions until every student is held accountable for his or her own success

(Continued)

Instead of . . .	Try to . . .
▶ Kicking misbehaving students out of the room	▶ Follow students to the hall, hold a brief conference, and then have them return to class to work
▶ Assuming that your students know how to study	▶ Teach study skills (see Section Five for tips on study skills) that are geared for your students and your course
▶ Expecting students to work because you have told them to	▶ Work with students to set and achieve personal goals (see Section Five for tips on setting goals)
▶ Hoping that your students will behave better	▶ Design a discipline plan for your classes and implement it

QUESTIONS FOR REFLECTION

Use the information in this section to guide your thinking as you reflect on these questions. They are designed to encourage you to think more deeply about the issues in the text or to discuss those issues with colleagues.

▶ After reading the list of common discipline mistakes that many secondary teachers make, do you recognize any that you may be doing? How can you handle this? What other mistakes could you add to the list?

▶ What role does having high expectations have in your classroom? How do you communicate your expectations for success to your students? How can you improve the way that you do this?

▶ After creating your discipline plan, what is the best way to begin implementing it? How will you be able to refer to and adjust it as the school year progresses?

SECTION THREE

Cultivate Your Role as a Classroom Leader

> **In this section you will learn**
>
> - How to improve your classroom leadership skills
>
> - How to set and achieve professional goals
>
> - How to be prepared for class each day
>
> - How to make your students pay attention to you
>
> - How to be aware of how you relate to your students

BECOME AN EFFECTIVE CLASSROOM LEADER

Although some of your colleagues may appear to have been born with a natural gift for teaching, that is certainly an illusion. Effective classroom leadership requires consistent and deliberate action as well as thoughtful planning. Because classroom charisma is not an effortless gift handed out to a select few but rather is a set of acquired skills, the effort you expend to cultivate your role as an effective instructional leader will reward you with a well-managed classroom filled with successful students.

It is no secret that the teacher is the most important factor in creating a discipline climate where students can thrive. If you are having a bad day, your students will, too. However, if you can project enthusiasm about your students and the subject matter even when you may not be at your best, then your students will be more likely to succeed than if you just slog though a tedious lesson. Self-reflection, professional attitudes, and attention to improving your classroom competence are just some of the integral elements you should consider in the cultivation of your role as a classroom leader.

STUDENTS SHOULD COME FIRST

Many teachers find that it is not always easy to be focused on teaching or students for the duration of the class. We all can experience legitimate distractions from time to time—an illness in our families or our own fatigue, for example. However, those teachers who are so distracted that they do not fully attend to their students will have to deal with many more discipline problems than those teachers who are focused on the activity in their classrooms. The questions below may help you gauge the level of distraction you may be experiencing each school day:

▶ Do you grade papers in class?

▶ Do you leave your cell phone on while you are supervising students?

▶ Do you find yourself without enough prepared handouts or other teaching materials?

▶ Do you check e-mail in class?

▶ Are you distracted during class by your family responsibilities?

▶ Are you distracted by routine paperwork chores such as book counts, attendance forms, or parent contact documentation?

▶ Do you spend class time on extracurricular activities such as clubs or sports that you sponsor?

▶ Do you confer with other teachers during class time?

▶ Do you conduct personal business during class?

Although there may occasionally be a valid reason for not putting students first, teachers who want to establish a productive learning environment focus on their classroom responsibilities and the welfare of their students. To reduce your classroom distraction and put your students first, try these suggestions:

▶ Learn to ask for help and to delegate whenever possible. Ask your students to assist you if it would make routine tasks such as collecting papers or collecting field trip permission forms quicker and easier.

▶ Arrive at school a few minutes early and stay a few minutes late. This practice will allow you to take care of many of the small tasks that can distract your attention in class if you are not fully prepared.

▶ Take care to use your planning time at school as efficiently as you can. For example, it is easy to spend too much time online unless you allot a specific time for this. Establish routines that will allow you to maximize the time that you have available for the tasks that make your classroom run efficiently.

VIEW YOURSELF AS A COACH

One of the most encouraging shifts in recent educational practices involves the changing role of the classroom instructor. No longer the disseminator of all knowledge, classroom teachers today know that a well-disciplined class is one where students are engaged in activities that lead them not only to the mastery of content knowledge, but also to the mastery of the skills necessary to unlock that information.

Two of the world's earliest legendary teachers, Socrates and Confucius, did not just deliver information, but rose to meet a much greater challenge: they inspired their students to seek knowledge. Twenty-first-century teachers can follow this noble tradition as they coach their students to explore and discover information on their own.

If you want to create a productive and orderly classroom, first assume the role of coach. Give your students the tools they need to research and think for themselves. Perfect your questioning skills. Encourage divergent thinking. Build instruction around essential questions so that your students can connect what happens in class with the world around them. Encourage your students to accept responsibility for their own learning with careful coaching rather than tedious lecturing.

THE IMPORTANCE OF ASSESSING YOUR PERFORMANCE

The demands of teaching secondary-level students can be particularly exhausting. By the end of a hectic week that could involve pep rallies, proms, home games, away games, college applications, field trips, dress code violations, cybercheating, and other adolescent turmoil, many of us long to forget about our school woes. Although giving in to this kind of fatigue is tempting, it will not make our problems fade away.

Just as our students need a systematic approach to their instruction, so should we take an organized and serious approach to cultivating our roles as classroom leaders. This is especially important when working with classroom discipline issues. When teachers remove the emotions that can accompany a bad week at school and look at their performance from every angle, then progress is possible.

Determining your strengths and weaknesses serves as an important step in gaining control of your classroom. When you are aware of what you are doing well and what you would like to improve, then you can set goals and work to achieve them. Your proactive approach to becoming the kind of classroom leader you would like to be also will enable you to remedy any negative discipline issues quickly.

In addition to the following list, you can use the exercises "How Well Do You Convey Your Enthusiasm?" and "Classroom Leadership Self-Assessment" to guide your efforts to assess your own professional performance. Whether your self-assessment is formal or informal, you can use several strategies to make this process as useful as possible:

▶ When you begin assessing your own performance, take care to focus on your positive qualities as well as on the areas that you would like to improve. Too often we focus on our mistakes instead of what we do well. Knowing your strengths will make it easier for you to use them to enhance your teaching.

▶ Look for patterns in your teaching. For example, do you always have a problem with the students in your last class of the day or is a particular day of the week calmer for you and your students than another?

▶ Gather information from a variety of sources and by using a variety of methods. This will provide a more objective view of how well you are doing than a limited approach can.

▶ Be careful to gather as many details as you can about a particular issue. For example, if you informally survey students and learn that they believe that your tests are too difficult, probe deeper. Find out where the difficulty lies and if it is really an issue with the way you design tests or with the way that students prepare for them.

▶ Remember that not every resource you use or every bit of evidence you may uncover as you evaluate yourself may be completely valid. Be as objective as possible when reviewing the information that you have gathered.

Teacher Self-Assessment

HOW WELL DO YOU CONVEY YOUR ENTHUSIASM?

Read the statements below and rate yourself to see how well you project your enthusiasm for your students and for your subject.

1. I use a system to make sure that I call on every student every day.

   Strongly Disagree   Disagree   Neutral   Agree   Strongly Agree

2. I make positive home contacts every week though notes, e-mails, or phone calls.

   Strongly Disagree   Disagree   Neutral   Agree   Strongly Agree

3. I have worked hard to foster a positive atmosphere in my class.

   Strongly Disagree   Disagree   Neutral   Agree   Strongly Agree

4. In my class, we recognize birthdays and other special events.

   Strongly Disagree   Disagree   Neutral   Agree   Strongly Agree

5. The main decorating motif in my class is a display of student work.

   Strongly Disagree   Disagree   Neutral   Agree   Strongly Agree

6. I take photos of my students and display them in the classroom.

   Strongly Disagree   Disagree   Neutral   Agree   Strongly Agree

7. I work around my less energetic times of day by pacing my instruction.

   Strongly Disagree   Disagree   Neutral   Agree   Strongly Agree

8. I like the subjects that I teach and try to instill that same feeling in my students.

   Strongly Disagree   Disagree   Neutral   Agree   Strongly Agree

9. I am a cheerleader for my school, my class, my subject matter, and my students.

   Strongly Disagree   Disagree   Neutral   Agree   Strongly Agree

10. I am aware of the power I have to make or break my students' day, week, year, and future.

    Strongly Disagree   Disagree   Neutral   Agree   Strongly Agree

Teacher Self-Assessment

CLASSROOM LEADERSHIP SELF-ASSESSMENT

Use these broad questions about your role as a classroom leader to evaluate your effectiveness in creating the positive learning climate that will lead to productive student behavior.

Read each question to analyze your effectiveness in that category. Use the space beside each one to record your score.

Rate yourself on a scale of "1" to "5." A ranking of "1" is the lowest score that you can earn and a "5" is the highest.

1. ____ Am I doing enough to prevent discipline problems from beginning?

2. ____ Are the daily routines in my class easy to follow?

3. ____ Are the class rules effective?

4. ____ Do I enforce the class rules consistently?

5. ____ Are my behavior and academic standards high enough?

6. ____ Are the plans I have for dealing with discipline problems workable?

7. ____ Have I helped my students set long- and short-term goals for themselves?

8. ____ Do I work with my students to help them achieve their goals?

9. ____ Do my students have enough relevant and challenging work to do?

10. ____ Is the instruction designed to develop higher-level thinking skills?

11. ____ Am I helping my students grow intellectually and socially?

12. ____ Am I using all of the resources and support personnel available to me?

13. ____ Do I include every student every day?

14. ____ Do I treat my students with sensitivity and respect?

15. ____ Do I present myself as a good teacher: concerned, committed, and professional?

HOW TO GATHER OTHER DATA ON YOUR CLASSROOM COMPETENCE

In addition to self-assessments, there are many methods you can use to gather data about your classroom leadership. Even though you should try to use a variety of ways to gather information, it is important that you use the methods that work best for your teaching situation. In the list that follows you will find some effective and flexible ways to assess your classroom performance. Choose the ones that appeal to you, adjusting them to fit your needs. After you have completed gathering this information, please see the "Sample Self-Rating Rubric" to begin to set goals that will improve your classroom leadership.

▶ **Set up an unobtrusive audio recorder to record yourself throughout a particular class.** When you review the recording, pay particular attention to concerns such as any bothersome speech patterns, how you react to various students, or your tone of voice.

▶ **Ask a colleague to observe you as you present a lesson.** You can either plan a general observation or ask for a targeted examination of a specific concern, such as the way your room is set up, your pacing, or the way you interact with various students.

▶ **Use a brief self-rating rubric to grade your performance throughout a class period.** Select the areas you want to examine and design a simple rubric to determine your strengths as well as your areas of concern.

▶ **Try a focused look at just one problem you may be experiencing.** Instead of a general assessment of your classroom competence, sometimes a more focused examination will provide useful data that can provide a solution for a classroom problem.

▶ **Provide students with an opportunity to make suggestions or comments.** Although this will vary from teacher to teacher depending on the maturity level of the students, a convenient suggestion box may provide a way to gather useful insights from your students.

▶ **Allow plenty of informal opportunities for students to communicate their opinions.** Exit tickets, journal entries, and other assignments that require students to reflect on class and their learning can yield a great deal of helpful information for you. Even an assignment as simple as asking students to create a class "Wish List" can yield useful information.

▶ **Offer an online survey to ask students to share their opinions about your performance.** One of the most user-friendly sites for this is Survey Monkey at www.surveymonkey.com. At this free site you can create a survey, have your students take it online, and then review the data analysis.

Teacher Self-Assessment

SAMPLE SELF-RATING RUBRIC

Warm-up activities:	A	B	C	D	F
Teacher activities:	A	B	C	D	F
Student activities:	A	B	C	D	F
Closure:	A	B	C	D	F
Class routines:	A	B	C	D	F
Procedures:	A	B	C	D	F

Teacher Worksheet

SETTING GOALS FOR IMPROVING YOUR CLASSROOM LEADERSHIP

Use the information you have gained from your self-assessment to focus your efforts to improve your classroom leadership. After you have determined your strengths and weaknesses, you can begin to set goals for improving the areas that are not as strong as you would like them to be.

By using the form that follows, you can begin your program of self-improvement in a systematic way. Here are the steps to take that will enable you to do this:

Step 1: Use the self-assessments in this section to determine your discipline strengths and weaknesses.

Step 2: Write out your problem as you perceive it to be in response to each question.

Step 3: List two strategies you think will help you solve this particular discipline problem.

Step 4: Begin to implement your strategies so that you and your students can benefit.

Since improving teaching skills is a daily process for even the most experienced teachers, you can photocopy this form and refer to it throughout the school year. An area of concern that you might need to work on right now may not be of the same importance to you later on.

Here's a sample from the reproducible to help you get started in your quest for improving how you manage the discipline issues in your class.

1. Is the instruction designed to develop higher-level thinking skills?
<u>I need to include more activities that are above the knowledge or comprehension levels.</u>

_____

Strategies

    a. Search online for suggestions about including higher-level activities in lesson plans.
    b. Include real-life and hands-on activities in every lesson so that students move at least to the application level.

2. Am I doing enough to prevent discipline problems?

_____

_____

Strategies

    a. _____

    b. _____

3. Are the daily routines of my class easy to follow?

_____

_____

Strategies

    a. _____

    b. _____

4. Are the class rules effective?

_____

_____

Strategies

    a. _____

    b. _____

5. Do I enforce the class rules consistently?

_____

_____

Strategies

    a. _____

    b. _____

6. Are my behavior and academic standards high enough?

_____

_____

Strategies

    a. _____

    b. _____

(Continued)

Teacher Worksheet *(Continued)*

7. Are the plans I have for dealing with discipline problems workable?

_____

_____

Strategies

a. _____

b. _____

8. Have I helped my students set long- and short-term goals for themselves?

_____

_____

Strategies

a. _____

b. _____

9. Do I work with my students to help them achieve their goals?

_____

_____

Strategies

a. _____

b. _____

10. Do my students have enough challenging and relevant work to do?

_____

_____

Strategies

    a. _____

    b. _____

11. Is the instruction designed to develop higher-level thinking skills?

_____

_____

Strategies

    a. _____

    b. _____

12. Am I helping my students grow intellectually and socially?

_____

_____

Strategies

    a. _____

    b. _____

13. Am I using all of the resources and support personnel available to me?

_____

_____

Strategies

    a. _____

    b. _____

14. Do I include every student every day?

_____

_____

(Continued)

Teacher Worksheet *(Continued)*

SETTING GOALS FOR IMPROVING YOUR CLASSROOM LEADERSHIP

Strategies

a. _____

b. _____

15. Do I treat my students with sensitivity and respect?

_____

_____

Strategies

a. _____

b. _____

16. Do I present myself as a good teacher: concerned, committed, and professional?

_____

_____

Strategies

a. _____

b. _____

AVOID UNREASONABLE EXPECTATIONS

Many teachers have a strong sense of idealism that draws them to education. Many of us draw a great sense of satisfaction from the thought that what we do in our classrooms makes a positive difference in the world.

When you consider how to improve the way you manage your class or conduct yourself as a teacher, keep in mind that you can't change everything all at once. In fact, there are some things that you just can't change at all. You can't make immature students grow up overnight or keep some of your students from occasionally making regrettable decisions, acting on impulse, or not keeping their priorities straight. Try to be reasonable in what you expect of yourself. Deciding to hold reasonable expectations for your performance is an important choice that can prevent stress and burnout.

Ask yourself if what you are trying to change is reasonable. If you can then decide to move forward, brainstorm several solutions and implement the one that appears to have the greatest chance of success. Set goals, work with purpose, change what you can, and you will soon see positive results.

HOW TO MANAGE YOUR STRESSFUL CAREER

Why do so many of us find our careers rewarding but stressful? Research shows that teaching used to be easier. Less was demanded of teachers, and students were easier to manage. Teachers are especially susceptible to occupational stress because we work in a rigidly structured career where students, administrators, parents, and the community all exert pressures on us. For most of us, these outside pressures are minor when compared to the internal ones that drive us to try to reach every student entrusted to our care.

As you feel your stress begin to build, you should act quickly to avoid the misery of challenges that have turned to distress. There are many strategies for coping with stress on the job as well as at home. Most of these suggestions can be divided into two categories: ways that will help you prevent stress from reaching dangerous levels and some simple techniques that you can use to change your attitude about your problems.

Techniques for Preventing Stress

▶ **Take advantage of professional development opportunities** to refresh your skills and attitude. Being a student again will sharpen your professional skills and broaden your perspective.

▶ **Take pride in being a good teacher.** Planning exciting lessons and carrying through with them won't leave you much time to brood on your problems.

▶ **Set professional goals for yourself and then work to achieve them.** Working toward the achievement of a goal will help you prevent or correct your teaching weaknesses rather than continue to suffer through them. This will keep you focused on something productive instead of your troubles.

▶ **Reward yourself when you have accomplished a particularly onerous task at school.** Remember that teaching is not a profession where recognition is always dependable, so you should take care of your own need for recognition for a job done well.

▶ **Plan relaxation time.** Too much pressure from the "should haves" will destroy even the most determined soul. Many people plan their work days very carefully, but let their free time fly by. Your personal life is just as important as your professional one.

- ▶ **Take time to enjoy your students.** Too often we rush through our teaching chores without taking time to appreciate the unique qualities of each child. Make every adolescent in your class into a hero at least once. Celebrate their achievements with them.

- ▶ **Take care of your health.** Eat well. Get enough rest to function successfully at work. Practice deep breathing exercises to stay calm. Exercise will help you cope with the effects of stressful situations too. Go outdoors and get moving. A sunshine-filled day will lighten a dark mood.

- ▶ Learn a lesson from those who have suffered great hardships and triumphed: **Live one day at a time.**

- ▶ **Set priorities for yourself and your workload** and use these to get your daily jobs done well. Divide your daily work into manageable tasks that can be accomplished in a reasonable length of time. After all, since this is an important skill that you teach your students, shouldn't you benefit from it also?

- ▶ **Learn to work well with the others in your department or your area of the building.** Creating a community at work will make the day more congenial for you and your colleagues.

- ▶ **Solve your problems as quickly as you can.** For example, if you are stressed because you have too many papers to grade, divide them into reasonable stacks and get busy. Deal with misbehaviors before they can get to you.

- ▶ **Politely say "no" when you are asked to do a task that will be too stressful.** Teachers are, by nature, helpful people. Sometimes this tendency causes us distress because we take on too much. Do your part to be a concerned and dedicated faculty member, but be realistic about the time you have available. Teaching your students well should be your first priority.

- ▶ **Be aware of what causes you to be stressed and deal with the problem.** Letting a stressful situation build up will only increase your stress level. Here are some problems you should handle before they grow too large: not enough supplies, difficult students, difficult colleagues, poorly managed paperwork, and poorly planned lessons.

Techniques for Changing Your Perception

Sometimes the best way to handle a stressful situation is to accept it as something you cannot change. Once this happens, you will need to take a further step and change the way you perceive this problem. A student we may regard as creative or funny may have another teacher who regards him as immature and irritating. The student hasn't changed, but the attitudes of the people who teach him have. One teacher enjoys this student; the other teacher is stressed.

There are many ways you can learn to see your job situation in a new light and increase the enjoyment you are able to find in your work day. Experiment with some of these techniques to see which ones will help you in your current teaching situation. Discard the ones that don't seem to fit your needs and find creative ways to incorporate the ones that will help you take the stress out of your job.

- ▶ **Have a colleague with whom you can share problems.** Talking with another teacher is helpful if that person is not one of those grumpy people who has a sour perspective on any problem. Having a colleague who will serve as an informal advisor or sounding board can help make sense of even the most complex problems.

- ▶ **Be sensible about your profession.** Everyone has bad days, sometimes even bad weeks. The important thing to realize is that your attitude about those days and weeks is what makes the difference.

- ▶ **Try your best, but be realistic about what you can and cannot accomplish.** Even the great teachers have had to realize they cannot reach every child every day. Give up those heavy loads of teacher guilt that we all carry around. We cannot make all of our students into happy and successful scholars in the course of a school term, no matter how diligently we try. Do your very best every day and do not allow yourself to feel guilty about all of the opportunities for improving your students' lives that you missed along the way.

- ▶ **Ask yourself: Is it the teaching profession that is making you miserable or is it the daily grind?** Rising at dawn and heading off to a job with such heavy responsibilities is not always easy, but many other careers are just as demanding and not nearly as rewarding. Before you allow your stress levels to build into burnout, consider carefully whether the grass is really greener on the other side of the career fence.

- ▶ **Remember that *you* determine the dominant mood in your classroom** and that no one, including a stressed-out teacher, has the right to ruin the learning opportunities for your students. A happy teacher can create happy students just as quickly as a grouch can offend every student in the room.

- ▶ **Refuse to take it personally when your students are disruptive or uninterested in a lesson.** The cause of the problem probably has nothing to do with you.

- ▶ **When you have problems at school, maintain your perspective.** Ask yourself what you did to cause the problem and what you can do in the future to avoid making the same mistake. Don't dwell on the things you have done wrong: learn from them instead.

- ▶ **When the task seems impossible, remind yourself that teachers made a difference in your life when you were younger**. You can do the same for your students. Our profession abounds with inspiring role models for you to learn from.

- ▶ **Make a list of the reasons that you chose education as your profession.** Tuck it away in a safe place, but carry it in your heart.

THE PROMISE OF PROFESSIONALISM

Veteran teachers often shake their heads at some of the things new teachers do in their classes that the wiser teachers wouldn't dream of doing once they have years of classroom experience. While there may be some validity to this attitude, all of us—new teachers and veterans alike—need to be aware of the professional responsibilities we assumed when we chose our profession.

Exactly what is professional behavior? It means being the very best teacher and employee that you can be every day. This is not always easy. Many things can distract us from our professional responsibilities. Poor planning, personal problems, lack of preparation, uncertainty about the right actions to take, stress, and fatigue are just a few. In order to be professional, we need to pay attention to these distractions and to the ill effects they can have on the discipline climate in our classrooms.

When we choose to conduct ourselves in a professional manner, we set an example for our students to follow that will also encourage them to behave in a productive way. Professionalism is an attitude that helps us earn the respect of our students because we send a message that we are in control of the classroom and of ourselves.

Consistently allow professionalism to be the underlying principle that governs your behavior toward your students. Use the following suggestions to improve the professional image you present to your students and to assume control of the discipline climate of your class.

▶ Dress neatly in a way that is comfortable for you but that is not distracting for your students. Because you are a role model of adult behavior, you should take your workday appearance seriously.

▶ Project an attitude of confidence even if you don't feel confident.

▶ Treat all of your students fairly. Not the same: fairly.

▶ Separate your personal self from your professional self. This attitude change will help you perceive criticism from your supervisors as helpful, not threatening.

▶ Support student organizations and teams at your school. The members of the community will notice and appreciate your efforts. Your students will, too.

▶ Acquaint yourself with the curriculum of the other grade levels in your discipline. If you are going to be an effective teacher, then you should know where your students are headed as well as what they are expected to have learned before they enrolled in your class.

▶ Make a daily list of the paperwork that needs to be done and resolve to get it all turned in on time.

▶ Be understanding and flexible, but not a pushover for too many ridiculous excuses.

▶ Repeat as often as needed: "I am in charge of this classroom. Unruly children are not the leaders here, I am."

▶ Teach your students the study skills they need to unlock the information in the textbook.

▶ Let your students do the talking. Teachers who ask questions instead of lecturing will experience far fewer discipline problems than those teachers who drone on and on.

▶ Be an example of a person who is always punctual. When you are late, you put an unfair burden on others who have to assume your responsibilities.

▶ Remind yourself that all teachers—young, old, cheerful, or tired—affect the classroom climate.

▶ Students without enough to do will quickly annoy all nearby adults. Perhaps this is the most common mistake teachers make: not giving students enough meaningful work to do.

▶ If you are angry enough to raise your voice in front of your students, stop and reassess the situation. Don't lose face in front of the class. Some of your students will be amused, some will be frightened, but all of them will lose faith in you.

▶ Be excited about learning. Communicate that excitement to your students.

▶ Ask questions if you are not sure about the best course of action to follow in a situation where you find yourself confused.

▶ Keep in mind that we don't teach a class; we teach individual students.

▶ Never forget that what you say in class today will be discussed at dinner tables all over town tonight.

▶ Use humor to lighten a heavy lesson. Allow your students to enjoy life with you.

▶ Treat all students with respect. Even the most difficult child has feelings that are easily hurt.

▶ Accept responsibility for student learning. Teach your students to accept responsibility for themselves as fast as you can.

- Don't join those legions of teachers who brag about how tough they are and how many students they have failed.

- Accept into your heart and soul that all students can learn, even those who seem impossible to reach. Don't give up on them.

- Be a force for positive change in your classroom. Don't allow yourself or your students to just drift through the term.

- Make lessons relevant and goals attainable.

- Learn from your mistakes. One of the hardest things about our profession is that it provides plenty of opportunities for this kind of learning.

- Have a good answer ready when a student asks, "Why do we have to learn this stuff anyway?"

- Have high expectations for your students. You must expect a great deal from them if you are to get a great deal from them.

- Promote cooperation as often as you promote competition.

- Don't allow students to curse in front of you. Don't tolerate even mild cursing.

- It's often the small details that separate professional from unprofessional behavior. Be punctual, accurate, and precise in your work.

- If a supervisor tells you that you have made a mistake, accept the correction with thanks. Work to correct the problem. Make sure your later success is evident.

- Focus on your students' excuses. What can you learn about your students and how they see you?

- Be consistent in your attempts to improve your students' behavior through patience and understanding. Don't give up on them.

- Make your lessons as involved with real-life experiences as possible.

- Help your students see the connection between their textbooks and their lives.

- Speak out against teen substance abuse *loudly* and *often*.

- Open and end each class in a spectacular fashion.

- Encourage your students to teach you.

- Make all students see that they are important to the success of the entire class.

- Take pride in your profession. Share this attitude with your students.

- Be an active teacher with an active class.

- Categorically refuse to accept certain behaviors such as name calling, insults, or other actions that will instantly disrupt your class.

- Treat your students as worthy individuals. Let them know you care for them.

- Make yourself aware of how your colleagues and students perceive you. Are you satisfied with the image you project?

- Be careful not to insult your students with unconsciously negative body language.

- Continually add to your knowledge about education. Read professional literature, attend workshops, and stay abreast of new developments in the field.

- Make your students, colleagues, and supervisors look good. Support other staff members with praise in front of students.

- When you make a mistake, admit it. Apologize and move on.

HOW TO BE PREPARED FOR CLASS EVERY DAY

Every decision we make as teachers is one that has the potential to affect the discipline climate in our classrooms in a negative or positive way. Making the commitment to be fully prepared for class every day is a sensible choice with the potential for significantly positive results. Students whose teachers are able to provide well-prepared and well-paced instruction are far more likely to stay on task than those students whose teachers are distracted by missing materials or poorly planned activities.

If you ever underestimate the importance of such a simple commitment on your part, consider the consequences of not being fully prepared. Here is a quick example of what can go wrong very quickly when something as simple as extra copies are not ready.

> A teacher arrives at school too late to make the ten extra handouts necessary for every student to have his or her own copy of the day's assignment. Chairs scrape as students find partners with copies to share and slowly settle down to work. Some students are especially distracted because they work more quickly than their partners and have to wait for their classmates to catch up before going on to the next page. Soon students realize that they are not going to be able to finish the assignment on time and either quit working or begin racing through it.

Even though the complex nature of our jobs makes it almost impossible to be fully prepared all the time, here are a few quick actions you can take to be fully prepared for class every day:

▶ Spend enough time at the start of the term planning instruction. With a broad overview of the semester as well as the various units you plan to teach as your guide, you will find it easier to work ahead and stay on top of the workload. After you have made your large-scale plans, then you should try to plan and prepare detailed instruction at least two weeks in advance.

▶ One way to make being prepared for class easier is to get in the habit of maintaining a calendar where you can record your meetings, duties, tasks, and lesson plans. Here are two excellent planning calendars that function well for teachers:

- **Do It Yourself Planner (www.diyplanner.com).** At this site you will find templates, suggestions, and even user forums to create your own planner or work calendar.

- **Mead School Supplies (www.mead.com).** Click on the "Teachers" tab to access a variety of useful planning products designed with busy teachers in mind.

▶ Be ready to be flexible. All sorts of things can cause delays, interruptions, or a change in plans. Create a folder prepared with general backup plan ideas that you can use all year. Consider including high-interest activities such as puzzles, games, and practice problems. In addition, you should also create backup plans with activities specifically related to the unit under study in your class.

▶ Make it a point to be as efficient as possible in how you manage paperwork. From grading papers to writing plans to documenting parent contacts, devise systems to stay organized. A helpful Web site with teacher-friendly suggestions for this is managed by Scholastic, Inc., at http://www2.scholastic.com. Browse the "Tools" selections under the "Teaching Resources" tab for various templates for to-do lists, calendars, and other planners.

▶ Create personal daily routines and work habits that will make it easier to stay organized. Some practical work habits for teachers include these:

- File handouts and other papers every day.
- Keep your classroom keys in the same place.
- Set aside a specific time for checking e-mail instead of just whenever you have a spare moment.
- Keep a notepad and pen in the same place so that you can easily write reminders or add to your to-do list.
- Have a routine for collecting student work so that it is easy for you to grade it quickly.
- End the day by leaving your desk clean so that your new day gets off to a good start.

▶ Ask students to keep their area of the room tidy, sort papers, staple or punch holes in handouts, and generally help manage the physical environment in the classroom.

HOW TO MAKE YOUR STUDENTS PAY ATTENTION TO YOU

It happens to every teacher at some time or another. We lose our students. Not physically, of course; it's pretty difficult to misplace thirty or so rambunctious individuals. But while their bodies are still in the room with us, their minds have taken a little vacation from the lesson we have so carefully prepared. If we're lucky, all that goes wrong is that their eyes glaze over and expressions of polite disinterest replace the focused attention that we strive to instill in our students.

If we're not lucky, pandemonium erupts and less enthusiastic teachers consider other career opportunities. The skillful teacher, however, will take pains to develop a full repertoire of strategies to cut the vacations short and put the class firmly back on track before too much vital learning time is lost.

Here are four mistakes many teachers make when trying to catch their students' attention. These mistakes are easy to avoid once you have made yourself aware of them.

Don't Talk Unless You Have Everyone's Attention

Many teachers talk *over* their students' activity. While students are getting materials ready, sharpening pencils, finding the page, or finishing a conversation, the teacher is in the front of the room giving directions or other information about the lesson for the day.

This is not a practice that encourages students to be self-disciplined or even polite. The message that it sends is that what the instructor is saying is not really important. It also usually results in either a student asking you to repeat the information or in students asking each other to explain what you have just said.

A Better Choice: Wait until you have everyone's attention before you address the class. Establish a signal with your students so that they know they need to stop what they are doing and listen to you. This can be an expression such as "May I have your attention, please" or another signal such as a place in the room where you go when you need to speak to the entire group. It's not enough simply to establish this procedure; you have to teach it to your class and then consistently reinforce it.

Don't Repeat Yourself

It's one thing to clarify information or explain directions; it's another to have to repeat yourself for students who are not in the habit of listening. Don't assume that your students are good listeners. Many have never been taught how to listen attentively.

A Better Choice: Say something once and teach your students to listen to you the *first* time. Take the time and teach listening skills throughout the term so that your students can develop them. Make this a part of the culture of your classroom and you will find yourself not having to repeat.

Don't Forget Your Audience

If you never vary the tone of your voice, if you mumble, if you talk with your back to the class, or if you talk to only one or two faces in the crowd, then you are more interested in what you are saying than in whether your students are learning the material. The best-planned lessons in the world are useless if you forget that you are talking to an audience of living, breathing adolescents who are quick to disengage from a speaker they don't find interesting.

A Better Choice: Recall those public-speaking tips from your undergraduate Speech 101 class and apply them. Videotape yourself or simply record your voice. Study your presentation to make sure you are reaching your audience.

If you give your students work to do while you are speaking that will force them to interact with you, then you can be sure of engaging their attention. A handout with key words missing or with outlined notes to complete will encourage students to stay on track while you are speaking.

Don't Assume That Your Students Are Ready to Listen Just Because You Are Ready to Speak

Many teachers tell their students to turn to a certain page in the book and then immediately begin talking about the material on that page while students scramble to find paper and pens to take notes. Your students need time to prepare themselves and to settle down before they can listen well.

A Better Choice: Wait. Allow your students to get their notebook pages dated and other materials ready before you begin talking to them. If you just want them to listen and not write, ask them to clear their desks of all writing materials and books. Set the stage if you want to capture their attention.

SHOW RESPECT TO GAIN RESPECT

No matter how interesting our subject, how dynamic our instruction, or how well-planned our procedures, if we do not have the respect of our students, we are poor teachers. Respect is one of those vital intangibles that is difficult to define. It's the constant delicate balance among the many roles we assume in our workday: disciplinarian, motivator, humorist, listener, advisor, evaluator, entertainer, guide, comforter, lecturer, and role model.

When students respect us, they don't see us merely as friendly adults who talk with them for several hours each week; instead we have met their ideal of what a teacher should be. Having your students' respect is one of the biggest assets you or any teacher can bring to school each day. Without it, all of your other efforts will not be successful.

How do we lose the respect our students are willing to extend to us? There are many ways in which the unwary teacher can cause students to lose faith. Here are just a few of the more obvious mistakes that are all too easy to make:

- ▶ Losing your temper
- ▶ Refusing to admit it when you make a mistake

- ▶ Treating students unfairly
- ▶ Assigning an insufficient amount of work
- ▶ Assigning work that is inappropriate or not challenging
- ▶ Treating students harshly
- ▶ Not knowing the material
- ▶ Being insensitive to students' needs
- ▶ Being emotionally unstable
- ▶ Not being a good adult role model

If these are the mistakes that are easy for teachers to make, how then can we earn our students' respect? The best way to ensure that we have earned our students' respect is to fulfill our roles as teachers. We telegraph our respect throughout the school day in the many small professional decisions that we make such as returning graded papers promptly, being prepared for class, and treating all students with dignity.

There is no better substitute for improving the way we teach than to be self-critical. When teachers examine the way they fulfill their classroom roles—assessing their own strengths and weaknesses—then they can work systematically to improve the areas where they are not as strong as they would like to be. See "Are You Too Permissive?" and "Determine What You Want Your Students to Say About You" to gather information about how permissive you are and exactly what you would like your students to say about you.

Teacher Self-Assessment

ARE YOU TOO PERMISSIVE?

One of the important areas teachers need to examine is how permissive we are. Do we let our students get away with misbehavior or are we too strict? Are we consistent in how we expect our students to behave? One of the most critical issues in earning student respect is the balance we must maintain between being too permissive and being too strict.

Use the items in this checklist to determine the areas where you are too permissive and where you may be too strict. Select the letter of the response that is closest to your own discipline style and fill in the blank. After you have finished all ten choices, check what your responses reveal about how permissive or strict you tend to be.

1. ____ Students jokingly insult each other while waiting for class to begin.
   a. Ignore the horseplay. Class hasn't started yet.
   b. Remind students of the procedure for starting class and the class rule about showing respect for others.
   c. Tell students to stop and to get to work.

2. ____ A student is lost in a daydream instead of finishing a reading assignment.
   a. Tell the student that if he or she doesn't get to work, there will be more to do for homework.
   b. Stay at your desk and wait to see how long it takes the dreamer to get back to work.
   c. Move to stand near the student.

3. ____ Students take too long to get their papers arranged for a test.
   a. Remind them to hurry.
   b. Start the test and let the slow ones catch up.
   c. Tell them they have one minute to get ready and then time them by watching the clock.

4. ____ Students ball up papers and toss them at the wastebasket while you are giving directions about an assignment.
   a. Shake your head, frown, and move near them.
   b. Stop what you are saying and reprimand them.
   c. Finish your directions. Go to the students and quietly ask them about the class rule they violated.

5. ____ Students chat while you are explaining the homework assignment.
   a. Ignore it.
   b. Stop and wait for them to pay attention.
   c. Tell them to stop talking and start paying attention.

6. ____ A student lacks a textbook, pen, or paper.
   a. Share materials from the class storehouse.
   b. Don't allow the student to complete the work in class. He or she can do it at home. This will help all students remember to bring materials next time.
   c. Allow the student to borrow from classmates.

7. ____ Students turn in sloppy or inaccurate work.
   a. Refuse to take it.
   b. Take it but give them a lecture about work habits.
   c. Require that they redo the work.
8. ____ Students are tardy to class without a good reason.
   a. Enforce your rules regarding tardiness to class.
   b. Refuse to let them in.
   c. Meet them at the door and ask why they are tardy.
9. ____ Students talk back rudely when you have reprimanded them.
   a. Send them to the office.
   b. Reprimand them privately.
   c. Ignore it.
10. ____ Students ignore you when you call for the class to quiet down to work.
    a. Keep asking until they listen to you.
    b. Raise your voice until no one can ignore you.
    c. Give the signal that they recognize as a sign that they need to get quiet.

What Your Responses Reveal About You

You might be *too permissive* if you chose these answers:

1. a
2. b
3. a
4. a
5. a
6. c
7. b
8. c
9. c
10. a

You might be *too strict* if you chose these answers:

1. c
2. a
3. b
4. b
5. c
6. b

(Continued)

Teacher Self-Assessment *(Continued)*

ARE YOU TOO PERMISSIVE?

7. a
8. b
9. a
10. b

The best way to deal with the issue of permissiveness is to make yourself aware of the areas where you may be inclined to be permissive rather than sensible in your approach. If you are still not sure of the best course to take, ask yourself these questions:

- ▶ Is this behavior appropriate?
- ▶ What will happen if I choose to ignore this behavior?
- ▶ What will happen if I choose to deal with this behavior?
- ▶ What message about future behavior am I sending to my students in the way I handle this problem?

Teacher Self-Assessment

DETERMINE WHAT YOU WANT YOUR STUDENTS TO SAY ABOUT YOU

Many secondary students have very clear ideas about what they expect from their teachers. If you want to be the kind of proactive and fair-minded teacher who has few behavior problems to deal with in the course of a school day, then it will be easier for you to establish a productive classroom atmosphere. One of the best ways for you to find out what your students expect from you is to informally survey them. You will probably find that the results of your survey will be similar to the following list of teacher traits that students value.

Use this list of the qualities that students value in their teachers to begin to examine how you measure up against your students' vision of the ideal teacher. If the quality is one that you already possess, place a checkmark in the blank. Since these are desirable traits, the more traits you can check, the better.

A good teacher

1. _____ Enjoys students

2. _____ Doesn't just hand out assignments, but teaches the material

3. _____ Assigns many different types of activities

4. _____ Has a great sense of humor

5. _____ Understands pupil problems and tries to help

6. _____ Acts like an adult and not a child

7. _____ Keeps promises

8. _____ Makes sure everyone understands how to do an assignment

9. _____ Is not too strict

10. _____ Is organized

11. _____ Spends time after school to help students

12. _____ Returns papers promptly

13. _____ Is friendly and fair

14. _____ Knows the subject matter

15. _____ Admits when he or she is wrong

16. _____ Stays open-minded

17. _____ Is enthusiastic about the subject

18. _____ Is willing to listen to both sides of an issue

19. _____ Does not allow much misbehavior

20. _____ Is polite to everyone all of the time

WATCH YOUR BODY LANGUAGE

Teachers who want to improve their classroom charisma know that much of their appeal is conveyed through their body language. Some experts even estimate that as much as half of what we want to communicate is done through the way we move our bodies. Paying attention to the nonverbal messages you send shows concern for your students. This, in turn, will make it easier for you to prevent many discipline problems.

To learn more about how your body language affects your presentation style, consider consulting one of these sources:

Pease, B., and Pease, A. *The Definitive Book of Body Language*. New York: Bantam, 2006.

Lieberman, J. *You Can Read Anyone*. Lakewood, NJ: Viter Press, 2007.

Nonverbal Signals You Should Avoid

- No eye contact with certain students
- Pointing at students
- Laughing while delivering a serious message
- Turning your back while a student is speaking to you
- Slamming doors, books, or anything
- Rolling your eyes as if in disgust
- Sharing "knowing looks" with other students when someone is having trouble with an answer
- Staying behind a desk or at a lectern for the entire class period
- Hugging students who clearly don't want to be hugged
- Snapping fingers at a student
- Jabbing a finger at a student's chest to make a point
- Ignoring students who fall asleep in class
- Staying seated for the entire class period
- Chewing gum or eating in front of students
- Speaking too rapidly, too loudly, or in a monotone
- Leaning away from students
- Talking on and on while ignoring body language signals from students
- Using a sarcastic tone
- Ignoring a student who is obviously tearful or angry
- Throwing anything at students, even in jest
- Never smiling
- Tapping fingers to show impatience with students
- Putting your hands too close to a student's face—violating his or her personal space
- Standing with your hands on your hips, obviously impatient or angry
- Not responding to a student's answer to a question or when a student speaks to you

Nonverbal Signals to Stop Misbehavior

You can also use nonverbal language to send a clear message that you are in control of the class and aware of your students' activities. You can use many signals with misbehaving students that will convey your message without distracting other students. These nonverbal messages are effective because they get your point across and do not interfere with the learning process. Here is a list of the nonverbal signals you can send to deter your students from misbehaving without having to say a word:

▶ Pick up your book or grade book and move to the front of the room

▶ Make eye contact with the student who is misbehaving

▶ Stand up if you are sitting and face the students who are off-task

▶ Turn music on or off

▶ Move to the board and write a message

▶ Hold up your hand with the palm facing the class

▶ Frown at students who are misbehaving

▶ Give a thumbs-up or thumbs-down signal

▶ Shrug your shoulders and shake your head

▶ Hand something to the misbehaving student

▶ Nod your head and raise your eyebrows

▶ Smile

▶ Put your hand on the object your student is touching

▶ Lightly touch the student on the arm or hand

▶ Move toward a student who is misbehaving

▶ Lean forward to show you are interested in a student's activity

▶ Stand or sit near students who are misbehaving

▶ Pause in the middle of what you are saying until an offending student stops talking

▶ Flick the lights or ring a bell as an arranged signal for attention

▶ Go to a designated area of the room where your students know they are supposed to stop talking when you are in this spot

▶ Glance pointedly at the clock when students either are being timed or are dawdling

▶ Point to the object you want them to focus on

▶ Hold up an interesting object to catch their attention and stop misbehavior

▶ Put your hand on the desk of a student who is being disruptive

▶ Raise your eyebrows and look surprised that one of your students would misbehave

KNOW YOUR AUDIENCE

Many teachers, in a rush to cover the mandated instructional material, find it all too easy to overlook one of the most important elements in maintaining a well-disciplined class: an attentive audience. Those teachers who are strong classroom leaders, however, carefully attend to the needs of their students throughout each class period. From adding in a quick two-minute wiggle break in the middle of a long assignment to switching from a fast-paced activity to a slower one near the end of a tiring class period, teachers who are sensitive to the whole group and the individual needs of the members of their classroom audience will experience far fewer disruptions than those teachers who ignore their students.

Many factors other than student ability and maturity level can affect the attention level in your class. Because you will find it easier to help your students if you are aware of the cause of their distraction or misbehavior, when a student or a group of students is not performing well, search for the underlying cause. Some of the negative factors affecting student performance that are easiest to monitor are

- The time of day that the class meets
- Classroom temperature
- The physical arrangement of the classroom
- Distracting school events
- Distracting personal events in students' lives
- The mixture of learning styles in the class
- Student attention span
- Student readiness level
- Prerequisite skills acquisition
- Student motivation
- Student interest in the material
- Class chemistry

Although the positive signs that indicate that your students are enjoying the lesson and learning the material are easy to spot, the negative signs are not always as evident, especially in older or well-behaved students. You should be alert to potential problems if you notice that your students are engaging in behaviors such as these:

- Fidgeting more than normal
- Making offhand negative comments
- Requesting to use the restroom or visit the clinic
- Working more slowly than expected
- Handing in incomplete or poorly done work
- Forgetting their materials or assignments
- Not making eye contact with you
- Making faces or eye contact with other students
- Slouching or turning away from you when you are speaking
- Frowning or staring vacantly into space

If you observe the above negative behaviors in your class, you should pay attention to their implications for the success of your discipline climate. Be careful to interpret them as accurately as you can, however. Many teachers who teach students from cultures different from their own can mistake nonverbal cues that are neutral or even positive in the student's culture for negative ones in the teacher's culture.

BE CAREFUL ABOUT YOUR LANGUAGE

A teacher's manner of expression is a powerful tool in creating a well-run classroom. Those teachers who have mastered the art of always speaking in a friendly, adult tone and who always seem to know just the right thing to say in just the right way experience far fewer problems than those teachers who find it necessary to shout just to be heard in class. One of the reasons for this is that many students have had few positive role models who speak to them in a kind, respectful, and mature manner. Because of their chaotic home lives, the only positive adult role models they may have are their teachers. With this in mind, the importance of being careful about how you speak to your students is clear. In the list that follows you will find a few tips to remind you of some of the mistakes you should skip when speaking to your students.

- ▶ Don't use a sarcastic tone. If it is disrespectful for your students to be sarcastic to you, then it is disrespectful for you to be sarcastic to them.
- ▶ Don't be too informal or playful, especially when you want students to settle down to work.
- ▶ Don't use a mocking tone to repeat what your students say.
- ▶ Don't create nicknames for your students that are not entirely positive, appropriate, and welcomed.
- ▶ Don't ask a student to repeat an ill-advised remark, especially in front of classmates.
- ▶ Don't use the same slang terms that your students do. While it is acceptable to speak informally, remember that you are an adult role model.
- ▶ Don't indulge in angry name calling.
- ▶ Don't forget to address other adults with respect and insist that your students do also.
- ▶ Don't neglect to monitor your own speech patterns for distracting verbal tics.
- ▶ Don't curse, even mildly. It is better to err on the side of restraint rather than offend with inappropriate language.
- ▶ Don't use double entendres that may be insulting, demeaning, or inappropriate.
- ▶ Don't forget that your tone is as important as the actual words that you use.

See this section's "Making Positive Choices" for more ideas about how you can make positive choices that can make your school year productive and pleasant.

Making Positive Choices

Instead of . . .	Try to . . .
▶ Checking e-mail during class	▶ Circulate around the room monitoring student progress and offering assistance
▶ Refusing to admit that you've made a mistake	▶ Solve what you can and focus on what you can change
▶ Allowing off-task behavior to escalate	▶ Pay attention to how permissive you may be
▶ Leaving in a rush at the end of the day	▶ Leave your desk clean at the end of each day
▶ Putting self-sticking notes all over your desk in an effort to stay organized	▶ Use a personal to-do list and a daily planner
▶ Wishing you were a better teacher	▶ Make a plan and implement sensible strategies to reach your goals

(Continued)

Making Positive Choices *(Continued)*

Instead of . . .	Try to . . .
▶ Making a quick, sarcastic reply	▶ Count to three before answering in a calm tone
▶ Feeling overwhelmed when you've had a bad day	▶ Be at least two weeks ahead in your planning
▶ Allowing too much horseplay during student down time	▶ Keep student down time to a minimum with well-paced lessons
▶ Remembering a student's unkind criticism of your lesson	▶ Offer students an online survey and solicit suggestions about how you are doing as a teacher

QUESTIONS FOR REFLECTION

Use the information in this section to guide your thinking as you think about these questions. They are designed to encourage you to think more deeply about the issues in the text or to discuss those issues with colleagues.

▶ How skillful are you at leading a class? What areas are you proudest of? What would you like to improve? Who can offer you help with your plans to improve?

▶ How well do your students pay attention to you? What suggestions from the list of ways to help students pay attention appeal to you? What techniques can you add to the list?

▶ Are you too permissive? How will you know if you are? How can you prevent the cycle of misbehavior caused by permissiveness from taking root in your class?

SECTION FOUR

Foster a Positive Classroom Environment

In this section you will learn

- How to create a positive classroom atmosphere

- How to help students cope with bullying

- How to use the three main elements of a classroom environment

- How to create a student-centered class atmosphere

- How to use class time wisely

ESTABLISH A POSITIVE CLASSROOM ENVIRONMENT

Although at first it may not appear as important as meeting state standards or maintaining a strong connection with students, establishing a positive classroom environment is also one of the key components in a well-run, orderly classroom. In this environment students can be safe, comfortable, and engaged. While it may be noisy and messy by the end of the period, a positive classroom still sets the stage for student success.

The three key elements of a positive classroom environment: keeping students safe, arranging the physical space into a workplace, and maintaining a brisk, businesslike pace, all prevent a great deal of misbehavior by sending an affirmative message to students. In a positive classroom environment, many smaller annoyances that can slowly erode the orderly and productive atmosphere that should exist are eliminated.

SAFETY MUST COME FIRST

No matter how beautifully decorated the room or how well-paced the instruction, if your students do not feel safe from harm, no learning is possible. Perhaps this overwhelming belief is the basis for the strong sense of shock that we feel when whenever there is a violent episode at a school. Above all else, a school should be a safe place for students and teachers alike.

How can we manage to keep students safe? The easiest factor to control is the physical surroundings. We can establish a place that is not only clean but free from obvious hazards such as broken glass and frayed electrical cords. Examine the following list of commonsense safety practices in order to determine which ones you can use to create a safe environment for your students and yourself.

- ▶ Don't leave matches or other fire starters where your students can take them.
- ▶ Discourage your students from taking such items as staplers from your desk. Instead, provide materials just for their use in another part of the room and teach students to respect your property.
- ▶ Lock out of sight all of your personal belongings as well as any money that you collect during the day.
- ▶ If your classroom is not in use, keep it locked. No room should be left unattended with students unsupervised.
- ▶ Keep teachers' textbook editions secure. If you should lose something of value, don't threaten your students. Instead, offer a reward for the first person to return it.
- ▶ Teach and enforce your rules and procedures on a daily basis until everyone understands your expectations.
- ▶ Organize your room so that your students can find what they need quickly and with a minimum of confusion.
- ▶ If possible, teach the class with your door closed. You will minimize disruptions from outside your classroom.

The next classroom safety element—the well-being of students—is not as easy to control as the physical environment. It requires teachers to use common sense to keep students out of danger. For example, we must be diligent in our awareness of each student's medical history so that students with allergies, asthma, or other medical conditions remain as healthy as possible. We also need to be aware of threats from outside the school such as a conflict in the neighborhood or a gang presence. Sometimes teachers are the first ones students turn to when there is a conflict with a family member or with a peer that is abusive or violent, and we must be able to act promptly and appropriately.

- ▶ Don't give your classroom or car keys to a student. Open the car door and the classroom door yourself and walk with students whom you ask to help carry things from your car.
- ▶ Pay attention to notes from a doctor or from a parent about a potentially dangerous physical condition.
- ▶ Report suspected guns or other weapons immediately.
- ▶ Have a zero tolerance policy for racial, cultural, or other prejudices.

▶ Keep scissors out of sight until you know your students very well. Even then be careful about potential weapons.

▶ Return parent phone calls on the same day you receive them. It is not only courteous and professional, but parents may have an important concern that needs to be addressed at once.

▶ Listen to students who say they feel unwell. Send ill students to the school nurse or office as quickly as you can.

▶ Keep adhesive bandages and tissues on hand for your students to use.

▶ Don't give students hard candy. It's too easy for someone to choke on it.

▶ Don't allow your students to have food or drinks in your classroom if this is against school policy.

▶ It's not wise to give out your home phone number to your students even though it is a friendly thing to do. The problems that need to be solved after hours can probably be solved with *you* making the calls, rather than your students phoning you.

▶ Stay at school with your students until their rides arrive if you are holding a group after school. They still need supervision. Don't give your students rides home from school.

▶ Realize that there is a reason that students misbehave. Do your best to discover and deal with that reason.

▶ Don't use too much cologne or aftershave. Some students may experience allergic reactions if you do.

▶ Openly take a stand against drugs, alcohol, and tobacco. Your students need to hear adults speak out against these substances.

▶ If you suspect that a student has been abused, act at once. Send the student to a counselor.

▶ Take seriously students who say they are suicidal.

▶ Pay attention to which students have left your room with a hall pass. You are responsible for the students assigned to your care. Keep your hall passes and other school passes in a safe place.

▶ Never accuse a student of serious misconduct or cheating without absolute proof.

▶ Come to work on time. Don't miss school unless you have to.

Because classroom safety is such an important aspect of school life, there is a great deal of information for educators online. Here are some Web sites that you may find particularly helpful in your efforts to create a classroom where students can feel safe and secure:

▶ The National School Safety Center (www.schoolsafety.us). Here you will find useful information, products, and many links to more information about what you can do to create a safe environment for your students.

▶ Keep Schools Safe (www.keepschoolssafe.org). Keep Schools Safe is an organization whose mission is to reduce school violence. You will find links to dozens of articles related to the topic.

▶ National Crime Prevention Council (www.ncpc.org). This site offers suggestions for teachers, students, parents, and others concerned with the issue of school safety. Use *school safety* as a search term on the home page to access the information related to schools.

HOW TO DETERMINE IF STUDENTS ARE STRESSED INSTEAD OF CHALLENGED

Although good teachers determinedly push their students to succeed through a combination of high expectations and hard work, it is sometimes difficult to tell when students are not just challenged to do their best, but genuinely stressed. The difference between the two is significant not just in terms of the mental health of individual students, but also in how your entire class functions.

Frustrations can cause otherwise pleasant students to act out at you and their classmates. They pick on each other with increasing frequency while the potential for disruptive and unproductive behaviors rises. Sometimes the frustration caused by stressed-out students can even escalate into violent behavior. When you are trying to determine the amount of stress that your students may be experiencing, consider some of these signals.

Stressed-out students tend to

▶ Engage in more name calling and negative interactions with each other

▶ Send you e-mails about their problems

▶ Complete fewer assignments

▶ Comment on their heavy workload

▶ Complain more than usual

Another method that you can use when you begin to notice the signs of distress among your students is to ask them to rank their problems on a scale of 1 to 5. This technique will provide an idea of how they are thinking, and it also lets students know that you care about what they are experiencing. "How Stressed Are You?" is a chart you can adapt to meet the needs of your students.

Student Worksheet

HOW STRESSED ARE YOU?

In the chart below, you have an opportunity to indicate what is causing any stress in this class.

Rank just how stressed you feel by circling the number in the middle column, with 1 being a very low stress level and 5 being a high stress level.

Topics	Ranking					Comments
Class activities	1	2	3	4	5	
Homework assignments	1	2	3	4	5	
Tests and quizzes	1	2	3	4	5	
Peer relationships	1	2	3	4	5	
Other	1	2	3	4	5	

PROTECT YOUR STUDENTS FROM BULLIES

It happens in the restrooms, in the hallways, at recess, on the playground, in the locker room, in the cafeteria . . . anyplace in a school where adult supervision is minimal. Generations of students have suffered verbal and physical abuse at the hands of other students. Unfortunately, too, bullying only gets worse as students enter the secondary grades.

How much worse? Each month thousands of secondary students report they have been attacked by a classmate at school. Many students report that they have been afraid to attend school at least once because of the threat of violence by a classmate.

Bullying is a serious and growing problem for educators. As more and more violent scenes are played out in our daily lives—reported to us through our news programs, enacted in television shows and movies, and portrayed in popular songs—we have a generation of children who are less sensitive to violence than preceding ones. Where incidents of bullying in the past may have involved ugly name calling or insults, today's bullying can result in a much more violent consequence: murder or suicide.

The worst aspect of the problem of bullying, however, is that many teachers admit they are slow to react when they observe a student picking on a classmate. These teachers either react unsympathetically when a complaint about a bully is made or simply turn away when they hear or see this type of abuse.

The weapons that make bullying effective in humiliating students are threats and fear. The misery that bullying brings to a hapless student who may simply be different from the others in the class far outweighs the sense that this is a normal part of growing up.

This policy of neglect would not be so surprising if teachers also felt safe at school, but many of us do not. Many secondary teachers report that they have been insulted, subjected to obscene gestures, or threatened by their students.

The first thing we need to do to stop this serious threat is to make sure we understand exactly what bullying is. Bullying can take three forms: physical abuse, verbal abuse, or cyberbullying. When physical abuse is involved, teachers are more likely to react to stop it. Verbal abuse is far more widespread and is often tolerated by teachers. Verbal abuse includes name calling, teasing, racist remarks, rumors, and other insults or slurs. Cyberbullying is a growing threat as more and more students use social networking sites to connect with their classmates.

There are eleven steps you can take in order to deal with the problem of bullying in general. These strategies are designed to be followed in sequence when you have to deal with an incident involving bullying in your class. Following these steps, you will find strategies for helping students who are victims of cyberbullying.

Step 1

Make sure your school's policy is clear and up-to-date on this issue. Every staff member should have a copy of the policy. Students should also be aware of the school's policy and the consequences involved.

Step 2

A positive step you can take with your students is to discuss the issue and to allow them to talk about their fears and beliefs on the topic of bullying. They can work together to establish peer-group support and to help each other see how wrong this type of abuse is.

Step 3

Be alert for the early signs of bullying. Often teachers only see the tip of the iceberg because bullies prefer to target victims in unsupervised areas. If, for example, you notice that several students have targeted one of their classmates for disrespect or that a student is having trouble making adjustments to your class at the beginning of the term, be alert that more may be going on than you see. Speak privately to the offending students to make sure they know that what they are doing is in violation of the school's policy on bullying.

Step 4

Make a special effort to patrol the areas in your school where bullying is likely to take place. Involve other teachers and administrators in this endeavor if a routine duty assignment schedule is not already in place.

Step 5

Continue to listen carefully and begin to document all incidents that you observe. Report your findings to an administrator or counselor.

Step 6

Put the school procedures into action when you speak to an administrator or counselor so that no time can be wasted in waiting for a response. Waiting for a response could allow the situation to escalate to more violence.

Step 7

Meet with the victim to discuss the incident and have that student write out a report of what happened. Just being able to talk about it with a concerned adult will help many victims.

Step 8

Lend your support to the victim. If an incident of physical abuse has occurred, act at once. Make sure victims are aware that you are working on their behalf.

Step 9

Meet with the bully and have that student also talk about what happened. Be firm, but don't lecture. Have that student also put the events of the incident in writing.

Step 10

Speak to the bully and his or her parents or guardians to let them know what you have witnessed or what has been reported. They should have a clear understanding that not only is the action not acceptable, but that the school has a policy against bullying and the incident has been reported to an administrator.

Step 11

Involve both sets of parents or guardians. Either have them come to school for separate conferences or send them copies of the written statements made by both students. Parents or guardians can be valuable resources in stopping this problem.

Cyberbullying

Cyberbullying is a relatively new harassment phenomenon that continues to spread as more and more students have access to social networking sites, cell phones, and other forms of electronic communication. Cyberbullying is just what its name implies: the harassment of one person by another through electronic means. For the classroom teacher, catching a cyberbully is difficult because our students' school computer time, if used productively, is spent in academic pursuits.

Cyberbullying is often more insidious than other types of bullying because it does not occur in just one place. Victims are never free from the threat as long as they carry a cell phone, check e-mail, or belong to social networking sites. Cyberbullies, too, are often more abusive and aggressive because they are not face to face with their victims. While the general advice about bullying offered above can make it easier for students to cope with physical and verbal abuse, it can also apply to cyberbullies.

While it is not our responsibility to police the way that our students use their personal electronic media to communicate with each other when they are not in class, teachers do have a privileged position in the lives of our students. We can offer aid and support when our students are the victims of cyberbullies. Here are the steps to follow with this kind of bullying:

Step 1

If a student confides to you that he or she is the victim of a cyberbully, the first step that you should take is to take the student's distress seriously. Talk with the student to learn the details of the harassment.

Step 2

Involve other professionals who can help your student immediately. Contact your school's technology support personnel and the administrator whose responsibility it is to cope with your school's fair use of the Internet policy to enlist their assistance.

Step 3

At this point, the other personnel should assume the primary role in helping your student with the issue. You should, however, continue to offer your support and encouragement to help the victim.

To learn more about what you can do to prevent and deal with digital harassment, several national organizations can offer you and your students advice and support. One of the foremost of these organizations is Wired Kids. This group maintains an informative and helpful site at www.stopcyberbullying .org. Another group is the Cyberbullying Research Center. Their site at www.cyberbullying.us offers constructive prevention and response tips for teens, victims, parents, and educators.

MAKING YOUR CLASSROOM SAFE BY ENFORCING SCHOOL RULES

There is a need for rules whenever people are expected to work in harmony. A school where all of the adults can agree on and abide by an established set of rules is a much more productive and pleasant place than a school where everyone does whatever might be workable at the moment. School rules are guidelines that can make life more agreeable for all of those people who are governed by them.

There is strength in unity. Teachers and students alike must abide by school rules. Although you may have important classroom rules, it is your responsibility to make sure your students know and understand the larger set of rules that governs their behavior. The suggestions that follow are designed to help you teach your students the importance of school rules and to guide you in enforcing them:

▶ Make sure you know and understand your school's rules. It doesn't do anyone any good to have rules in a faculty handbook if you don't make yourself thoroughly familiar with them.

▶ The time to begin to teach school rules is at the first class meeting. Waiting for a week or two sets a bad precedent that will make changing student attitudes more difficult. Don't assume that your students know the rules; take the time to make sure everyone understands them. Your students should not break rules because no one cared enough to teach them.

▶ After you have made sure your students know what the school rules are, go a step further and make sure your students understand the need for everyone to work together.

▶ Don't only tell your students the benefits of following the rules. Instead, get them to work together to generate a list of the positive things that happen when all students cooperate in following the rules. Post this list as a reminder to everyone.

▶ Another effective way to make students see the need for cooperative behavior is to have them survey adults in the community about the rules that govern their workplaces. This will help students see that rules are a part of an adult's workday and not just a set of arbitrary tortures for adolescents.

▶ Follow the rules yourself. If your students can't chew gum or drink soda in class, then you shouldn't either. Model the behaviors you want your students to have.

▶ Set a positive climate for enforcing school rules by praising your students when they follow them. When all students are on time for class or are particularly well behaved at a pep rally, for instance, take time to thank them for their cooperation.

ESTABLISH A PHYSICAL ENVIRONMENT CONDUCIVE TO LEARNING

Just as safety is vital to a positive learning environment, the second key element is the way that you arrange the physical space of your classroom. During the current budget crisis in education, it's not always easy to arrange rooms in the ways that we would like. Drastic spending cuts have all but eliminated the bulletin board supplies and other materials we had grown accustomed to in more affluent times. Broken desks and other equipment are not replaced; equipment for displaying student work is in short supply; and increased class sizes make arranging desks a challenge.

Other problems also affect how we set up our rooms. Because we have students with diverse needs, we need to be responsive to a wide variety of physical needs and learning styles. We struggle to make a workable physical environment in spite of overcrowded classes, budget cuts, and having to share classroom space with other teachers and their pupils. As difficult as it is to arrange the classroom, however, creating an environment for learning has such a significant impact on the discipline climate in your room that the effort is worthwhile.

However, even with these serious problems, there are many things teachers can do to create an environment that encourages positive discipline. Your room should reflect a pleasant, professional attitude and encourage your students' efforts to be successful. Careful planning and organization will ensure that your students are comfortable and ready to work while they are in your room.

When you are deciding how you want your room arranged, consider three important elements: the traffic flow, the space you need for yourself, and the physical arrangement of the desks.

Traffic Flow

The first of these elements, traffic flow, has a serious impact on classroom management. Concerns that appear minor when you first begin thinking about them can soon escalate into major distractions if not attended to. If the trash can or recycle bin is in the back of the room near your desk, for instance, instead of near the door, students will not be able to dispose of trash on the way out at the end of class. Instead they will make trips to the back to dispose of trash, causing a distraction for other students. Five strategies are listed here to help you consider the problems of traffic flow in your class and how you want to begin to solve them.

Strategy 1

The best way to begin dealing with the problems of traffic flow is to identify the routine events that are predictable in your class. You should plan the most efficient ways for your students to do each of these routines. If you put a stapler and hole punch near the trash can, for example, students will mill around less than if these three items are in different areas of the room. You can increase the efficiency of your design by placing them near the door and adding a tray for students to put their completed work in. Adding a bookcase or table for shared supplies and a bulletin board for school information will create an efficient student area and reduce the unproductive traffic in your class.

Some of the routine events in your class that you can plan for will probably be

- ▶ Entering and leaving class
- ▶ Passing out papers
- ▶ Using the stapler or hole puncher
- ▶ Sharpening pencils
- ▶ Disposing of trash
- ▶ Getting materials

- ▶ Speaking with you privately
- ▶ Picking up a hall pass
- ▶ Getting papers back from you
- ▶ Checking information on the bulletin board

Strategy 2

Another routine event you can predict and you need to consider in setting up your room is a relatively private place for students to talk with you and to pick up hall passes or other paperwork. If you place your desk at the back and add an extra chair beside it facing you and turned away from the class, then you have created the space that you need for this.

Strategy 3

Instead of having students pass papers to the front of the room for you to collect, it is much more efficient to direct the flow of papers to the student nearest your desk. Have that student neatly stack them on your desk. You will not only be more efficient, but you will also reduce the confusion in the class because you will still be able to monitor and move around the room instead of waiting for papers to come to you.

Strategy 4

If passing out texts or work folders is a routine event in your class, place them near the door for students to pick up as soon as they enter. The area near the door is often an area that is overlooked when teachers set up their rooms, but it is an area that can be extremely useful if you plan carefully. You can also use this area to post your syllabus or the homework reminders you want students to notice on their way out.

Strategy 5

In addition to the disruptions that come from within our classrooms, you can reduce interruptions from without by placing an envelope or folder outside your door if your district's fire code permits. People can leave papers and notes for you there rather than interrupting the flow of instruction.

The Space You Need for Yourself

The space you need for yourself is another important element to consider when you are setting up your classroom. You need a convenient place to work and to store the materials you will not need to share with your students. Teach your students not to take anything from it without asking your permission first.

The most obvious mistake that many teachers make when setting up a room is to place the teacher's desk at the front of the room in front of the board. If you place your desk at the back of the room instead, you will be able to monitor students from your seat during quiet times. You will also discourage students who might be tempted to pick up a teacher's edition or other personal items from your desk as they crowd past.

The Physical Arrangement of the Desks

The third element to consider when creating your desired physical environment is the arrangement of student desks. The configuration of student desks will play a large part in the success or failure of the discipline climate that you establish in your classroom.

Some arrangements, such as small groups or circles, encourage students to talk with each other. Others, such as the traditional arrangement of rows facing the front, encourage students to focus on the teacher. Throughout the term you and your students will probably use different arrangements for different purposes, but there are a few principles that should guide you in deciding which arrangement will work best for you at any given time.

▶ First of all, you must be able to see every pupil's face. A well-organized grouping where half of the class sits with their backs to you is not a functional one if you want to catch and hold their attention.

▶ Your students must also be able to see you. If you have to speak from a point where a student's view of you is blocked, then you should reconsider the desk arrangement.

▶ Another important consideration when setting up desks involves the distractions in your classroom. If your students use pencils, don't block the sharpener. Other distractions to work around can include the door, the trash can, blasts of hot or cold air from vents, areas where materials are stored and shared, computer screens, noise from the hall, and your desk.

▶ Another point to consider when you're deciding how to arrange desks is movement. Will you be able to move around the room easily? Will your students?

▶ Pay attention to where you spend most of your time in a class period. If you are like most secondary teachers, you probably spend most of your time at the front of the room. This will affect the desk arrangement because you will need to be able to arrange the desks in such a way as to encourage all students to stay on task.

▶ Be careful not to place student desks too near a wall or a chalkboard. These areas are often targets for vandalism.

▶ Even if your room is overcrowded, you should plan to have at least one extra desk if at all possible. You will find that it will come in handy if you need to isolate a student or if you have a classroom visitor.

▶ Many teachers have found that starting the term with seats in traditional rows is a good idea. Such an arrangement is orderly and businesslike. It sends the message that you want students to focus on you and not on each other; thus it promotes an orderly climate from the beginning. If you number the desks, you will find it easier to arrange a seating chart and to put the room back in order after students are finished working in groups.

▶ As the term progresses, you will need to move students into various activities. You will need different patterns for small-group work, class discussions, debates, and guest speakers.

▶ It is important to make a final test of your seating chart and of your room arrangements before the term begins. Sit in the desks in your room. Can you see the board? Can you tolerate the glare? What about the other distractions? Will your students be comfortable and productive in the environment that you have created for them?

▶ An excellent source for classroom configuration inspiration is to use the "Images" feature of the Google search engine. Use *classroom layout* as a search term and you will have access to dozens of useful images of ways to configure your classroom.

In addition, at the sites listed here you will find many useful ideas that you can use as you arrange your classroom so that your students are safe, comfortable, and able to work well with each other and with you.

▶ Scholastic (http://teacher.scholastic.com/tools/class_setup). At Scholastic's site, teachers will find an easy-to-use interactive blueprint where you can design a variety of classroom layouts.

▶ 4Teachers (http://classroom.4teachers.org). On the "Classroom Architect" page you will find an interactive blueprint that allows you to design a personalized layout for your classroom.

SEATING ARRANGEMENTS

Arranging the furniture in your classroom into functional and attractive patterns is an exercise in futility if you don't use a seating chart. No matter how skillfully you set up the physical environment, no matter how well-planned your lessons, no matter how dynamic your delivery, if your students don't focus on learning, then they are wasting their time and yours.

Anyone who has ever stood in front of a class with no seating chart has watched what can go wrong when students choose to sit wherever they please. Students from the same neighborhood choose to sit with each other—resulting in painfully obvious ethnic divisions. Students fight over seats. Talkative students sit together so that they can chat with greater ease. Unmotivated students sit in the back in a quest for anonymity. Easily distracted students invariably choose seats near the door, pencil sharpener, or window. Students with special needs who should sit near you wind up somewhere in the middle where they are quickly lost. The noise level reaches new heights.

There are many convincing reasons to use a seating chart. Putting your students in assigned seats right away shows them that you are organized and well-prepared from the first day forward. You can begin with an alphabetical arrangement since you may not know your students. This seating arrangement will enable you to learn names quickly.

Seating charts also allow you to mix your students into a team instead of allowing them to sit in cliques. Assigned seats can be used to mix low-ability students with high-ability ones, distraction-prone students with peers who stay on task, talkers with quieter students, and boys with girls.

You can also use seating charts to handle medical problems smoothly. Students with poor vision or who need extra help can get it if you arrange the room to accommodate their needs. You can also cope with the difference in the sizes of your pupils if you assign seats to make sure that tall students are not blocking the view of shorter ones. You can also deal with the physical size of your pupils with greater sensitivity. If a student is extremely large, that student will be uncomfortable in a small desk.

With a seating chart, you can move the pupils who need help staying on task near where you spend most of your time. Placing these pupils near you and away from attractive distractions will help them stay on task.

Assigning seats also provides security for those timid students who don't want to argue with more aggressive classmates over seats. This is especially important with those students who may want to sit near you to concentrate, but who aren't comfortable enough to speak up about it. Assigning seats removes another barrier between your students and their chances for a successful day in your class.

SHARING CLASSROOM SPACE

One inconvenient side effect of the recent economic downturn is more schools that are too crowded to be comfortable for students and teachers. More teachers than before travel from room to room instead of having a classroom for their own use. While this type of scheduling may solve some schoolwide problems, it can create others. In particular, discipline problems can arise quickly when teachers are unprepared to share classroom space with colleagues. Without careful preparation, teachers who have to share space with other teachers can expect issues such as these to cause discipline problems:

▶ The desks may not be arranged so that your students can work efficiently.

▶ Your students may lose class time because their materials may not be easily accessible.

▶ The desks may be the correct size and kind for the other teacher's students, but not for yours.

▶ There is not enough board space allotted for your use.

▶ It is impossible for you to display your students' work or even to post reminders and other information.

▶ Your students have trouble locating you when they need to speak with you.

Fortunately, there are several sensible solutions to this issue that may help you minimize the discipline problems caused by sharing a classroom.

▶ Because the potential for losing papers, books, and other important supplies is greater when you move around, make it a point to have your instructional materials as well-ordered as possible. Try to carry extra copies when you can.

▶ Make sure your students know where to find you between classes, during specific periods of the day, and before and after school.

▶ Talk with the teachers whose classrooms you share. Discuss the space that you and your students need as well as how you can solve potential problems. Your conversation should cover basic topics such as sharing classroom keys, allotting board space, and arranging desks as well as more complex ones such as who will assume responsibility when students leave personal belongings behind.

▶ Be careful to be on time to class even when you have to travel in crowded halls. An unsupervised classroom is a place where misbehavior can quickly escalate.

▶ Consider using a class Web page to create a virtual classroom. Post reminders and display student work, photos, and other items that you can't display in your physical classroom. Even if you post only a few items, you will make it easier to connect with your students and prevent discipline problems.

OVERCROWDED CLASSROOMS

In the recent past, many teachers have had to cope with classes that were just slightly above the recommended size for the grade and subject. However, today's widespread and severe budget cuts have created critically overcrowded classrooms that would have been unthinkable just a few years ago. As inevitable as overcrowded classes may be, the discipline problems associated with them are not. Overcrowded classes can be managed successfully by those teachers who meet the unique challenges they present.

Even though we know that smaller classes are the preferred option for our students, a positive discipline climate and a pleasant learning environment are possible in overcrowded classes. The following strategies can start you on the way to successfully managing the problems of overcrowded classes.

▶ Even if you are not easily intimidated, confronting a large group of students who have been crammed into a classroom designed for a much smaller group can be more than a little discouraging. Unless you immediately assume a strong leadership role, you will be so outnumbered by your students that they will be in charge of the class, not you.

▶ The room arrangement is very important in overcrowded classes. Make sure you have enough desks. Move all equipment that you don't need to use right away to storage and do whatever else you can to further reduce the claustrophobic effects of clutter in the room.

▶ Pay careful attention to traffic patterns and student movement. Try to reduce this as much as possible. Teach your students to dispose of trash at the end of class and to sharpen pencils only at the start of class.

▶ An overcrowded class requires more monitoring than a smaller one. Teach your students that they are to place their book bags under their desks rather than in the aisle to make movement easier.

▶ A seating chart is an absolute must in an overcrowded class if you want to reduce the amount of off-task behavior. A structured environment will reduce the number of problems you will face.

▶ Prepare yourself for the noise level. A large class can be a noisy class if you don't establish some guidelines early in the year with your students to help them control the noise level.

▶ Be extremely organized and a model of efficiency for your students who could be tempted to use overcrowding as an excuse not to do their best. Keep your personal space in good order and insist that your students leave their area tidy at the end of class. Encourage them to check to make sure their classmates don't leave personal belongings behind when class is over.

▶ It is important for you to avoid confusion and the discipline problems caused by failure to return papers promptly. Although it takes longer to grade papers for a large class, your students may feel lost in the crowd if you allow papers to pile up before you give them the feedback that all students need in order to stay focused on learning during class.

▶ Routines are very important in a large class. Establish and teach them early in the term. Students should be able to predict what they are supposed to do in your class even though many students are in the room.

▶ Allow no horseplay. Even though you may be inclined to allow students some leeway in playing around, this is not a good idea when there are too many students in the room. Horseplay in a crowd is wasted time as well as dangerous.

▶ Be especially careful in a crowded class to prevent the cheating that can happen because students have to sit close together. Provide a cover sheet and monitor carefully to prevent problems.

▶ Enlist your students in a sense of togetherness and encourage a spirit of cooperation in solving the problems caused by an overcrowded class. A sense of humor and a positive attitude on your part will set a pleasant tone for your students to model.

▶ It is important for you to speak with every student each day. Greeting them at the door is a good beginning to solving the problems of having to keep in touch with many students. Make a point to let your students know that you are aware of them as people, not just as faces in a crowd.

▶ Creating permanent teams of study buddies is a good way to give students a sense of togetherness and connectedness in the midst of the larger group. When students have a few partners to turn to for help and support, they will feel like a part of the class instead of being just one of many.

- Courtesy to each other and to you is especially important in a large class. Teach the importance of courtesy to the students in a large class and insist that they treat everyone with politeness. A large courteous class is much better and easier to deal with than a small rude one.

- Your attitude is the most important factor in coping successfully with the demands of a large class. It's not the number of students occupying seats in the room, but the careful planning, interesting lessons, and sincere effort to connect with each student each day that will determine the success or failure of the discipline climate in a class.

DEALING WITH NOISE LEVELS

One of the most important aspects of a productive classroom environment is establishing a plan for coping successfully with the various noise levels that can occur in a class period. Maintaining an acceptable noise level in a classroom is not always an easy task. Our students seem to thrive in a noisy world full of ringing phones, conversations, and noise, noise, noise—and the louder the better.

Unfortunately, this noise tolerance on the part of our pupils can have an adverse effect on the orderly, productive classrooms we want to have. More than one teacher has had the unpleasant experience of having to shout to be heard above pandemonium.

You can have a classroom where the noise level is under control by teaching your students how to achieve the acceptable noise levels you want in your classroom. The following strategies can help you and your students as you learn to work together to create a classroom where the only noise is the sound of great minds at work.

- Begin to teach the various types of noise levels to your students by dealing with distance. Teach them to pay attention to the one-foot voice, the two-foot voice, and a whisper. Model these acceptable levels and monitor until your students have internalized them.

- Tell your students which noise levels are acceptable for each assignment you give them. Be specific and clear.

- Play soft instrumental background music at a volume that can be heard all over the room. This will tend to quiet most students if you tell them that you always need to be able to hear the music over their voices.

- Plan ways to signal your students when the noise level reaches an unacceptable level. Some prearranged signals could be a gesture, a warning word from you, a warning mark on the chalkboard, or a quick flick of the light switch.

- Monitor noise levels by moving around the room frequently to help students stay focused and working quietly.

- When pupils are working in groups, teach them to talk only to the other people in their group so that they won't have to raise their voices to be heard. You can also put a student in charge of the noise level for that group.

- Take noise level into account when you plan. If a lesson is going to be a very loud one, you might consider moving to a location where you won't disturb the other people or classes around you.

- Make sure your students understand when noise is unacceptable. Many of your students will think nothing of talking when you are giving directions or during a movie or even during a test unless you teach them not to do this.

- ▶ Teach your students to be attentive listeners. If you teach your students how to listen well, then you will be closer to reducing side talking and background noise when these are inappropriate.

- ▶ When your students are working together, keep the noise level down by putting them physically close to one another. Sounds simple? Many teachers overlook this easy way to control the volume.

- ▶ Adjust your attitude about noise if you need to. Many students are comfortable working in noisier environments than adults can tolerate easily. If you find yourself fretting about noise, examine your attitude before you make any sweeping changes.

- ▶ Arrange your room into loud and quiet areas on days when a variety of student activities will be in progress at the same time. Students who need to talk can feel more comfortable doing so if they move to an area of the room where they won't disturb a student who needs more peace and quiet to concentrate.

- ▶ Lower your own voice. If you speak quietly and command attention at the same time, then your students will quiet down in order to hear what you have to say.

- ▶ Distinguish between good noise and bad noise. A noisy class may either be one where there's a lot of productive talking and on-task behavior or one where students are rudely ignoring the instructional directives for the day.

PROMOTING CLASSROOM OWNERSHIP

When secondary students feel that a classroom is a place designed with their welfare in mind and that they can have a voice in the way it is managed, they are more likely to work in harmony with each other and with you. In a classroom where students feel a strong sense of ownership, they have opportunities to work together for the common benefit of everyone involved. This cooperation, in turn, reduces much of the student-to-student tension that can mar any lesson. The pleasant atmosphere of trust generated when a teacher solicits assistance and advice from students will reduce the small grievances that students can accumulate.

Finally, the greatest benefit you will notice as you involve your students in activities that promote classroom ownership is that those activities move your students closer to becoming self-disciplined. Helping students learn to assume responsibilities that benefit others will move students toward becoming self-directed learners whose focus is on learning and not on misbehavior.

If you want to promote a sense of classroom ownership among your students, there are several quick actions that you can take to involve them in appropriate ways:

- ▶ Ask their opinions. A quick, "What do you think we should do about this?" is a sure way to involve students in the subject under discussion.

- ▶ Delegate as many routine tasks as you can.

- ▶ Keep the room clean so that students will have a reason to maintain it. If your students hear you comment that you keep the room tidy for their benefit, they will be more willing to pitch in.

- ▶ Create an inclusive classroom atmosphere by displaying student work and items of interest to them. This lets students know that you value them and appreciate their efforts.

- ▶ Offer choices when you can. For example, if you routinely play music while students work independently, before making a selection, you could ask which of two choices they would prefer.

- ▶ Enlist student help in establishing procedures for taking care of routine activities such as moving chairs into groups, turning in assignments, or posting homework notices on a class Web page.

CREATE A STUDENT-CENTERED CLASS ATMOSPHERE

There are many names for this teaching phenomenon. *Student-centered learning*, the *user-friendly class*, and *invitational teaching* are just three of them. Whatever the name, the result is the same: a place where students and teachers can work in a safe and pleasant environment as partners in the exciting process of learning and preparing for the future. The important word here is *partners*.

These havens exist everywhere and anywhere. You don't need a huge operating budget, gifted and willing students, or cooperative colleagues to make your classroom a friendly place. What you do need is the right attitude, a clear vision of what you want to happen, and the willpower to put your plans into effect.

In a student-centered class, your pupils are not just passive receptors of your expert knowledge. Instead, you and your students work together to discover and learn. Although a student-centered class is often noisy and full of activity, much more learning is going on than in the more traditional classrooms.

Make no mistake: the teacher still needs to be a strong and powerful force in the classroom—probably more so than in a traditional class. However, your role now is that of facilitator, collaborator, and coach working with students, rather than being the expert who holds and withholds the information that students need.

STRUCTURE YOUR CLASS TO USE TIME WISELY

The third element necessary to create a productive classroom environment involves how you use the time your students have with you. Using class time for focused learning activities is an effective way to establish a productive atmosphere for your students. From the beginning of class until the end, you can pace instruction and activities so that students are engaged in learning instead of misbehavior.

QUICK TIPS TO MAKE EVERY MINUTE COUNT

▶ Plan and teach lessons that are focused around a clearly stated objective that is published for your students.

▶ Teach your students that you are the person who decides when class will begin and end—not a bell. This will reduce disruptions and wasted time near the end of the class period.

▶ Don't call roll out loud. Check attendance by scanning the room while your students are working independently.

▶ Assign an appropriate amount of work. Fifty math problems may not be as effective as fifteen done correctly. Finding the appropriate pace of a lesson is not an easy thing to do, but careful pacing will prevent frustration and wasted time.

▶ Provide alternative assignments for those students who finish an assignment ahead of the others. Many students waste precious time waiting for others to finish.

▶ Make sure the topics you assign are relevant and necessary for your students' immediate and future needs. Your students should understand their importance.

▶ Plan your classes so that students are engaged from the minute they enter the room until you dismiss them. Giving "free time" at the end of class is a practice with enormous potential for trouble.

- Stay on topic. Resist the temptation to be distracted during a lesson by students who want to chat or otherwise stray from the topic.

- Establish and follow a routine set of procedures for daily classroom chores. When students know how to manage classroom routines, they will be more likely to stay on task.

- Be careful not to interrogate students who are tardy or who are otherwise misbehaving in front of the class. Work to minimize disruptions, not call them to the attention of everyone else.

- Be flexible. Many teachers who are well organized like to stick with a lesson plan even if it isn't working. This is evident in those classrooms where students are sleeping, tuned out, or disruptive. Don't be afraid to change a lesson plan in the middle of class if you see that your carefully made plans are not working. Always have a backup plan.

- Plan lessons that are exciting and have real-world applications so that students will stay focused.

- Give immediate feedback so that students know how they're doing and can proceed with confidence. Research shows that the sooner students know how they did on an assignment, the better.

- Become the most organized and well-prepared teacher that you know. Don't waste your students' time because you are not ready for class.

- Arrange your activities so that your students can work together as often as possible. Students who are taught to work well together are much more likely to be productive than those students who never have a chance to collaborate successfully with others.

- Strive to interact positively with every student every day. Show your students that their welfare is important to you if you want to encourage on-task behavior.

- Recognize that not all of your students will have the same abilities and background knowledge. Many teachers waste precious time because they assume students have common background knowledge and can learn at the same rate. If you spend time assessing your students' previous knowledge before beginning a unit of study, you will be much better at designing lessons that will fulfill the needs of each student. Build in lesson components that will address the varying learning rates of your students.

- Don't allow small misbehaviors to continue or to escalate.

- Raise your students' awareness about the importance of using time wisely.

- Teach your students the skills they need to become self-disciplined. If your ultimate goal is that your students will govern their own behavior, then you need to spend time teaching the social skills that will lead to this. Students who are not self-disciplined waste everybody's time with misbehavior and unproductive activity.

THE FIRST TEN MINUTES OF CLASS

The first ten minutes of every class are crucial in getting your students off to a constructive start. During these first minutes you establish the tone of the class for your students whether you realize it or not. If you have completed the careful preparation that is required for a successful class, then this brief time can be used to get your students focused on learning.

Students who are focused on learning and achieving instead of trying to figure out what they are supposed to do will be less likely to engage in disruptive misbehavior. During the first ten minutes of class you can avoid many discipline problems by providing your students with a comfortable and predictable routine that varies in content but gives them the necessary stability to perform well academically and behaviorally.

Help your students focus their attention on the activities in your class by giving them a brief exercise designed to capture their interest. There are many small assignments that your students can complete in the first ten minutes that will prevent behavior problems when they focus on the day's lesson or will review the previous day's work. The following suggestions can be adapted to fit the needs of your students and of the day's lesson. You can ask your students to

- Make a quick outline of their notes
- List important facts from a previous lesson
- Review a classmate's planner to make sure the homework assignment was recorded correctly
- Quiz each other
- Create three practice problems and give them to a classmate to solve
- Write a paragraph
- Predict the day's learning
- Draw a diagram, flow chart, bar graph, or other graphic organizer
- Make a set of flash cards
- Write a fact on the board
- Combine information with another student
- Draw a cartoon
- Summarize the reasons that something happened
- Judge the suitability of something
- Illustrate important information
- Create a test question
- Write marginal notes for an essay
- Take a miniquiz
- Write a review of the previous class in fifty words or fewer
- Use a highlighter on their notes
- Create a mnemonic device
- Read a newspaper or magazine article
- Label a map
- Review a classmate's homework assignment to fill any gaps
- Listen to an audio clip related to the lesson
- Brainstorm ideas for an essay
- Watch a slide show
- Scan the day's reading assignment
- Make a list of reasons to study the day's topic

- ▶ Solve a puzzle
- ▶ Explain an illustration

If your students have access to computers, the start of the day's classes can involve warm-up activities that require them to use a computer. Here are some brief electronic activities for the start of a class period for you to adapt for your classes. Have students

- ▶ Review electronic flash cards
- ▶ Watch a video clip related to the lesson and respond
- ▶ Engage in an instant message dialogue with a classmate explaining one aspect of the previous day's lesson
- ▶ Solve an online interactive puzzle
- ▶ Play an online interactive word game
- ▶ Update their electronic planners
- ▶ Use the reminder or note feature of their computers to list five key facts or definitions
- ▶ Annotate an electronic text
- ▶ Create a quiz for a classmate to take
- ▶ Complete an online survey
- ▶ Complete an online review quiz
- ▶ Make Twitter postings about the lesson they are about to study
- ▶ Send a copy of their notes from the previous class to a classmate to review or highlight
- ▶ Create a mini slide show about the five most important terms in the upcoming lesson
- ▶ Post a quick question or prediction on a class wiki

REDUCING DISRUPTIONS THROUGH EFFECTIVE TRANSITIONS

Because students have grown accustomed to the fast pace of modern life with its intense barrage of distracting messages, they can grow bored very quickly with a lesson that seems to last too long. Wise teachers have learned to create a positive learning environment by designing daily lessons around several brief activities. While this decision is a very sensible reaction to the discipline problems caused by student disinterest, it can create problems of its own: transition periods where students with nothing to do waste valuable learning time by entertaining themselves and each other with inappropriate behavior.

Transitions are difficult because they require that students mentally close out one task, prepare for the next one, and then refocus their mental energies on the new topic. Some students find it difficult to do this several times during one class period.

One useful technique for increasing the level of student concern about wasted time during transitions is to set a time limit for the transition and to actually time your students. Students who are told by a teacher that they have only one minute to switch from one activity to another are more likely to move more quickly than those students in a less-structured situation.

You can also reduce the number of discipline problems in your classroom if you design activities that flow naturally from one to the next with minimum interference from you. Your students become self-disciplined when they assume the responsibility for following the directions and making the transition an integral part of the lesson.

Another way to encourage self-discipline during transition times is to provide your students with a checklist of the things they need to accomplish during the class period. Early in the term you should teach your students how to use a checklist to keep track of their daily tasks.

A final solution to the problem of wasted class time is to give students productive activities to convert their useless waiting time into learning opportunities. Even these small blocks of time can be productive and enjoyable for you and your students if you use brief learning activities to keep students involved in actively thinking and learning.

ACTIVITIES TO KEEP STUDENTS ENGAGED IN LEARNING DURING TRANSITION TIMES

These activities are ones that turn time that would otherwise be wasted in your classroom when students are forced to wait for others to begin class, to settle down to work, or to finish an assignment into constructive experiences. Even though these activities are designed to be brief, their impact on the productivity in your classroom can be significant.

Students will often find these activities exciting enough that they will do them without protest and look forward to the break in routine. The activities here are written in the form of directions for students to follow. Adapt, adjust, or add information to use these to create other activities that will keep your students involved in productive learning all period long.

- ▶ Look over your notes from yesterday's lesson. Circle the key words.
- ▶ List five things that you can recall we did in class yesterday.
- ▶ Pick a partner and play a quick game of "Hangman" with your vocabulary words from this unit of study.
- ▶ List the key ideas in today's lesson.
- ▶ Make quick flash cards to review the vocabulary words we have studied this week.
- ▶ List the steps in . . .
- ▶ Predict what caused . . .
- ▶ Open your book and read the first three paragraphs from yesterday's lesson. What is something new that you learned today that you hadn't realized yesterday?
- ▶ List ten words associated with the lesson we are currently studying.
- ▶ What is your objective for this class today?
- ▶ Write out a study skill that you have recently mastered.
- ▶ Time a classmate while that person intently reviews yesterday's lesson. Switch roles and repeat.
- ▶ Scan your text and find . . . (Provide your students with specific facts or information to seek. This is an excellent review technique.)
- ▶ Predict what will happen next.

▶ Here's your word of the day: _____. Copy and define it and then use it correctly in a sentence.

▶ What is the most important quality for a good student to have?

▶ Provide another example of your own for . . .

▶ Supply the missing words in this cloze exercise. (Find a reading assignment that is appropriate for your group and then cloze it.)

▶ Unscramble these vocabulary words.

▶ Match the items in column A with the items in column B.

▶ Find the similarities in these two photographs.

▶ What do you need to accomplish this week? Make a "To Do" list for this week's activities.

▶ Write a set of instructions for . . .

▶ Looking back over this week, what did you really learn?

▶ List ten things you learned in class today.

▶ Read this short newspaper article and respond to it in your journal.

▶ Practice the process of elimination on these multiple-choice questions.

▶ Complete these analogies that relate to the lesson we are going to study today.

▶ Tell why a change in _____ occurred.

▶ Brainstorm every possible solution you can think of for . . .

▶ Design a _____ to _____.

▶ Judge the value of . . .

▶ Make a proposal to . . .

▶ Describe what would happen if . . .

▶ Look over the first three paragraphs of your homework reading for last night. Write a brief paraphrase of them.

▶ List the factors you would change if . . .

▶ Describe the turning point in . . .

▶ What are the underlying principles of the lesson we are studying?

▶ What is the correct procedure for . . . ?

▶ Justify the rule about . . .

▶ Defend your position on . . .

▶ Defend your teacher's position on the topic of . . .

▶ How can you modify _____ so that it is more efficient?

▶ Proofread this paragraph and make as many corrections as you can.

▶ What solutions do you have for the problem of _____ ?

▶ Demonstrate the proper way to _____.

▶ How does what you learned in this lesson really apply to your life?

▶ Why is it necessary for successful people to use time wisely?

- Choose a partner and show that person how to use one fact from the lesson that you learned in this class yesterday.
- There are seven errors in the reading passage you were given as you came into the classroom. Can you find them all?
- Take two of the vocabulary words you have been studying this week and use them both in the same sentence.
- Write one of the key words from this lesson on a scrap of paper. Pass it to a classmate. Time that person for one minute to tell you five important things about the word.
- Why is it useful to learn the information in the unit we are now studying?
- Pick a partner and brainstorm a list of all the ways you can use the information that you have learned in this class in the last three days.
- What did you learn in another class this week that you can use in this class today?
- What have you learned in this class lately that you can apply to another class?
- Take the items on the board and group them according to criteria that you devise based on the information in yesterday's lesson.
- What are some of the assumptions you had about today's class?
- Using what we learned in class today as proof, justify the reason for . . .
- Create a word search puzzle that you will share with a friend tomorrow. Use the key words from today's lesson.
- Use all of your vocabulary words to create a quick short story.
- Create a fair test question about the information you have learned today.
- Take a list of words and create relationships among them.
- Design a question about the lesson that will absolutely stump a classmate.
- List as many ways as you can in which you are like the people we have studied in today's lesson.

Many of these activities can easily be adapted for those students with computers. For example, instead of just listing facts or words, students can create word clouds at Wordle's home page at www.wordle.net or make a short puzzle at Discovery School's Puzzlemaker page (www.puzzlemaker.com.).

THE LAST TEN MINUTES OF CLASS

The last ten minutes of every class period can be ones where your students are either engaged in misbehaviors of varying degrees of seriousness or engaged in positive and productive behaviors that indicate self-discipline. You can take several steps to ensure that your class provides your students with a sense of satisfaction.

First of all, establish a routine for the end of class so that students know

- You won't detain them.
- They have to clean up after themselves.
- They are expected to continue their good behavior.

- They have a very limited amount of time to pack up their things.
- There is a closing exercise for them to complete every day.
- They will be dismissed at a signal from *you*, and not by the bell.

There are many benefits from having a well-structured closing to your class. The biggest benefit, of course, is the marked reduction in misbehavior. Here is a simple two-step plan for ending class that you can follow if you want those last minutes to be as productive as the earlier ones.

Step 1: Closing Exercise (8 Minutes)

There are many last-minute exercises you can have your students do in the brief time that you allot for this. Here are some suggestions to help you design closing exercises that will work with your students. Ask your students to

- Chain together five facts that they learned in class today.
- Study a photograph and relate their observations to what they learned in class.
- Survey a classmate about the information in the lesson.
- Write a brief assessment about their knowledge at the end of class.
- Relate two quotations to each other and to the lesson.
- Prove that they have learned at least three key ideas today.
- Recall and share a fact with the rest of the class in a round-robin activity.
- Link what they have learned today with another subject.
- Generalize from a list of facts or key ideas.
- Review a list of key words for the next day's assignment.
- Write a quick explanation of the most interesting aspect of the day's lesson.
- Learn a new word related to the day's assignment.
- Participate in a rapid-fire drill on the relevant facts from the lesson.
- Do a quick vocabulary review or spelling bee.
- Play a game for bonus test points.
- Explain the directions for the homework assignment one more time.
- Discuss a final thought for the day that you have hidden on the board under a sheet of paper all period long.
- Do some independent research about the topic under study.
- Read and comment on a brief passage related to the day's topic.
- Discuss a provocative cartoon.
- Thank someone in their group for a specific action.
- Predict what they will learn at the next class meeting.
- Write down five things they learned in class and share their list with a classmate.

Step 2: Dismissal (2 Minutes)

After the closing exercise has been completed, you should have two minutes for your students to get ready to be dismissed at your signal. During this time they should have a daily routine to follow. The routine you establish for them should include

- ▶ Disposing of the trash that has accumulated during the class period
- ▶ Stowing away books and materials
- ▶ Checking under desks to see that nothing is left behind

It is perfectly okay to allow talking at this time if students stay in their seats and keep their voices down. You can teach this part of the closing routine to your students by timing them often at first and rewarding the class for successfully completing it.

One mistake that many teachers make is to allow students to jump up and bolt for the door when the bell rings. You need to teach your students that *you* will dismiss them and that they should wait for your signal. You do not need to detain them after the bell has rung in an obvious power display in order to make the ending of your class productive.

At the very end of class, you should move to the door and speak to every student as the class leaves. By doing this you will prevent any last-minute flare-ups of misbehavior. You will also show your students that they have a teacher who models the concern and courtesy that they need to leave the class with a feeling of well-being. See this section's "Making Positive Choices" for more ideas on how to make choices that will help you foster a positive environment in your classroom.

Making Positive Choices

Instead of . . .	Try to . . .
▶ Allowing students to take items from your desk	▶ Set up an area where students can use a stapler, hole puncher, or other shared supplies
▶ Delaying action when students say they are not feeling well	▶ Take their claims seriously and immediately send ill students to the clinic or nurse
▶ Pretending not to hear students talking about underage drinking	▶ Speak to students about your school's policy concerning substance abuse and underage drinking
▶ Allowing students to mill around before class starts	▶ Have a focusing activity in place at the start of class
▶ Ignoring bullying when the victim doesn't seem to mind	▶ Take a stand against all types of bullying
▶ Not acting quickly when a student reports cyberbullying	▶ Take all reports seriously and involve an administrator immediately
▶ Dealing with distracted and off-task students	▶ Create a seating chart that will help all students focus
▶ Creating an unsafe situation when sharing a classroom with another teacher	▶ Always be on time to make sure students are supervised
▶ Coping with student tension	▶ Promote a sense of class community through shared responsibilities
▶ Asking students over and over to be quiet	▶ Arrange signals to help students control their own noise levels

QUESTIONS FOR REFLECTION

Use the information in this section to guide your thinking as you contemplate these questions. They are designed to encourage you to think more deeply about the issues in the text or to discuss those issues with colleagues.

▶ How safe is your classroom? What do you need to do to ensure the safety of all of the students in your care? How can you prioritize the steps you need to take to accomplish this?

▶ Is your class student-centered? How can you improve the layout of your class so that every student can be fully engaged?

▶ How well do you use the time that your students are with you? Would any of the activities in the lists in this section appeal to you and your students? How important is using time wisely in your teaching practice?

SECTION FIVE

Promote Self-Discipline

In this section you will learn

- How to help students become self-disciplined learners
- How to increase the positive interactions you have with students
- How to help struggling students overcome obstacles to success
- How to teach students to set and achieve goals
- How to use behavior contracts successfully

MOVING BEYOND CROWD CONTROL TO PROMOTE SELF-DISCIPLINE

If the ultimate purpose of the enormous amount of energy, thought, and effort that we pour into our discipline policies and practices is to create students who are self-directed, at what point will we know we have been successful? Unfortunately, as with most of our dealings with adolescent students, the process is not always an easy one. Often, just when we think that all of our discipline goals have been met, something will happen in class to remind us that our students still need us to help them keep from straying off-task.

In spite of the impossibility of knowing for certain just how successful our attempts to help students assume responsibility for their actions will be, we must work toward that goal. We should not only direct our students so that they understand what they should do, but we must encourage them to be willing to do the right thing at the right time.

Moving students toward the goal that we have for them—that they will become self-disciplined learners—is not a task that can be rushed. Fortunately, we have countless chances to help students in their efforts to become self-disciplined. If you want to help your students mature into accepting personal responsibility, you could pick two or three of these techniques to use now. When they have become an integral part of the culture of excellence you want to promote in your classroom, then you could try some of the others.

Model the Behavior You Want Your Students to Have

Our actions certainly speak louder than our words when it comes to teaching our students the behaviors we want from them. This is particularly true of self-directed behaviors. If we want students to be articulate, then we must be articulate. If we want their work to be neatly done, then the handouts we give them must be models of neatly done work. If we expect our students to come to class on time, then we must encourage that promptness through our own punctuality. Secondary students need strong positive role models who will show them the way to succeed. One of the greatest gifts we can give our students is to be the kind of role model they need day after day.

Maintain High Standards for All of Your Students

We are not going to be successful in moving our students toward self-directed behavior unless we have high academic and behavior standards for them. If students are going to stretch their limits and grow, then they need to be challenged to do this. If you want to see just how capable your students can be, then set limits that are difficult but not impossible. You don't have to expect perfect academic or impeccable behaviors all of the time, but too often our students are much more capable than we give them credit for being. It is especially important to maintain these high standards when students seem to struggle or when less-capable students are included in the class. It is a disservice to the students to lower our standards instead of helping students rise to meet them.

Connect Effort to Success

Too often teachers hear students exclaim, "But I studied! I should have an 'A' on this!" when they have spent just a few minutes looking over their notes while texting, watching television, updating a playlist, and browsing online. To help students mature in their thinking and to become self-disciplined, caring teachers make the effort to show students that success requires effort. Discuss how long they really studied and which techniques they used. Encourage them to use the monitoring charts in this section. Ask questions designed to make students reflect in a productive way about the effort they exert. Students who can see that their success is the result of their effort are far more likely to succeed than those who cannot.

Motivate Your Students to Work Well

It is important for all of us to recall our own school years when large parts of the day were not as interesting for us as others. What made the difference for many of us was a determined and caring teacher who motivated us to want to learn. These were the teachers whose homework we always did no matter what. We arranged our dental appointments around their classes because we did not want to miss even one day. What a contrast to those other classes where we perfected the fine art of sneaking peeks at the clock to see if another thirty seconds of tedium had passed yet.

The difference in those classes was not only in the subject matter under study. Those teachers who cared enough to motivate us to learn made the difference. We, too, can motivate our students to want to succeed. Hundreds of techniques are at hand for those teachers who use a bit of creativity to catch and sustain student interest. If you want your students to want to become self-disciplined, it is up to you to include as many motivating factors in each lesson as you can.

Be Encouraging and Positive with Your Students

Students whose teachers make it abundantly clear that they have confidence in their ability to succeed are students who are more apt to become self-disciplined than those whose teachers doubt their students' abilities. If you want positive actions from your students, then you must show your own positive side. This does not mean you need to be falsely cheerful or flatter your students; both of these tactics will surely fail with a spectacular thud. Secondary students are fragile creatures who need strong doses of support and encouragement (just like their teachers) in order to be at their best. If you want to help them move toward self-discipline, encouragement and a positive approach are critical for success.

Hold Your Students Accountable for Their Actions

In addition to high expectations and encouragement, you must make students aware that there is also some level of negative consequence for their actions. It isn't enough simply to have high standards for your students. You also must hold them accountable for their success or lack of it in meeting those standards.

Teachers can use many techniques to make sure students are learning to accept responsibility for their own success. These techniques should be part of the overall scheme by which you encourage students to perform at their best level academically and socially. If we never hold students accountable for their actions, then they will not develop into the resilient and self-disciplined pupils that we want them to be.

BECOME A CONSISTENT TEACHER

Consistency is one of the most important variables in managing student behavior because it allows students a safe framework within which to operate while they struggle to become self-disciplined learners. Consistent classroom management allows a teacher to create a predictable environment where students know what to expect and thus can make choices based on established rules, boundaries, and consequences.

If we want our students to become self-disciplined, we must create a consistent environment for them. They have to know what to expect from their classmates and from their teachers if they are going to make intelligent decisions. Even though consistency is so very important to the discipline climate in a classroom, it is also one of the most difficult struggles that many teachers face daily. Teachers have to make hundreds of decisions each day. Most of these, many of them critical to the future success of our discipline climates as well as to the success of our students, will be made in front of a room full of lively teenagers. We seldom have time for thoughtful reasoning because we have to think fast on our feet. No wonder it is so difficult to be as consistent as we should be every day. Here are some of the common mistakes in consistency that many of us find it all too easy to make:

- We overlook a broken rule "just this once."
- When students have missed several days, we find it difficult to hold them to the same academic standards for make-up work that we would have had if they had been there for class.
- We call one child's parents or guardians to report misbehavior that we have allowed from other students.
- We allow a good student to slip into class tardy, while we are on the alert for other students who try the same thing.
- We expect less of the students whom we perceive to be less able than others.

If you want to become more consistent in the way you manage your class, some easy techniques can help you get started. Here are several quick ones for you to begin to use to create the consistent environment you want for your students:

- Create routines and procedures for the day-to-day operation of your class and enforce them.
- Post your class rules and teach them to your students.
- Enforce your class rules for all students every day.
- Be a prepared and organized teacher so that you will find it easier to make those tough quick decisions each day.
- Expect the same high standards for behavior and academic performance from every student.
- Intervene early when students are having problems.
- Listen carefully to your students, but don't be a pushover for too many excuses.

TEACH STUDENTS HOW TO MONITOR THEMSELVES

One of the most powerful techniques for teachers who want to direct their students to become self-disciplined is to teach students to monitor themselves. When students monitor their own behavior, the responsibility for improvement and success rightfully shifts from teacher to student. When your students learn to monitor themselves, you no longer have to assume the role of overbearing adult in charge of a room full of students who have perfected the art of learned helplessness. Instead you become a learning partner with your students. Below you will find a list of strategies or activities that you can adapt to help your students stay on track by monitoring their own progress.

- Offer rubrics in advance of an assignment.
- Give students checklists of tasks to be accomplished.
- Ask students to reflect on their learning or on their work habits.
- Set and work toward a goal.
- Make frequent progress checks.

- ▶ Allow students to see their grades at least weekly.

- ▶ Encourage students to chart their grades.

- ▶ Have students break assignments into smaller parts and set their own due dates for each small part.

- ▶ Give students a syllabus so that they can plan their work.

- ▶ Have students complete admit tickets with their plans for the day's work.

- ▶ Ask students to assess their own strengths and weaknesses.

Ask students to keep a list of what they have learned and what they still need to know in a unit of study.

Here you will find five brief forms that you can offer your students to help them develop their skills at self-evaluation. The forms are designed to help your students set and achieve goals for their academic progress, time management, and self-advocacy. You can use them all at once, at the end of a grading period, or throughout the school year as appropriate for your students.

Student Worksheet

YOUR CLASS GOALS

Name: _____ Class: _____

1. Record the grade goal you have for this class.
2. List the strategies you need to use to meet your goal.
   a.
   b.
   c.
   d.
   e.
3. Keep a record of your progress here:

Date	Assignment	Grade

Student Worksheet

ASSIGNMENT CHECKLIST

Name: _____ Month: _____

Darken each block as you complete and turn in that assignment.

Week	1	2	3	4	5	6	7	8	9	10	11	12	13	14	15
1															
2															
3															
4															
5															
6															
7															
8															
9															
10															
11															
12															
13															
14															
15															
16															
17															
18															
19															
20															
21															
22															
23															
24															

Remarks:

Student Worksheet

MY GOALS FOR TODAY

Activity	When I Will Do This	Who Can Help

Student Worksheet

THE PROGRESS OF MY GRADES

Draw a line from your weekly average each week to graph your progress. Use what you learn to adjust the way you prepare for class.

Week 1	Week 2	Week 3	Week 4	Week 5
100	100	100	100	100
95	95	95	95	95
90	90	90	90	90
85	85	85	85	85
80	80	80	80	80
75	75	75	75	75
70	70	70	70	70
65	65	65	65	65
60	60	60	60	60
55	55	55	55	55

Student Worksheet

SELF-EVALUATION FORM

Name: _____ **Date:** _____

Rate your behavior today on a scale of 1 to 3:

A "1" means you were not as successful as you would like.

A "2" means you are getting better at the behavior.

A "3" means you were successful at that behavior.

1. _____ I followed written and oral directions.

2. _____ I did not make careless mistakes.

3. _____ I turned in all work on time.

4. _____ I worked independently.

5. _____ I paid attention to the lesson.

Circle the number that best reflects the percentage of class time you were productive today:

10%   20%   30%   40%   50%   60%   70%   80%   90%   100%

What did you do in class today that helped your self-control?

_____

_____

_____

Questions That Can Encourage Self-Discipline

Although there are many different approaches to encouraging students as they develop into self-disciplined learners, one of the most valuable of these involves asking thoughtful questions that require students to analyze their progress. When we ask our students to reflect on their work habits, their efforts, and their successes and failures, we provide guidelines to help them develop the habits of mind that will lead to self-discipline. In the brief list that follows, you will find questions that require students to consider how they approach their work.

- ► Do you understand what to do to succeed on this assignment?
- ► How can you replicate this success on tonight's homework assignment?
- ► What good work habits are you proudest of?
- ► What are your weakest work habits? What can you do to overcome them?
- ► What do you tell yourself when you are feeling lazy, but have lots of work to do?
- ► What is important about the approach to your work that you take?
- ► What do you do that makes it easier for you to complete your work well and on time?

FOCUS ON YOUR STUDENTS' STRENGTHS

It is no secret that the relationship we build with our students affects their success. A positive relationship with our students is one of our strongest defenses against disruptive behavior.

Often we try to stop misbehavior with a flurry of negative commands and injunctions against behaviors that students find more natural than the more formal or productive ones we try to teach. Most secondary students can recite dozens of things they know they should not do. If those same students are asked to name their five greatest strengths, however, many would be at a loss.

While it would be wrong to unfairly praise or encourage students for behaviors that do not promote future success, the negative attitudes that many of us carry with us to school are just as wrong. Although it is natural that we should spend so much time in our profession dealing with the errors our students make or with the things they should not do or with what's wrong, we do need to balance this negativity by focusing on our students' successes or strengths as well.

The long-term rewards that accrue when we focus on our students' strengths are partly the result of a self-fulfilling prophecy. When our students believe they can do some things correctly, they are going to be brave enough to take that extra risk that will generate even more success. Hateful or unkind comments, however, will destroy even the bravest student's confidence.

There are many ways to begin to include a more positive focus on your students' strengths in your lessons:

- ► Pay your students sincere compliments whenever you can. This is a pleasant and productive habit to encourage in them also.
- ► Use positive body language to convey your respect and sincerity when you talk with students.
- ► Make eye contact. Pat a shoulder or a hand. Make sure your expression is pleasant.
- ► Ask students to share a hidden talent or skill with you.
- ► Be generous with praise. Students who are aware of what it is they are doing correctly will want to repeat it.

- Open class by having students explain what they did well on their homework assignments.

- End class by asking students to share the most important things they learned that day.

- Ask students to tell others what they did right on a difficult assignment so that the good news can be shared for the benefit of everyone.

- Do not compare one student with another, especially if you pit one student's weakness against another's strength.

- Hand out brightly colored pieces of paper and ask the students to write down a contribution they can make to the class. Post these contributions for all to see.

- When students go over returned papers, have them correct their errors and list the things they did right, too.

- An easy way to make sure all students have the extra help they need is to have the student experts in the room share their expertise with others.

- Having students set and achieve goals is a good starting point for identifying the strongpoints of each one. When students have a purpose for working, they tend to work well.

- Be careful that the strengths you compliment your students on are ones that are appropriate for their age level, unless you inadvertently want to either insult them or send a message that your standards are very low.

- Ask students for their advice or opinions. Students often have important insights and solutions to problems that surprise many adults, even those who know them well. Be obvious when you tap into this resource.

- Classes seem to take on a personality of their own. Use this to your advantage when you can. If classes are very talkative, turn this into a strongpoint by giving the students opportunities for debate and discussion. Make sure you focus on their strengths while you help them eliminate their weaknesses.

INCREASE POSITIVE INTERACTIONS WITH YOUR STUDENTS

One of the most effective ways that experienced secondary teachers have found to promote self-discipline in all of their students is to increase the positive interactions that they have with each one. While it is very easy to have a positive relationship with those personable students who care about their work and who make it clear that they value their teachers, it is not always easy to have the same positive relationship with those students who struggle with class requirements, are impulsive, have attention deficit disorders, or who are underachievers.

Even though it may not be as effortless as the relationships you build with the more successful students in your class, it is even more important that you work to have a positive relationship with every student—especially those who need you most. Those students who find school difficult need even more positive interactions with their teachers than those students for whom school seems to come easily. Below you will find some strategies that can help you increase the positive interactions you have with all of your students.

HOW TO ENCOURAGE STUDENTS WHO ARE STRUGGLING

While insufficient self-discipline may be just one of the reasons students are unsuccessful, undiagnosed learning difficulties, family problems, and a lack of background skills or knowledge may also contribute.

Although it is sometimes impossible to know why some students struggle with their assignments while others breeze through them, the effect of the struggle is painfully clear. Students who believe that they have no chance of passing a class seldom continue working until the last day of the term. Unfortunately, even just one student who is not successful can have a detrimental effect on all of the students in the class as that student attempts to sleep though class, becomes argumentative, or disrupts the work that others are attempting to accomplish. While every case is different, you may find some strategies successful in mitigating the damaging effect that students who are struggling may create for themselves and for the rest of the class.

Students Who are Struggling, but Who Have a Chance to Pass the Course

Step 1: Make it clear that you and the student must work in partnership if that student is to successfully complete the course. Decide on times when you can meet together to ensure that the student knows what to do and how to succeed. Stress that you are willing to help the student, but that the student also has responsibilities. Consider an assignment contract similar to the contract in "Setting Short-Term Goals" later in this section to make your expectations as concrete as possible.

Step 2: Communicate frequently and openly with the student and his or her parents or guardians. Be straightforward about the situation and about what the student must accomplish to pass the course. Provide frequent updates so that everyone can stay informed.

Step 3: Make sure that the expectations that you have for the successful completion of the work are clear. Discuss the types of assignments, the quality of the work that is acceptable, and the due date for each assignment. Be as explicit as possible.

Step 4: Work with the student to focus on study skills as well as learning the material for the course. Arrange for peer tutors and other possible remediation assistance.

Students Who Are Struggling, but Who Do Not Have a Chance to Pass the Course

Step 1: Be very careful to make sure that there is no way at all for your students who are in this situation to pass the course. The time you spend double-checking your calculations will be amply rewarded if the student does have a chance to pass.

Step 2: Take extra care not to humiliate the student even further. Even though these students may act as if they do not care about school at this point, they are usually deeply embarrassed and filled with self-doubt.

Step 3: Inform parents of the situation and the student's responsibilities for the duration of the course. Make it clear that you are not giving up on their child, but continuing to offer instruction.

Step 4: If the student is not interested in completing assignments that the other students are required to do, consider offering remediation work that could make it easier for the student to retake the course successfully.

Step 5: Find a common ground to work together successfully with this student. Use a contract or come to some form of clearly expressed agreement with the student so that behavior expectations are clear. A student who is failing a class should not be allowed to sleep or to disturb others.

HOW TO HELP IMPULSIVE STUDENTS

Students with this learning problem are easy to recognize in any classroom. They are usually the ones soaking up all of the negative attention. Impulsive students may act before thinking. They may spend too much time in an unproductive attempt to get organized at the beginning of an assignment. The floor around their desks may be littered with piles of balled-up paper that has been hastily scribbled on and discarded.

These students disturb others by calling out answers without regard to whether they are right or wrong. These are the students who seem to live frantic lives in a state of near crisis. Every request to leave the room is an emergency. Every bad grade is a sure sign they are going to fail the entire course. Undone homework—a nightly problem—is someone else's fault. They are fidgety and forgetful and their own worst enemies.

Impulsive students require the utmost in patient firmness from every teacher. With the help of sympathetic teachers and other adults, these students can be transformed into well-behaved and successful students. If you have one of these students, consider trying some of the strategies suggested here to help them develop self-discipline and work productively.

> ► Replace their negative behaviors with more appropriate ones. Teach them the correct behavior to follow in your class for the various times when impulsive students seem to have the most trouble staying focused. For example, be firm about expecting these students to remain seated while you are speaking to the entire class.

> ► Be very specific about what is and what is not acceptable behavior. Begin consistent reinforcement as soon as you do this. If you are not consistent, you will only confuse impulsive students.

> ► Insist that they use a daily planner. Hold impulsive students accountable for keeping track of their work.

> ► Don't accept excuses that are clearly inappropriate. Impulsive students need to be sure of the boundaries of acceptable and unacceptable behavior. Be concrete and specific.

> ► Make sure they see their assignments as small steps that lead to something bigger and that these small steps need to be accomplished one at a time.

> ► Use plenty of positive reinforcement to build confidence and to reassure impulsive students that they are on the right track. They need a lot of positive attention to replace the negative attention they have been used to receiving.

> ► Impulsive students also usually respond well to a behavior contract because it is very specific about what they will be expected to do.

> ► Teach impulsive students to self-evaluate. They are usually so busily engaged in negative behavior that they haven't had a chance to learn this very natural act.

HOW TO ASSIST STUDENTS WITH ATTENTION DEFICIT DISORDERS

Painfully evident in many cases, students with any of the broad spectrum of attention deficit disorders (ADD) can feel out of place and defeated as they endeavor to succeed in school. Similar to the students who are too impulsive, these students may experience difficulty staying on task in class. Although this disorder is a complex one, a caring teacher can take several simple actions to make it easier for students with attention deficit disorders to develop the skills that will enable them to become self-disciplined.

▶ By the time these students are in secondary school classes, they may have had such chaotic times in earlier years that they do not have adequate work habits or study skills. Early in the term, work with them to establish clear procedures and routines to make their school lives easier. Keeping an organized notebook, recording assignments in an assignment notebook, and managing study time are all important skills for students with ADD.

▶ Adopt a proactive stance when you design instruction to try to anticipate the problems that your ADD students could have. For example, try to make your directions as clear as possible by using at least two modalities to present them. Review them several times at the beginning of an activity to make sure that your students with ADD know what they are supposed to do.

▶ Simplify their lives by teaching them how to manage their materials. Teach these students how to get organized and then check their materials every day. Discourage them from the distractions that seem to go with these students: phones, cosmetics, dried-up pens, personal notes, or countless locker combinations on tiny scraps of paper. It will take weeks of checking before the older, disorganized habits are replaced by better ones, but be persistent.

▶ Encourage your ADD students to explore alternative forms of instruction: reading along with an audio version of the text, using a computer, or peer tutoring, for example.

▶ Make frequent progress checks to ensure that these students know what to do and how to do it well.

▶ Talk to parents or guardians about what they can do to help at home. Sometimes something as simple as showing adults a record of homework assignments each night or teaching their children to put their packed book bags by the door will help reinforce organizational skills.

▶ If you notice that a student with ADD is struggling to stay on task, be quick to offer assistance. Often a wiggle break or brief change of scenery will enable them to focus better. Alternatively, you could offer a checklist or other organizer so that students can work in a systematic fashion.

HOW TO SUPPORT STUDENTS WHO ARE UNDERACHIEVERS

One of the most frustrating types of students to teach, students who are underachievers—those who can do their work, but who choose not to—often don't neglect their work because they do not care about school. Instead, quite the opposite is true: underachieving students are often paralyzed by a lack of self-confidence. They want to do well, but doubt that they will be able to.

You can help these students develop self-confidence and self-discipline by adopting a matter-of-fact attitude that removes some of the negative emotions they may be experiencing as they contemplate their work and their failure. Several effective strategies will allow you to support your underachieving students who struggle with self-discipline:

▶ Reward and encourage improvement. Mark progress as it happens so that these students will have a reason to keep trying. These are the students in your class who become easily discouraged. Keep them upbeat and positive in their belief that they can overcome their negativity.

▶ As often as you can, increase the amount of intrinsic motivation in each assignment so that the appeal of the work may help the underachiever stay on track.

▶ Be quick to intervene at the beginning of an assignment if you notice that a student is having trouble getting started. Their lack of self-confidence makes it difficult for underachievers to begin work.

- Do not be a pushover for excuses. In a matter-of-fact manner direct or redirect the student to stay focused, turn in missing assignments, or begin working.

- Be aware that when this student tells you "I did it, but I left it at home," that the student is probably telling you the truth. Lack of belief in his or her own self-worth makes it difficult for the underachiever to submit work that may not be perfect. Work on this issue with parents or guardians as well as with the student.

HOW TO HELP STUDENTS MAKE UP MISSED WORK

Very few students have perfect attendance. When students are absent for even one class period, the problem of making up missed work begins and doesn't seem to go away until the last bell of the term rings.

Failure to make up work can be a miserable experience that leads to serious discipline problems for teachers, parents, and students. When students do not make up their work promptly, their grades begin to drop and their desire to do well in class seems to vanish as they grow more and more overwhelmed.

The problem of make-up work does not have to be a tiresome task or a discipline problem for you and your students if you establish a fair policy, post it, teach it to your students, and then enforce it consistently. Here are some guidelines that will help you do all of these:

- Make sure your policy is reasonable, workable, and in line with your school's policy.

- If you provide your students with a syllabus, encourage them to follow it as closely as they can while they are absent to try to stay caught up.

- Encourage your students to make up missed work as quickly as possible. Praise students who do so.

- Discuss the issue of make-up work with your students. This will help you and your students in defining the limits of responsibility as well as in generating solutions to this problem.

- Be sure to inform the parents of your students of your make-up work policy at the start of the school term.

- Whenever you pass out handouts, put the leftover copies in a special folder for the convenience of those students who are absent. Encourage your students to check this folder when they return so that you won't have to search for extra copies for them.

- Keep all returned papers for absent students in a folder. You will have the papers right at hand when your students return.

- A useful strategy is to divide your students into study teams. In each team, students share the responsibility for helping each other make up missing work by calling absent members, taking and sharing legible notes, reviewing the difficult parts of an assignment, and just providing a bit of extra support.

- Set aside a generous amount of time each week when you will be available to your students for make-up work. Post this information and make sure that it's also available for parents or guardians. Your students and their parents will appreciate this extra time and effort on your part.

- Although the practice of allowing students to make up missed work during class time is certainly convenient for teachers and students, what you are really doing is causing that student to miss yet another day's work. Consider setting aside time before or after school for students to make up missing work instead.

- Have your students rotate the task of recording the daily events from each class on a large calendar. This quick summary of what was done in class will help the absent class members quickly get back on track.

- Set aside board space where you can keep a running record of missing work. In this space you could post your syllabus if you use one or a calendar with the daily assignments on it; a list of the students who owe missing work; and the final date on which you will accept missing work from them.

- For long-term projects, you could post a modeling chart where you can mark off assignments as they are completed. Your students can check this chart to see what work they still need to complete. This is useful even for older students who have trouble staying organized and managing their time wisely.

- Always make time to talk with your returning students about the work they owe. Make sure they understand what they need to do in order to complete the assignments satisfactorily and get back on task quickly.

- A time-consuming but very effective technique to keep students on track is to contact a parent if a due date for missing work is nearing and the student has made no effort to complete it. The word will get around quickly that you are serious about make-up work.

- Don't allow students to make up work past your time limit simply to raise their grades. Enforce a reasonable policy and you will teach responsibility.

- If many of your students are absent due to an epidemic or some other catastrophe, adjust your instruction and make-up work expectations.

- Be prompt, detailed, and accurate when you are asked to send assignments home for a sick child. Writing a friendly note and offering assistance in making up missed work is courteous as well as professional.

- When you assign a big project, give consideration to how you will grade ones that students turn in late. Bear in mind that students who are not prepared will use absence as an excuse to create an extension for themselves unless you establish, teach, and enforce a policy for this situation. One solution is to deduct a certain number of percentage points for each day the project is late. Be sure that all of your students know about this in advance.

- Be consistent in teaching students to accept responsibility for missing work by asking them what steps they need to take to complete the assignment before the final due date.

- There will always be situations where you have to use your best judgment. For example, if a student is absent because of a serious illness or because of the death of a family member, you should treat that student with compassion. You need to consider the overall benefit to the child and adjust the make-up work.

- Issue reminder slips to students upon their return so that they have a written record of what they owe.

PROMOTING SELF-DISCIPLINE THROUGH IMPROVED SELF-IMAGE

A healthy self-esteem is not handed out at birth—not even to those enviable individuals who were born with such advantages as intelligence, beauty, good health, and loving families. A positive sense of self is something that caring adults help young people develop.

In secondary classes it is particularly apparent that students who are confident in their ability to master the daily challenges of school find it easier to succeed. When we boost this attitude in our students, our students learn more and behave better.

The reasons for this are not hard to determine. When students regard themselves as capable learners, they act in ways that perpetuate this belief. They resist the negative effects of peer pressure and learn to develop the social skills that will help them be positive members of the class. Self-confident students are courteous, willing to offer help, tolerant of others, and willing to take risks.

Promoting self-esteem in our students is not something that should replace the curriculum; instead, it should be a natural part of the positive approach that we take with our students. When we let them see that we are concerned about them, we take an important first step.

It is also important to remember that in school self-esteem must be based on achievement—particularly for secondary-level students. It can't be founded merely on personal qualities, but must be solidly based in the sense of satisfaction that comes from doing a job to the best of one's ability.

Although there are some simple activities that we can do to help our students focus on their successful achievements, the best ways to bolster a healthy self-image are the ones that will appeal most to your students. In the following lists, you will find general guidelines to help you work with your students. You will also find simple suggestions for specific activities so that the improved sense of self-esteem you want to foster will arise naturally from the positive relationship you develop with your students.

General Guidelines for Helping Students Develop a Healthy Self-Image

▶ Improve your listening skills. Students are acutely sensitive to the nuances of body language. Treat your students as if they are important people in your life. Attend to what they say, even in the frantic press of daily activities.

▶ Pay attention to the way you talk to students. Use a pleasant, soft voice. Be friendly as well as firm with them. Encourage them through specific praise and encouragement, not just by saying, "Good job!" no matter what a student does. It is also important to avoid needless negativity with students. For example, instead of saying "Don't interrupt me," try saying "I'll be with you in a minute" if you want to send a more positive message.

▶ Offer help to those students who need special help and encouragement. Some students need that extra tutoring session or a bit of extra time with you in order to become competent in your class.

▶ Hold your students accountable for participation in class. Do not let them sleep, refuse to work, neglect to make up work, forget homework, or ignore what you have assigned for all of your other students. Students who opt out of participating in class may be relieved for the moment, but they are not going to feel good about themselves or about your class if you allow this behavior.

▶ A great deal of personal reward can be found in activities that help others. Involve your students in class activities that are geared to helping other people. Students who tutor each other or younger students, collect money and goods for the needy, participate in an Earth Day cleanup, or are involved in other compassionate and helpful activities will reap tremendous benefits in the form of improved self-esteem.

▶ Create a team spirit in your classroom. Students should feel they are part of a special group. When a class develops this strong sense of identity for themselves, everyone benefits from the confidence-enhancing effects.

▶ Use praise and rewards to keep students focused on their accomplishments. Take a no-nonsense approach to how you provide correction for your students, but be gentle. Over and over again, research and common sense both prove that it is the positive actions we take with our students that promote a productive classroom climate. Students who have teachers who show sincere approval for their actions are more successful than those students whose teachers intimidate them into compliance.

▶ Structure your lessons so that students have opportunities to succeed and then to enjoy the feelings of accomplishment that accompany success.

Simple Activities That Will Boost Self-Esteem

▶ Have students create a class *Who's Who* entry about each other. Include the hobbies, interests, and skills of each one in an effort to help students learn to relate to each other in a positive way.

▶ Another way to increase the team spirit atmosphere in your room is to have students bring in words and photographs that reflect their interests, talents, and skills. Use them to create a large wall collage to display the positive things your students have in common.

▶ Create opportunities for students to reflect upon and recognize the contributions of their classmates after a shared assignment, project, or discussion. Teach the importance of recognizing each other's accomplishments.

▶ Set aside space to create a "Wall of Fame" in your classroom where you can display excellent work.

▶ At the end of class, ask students to tell you something important that they did well or learned.

▶ Ask students to describe the most difficult part of a lesson and what they did to overcome that difficult part.

▶ Take photographs of your students while they are working well and display them.

▶ Ask students to share with you or with class members three things that will help them have positive feelings about themselves or their work.

▶ After a particularly long or difficult unit of study, hold an awards ceremony to celebrate its successful completion.

▶ At the end of the year, ask students to write a letter to a future teacher describing what they learned in your class.

▶ Ask students to list the ways they can accept personal responsibility for becoming successful in school.

TEACH YOUR STUDENTS TO SET AND ACHIEVE GOALS

According to the American dream, anyone who wants to be a success can achieve that goal through a combination of persistence, hard work, and determination. Sadly, the philosophy of violence and hopelessness permeating much of the popular culture avidly consumed by adolescents seems to have robbed many of them of the optimistic view of the future that guided so many earlier Americans to successful lives.

The widespread acceptance of this pessimistic attitude is not limited to inner-city street gangs. Teens who live in rural poverty, teens who are pregnant, teens who live in troubled homes, teens with substance abuse problems, teens in trouble with the law, teens who are unloved—almost every young person living in our country is at risk from this devastating hopelessness.

Adolescents need powerful and consistent messages from the caring adults in their lives to combat this national mood of weary despair. One of the most important tasks we can accomplish for our students is to help them grow and achieve their dreams.

If we are going to be successful at combating the negativity that seems to be widespread among teens, we need to help them strengthen their feelings of self-worth by teaching them to set goals and then work to achieve them.

There are many benefits to teachers who do this. The most important one is the positive and purposeful class atmosphere that results from students who have a reason for attending school and have direction in their lives. This benefit has a profound effect on both teachers and students.

Here are some of the other benefits that can happen when teachers encourage students to become goal-oriented:

▶ We can give support to students who are making serious efforts to learn to take control of their own lives and to achieve their dreams.

▶ Our students will understand that what they do now will have an impact on their futures. They come to realize that there is a clear cause-and-effect correlation between their present and their future.

▶ Students with clear goals have a reason to come to school and to learn. They are working for something, not just enduring another weary day at a desk. They achieve more than those students without goals.

▶ Students will come to believe in their ability to make the productive choices that will help them fight peer pressure. The certainty of their decisions will help reduce many frustrations.

▶ Students who work toward achieving goals will learn to be successful. They will also learn that success comes from the act of taking responsibility for one's own actions and not from chance.

There are several ways you can begin the process of directing students to their futures. The most effective way is to begin with a structured lesson that will accomplish more than informal moments here and there. Here are ten steps for designing lessons that will help students establish goals and learn to work to accomplish them:

Step 1: Begin by having the students discuss some of the famous people they know about. They can do this in a large-group or small-group discussion. Ask them to brainstorm about the qualities that cause some people to be successful. Eventually lead students to see that success does not happen by chance, but is created through planning and goal setting.

Step 2: Have the students determine what personal qualities they already possess that could be classified as strengths and interests.

Step 3: Have the students visualize their futures by imagining what they would like for their lives to be like five years and ten years from the present.

Step 4: Use the "Setting Long-Term Goals" form that follows or design a form of your own to have students write down the big goals they have for the future. Have them commit their dreams to paper along with the behaviors they will need to achieve their goals. Stress that long-term goals are those that are five or ten years away.

Student Worksheet

SETTING LONG-TERM GOALS

Name: _____ **Class:** _____

Goal 1: _____

    Date when I will achieve my goal:_____

    Steps I will have to take to achieve my goal:

    1. _____

    2. _____

    3. _____

    A problem I will have to manage to achieve my goal:

Goal 2: _____

    Date when I will achieve my goal: _____

    Steps I will have to take to achieve my goal:

    1. _____

    2. _____

    3. _____

    A problem I will have to manage to achieve my goal:

Step 5: Monitor carefully to make sure students' goals meet these criteria for success:

▶ Goals should be specific.

▶ Goals should be realistic.

▶ Goals should be easy to explain.

▶ Goals should be something the student really wants.

▶ Goals should be attainable.

Step 6: Have students focus next on the mid-term goals they have to meet in order to achieve their long-term ones. Students can fill out the sample form provided in "Setting Mid-Term Goals" or you can design one of your own. Stress that mid-term goals should be anywhere from six months to a year away.

Step 7: Next have students begin on the short-term goals that will help them get started on the way to a successful future. Again, you can use the form included here or design one of your own. Short-term goals are ones that students can accomplish today or within the week. Use the sample form "Setting Short-Term Goals."

Step 8: After the students have committed themselves to their goals on paper, your next task is help them learn to become goal-directed. It's not enough to just write them down; people must learn to work to achieve their dreams. Do this by having the students keep their goal commitments in their notebooks so that you can refer to them throughout the term.

Step 9: Help your students understand that the only way to reach a long-term goal is by taking a series of smaller steps that lead from short-term goals to mid-term ones to the final ones.

Step 10: Spend just a few minutes each day revisiting, reteaching, and refining your students' goals. You don't have to spend more than a few minutes each week on helping your students stay focused on their weekly goals. This time will be regained several times over through the increased productivity of your students.

Other Activities You May Include

▶ Help students who are having trouble staying focused identify the behaviors that are interfering with their goals. After they have done this, help them generate solutions to those problems.

▶ Review their goals every now and then to see if students need to change direction. Are they taking the right steps? Are they still committed to these goals?

▶ Ask the students to determine the next steps in their personal growth. Do they need to seek more information about the goals they have for themselves? Do they need to find a mentor who will help them with guidance and support?

▶ Practice goal-setting techniques in the assignments you give your students. When they have a large project, ask them to break it down into smaller parts and then to set goals and timelines for each stage of the assignment.

Student Worksheet

SETTING MID-TERM GOALS

Name: _____ **Class:** _____

Goal 1: _____

    Date when I will achieve my goal: _____

    Steps I will have to take to achieve my goal:

    1. _____

    2. _____

    3. _____

    A problem I will have to manage to achieve my goal:

Goal 2: _____

    Date when I will achieve my goal: _____

    Steps I will have to take to achieve my goal:

    1. _____

    2. _____

    3. _____

    A problem I will have to manage to achieve my goal:

Student Worksheet

SETTING SHORT-TERM GOALS

Name: _____ **Class:** _____

Target dates: _____ until _____

Goal 1: _____

How will I know when I have achieved my goal?

What specific steps must I take to achieve my goal?

1. _____

2. _____

3. _____

4. _____

What behavior might interfere with my goal?

Goal 2: _____

How will I know when I have achieved my goal?

What specific steps must I take to achieve my goal?

1. _____

2. _____

3. _____

4. _____

What behavior might interfere with my goal?

TEACH STUDENTS TO MAKE GOOD DECISIONS

It's ironic. One of the most frequently voiced complaints by adolescents in their endless struggle for independence is that too often they face unnecessary restrictions imposed by the powerful adults in their world. The irony of this situation lies in the misconception that many teens have about their lack of power.

Teenagers today have to make choices that were unthinkable in earlier times. We routinely expect even the most vulnerable and ill-prepared adolescents in our society to deal with issues and problems that have a serious impact on their lives and on our own. We don't find it unusual that students plan their own school schedules, select and purchase their own clothing, drive their own cars, fix meals for themselves and other family members, care for siblings, or get themselves off to school each morning. For many teens, these choices are tough, but routine. Many handle them with surprising ease. Others do not.

The gamut of decisions that today's students have to make is not only tough, but sometimes unforgiving. Adults are no longer shocked at finding exhausted students working long hours in after-school jobs, involved in violent crimes, experimenting with illegal drugs, or being sexually active. Unfortunately for the secondary teacher, too often these choices overwhelm students who are not prepared to handle the responsibilities that go along with so many options. The impact of students who make poor decisions for themselves can be devastating on a classroom.

However, one of the most joyful tasks teachers can undertake is to guide students as they learn to make sound decisions in our classrooms and, ultimately, in their lives. Luckily for us, many nonthreatening opportunities exist for teachers to help students make good decisions in the course of a school day. There are many advantages to giving students safe options as often as possible. Here are just a few of them:

> ► When we allow our students opportunities to make choices and then to discuss the consequences of those choices with us, we teach them to think about the actions they take.

> ► Options increase students' problem-solving abilities while reducing the need for time-consuming and unpleasant power struggles.

> ► Giving students choices can allow them to share ideas while working toward a common goal—a skill they will need as good employees when they are adults.

> ► Allowing students to have frequent options shows that you value their opinions, respect their uniqueness, and have faith in their ability to succeed. All three of these will increase your chances of having a peaceful and productive classroom.

If we want our students to become more self-disciplined, then we should help them realize they have tremendous power and control over almost every aspect of school life. This power and control lies in their attitude. They can choose how they do their work, regard their classmates, and treat their teachers. In fact, they have choices throughout their school day through their attitudes. Students with a positive attitude about their school day are pleasures to teach. Students with a negative attitude create our discipline problems.

We can help the students in our classes make good choices about their attitudes by explaining this concept in terms of small steps. Many small good choices can add up to a positive pattern. We can and should offer all of our students plenty of opportunities to make wise decisions.

You do not have to lose control of your class while you help students make good decisions. It would be unwise to abandon your classroom to the whims of your students. The best way to promote sound decision making is to give students a limited range of choices. For example, instead of saying, "Do you want homework tonight?" try, "Do you need to do exercise three or exercise four or both of them for extra practice at home tonight?"

Here are some other safe ways to begin thinking about how you can give your students options. Making choices such as these will lead students to make good decisions for themselves as they struggle toward an independent adulthood.

- ▶ "Which of these two assignments do you need to do first?"
- ▶ "How should the teams for this task be set up?"
- ▶ "Which day would be better for the test on this unit?"
- ▶ "You may be excused from the room three times this month. How can you use those passes wisely?"
- ▶ "Do you need to do this now or can it wait a few minutes?"
- ▶ "Do you need more practice on this or should we count the next activity for a grade?"
- ▶ "What could be a more efficient way to arrange our supplies?"
- ▶ "What would be a better way to express that?"
- ▶ "We have these things to accomplish next week. Would you like to help me plan on which days we will do them?"
- ▶ "What should we do about students who choose to break this rule?"
- ▶ "You can have either the essay format or the objective format for your test. Which one would you prefer?"
- ▶ "In what order do you want to answer questions?"
- ▶ "Which nights next week will be better for you to do this homework assignment?"
- ▶ "When someone is rude, what can you choose to do instead of responding with rudeness yourself?"
- ▶ "You have ten minutes left. Please do either exercise A or exercise B."
- ▶ "There are five essay questions for you. Answer any three of them."
- ▶ "Would you like to do your review drill orally or in writing?"
- ▶ "If you continue to do that, what will the result be?"
- ▶ "Since you didn't do well on that quiz, what could you do now to make sure that you will do better on the test?"
- ▶ "What is one choice you can make right now that will improve your future?"

CREATING SELF-DISCIPLINED STUDENTS THROUGH PROBLEM-SOLVING ACTIVITIES

One of the best ways to help students make the transition from being part of an unruly mob to being trusted and valuable members of a community of self-directed learners is to involve them in making choices and decisions that solve problems. At this point in their lives, students are faced with countless important decisions.

Many times their futures depend on these choices. Many teens have to make important decisions about their careers, where they want to go to college, if they want to go to college, and other life-choice issues. Then they also have the tremendous additional pressures facing teens today: substance abuse, sexual activity, peer relationships, and self-confidence issues.

If what we want from our students is clear thinking on these issues and the ones that concern our subject matter and the behavior that we expect from them in class, then we need to give them plenty of practice in making viable decisions. There are several important things we can do to make this process part of our classroom:

▶ We can teach students to recognize a good idea. Although there are many ways to determine this, we can at least show our students the necessity of looking ahead and predicting outcomes based on what they can anticipate as results.

▶ We can teach students how to generate ideas by showing them how to brainstorm until they have exhausted all of the creative avenues available to them.

▶ We can give students opportunities to have a voice in the decision-making process in our classrooms. Students who are on the way to becoming self-disciplined need the supervised practice in generating, evaluating, and implementing solutions to problems that we can offer.

If you are working toward having your students make wise choices for themselves as part of the classroom-management practices you use in your room, there are many opportunities to involve your students in problem-solving activities. Some problems you might have students solve include the following:

▶ Improving the way they handle homework assignments

▶ Improving student behavior in the public areas of the building: cafeteria, bus ramp, parking lot, hallways, restrooms

▶ Arranging a new due date for an assignment

▶ Changing the rules of the class

▶ Planning class activities such as field trips or banquets

▶ Managing projects they have to complete as a group

▶ Managing class routines

▶ Improving student behavior in class

▶ Solving a community issue or problem

▶ Researching information about a topic

▶ Obtaining more materials needed for class: software, computers, calculators, books, tapes, magazines, pens, and so on

▶ Improving the traffic patterns in class

▶ Establishing a peer-tutoring support system

▶ Resolving peer conflicts

▶ Monitoring shared materials

BEHAVIOR MODELING THAT CAN TRANSFORM YOUR CLASS

Long a staple of elementary classrooms, behavior modeling charts have a definite place in secondary classrooms also (see the "Behavior Modeling Chart" that follows). Behavior modeling works by making students aware of their behavior. When their progress is visible, students have a clear idea of class expectations. No longer are their teacher's admonitions vague, but they are precise and real.

One of the most effective ways to use a behavior modeling chart is to display a positive behavior that you would like students to improve. Simply making their effort and success rate visible has a productive effect. When various classes are displayed, a subtle competition begins that can increase positive peer pressure. Many teachers have found behavior modeling an effective method of improving behaviors such as these:

- ▶ Homework completion
- ▶ Bell work completion
- ▶ Neat work
- ▶ Time on task
- ▶ Productive transitions
- ▶ Skill or practice accuracy

Teacher Worksheet

BEHAVIOR MODELING CHART

Number of Students Who Do This										
Behavior	M	T	W	Th	F	M	T	W	Th	F

Additional Notes:

USE BEHAVIOR CONTRACTS TO PROMOTE RESPONSIBILITY

The idea of written contracts between students and teachers has been a proven success in classrooms for many years. Whether it's the promotion of positive behaviors or the elimination of negative ones, contracts are one of the most effective tools a creative teacher has.

Contracts between teachers and students can be as varied as student interests and your own creativity allow. You can easily add your own unique touches to the standard formats suggested in this section to help your students find success.

Although contracts differ from teacher to teacher and from situation to situation, they generally have common characteristics. Basically each contract should include

- ▶ Name of the student
- ▶ Name of the teacher
- ▶ Beginning and ending dates
- ▶ Specific tasks to be performed
- ▶ Degree of success expected
- ▶ Immediate rewards
- ▶ Future rewards
- ▶ Consequences
- ▶ Witness signatures
- ▶ Student and teacher signatures
- ▶ Any extra notes pertaining to a specific contract

Don't be afraid to have fun with a contract if the situation warrants. Use legal language and an elaborate typeface. Illustrations and places for students to make addendums also create interest. Do whatever you can to catch your students' attention and motivate them to improve the behavior in the contract or perform whatever task is required by it. Although there are as many different types of contracts as there are teachers who use them, the most common ones deal with assignments, the behavior of individual students, and the behavior of an entire class.

Assignment Contracts

Assignment contracts are special types of behavior contracts that can be especially effective for reviews, drills, work that is easily self-checked, when you sense that a class would like more choice in making decisions about their work, when you have a mature class, or when you want to help students reinforce their skills. There are many ways to design these depending on what you want each one to accomplish. In particular, these are excellent for students who like to work independently within a comfortable framework of your expectations.

Assignment contracts allow students choices about what they want to work on each day. In this type of contract, you decide what type of work needs to be done, but the students are allowed some freedom in deciding the order in which it is completed. In general, this contract should not last longer than a week before you bring everyone together for a common pooling of knowledge and review before assessing progress.

Teacher Worksheet

SAMPLE ASSIGNMENT CONTRACT

I, _____ , agree to complete all assignments necessary to earn a grade of _____ for this unit of study.

I realize that all of the assignments must be completed to the degree of proficiency required, checked daily, and that all assignments must be turned in by the date indicated for the grade that I choose.

My goal is to earn a grade of _____ on this unit of study.

Work required for an "A":

1. Any ten of these exercises by _____ :

   a.

   b.

   c.

   d.

   e.

   f.

   g.

   h.

   i.

   j.

   k.

   l.

2. Any three of these by _____ :

   a.

   b.

   c.

   d.

   e.

3. Successful notes on Chapter _____ by _____ .

4. Quiz on _____ with a score of _____% or higher on _____ .

5. Quiz on _____ with a score of _____% or higher on _____ .

6. Final test with a score of _____% or higher on _____ .

(Continued)

Teacher Worksheet (*Continued*)

7. Two projects from this list:

   a.

   b.

   c.

   d.

   e.

Work required for a "B":

1. Any eight exercises

2. Any two choices

3. Successful notes on Chapter _____

4. Both quizzes passed with a score of _____% or higher

5. Final test with a score of _____% or higher

6. One project from the list

Student signature: _____ Date: _____

Behavior Contracts

Behavior contracts are designed to help solve discipline problems that are usually the result of a student's bad behavior or work habits (see "Sample Behavior Contract 1" and "Sample Behavior Contract 2"). Talking back, not doing homework, and other habitual misbehaviors respond well to this type of contract.

Begin with steps that are easily and quickly met. It is better to create a series of short contracts rather than one long contract since the object here is to help the student improve behavior; this is accomplished more readily in small, easily achieved steps. It is also effective to begin with tangible rewards rather than intrinsic ones in order to get the student used to the new behavior.

Make sure the student understands the problem that has resulted in the need for a contract and the alternative solutions to which you can both agree. The agreement between you must be explicitly stated in the written contract. Another effective technique is to ask the student to restate the terms in his or her own words.

You can also enter into a contract with a parent and a student when the need arises. If a parent is actively involved in the solution to a problem, having that parent sign the contract is a good idea. The student will also take it more seriously.

In addition to using behavior contracts as tools in solving major behavior problems, you can also use them to help eliminate minor disturbances. The reason that behavior contracts work well on these smaller problems is simple: they force a student to attend to the problem. Once a student sees the problem behavior written out and agrees to take steps to solve it, that student is then aware of not just what's wrong, but how to fix it. Behavior contracts work because they give students alternatives to misbehaving. The following list of disruptions are examples of the kinds of misbehaviors that can be improved with contracts:

- ► Tardiness to class
- ► Forgetting to do homework
- ► Putting one's head down during class
- ► Speaking without raising a hand
- ► Mild and habitual backtalk to the teacher
- ► Not following the procedure for beginning or ending class
- ► Writing on the desktop
- ► Excessive restroom requests
- ► Work not done neatly
- ► Not having books and materials in class
- ► Habitual inattention
- ► Unorganized notebooks and materials
- ► Chewing gum
- ► Mild rudeness to other students
- ► Balling up paper when the teacher is talking

Teacher Worksheet

SAMPLE BEHAVIOR CONTRACT 1

I, _____ , hereby declare on this date,

_____ , that I agree to do the following:

_____

_____

My efforts at meeting this goal will be considered acceptable and complete when:

_____

By successfully completing the terms of this contract, I will be rewarded by:

_____

Student signature: _____ Teacher signature: _____

Teacher Worksheet

SAMPLE BEHAVIOR CONTRACT 2

Contract between _____ and _____

                              Student   Teacher

_____ agrees to

_____

Rewards: _____

Consequences: _____

Dates for checking progress: _____

The terms of this contract will end on this date: _____

Student signature: _____ Teacher signature: _____

Group Contracts

Using behavior contracts to motivate groups to perform better is an efficient way to create a positive classroom climate. Having an entire group sign a contract creates a sense of camaraderie that makes students work together for the good of all.

Some teachers use group contracts after the set of classroom rules has been determined. You might have your students sign individual copies to keep in their notebooks, while you have the class sign one large copy that is posted. Use a contract to have students set successful goals for themselves at the beginning of each grading period (see the "Sample Group Contract" that follows). In addition to the grade they want to earn, have your students list the steps they need to take in order to meet their goals.

When your students are in groups, they will enjoy contracting out who is responsible for which tasks. When each member of the group sees the jobs to be done written out, the chances for the successful completion of those tasks become greater as students begin to see their part in the whole of a project. Signing a contract with group members creates a sense of responsibility in each member.

A good way to create a team spirit is to set up a contract in which all of the members work toward a common goal. For example, you might want to promote certain behaviors and eliminate others. If your incentive is appropriate, your students will help each other reach that goal.

Student Worksheet

Class Rules Contract for the Entire Class

We, the undersigned, understand the behavior expectations for this class and intend to faithfully abide by and be guided by them for the betterment of all concerned.

We hereby sign in good faith: _____

Witnessed this day,

Signature of Teacher: _____

HOLD STUDENTS ACCOUNTABLE FOR THEIR OWN SUCCESS

In recent years one of the focal points in educational reform is the idea that to improve our students' chances for successful futures, we must set high standards for all of them, not just the ones who cause less trouble than others. Although this truth is surely self-evident, it is not the entire truth. It is not enough to have high expectations for our students if they do not know how to rise to meet those expectations.

We must hold our students accountable for meeting or exceeding the high standards that we have created for them. Setting high standards is simple. Holding students accountable for their success is not.

No matter how difficult it may be, however, helping students reach high standards is critical to the discipline climate in a secondary classroom. When students feel a sense of urgency about their work, they tend to be too busy to disrupt class. When a helpful and positive teacher is involved with hard-working students, the discipline climate reaches the potential we want for our students and for our own satisfaction.

▶ Be clear with your students that you expect excellent behavior and work from them *at all times*.

▶ Involve parents or guardians as often as it takes for you to create an effective team of caring adults who want to help a child succeed.

▶ Create a wide variety of fair assessments. A few objective tests or quizzes are not fair ways to hold students accountable for their learning. Employ as many effective ways to evaluate student progress as you can to meet the needs and abilities of your students.

▶ Convey your faith in the ability of your students to achieve the standards of excellence you have established for them. If they think you doubt that they can succeed, then your students will give up.

▶ Teach your students how to do their work. Students should be taught the study skills they need to reach the standards you have for them.

▶ Call on every student every day. Allow no student to be invisible in your classroom.

▶ Make sure your comments on assignments are geared toward helping students correct their errors and improve their performance.

▶ Be a good role model of the values you want to instill in your students. Hold yourself accountable for high standards and be the good example that your students should follow.

▶ Foster responsibility through the daily routines and procedures you establish for your students. Involve them in routine classroom-management tasks.

▶ When students have completed an assignment, give them another assignment to begin right away or allow them to choose among acceptable alternatives. No student should waste time by having nothing to do while others finish an assignment.

▶ Review the material at the start and end of class so that students are aware of what they should focus on learning.

▶ Establish clear procedures to manage students who need to make up work, students who do not turn in completed work, students who do not complete homework assignments, and students who do unacceptable work.

▶ Teach your students to pace themselves by paying attention to the time it takes for them to complete various types of assignments. Teach them how to estimate the amount of time it will take to complete assignments and how to time themselves.

▶ Consistently enforce class rules, expectations, and procedures.

▶ Keep your interactions with individual students brief enough so that your attention can stay focused on the rest of the class as well. Don't allow your time to be monopolized by one attention-seeking student at the expense of the others in the class.

▶ Make sure your students know that you pay attention to them. Students who know their teacher is paying attention to their behavior are not going to misbehave as readily as those students who believe they can get away with bad behavior.

▶ Teach your students to be organized and systematic in how they approach their work.

▶ Encourage a team spirit in your class. If a student has reached success through hard work, then have that student share his or her newfound expertise with others who may still be struggling.

▶ Refuse to repeat yourself needlessly. Set high standards for listening skills by thinking before you speak and by making sure your students are listening.

▶ Hold your students to the same behavior standards for substitute teachers that you expect when you are in the room. Discuss this with them in advance of the time when you will be absent; you will find that your students behave much better than if you adopt a "kids will be kids" attitude.

▶ Refuse to allow your students to sleep or to do homework for other classes in your class. They should be doing *your* work in *your* class.

▶ Make it a point that you expect 100 percent accuracy in student work. Some students will aim to just get by with a minimum of work unless you encourage them to do otherwise.

▶ Have students edit or double-check each other's work before turning it in. Peer editing works best if you provide students with a checklist of standards to follow while proofreading.

▶ Be very specific about your criteria for success on an assignment so that students have a clear path for excellence before they begin to work.

▶ Instead of having all of your students shout out answers in an oral activity, ask them to write their responses first and then answer when you call on them. This will force everyone to think before responding.

▶ Plan the procedures you want your students to follow in case they don't have their materials or textbooks in class. Don't allow students to get away with not working because they don't have their materials.

▶ When you are moving around the room to monitor activity, ask your students to underline the answers they think are correct and circle the ones that puzzle them so that you can work together to make sure they understand how to do all of their work well.

▶ If you find that some of your students are reluctant to finish their work on schedule, contact their parents or guardians. If students know that their progress is being monitored at home as well as in class, they usually perform better.

▶ If you see that students have trouble grasping an assignment, reteach the material. Don't allow students to rest on their ignorance.

▶ When students miss the answer to a question, ask them to write the correct answer on their papers. Students should be held accountable for correcting their papers.

▶ Make neatness an important component of the work in your classroom. You don't have to be a perfectionist, but you should expect your students to turn in neat work.

To learn more about how to help your students develop self-discipline, see this section's "Making Positive Choices."

Making Positive Choices

Instead of . . .	Try to . . .
▶ Expecting less of those students who struggle to succeed in school	▶ Encourage every student by maintaining high expectations for all
▶ Imposing only your work ethic and standards on your students	▶ Show students the connection between effort and success
▶ Neglecting to have negative consequences for infractions of class rules	▶ Hold all students accountable for their behavior—both positive and negative
▶ Overlooking broken rules	▶ Be consistent in the enforcement of rules
▶ Being a pushover for too many excuses	▶ Listen carefully and verify students' statements when necessary
▶ Suffering through your students' learned helplessness	▶ Empower your students by teaching them to monitor themselves
▶ Dwelling on the negative behaviors of your students	▶ Focus on how you can use their strengths to make positive changes
▶ Standing by as your students make bad decisions	▶ Teach students how to make good choices for themselves by giving them options
▶ Allowing students just to drift through the school year	▶ Teach students to set and achieve goals
▶ Allowing students to fail your class	▶ Push students to take responsibility and make positive changes instead of choosing to fail

QUESTIONS FOR REFLECTION

Use the information in this section to guide your thinking as you reflect on these questions. They are designed to encourage you to think more deeply about the issues in the text or to discuss those issues with colleagues.

▶ What are your students' strengths? How do you capitalize on this knowledge to help all of your students?

▶ What goals do your students have for themselves? How do you keep them focused on the future? What techniques work well for you and your students?

▶ What kinds of difficulties do your students have in regard to their school work? How do you offer support to those students in your class who may be struggling?

SECTION SIX

Use Classroom Management Systems

> **In this section you will learn**
>
> * How to create classroom rules
>
> * How to set fair and appropriate limits
>
> * How to use classroom policies to guide student behavior
>
> * How to teach students to follow class rules, policies, and procedures
>
> * How to design effective procedures to manage class activities

CLASSROOM MANAGEMENT DECISIONS YOU WILL HAVE TO MAKE

As a vital part of a discipline plan, your classroom management decisions are a positive approach to help students become self-disciplined. Using a combination of rules, policies, and procedures to run the day-to-day business of your classroom will create a system of expectations that allows students to function well within the boundaries established by a familiar framework.

While all three elements of a classroom management system should work together, each differs from the others in significant ways. Classroom policies differ from procedures in that policies are broad in scope whereas procedures are more action oriented. Policies differ from rules in that rules govern broad aspects of student behavior while policies cover more specific topics.

Table 6.1 shows how the three elements of a classroom management system would work together to create a positive learning environment in a classroom where students have access to laptop computers.

When you begin planning how you want the daily business of your classroom to run, you will have to make carefully considered decisions about the rules, policies, and procedures that can make your

Table 6.1. The Interaction of the Three Elements of a Classroom Management System in a Laptop Classroom

Policy	Rule	Procedure
"In this class, you may not download music. This is part of the school district's acceptable use policy you signed at the start of the term."	"Use your class time wisely."	"Please wait until I am finished giving directions before you open your laptops."

class productive. To begin this process, try brainstorming all possible answers to the questions below. Thinking through these issues with this technique should allow you to make decisions that will impact your classroom in a positive way.

▶ How much off-task behavior am I comfortable allowing before I feel that my students are negatively affected?

▶ What behaviors are most offensive to me? How should I prevent them?

▶ What can I do to promote more on-task behaviors?

▶ How structured should the class environment be? Am I comfortable with some down time at various times during the period? If not, what will I do to prevent it?

▶ How will I make sure that my students know and understand the rules, policies, and procedures in my classroom?

▶ Are my classroom rules, policies, and procedures in line with the school and district ones?

▶ How will I enforce the rules, policies, and procedures of my classroom?

HOW CLASSROOM RULES, POLICIES, AND PROCEDURES PROMOTE SELF-DISCIPLINE

Anyone who has ever substituted for a colleague who was absent knows how important classroom procedures are. Those classes where students know what to do and how to go about it are pleasant and productive places. By the time students are in secondary-level classes, they are ready to assume responsibility for many routine tasks.

In a well-managed secondary class, the wise teacher will use the abilities of all students to the best advantage in creating a self-disciplined classroom environment. The following list gives several reasons that should convince you that taking the time to establish and teach your students to follow routine procedures is a sound way to get students to govern their own actions:

▶ Students begin on-task behavior as soon as they enter the room and continue to be focused throughout the period.

▶ Students understand exactly what you expect of them every day and what they have to do to meet those expectations.

▶ Students can focus on relevant learning activities rather than on how they are supposed to complete daily chores.

- Students learn how to be better organized themselves by watching an adult model efficient behavior in the workplace.

- Students assume responsibility for their own work without being nagged by yet another impatient authority figure.

- Students are comfortable and happier when they work within the framework of classroom procedures. Comfortable and happy students are less likely to be disruptive.

- Students interact with each other and with you in positive ways because you have established an atmosphere of mutual cooperation in your classroom that makes this possible.

A SIMPLE TECHNIQUE TO MAKE RULES, PROCEDURES, AND POLICIES EASY TO REMEMBER

One of the best ways to ensure that your students are attending to the rules and other important information that you give them at the start of the term is to have them fill in a worksheet as you go over the rules and information. This practice has several advantages over just talking to your students.

One advantage is that it forces students to become active learners while you are teaching them the rules, procedures, and expectations you have for them. Instead of passively listening to yet another teacher drone on and on about how they are supposed to act, your students will be forced to attend to what you are saying.

Another advantage is that your students will have a written record of just what they are supposed to do. When a student breaks a rule, you can ask that pupil to check the rule on the handout. Because they have written the answers themselves, students are far more likely to recall them.

A final advantage of such a worksheet is that you communicate to your students early in the term that you are a serious teacher who has given much thought to the way you want your students to act in class. When you are able to effectively communicate this to your students, you are then on your way to helping them become self-disciplined.

SETTING LIMITS AND ABIDING BY THEM

"But you said!" "That's not fair!" "Are you sure?" "How come we have to do that?" It's clear from reactions like these that many students are used to arguing with the authority figures in their lives. From the howls of protest when we make unpopular decisions to endless debates about possible answers on a test, many secondary students are clearly accustomed to getting their own way if they nag loudly enough to wear out their exhausted teachers.

Here is what can go wrong when teachers do not abide by their own standards:

Step 1:   You ask students to cooperate with you.

Step 2:   You wait while they disregard your request.

Step 3:   You repeat your request in a louder voice.

Step 4:   You wait while they disregard your request again.

Step 5:   The cycle repeats itself until you lose your cool or just give in to their demands.

Although it is sometimes difficult, try to accept the fact that teenagers will test every decision you make, will argue endlessly if given an opportunity, and will continue to push every limit possible even on the last day of class. When you are aware that your decisions will be tested, it will be easier for you to set limits.

Even though failing to set and abide by firm limits in a classroom can create a cycle of unproductive behavior, you can avoid this problem. One helpful approach is to remove as much of the emotion from the situation as you can. It's not always easy to resist when students appear ready to stage a tantrum, but those teachers who can take a calm and straightforward approach will find it much easier to deal with student misbehavior.

Another way to manage the issue of setting limits is to take time when you create a rule, policy, or procedure to put yourself in the place of your students and anticipate what could go wrong during enforcement. Planning how to handle possible protests will make it easier for you to convince your students to cooperate.

You should also be careful not only to be fair, but to make sure that your students perceive your decisions as fair. Make it a point to preempt student challenges by letting your students know that you intend to be fair to everyone in the class when you make decisions that affect the entire group.

Resist the temptation to be a pushover. Many teachers give in more frequently than they should in an effort to be agreeable to their students. In the long run, this will fail as students continually struggle to gain their own way. Adopt the stance that while you are friendly, you are also a firm teacher. Project a matter-of-fact attitude whenever you have to relay the enforcement of an unpopular decision and you will find that setting limits and abiding by them is not as difficult as it seems.

HOW TO SAY "NO" WITHOUT BEING NEGATIVE

Classroom teachers spend their days bombarded by a steady stream of requests from students who want to go to the restroom, the office, a locker, the clinic, or to call home, open a window, shut a window, sharpen pencils, and hear the directions just one more time. Fielding these entreaties tactfully requires that we make quick decisions not only about whether the request is a sound one, but also about how our response will affect the entire class as well as the student making it.

One of the most useful skills that a secondary teacher can develop is the ability to refuse a student's request without causing offense. Although it may seem impossible, this is not as difficult as it appears. Instead of abruptly refusing, try one of the statements or questions that follow. Each one is designed to deny a student request in a pleasant, nonconfrontational way that preserves the student's dignity.

- ► Let me think about that for a little while.
- ► Let's talk about that after class.
- ► Let's finish this first.
- ► I don't think this is really necessary at this time.
- ► I don't think that is the best decision because . . .
- ► Are you sure that's a wise choice?
- ► What do you think?
- ► Could you give me a moment?

- Can this wait?
- What are the pros and cons involved in your request?
- How are you planning to do that?
- How will you accomplish that?
- Can you tell me why that would not work?
- Would you ask me again in a moment?
- Have you finished your assignment?
- How will that help you achieve your goal?
- Who else have you asked about this?
- Are you sure that's wise?
- Why don't you give that some more thought?
- Why are you asking?

CREATE CLASSROOM RULES

You may be tempted not to take the time to create classroom rules if you think students who are in secondary school should already know how to behave properly. You're right, they should. But they don't.

Even older students do not always know what you expect from them, and they are not talented mind readers. To complicate matters further, other teachers have different behavior expectations for the students whom you share. Why should we go to the trouble of creating a set of rules for our students? The first issue you have to resolve when you begin to consider your rules is just why you need them. There are several sound reasons for establishing a set of rules that will guide your students.

Rules show your students the importance of good behavior if they are to work productively. If you want to increase the number of positive behaviors in your class and decrease the number of negative ones, then you need to make students aware of the necessity of committing themselves to choosing to follow the established standards of the class.

Rules give students and teachers a common language for the set of expectations that each has for the class. Even the most experienced educators can be surprised at the gap between the behaviors they believe that their students should exhibit and the behaviors those students engage in when they are left to just figure things out for themselves.

Students and teachers need rules spelled out clearly if they are to work together to generate a balance between permissiveness and punishment. Rules do this when they are consistently and fairly enforced. Your students will stop constantly testing your decisions, and everyone can work in harmony.

Because rules set limits and provide guidelines, they can protect our right to teach and the right of all students to have a positive environment for learning. Rules make us secure because they protect the safety of students, teachers, and property.

As a final argument for taking the time and going to the trouble to create a set of rules, consider your students. Even though they appear to be in a state of constant rebellion against all types of authority, students do not want—nor do they need—total freedom. The pupils in your class want guidance from caring adults who show them respect and consideration.

How to Involve Students in the Process of Creating Rules

In addition to understanding why you need classroom rules, another factor you need to give some serious attention to when you create rules is how involved you want your students to be in the process. Experienced teachers will agree that the best possible way to create class rules is with the wholehearted cooperation of all students. The reasons for this are simple. When your students have a say in deciding what the class rules should be, you show trust and confidence in them. Another reason to involve a class in this process is that students will be more likely to follow rules that they have created for themselves. There will be a group pressure in place that keeps many students from breaking the group's rules.

If you do decide to allow students to create rules for themselves, begin by asking a series of questions designed to get them thinking about what could benefit them all. Some questions to ask include

- ► What makes a student behave well in some classes?
- ► What behaviors do you notice students with good grades exhibiting?
- ► What are some behaviors you know will hurt a student's chances of doing well?
- ► What limits should we set to make sure everyone can do well?
- ► What rules do you think would work well for us here?

What to Do When You Don't Want to Involve Students

If you are not comfortable with allowing your students to create class rules, then don't involve them. Some classes start the term unable to successfully handle the mature responsibility of such a procedure. If this is the case for your class, you can still involve them in creating rules, but this can be done later in the term when they have settled into the routines of your class.

In this case, you should create a workable set of rules for them at the start of the term, teach these rules, and consistently enforce them. When you are ready for your students to participate in creating or refining rules for themselves, you can have the students examine the current rules and modify them.

State Rules Positively

After you have begun the process of getting your students to think about the areas you would like to have the rules cover, you are then ready for the second step: how to state them.

State your class rules in a positive way. Instead of saying "Don't write on the desks," phrase the same thought as "Show respect for the property of others." With this slight change in wording, the emphasis is now on what your students *should* be doing, not on what they should *not* do.

Instead of stating "Don't play around before class starts," try "Be in your seat and working when the bell rings," so that the tone is pleasant and the directive is broad enough to cover a wide range of activities. The positive message conveys a tone of mutual respect that is lacking in the "do not" statements.

Determine If Rules Will Be Successful

Because rules are such a vital part of the success of a classroom management system, you should take care that the ones you create to help your students stay on track are the best possible ones for your teaching situation. To be effective, classroom rules have to do several things all at once. They must

- ▶ Cover the entire range of possible student misconduct
- ▶ Appeal to students
- ▶ Fit within a school district's policies for student behavior
- ▶ Be stated simply enough for all students to understand them
- ▶ Be enforceable
- ▶ Satisfy the parents and guardians of our students
- ▶ Create an orderly classroom
- ▶ Be as fair to as many people as possible
- ▶ Be easy to remember

If you are still not sure whether your rules are appropriate for secondary students, here are a few examples that might help you determine if your classroom rules will lead to self-directed learning:

- ▶ Bring your materials to class every day.
- ▶ Be prepared to do your best in class each day.
- ▶ Respect the personal rights and property of others.
- ▶ Help your classmates and yourself by respecting the learning environment.

It is also important that you select just a few rules so that your students will have no trouble in remembering and honoring them. You will find that it is easier for you and your students to follow a few broad rules rather than a larger number of detailed ones. If your rules are reasonable, few in number, broad in scope, and stated positively, then you are well on your way to creating a positive classroom atmosphere.

Determine Appropriate Consequences

After you have created the rules and stated them in the best way possible, you now have to consider the consequences your students will face if they break them. Begin this by discussing with your students the intangible rewards everyone will enjoy when they follow the rules.

Ask your students for their advice on assessing how the rules should be enforced. Be careful to state that you intend to take their comments under advisement so that you are not forced to agree to anything on the spot with which you are uncomfortable. Don't give in to student pressure that could compromise the strength of your carefully thought-out rules.

Make sure the consequences are ones you can enforce comfortably. They should fit the infraction in a natural way. Consequences should also follow a simple pattern of escalating penalties for escalating offenses.

For example, asking a student who is tardy to class one time to stay after school for an hour is not appropriate because it is excessive. A more appropriate consequence would be a warning for the first tardy to class, an e-mail to a parent or guardian for the second time, and a fifteen-minute detention for the third time. The penalties are not only appropriate, but also grow more severe with each infraction of the rule.

If you are still not sure about the effectiveness of the classroom rules you have established, use the questions in the following list to guide you as you examine each one:

▶ Is each rule necessary to the smooth management of your class?

▶ Is each rule reasonable and age appropriate?

▶ Are you willing to consistently enforce each one?

▶ Is each one stated as positively as possible?

▶ Are your class rules consistent with school policies?

▶ Can your students recite the rules from memory?

▶ Are students committed to honoring the rules?

▶ Do your students understand the consequences and rewards associated with each one?

▶ Are the consequences appropriate?

▶ Can your students cite examples that define each broad rule?

HOW TO TEACH CLASSROOM RULES SUCCESSFULLY

A perfect list of rules is useless if your students don't know them or don't understand them. You will find that most broken rules are momentary lapses on the part of students. You can help them with this by raising their awareness of the rules and of the importance of following them. The way to do this is to teach the rules. You will also find that one of the three important areas concerning classroom rules, teaching them, is the most important if you want an orderly classroom. It's also the easiest one to overlook as you focus your energy on teaching the material in your curriculum.

Use the following techniques to establish a balance between being firm and showing respect for your students. This is not a one- or two-day event, but rather a process that continues until the end of the term. Use these strategies to get started in the right direction and let your creativity and teaching skills take over as you make sure your students understand what they are supposed to do to honor the rules in their classroom.

▶ Design a plan for teaching the rules to your students just as you would design a lesson plan to teach any other information. Explain the behavior, model it, have students practice it, and then reinforce it.

▶ Be friendly, serious, and firm when you introduce the topic of classroom rules to your students. Now is not the time to confuse your students by treating the subject lightly.

▶ Enlarge a copy of your rules and display it. There should also be a copy in each student's notebook.

▶ Compare the classroom rules that govern your students with the rules of the workplace. Relate classroom rules to the world of work as often as you can so that your students understand that the rules they follow in your class are similar to the ones they will live by when they are adults.

▶ Focus on teaching and reinforcing class rules during the first few weeks of the term to ensure that your students take them and you seriously. Don't neglect to return to the rules as needed throughout the term.

- Enhance your presentation of classroom rules by involving your students in active roles. Rather than sit through a boring lecture from you, they can role-play situations where rules are broken, list the positive and negative consequences of the rules, or hold a debate about the need for various rules.

- Check for student understanding of the rules by having your students explain the rules to you. This would be a good time to have them think of new examples or benefits for each one.

- Hold sessions periodically where you and your students review the rules that they have listed in their notebooks. Checking for understanding every now and then will make students aware of the rules of the class and thus be better able to abide by them.

- Offer alternatives to students who break class rules. Teach them not just to stop a negative action, but to replace it with a positive one. You encourage self-discipline and redirect student energy when you do this.

ENFORCE CLASSROOM RULES

Enforcing your classroom rules is as important a step in creating the kind of classroom environment you would like to have as are creating and teaching them. Effective enforcement of the rules will make the difference in your classroom between order and disorder and between a positive or a negative atmosphere.

Much of what we already know about enforcing classroom rules is simply common sense: you have to be consistent in enforcement from the first day of the term until the very last day. If you are not consistent, you will confuse students. They will not be able to see the connection between the rule and their behavior unless you bring it to their attention through consistent enforcement.

Here are some strategies designed to help you be more effective at enforcement. Use them to encourage your students to follow the rules that govern your class.

- Deal with a broken rule immediately. Waiting will confuse students who are expecting to see you take action.

- Don't threaten students who break a rule. Calmly enforce the rule.

- Don't lecture, argue, fuss, or give undue attention to rule breakers. Enforce the rule.

- Be clear with your students. When you have a rule, mean it. Show this by making sure you enforce all rules.

- Call parents or guardians if you see that a student is having problems with a particular rule. They can be very helpful when asked to intervene early.

- When a student breaks a rule, follow a quick five-step procedure:

  Step 1: Have the student state the rule. Ask, "What rule have you broken?"

  Step 2: Clarify the rule so the student can see that it applies to this situation.

  Step 3: Ask the student to tell you the reason for the rule.

  Step 4: Have the student tell you the consequence.

  Step 5: Put the consequence into action.

- When a student has broken a rule for the first time, question the student privately to make sure he or she understands which rule was broken.

- Be aware of the trouble spots in your class day. Before class, transition times, and when some students finish an assignment before others are often times when students have trouble following class rules.

- Check to see why your students are breaking a rule. Students may misbehave because they need attention from you or their peers. Students also misbehave because they need more clearly defined limits or because they are lacking sufficient motivation to improve their behavior.

- Sometimes students don't observe rules because doing so is not a priority for them. You must make it a priority for your students to be governed by class rules. Doing so will help your students be self-governed.

- Be patient. Your students are going to backslide as well as perform better than you expect. Enforcing rules is a long-term commitment.

- One way to make enforcing the rules easier for everyone is to keep the infractions small. Try to keep situations from escalating into major disruptions whenever you can.

- When you enforce rules, don't tell the offending student the rule he or she has just broken. Instead, ask the student to recall the rule for you. This is more effective in creating a permanent change.

- Don't hesitate to put the rewards and consequences for your class rules into place. Having a class reward early in the term will show your students that you are serious about the rules that govern your class.

- Call attention to good behavior as often as you possibly can. Rewards can be an effective way to encourage students to follow rules.

- It is tempting to make exceptions to your rules. Before you make exceptions, think carefully. You have to balance the needs of the group with the needs of the individual student who broke the rule.

- One effective technique to enforce rules consistently is very easy: Chart the rules that are frequently broken. Simply make a checklist with a grid to record each infraction as it happens. You can do this by writing the rule on the board and putting a check mark next to it whenever it is broken. Often the act of recording the infractions will serve to make students aware of the rules they often break.

- If you find you are having trouble enforcing a particular rule, you may want to ask yourself these questions to see how to get back on track:

  Question 1: Do all students understand this rule?

  Question 2: Is the rule too vague or too broad?

  Question 3: Do students understand and accept the need for this rule? Can they see how it is necessary for the smooth running of the class?

  Question 4: Has your enforcement of this rule been consistent or have you sent a confusing message by allowing too many exceptions?

POLICIES THAT GUIDE YOUR STUDENTS

In addition to rules and procedures, the policies that you create for your students are a key component of a successful classroom management system. Begin by making sure that you are aware of the district and school policies that affect your students and that your classroom policies operate in harmony with those. In addition to these broader policies, you should establish policies that can serve as guidelines for your students to follow while they are enrolled in your course.

For example, your school district may have a policy that all make-up work should be completed within five days of a student's return to class. It could be your classroom policy that you are available two days a week after school to help students make up work. Because policies, like rules and procedures, will differ from classroom to classroom, it is important that you make it easy for your students to know what they are.

Some of the areas that you may need to design policies for include these:

▶ Food in the classroom

▶ Class discussions

▶ Missing work

▶ Types of appropriate homework help

▶ Homework

▶ Conflicts with classmates

▶ Lost textbooks

▶ Student portfolios

▶ Blog and wiki responses

▶ Seeking assistance

▶ Tardiness

▶ Technology use

▶ Grading policies

ESTABLISH CONTROL THROUGH CLASS PROCEDURES

One of the easiest ways to decrease the amount of negative behavior and increase the amount of positive behavior in your class is to provide a businesslike set of class procedures for your students. Being consistent in the way you manage routine tasks will save you and your students valuable hours of wasted time and eliminate many of the discipline headaches that a less-organized class experiences.

At the beginning of the term, establish a few simple procedures for routine classroom activities and then spend a sufficient amount of time teaching these procedures to your students. The extra time you spend teaching your students how you want them to perform these procedures will reward you with saved class time, less confusion, comfortable students, and more efficient learning. All of these, of course, result in a marked decrease in discipline problems and an increase in productive activity.

Make sure, also, that your students understand why it is necessary to follow these procedures so that their cooperation can be wholehearted. In addition to the procedures described in this section, you should consider establishing procedures for these classroom activities:

▶ Beginning class

▶ Ending class

▶ Cleaning work areas

- ▶ Recycling or disposing of trash
- ▶ Formatting written work
- ▶ Recording homework
- ▶ Asking for assistance
- ▶ Attending to media presentations

Passing Out Papers

At the start of class, have all of the materials that you and your students will need for class ready so that no one will have to wait while you shuffle papers. Either give your students the handouts for the day as you greet them at the door or place all of your students' work in folders that they can pick up at the start of class.

Shared Supplies

Establish a shared bank of materials and supplies such as pens, pencils, paper, and extra textbooks so that those students who find themselves unexpectedly caught short will be able to settle down to work quickly. While there are many ways to set up such a bank, one of the easiest is to have students who want to participate bring in materials that can be shared. Put a student or two in charge of collecting the materials and maintaining the collection. Before class starts, students who need to borrow items will check with those classmates who are in charge. At the end of class, the students who are in charge assume responsibility for ensuring that the borrowed materials are returned. This system allows students to work together to solve a problem that has immediate consequences for them. It also promotes self-discipline rather than involving you.

Giving Directions

- ▶ At the start of class, have written directions on the board in the same place each day so that your students know what is expected of them.
- ▶ Use numbered step-by-step directions to keep students on task. Word the information as simply as possible.
- ▶ Develop a few key words in your directions that will serve as signals for your students.
- ▶ Check for understanding when you go over directions with your students. Often, in spite of our best efforts, what we think we are saying is not what our students understand at all.
- ▶ Provide your students with a checklist if the directions are lengthy or complicated so that they can cross off each task as they complete it.

Students Leaving the Room

- ▶ Be reasonable, but be clear in your expectations that leaving the room is not to be a daily occurrence without just cause.
- ▶ Establish and follow a fair policy for students who need to sign out of your room.

▶ Set a limit on the amount of time that students may spend when they have checked out of your room for any purpose.

▶ If you are fortunate enough to work in a small or peaceful school where generic hall passes work well enough to be approved by your supervisors, then use one. If not, be sure to complete an official hall pass with the student's name, destination, and the time he or she left the room. An official pass will make students more aware of the necessity to hurry back and not stray from the intended destination. In either case, students should not leave the room without a pass from you.

▶ Make sure students who are leaving know when they are expected to return.

▶ Collect the hall passes when students return and note the time of return. File these passes just in case you need them later for documentation purposes.

▶ Sometimes students who see their sign-out times noted on a chart (see "Student Sign-Out Sheet") will be more careful not to abuse the privilege because a chart increases their awareness of the amount of time they actually lose from class when they need to leave the room.

Teacher Worksheet

STUDENT SIGN-OUT SHEET

Class: _____

Beginning Date: _____ Ending Date: _____

Student Names	Time in Minutes That Students Were Out of the Room											
	1	2	3	4	5	6	7	8	9	10	11	12
1.												
2.												
3.												
4.												
5.												
6.												
7.												
8.												
9.												
10.												
11.												
12.												
13.												
14.												
15.												
16.												
17.												
18.												
19.												
20.												
21.												
22.												
23.												
24.												
25.												

Collecting Papers

▶ Create a pattern for paper collection. Students should either pass their papers to someone sitting near your desk or to the same collection point every day so that no one will have to get up and walk around. Passing papers to the front of each row is not as efficient as having all papers passed to a central collection point.

▶ If you choose to collect papers when you stand at the door at the end of the class to dismiss your students, ask them to tell you one relevant fact from the day's lesson as a final review as each one hands you a paper.

▶ Encourage the student who dawdles over a test to finish by setting a reasonable time limit for completing it.

▶ Encourage your students to produce accurate, neatly done work. It saves time when they do a job right the first time rather than having to do it over.

Checking Attendance

Never waste your students' time by calling the roll out loud. While taking attendance is very important, it should be done in the most efficient manner possible. Calling the roll every day is not efficient because it provides students with limitless opportunities to misbehave as they sit with nothing to do but watch you and the rest of the class interact one person at a time. You should check attendance by referring to your seating chart either while your students complete their start-of-class assignments or later in the class period.

Making Up Missed Work

The problem of make-up work does not have to be a tiresome task or a discipline problem for you and your students if you establish a fair policy, post it, teach it to your students, and then enforce it consistently. For more information on helping students make up work, see Section 5. Here are some guidelines that will help you do all of these things:

▶ Be sure to inform the parents or guardians of your students of your make-up work policy at the start of the school term.

▶ Encourage your students to make up missed work as quickly as possible. Praise students who do so.

▶ Whenever you pass out handouts, put the leftover copies in a special folder for the convenience of those students who are absent. Encourage your students to check this folder when they return so that you won't have to search for extra copies for them.

▶ Set aside time each week when you will be available to your students for make-up work. Post this information and make sure that it's also available for parents or guardians. Your students and their parents will appreciate this extra time and effort on your part.

▶ Have your students rotate the task of recording the daily events from each class on a large calendar. This quick summary of what was done in class will help the absent class members quickly get back on track.

▶ Always make time to talk with your returning students about the work they owe. Make sure they understand what they need to do in order to complete the assignments satisfactorily and to get back on task quickly. You can use a list such as that shown in "Missing Work Reminder List."

Student Worksheet

MISSING WORK REMINDER LIST

Student's Name	Missing Assignment	Due Date

Fire Drills, Emergencies, Bomb Threats, and Lockdowns

At least once during the first week of school and at unpredictable intervals thereafter, you and your students will be evacuated from your building or will have to practice what to do in a lockdown situation. Minimize the potential for trouble in these events by planning ahead and teaching your students some basic behaviors you would like to see during these times.

Convey the seriousness of the situation to your students so that they can see the importance of it too. Your attitude should be consistently serious throughout the preparations for building evacuation or lockdown drill.

Make sure to have a roster handy to call roll to make sure all of your students are safely out of the building or in their assigned positions for a lockdown drill. Teach them that you will call roll to provide for their safety and that you expect them to answer quickly. They should answer the roll by saying "Here" or some other agreed-upon signal so that you can do this with no fuss.

Good Citizenship

If your school is one where students are expected to display good citizenship practices during the "Pledge of Allegiance," then you need to make sure this part of the school day is an occasion where your students show a respectful attitude for the rights of others and for the citizenship responsibilities of all. Teach your students that you want them to stand quietly and respectfully during this activity. If you have students who refuse to participate, take their objections seriously. Contact their parents or guardians to make sure there is a valid reason for this refusal. Refusing to recite the "Pledge of Allegiance" is not a class disruption; however, disturbing others who want to participate in the recital is a disruption. Make this clear to both the students who refuse and to their parents or guardians.

A Visitor in the Classroom

Be clear with your students about what you expect them to do when there is a visitor in the room. Stress the importance of polite behavior toward guests. Teach your students that you want them to keep working when a visitor enters the room. Stress that they are not to call out the person's name or make other disruptive noises or gestures. Their behavior should remain the same as it was before the visitor entered the room. To learn more about the positive choices you can make as you develop the classroom management systems that will work best for you and your students, see this section's "Making Positive Choices."

Making Positive Choices

Instead of . . .	Try to . . .
▶ Spending the school year correcting your students for making minor mistakes	▶ Teach rules, policies, and procedures
▶ Repeating commands for your students to ignore	▶ Set limits and stick to them
▶ Snapping in annoyance at a student who is misbehaving	▶ Remember to respect your students' feelings and dignity at all times
▶ Assuming that your students know how to behave in class	▶ Teach students what you expect of them
▶ Having too many "do nots" in your rules	▶ Take care to state rules in a positive way
▶ Assigning excessively severe consequences	▶ Make sure that you have planned appropriate consequences

(Continued)

Instead of . . .	Try to . . .
▶ Being inconsistent in how you enforce rules	▶ Begin by enforcing schoolwide rules
▶ Wasting your students' time in confusion	▶ Have clear policies and procedures that govern the running of your classroom
▶ Permitting students to not work because they do not have the materials necessary for class	▶ Establish a shared materials bank for all students to use
▶ Allowing students to goof off during fire and other emergency drills	▶ Impress upon the students the importance of safety and cooperation when they participate in drills

QUESTIONS FOR REFLECTION

Use the information in this section to guide your thinking as you reflect on these questions. They are designed to encourage you to think more deeply about the issues in the text or to discuss those issues with colleagues.

▶ How do you tell your students *no* without sounding negative? How important is this in your classroom?

▶ What limits do you need to set for your students? How do you adjust those limits as the school year progresses?

▶ What procedures, rules, and policies do you find most important or helpful in maintaining a positive class atmosphere?

SECTION SEVEN

Create and Maintain a Partnership with Students' Families

In this section you will learn

- How to establish positive relationships with families

- How to know what to expect from your students' families

- How to hold effective conferences

- How to maintain accurate documentation of home contacts

- How to communicate well with the families of your students

WHY ALL TEACHERS NEED THIS POSITIVE RELATIONSHIP

Many secondary teachers think that because their students tend to project an air of independence that they are self-sufficient creatures. Most are not. They belong to families of various sizes and types. Your students are, in fact, very dependent on their family members. Because of this strong family bond, you should never underestimate the importance of dealing successfully with the parents or guardians of your students. Not only do they have the right to be informed about their child's academic and behavioral progress, but they can also be enormously helpful. After all, these are the people who know more about your students than anyone else.

Secondary students have parents or guardians who are as concerned about the welfare and educational status of their children at this point in their lives as they were when they were younger. These are the people who want the best for their children and who look to teachers for help in navigating the turbulent waters of adolescence.

Without doubt, family support has a significant impact on students' attitudes about school. Many secondary teachers realize early in their careers that those students whose families are involved in their education consistently perform better academically than those students whose parents or guardians are not as involved as they should be.

Establishing a good working relationship with parents also makes a productive classroom discipline climate much easier to achieve. When students know that the important adults in their lives are united in their attempts to help them achieve their potential, they are less likely to misbehave and more likely to achieve success. Some other benefits of working well with the parents or guardians of your students include these:

▶ The job of coping successfully with every student in a class is just too complicated to do it without help. We can't be knowledgeable about every aspect of a child's life. It only makes sense to turn to those who know more than we do.

▶ Strong adult influences can help students fight negative peer pressure. The more adults that we can enlist in our efforts to create a positive classroom, the better.

▶ Our students learn polite behavior and positive interactions by watching how adults relate to each other. When students see that teachers and parents or guardians work together well, misbehavior tends to decrease.

▶ Behavior—both good and bad—does not occur in a vacuum. A pupil's behavior is often influenced by what has happened earlier in the day, the week, or even the year. Working closely with family members will help us understand our students' behavior.

Working well with parents and guardians is just good sense if you want to create a positive learning environment in your classroom. If you make a point of helping family members feel successful about their children, you will find them more willing to work cooperatively with you. Everyone wins when this important relationship is a strong one.

POSITIVE ATTITUDES TO HELP YOU WORK WITH PARENTS AND GUARDIANS

As you work to establish and maintain the important positive bond between school and home, there will be obstacles. While most of the parents or guardians of your students will have a positive attitude about school and your class, inevitably there will be those who do not. When this happens, it is easy to retreat, complain, or even cease trying to communicate with them. Because of the detrimental effect of these reactions on your students, it is important that you respond as a competent, confident professional educator. To make this easier, adopt these attitudes:

▶ While you may see a student only a few hours a week, family members have much deeper insights into a student's personality. When you can work together successfully, they will be able to share those insights with you. Everyone wins when this happens.

▶ Even parents or guardians who don't seem very involved may care very deeply and certainly will want the best for their child.

▶ While you may disagree with their approach to parenting, you will find that if you approach your students' families with respect, you will find it easier to work together. Helping them maintain their dignity in awkward situations will only generate more cooperation and goodwill.

- When there is a problem at school, don't forget that the negative reactions of parents and guardians may arise because they are embarrassed, worried, frustrated, unsure of what to do next, or angry. Allow time for listening to these reactions before working together to resolve the problem.

- Remember that your goal in working with parents and guardians is to create capable, successful students who enjoy school, learning, and your class.

AVOID CONFRONTATION WITH A TRANSPARENT CLASSROOM

One of the easiest ways to maintain a positive working relationship with the parents and guardians of your students is to make sure that your classroom is as transparent as possible. With today's technology, making sure that everyone knows firsthand what is happening in your class is easier than ever. When teachers take the time to communicate directly with the parents and guardians of their students, the trouble that can follow miscommunication diminishes.

One frequent complaint that parents and guardians have involves homework assignments and project due dates. Take extra care to make sure your homework policies are published in several different ways and that project due dates are announced well in advance. The parents and guardians of your students should not have to struggle to find out what their child's homework is and when the work is due.

Some of the ways that you can make sure students and their parents or guardians are aware of the expectations, rules, policies, procedures, and activities in your class include these:

- Send home notes frequently

- Maintain a daily class log or calendar

- Use the bulletin board space in your room to post information

- Photograph your students at work

- Publish a syllabus so that students and their families can plan ahead

- Send home progress reports frequently

- Return all phone calls promptly

- Make sure parents and guardians know that they are welcome to visit your class

- Create slide shows of your students at work for parents and guardians to view at open house or other schoolwide meetings

- Invite parents or guardians to visit your class for special occasions such as guest speakers, field trips, and exhibits of student work

HOW TO GENERATE A POSITIVE WORKING RELATIONSHIP

Use the following strategies to improve how you present yourself to parents or guardians so that you can establish the kind of successful working relationship with them that you want.

- At the start of the term, send home a letter that explains the most important rules, policies, and procedures in your classroom. In particular, be very careful to explain your homework policy if you want parents or guardians to help you with this area. See the "Sample Introductory Letter" that follows for a sample letter you can adapt for your classes.

Teacher Worksheet

SAMPLE INTRODUCTORY LETTER

Dear Parents or Guardians,

I am looking forward to a new school term as your child's English teacher. This will be an exciting time for my students and for me. We will study vocabulary, literature, writing, usage, and study skills in preparation for a successful completion of the state standardized tests next spring. I have planned many activities throughout the course of the year that I hope will help my students succeed academically.

Students and their parents or guardians are naturally curious about the amount and types of homework to be assigned this term. There will be homework assignments almost every night. You should expect to see your child spending thirty minutes reviewing, reading, working on projects, studying, or writing essays. A copy of the schedule will be given to each student to keep in his or her binder as well as posted on the class Web page. In addition, students are expected to copy their assignment into their assignment notebooks at the start of class each day.

When you have questions, please feel free to e-mail me at _____ or to call me at school. Our number is _____.

I am looking forward to working with my new students this year. I am also looking forward to meeting you and working with you to help your child succeed.

Best wishes,
Mrs. Thompson

▶ Make sure that all written correspondence is neat, legible, and carefully proofread so that you appear as professional as possible. Readers should pay attention to your message, not question your expertise.

▶ Contact parents or guardians when their children are successful as well as when you need their help in solving a problem. When they hear good news from school, parents or guardians realize you are trying to help their children be successful. When they only hear from teachers when there's trouble, they quickly learn to dread conversations with us.

▶ Be a good listener when you talk with parents and guardians. Often they are as confused and worried about a child's behavior as you are. Listen carefully; together you can be a strong team.

▶ If there is a death in the family or another kind of emergency, offer assistance in helping your student through the crisis. This small gesture will let them know you care about the welfare of their child.

▶ Encourage parents or guardians to visit your class as volunteers or as guest speakers.

▶ If a parent or guardian requests weekly or even daily progress reports, comply with this request willingly. If you are not able to send progress reports electronically, set up a system where the student is responsible for bringing you a paper to sign at the end of class each day or week with the requested information. You can make this even easier for yourself if you use the "Student Progress Checkup Form."

Student Worksheet

STUDENT PROGRESS CHECKUP FORM

Student name: _____ Class: _____

Date	Teacher Comments	Parent Comments

- It's not a good idea to give out your home number. You should protect your privacy and personal life. Keep relationships with parents or guardians on a professional level.

- If a parent or guardian calls you, return the phone call as soon as possible. Do not let even twenty-four hours go by without talking to the parent or guardian. To do otherwise is not only rude, but harmful to your relationship with the child and his or her family.

- Sometimes parents and guardians allow their own unpleasant experiences with school or with their child's previous teachers to color their view of you. Be as positive, responsive, patient, and professional as possible to help them overcome their negative feelings.

- Be quick to involve parents and guardians when there is a problem with a student. Many parents and guardians complain that teachers let problems get out of hand before calling home. This is understandably easy to do if you and the student are trying to work out the problem or if it does not seem to escalate, but it is not a good practice. If you notice a drastic drop in a grade, for example, notify the parent or guardian as soon as possible.

- If a student's problem is a serious one, set up a conference so that you can discuss the situation face to face. Be as flexible as you can in arranging time for this conference and make sure the parents or guardians have plenty of advance notice about meeting times.

- When you have to call home about a problem, be as specific as possible. Don't say that the child is "acting funny," for example. Instead, give examples of what the child has done that causes your concern.

- Call parents or guardians at work if necessary. When you get them on the line, have the courtesy to ask if they have the time to talk to you at that moment.

- When you call a parent or guardian at work, be very careful about the message that you leave. Do not involve a parent or guardian's coworkers in the personal business of one of your students. This violates the child's privacy and is unprofessional on your part.

- Have a specific goal in mind when you contact a parent or guardian. Don't ramble in your explanations. Try to keep the parent focused on solving the problem also.

- Make sure you have followed school rules and have the proper documentation in place when a parent or guardian calls to question you about a concern.

- Never become confrontational with parents or guardians, even when they are confrontational with you first. Instead, show your professionalism by projecting concern and caring. If they still are confrontational, politely adjourn the conversation to ask for assistance from a supervisor.

- Never talk about another person's child when you talk with a parent or guardian. This is not only unproductive and unprofessional, but it will also get back to the child or the other parents quickly.

- Immediately document any contact that you have had with a parent or guardian whether it's a phone call, conference, or letter. If an e-mail is more than just a routine inquiry, be sure to save it. You may need this information later.

- Write a thank-you note after a conference or after a phone call to thank the parents and guardians for their concern and time.

In addition to writing your own notes, you can try some of the many free templates that are available online. You will find the ones at Education World (www.education-world.com) particularly easy to use. Use *Teacher Tools and Templates* as your search term to find dozens of free templates for notes, forms, and letters.

Another useful Web site with templates for teachers to use to communicate with the parents or guardians of their students is a site for teachers run by teachers: Teacher Tools (www.teachertools.org). At the Teacher Tools home page, click on "Forms and Letters" to access many free printable templates and notes.

WHAT YOU CAN EXPECT FROM YOUR STUDENTS' PARENTS AND GUARDIANS

Even though the ideal parent or guardian would be informed, supportive, caring, and cooperative while providing a stable home environment and supervising homework, few individuals can meet these lofty ideals. Instead, the parents and guardians of our students are people much like ourselves. They want to do what is best for their children and don't always know exactly how to go about it.

Some are overly involved in their children's lives and extremely sensitive to the smallest problem— real or imagined. Some will have a negative view of you because of their own unpleasant past experiences with school. Still others will experiment (successfully or not) with the degrees of independence that they allow their children as they move into secondary school. Still others will be positive and supportive allies.

Despite this complicated variation, one thing is certain: creating a successful relationship with the parents and guardians of your students is up to you. It is the classroom teacher's responsibility to reach out to the significant adults in our students' lives. It is our job to make sure that every parent or guardian feels confident that we want to work with them for a common goal: the success and well-being of their children.

WHAT YOUR STUDENTS' PARENTS AND GUARDIANS SHOULD EXPECT FROM YOU

In order to create the mutually beneficial relationship that you should have with the parents and guardians of your students, you should be aware of the expectations that they may have of their children's teachers and of you in particular. When you are aware of what they expect and need from you, then it will be easier for you to rise to meet the challenges involved in establishing this important relationship. Here are just a few of the qualities and behaviors that your students' parents and guardians should expect from a caring teacher.

The parents and guardians of your students want you to

- ▶ Care about their child's well-being and treat him or her as a worthy individual
- ▶ Provide them with up-to-date and objective information
- ▶ Listen respectfully to their concerns
- ▶ Prepare their child for a successful future
- ▶ Conduct yourself as a professional educator and as a suitable role model
- ▶ Make sure their child is safe when he or she is with you

- ▶ Uphold the community's standards and beliefs
- ▶ Communicate with them in a timely fashion
- ▶ Maintain an orderly classroom where learning is the primary activity
- ▶ Help their child be successful academically

HOLD BENEFICIAL CONFERENCES

Parent conferences can produce high-level anxiety for all of the parties involved: parents, teachers, and the students who are the cause of the occasion. Parents and guardians who are summoned to school may feel that their years of child-rearing decisions are under attack. Teachers dread that parents will question every decision that they've made since student teaching and then call in auditors to check over their grade books. The students who misbehaved to the point that the important adults in their lives are meeting—usually behind closed doors—relive every mistake that they've ever made since kindergarten while they wait to see just how long they'll be grounded. At least that's what happens on television sitcoms.

Of course, the reality of conferences is quite different. There are many different ways for parents and teachers to meet to work together for the well-being of a child. The most informal way is a chance meeting, perhaps in the mall or at a social gathering. Parents and teachers can also get together at parent-teacher functions and back-to-school nights. A more structured conference happens when a parent and a teacher speak with each other on the phone to solve a problem that has arisen. The most formal and structured type of conference is also usually the most effective: a face-to-face meeting.

Teachers who want to communicate well with parents or guardians realize that they want to be reassured that their child is doing well and can succeed in school. Even though this may not be the current state of affairs with their child, families want teachers to work with them and with their children to make this happen. We need to connect solidly with the parents or guardians of our students if we intend to create a positive learning climate in our classrooms.

One way to have a beneficial conference is to make sure our goals for the conference are clear. There are several important goals for every successful parent conference:

- ▶ You should present yourself to parents or guardians as a friendly teacher who has their child's best interests at heart.
- ▶ You should strive to create an inclusive atmosphere of cooperation and friendliness.
- ▶ Parents should leave with a sense of satisfaction because all of their questions have been answered and all of the points they wanted to cover were addressed.
- ▶ Both parties should have a sense of mutual respect and an understanding of each other's problems.
- ▶ A workable solution to the problem has been agreed upon and everyone involved intends to work together to help the student.

In addition to these goals, there are many other things you can do before and during a conference to make sure that the result is what you want it to be. By working together with parents and students, you can have the peaceful and productive classroom climate that you want. The very best public relations instrument that any teacher can have is a room full of well-behaved and satisfied students busily engaged in the task of learning.

Before the Conference

▶ Make sure you have a clear purpose for the conference.

▶ Plan the points you want to cover.

▶ Gather samples of the student's work.

▶ Establish a rough estimate of the student's strengths and weaknesses as well as any special aptitudes.

▶ Find out about the student's performance in other classes.

▶ Try to anticipate any questions and concerns the visitors may have.

▶ Create a seating arrangement that will be comfortable for visitors. Sitting together around a table is much more comfortable and friendly than expecting parents to sit in student desks while you sit at yours.

▶ Make sure you have pen and paper for taking notes. Have some handy for parents and guardians, too.

▶ Create a plan of action that you would like to discuss.

▶ Make sure you remain calm before and during the conference. Becoming agitated will interfere with the rapport you want to establish.

▶ Make a neat "Do Not Disturb" sign and post it on your door so that you can meet with parents or guardians without distractions.

During the Conference

▶ Be considerate. Meet the visitors in the school office and escort them to your room unless you are sure they know the way.

▶ Be prompt.

▶ Greet them cordially and express your appreciation for the fact that they came to the conference. This will create a tone of goodwill that you should strive to maintain throughout the conference.

▶ Do not try to impress parents and guardians with your knowledge of educational terms and jargon. Use language that will make them feel comfortable.

▶ Begin the conference with positive remarks about their child. Talk about the student's potential, aptitude, and special talents. Focus on strengths even if the reason for the conference is a serious breach of conduct. Do not lose sight of the fact that this child is very important to the parents.

▶ Convey the attitude that the child's welfare is your primary concern.

▶ State the problem in simple, factual terms and express your desire to work together on a solution for the good of the child.

▶ Allow upset or angry parents and guardians to speak first. After they have had the opportunity to say all of the things that they have probably been mentally rehearsing on the way to school, then and only then can they listen to you or begin to work on a solution to the problem.

▶ Show examples of the student's work that illustrate the problem. If the problem is not directly work-related, be prepared to discuss specific examples of misbehavior.

- If this is a problem that you have talked about before, perhaps informally or over the phone, share any improvement.

- Be specific about what you have done to help correct the situation.

- Listen carefully to the parents and guardians. If you want a solution to the problem, give them your full attention throughout the conference. Your nonverbal language is crucial to the success of a conference. Be attentive, friendly, and positive.

- Encourage parents and guardians to express their ideas. You need their insight and help if you are to solve problems students may be experiencing in your class.

- Ask questions that will direct their thinking. These questions can also keep everyone focused on the problem at hand and on solutions to it.

- Summarize the points of the conference at the end. Be sure to outline what you will do and what they will do to help their child be more successful in school.

- Determine how you will follow up on the conference and keep the parents up-to-date.

- Express appreciation again for their concern and the time they have spent with you in the conference.

After the Conference

- Immediately document the conference either with your notes or by filling out the "Contact Documentation Form" that follows. Don't wait to do this because your memory may play tricks on you later.

- Write out the steps that you, the student, and the parents or guardians will take now that the conference is over.

Mistakes to Avoid

- Don't make parents and guardians defensive and don't become defensive yourself.

- Don't talk about other students or compare one child to another.

- Don't talk about other teachers, the principal, or the school district unless you are complimentary.

- Don't become angry. It won't accomplish anything.

- Don't try to outtalk parents or guardians. They need to feel comfortable expressing themselves around you. Don't interrupt, either. Both trying to outtalk and interrupting are bad manners.

- Don't make parents and guardians uncomfortable by asking questions that are too personal.

- Do not allow them to become abusive. Sometimes angry parents lose control. As soon as you see this happening, end the conference as gracefully as you can and involve your supervisor. Do not remain alone with parents who are angry to the point of abusing you.

- Don't neglect to document the conference and file your notes.

- Don't neglect to follow through on the promises that you have made to the parents during the conference.

- If you have learned confidential information during the conference, keep it confidential.

DOCUMENTING HOME CONTACTS

Sometimes it appears as if the stacks of paperwork that teachers are expected to manage reach the ceiling. There are countless forms for just about every interaction we have with our students. It is an unfortunate part of the discipline process that we have to protect ourselves in this way, but we do. It's just good sense to keep accurate records of when you have communicated with the parents or guardians of your students. Especially at the end of a school term, you might be expected to provide proof that you have enlisted the aid of parents or guardians as well as others in your efforts to help a particular student.

In June you may not remember that you contacted a student's home in September. It is horrifying to think you could be accused unjustly of not doing all that you could to help a student, but it can happen. It does occur every year in countless cases where frustrated people look for a simple cause to a complex problem.

Just a few minutes of planning and paperwork will save you time, enhance your professional credibility, and prevent problems when someone wants proof that you have fulfilled one of your most important professional duties.

Since so much of the paperwork we have to do is time-consuming and tedious, it pays to make it easy whenever we can. Keeping a record of the times you communicate with parents or guardians does not need to be time-consuming. One way to do this is to document contacts in a standard format.

Photocopy the "Contact Documentation Form" that follows so that you have one for each student. Whenever you communicate with a parent or guardian, simply fill out the form and file it in a folder with the other paperwork you have for that particular student.

Teacher Worksheet

CONTACT DOCUMENTATION FORM

Student: _____

Parent: _____

Date and time of contact: _____

Type of contact:

_____ Phone call

_____ Letter

_____ Detention notice

_____ Home visit

_____ Informal meeting

_____ Meeting with administrator

_____ Meeting with counselor

_____ Other: _____

Person initiating the contact: _____

Topics discussed: _____

Steps parent will take: _____

Steps teacher will take: _____

Additional notes:

MANAGE ELECTRONIC CORRESPONDENCE

In recent years, more and more teachers have discovered the ease and efficiency of using e-mail to communicate with the parents and guardians of their students. Communicating via e-mail is quick and direct. No longer do teachers have to rely on preparing laboriously handwritten notes that mysteriously disappear before reaching home.

Using e-mail can offer other advantages for busy teachers as well. We can send a brief reminder about upcoming assignments to an entire group or just one student. Parents can ask quick questions and receive a prompt response. Many concerns and problems can be dealt with without delay while they are still manageable. The ease of this type of immediate communication makes it easy for us to relate well to the families of our students. As in all written communication, nuances of expression can be lost and misunderstandings can occur as what you have written quickly is misinterpreted. The speed of replying can make it harder to ensure that what you write is carefully expressed and proofread.

Responding to e-mail at school can also consume valuable time during your planning period. This is especially frustrating when some parents or guardians expect instant responses to their messages. Sometimes, too, students as well as their family members expect you to answer e-mail questions late at night.

Fortunately, the problems of managing electronic correspondence can be successfully managed with careful planning. To avoid having e-mail consume too much of your time at school, be straightforward. While you cannot realistically set limits on the amount of e-mail you need to handle at school, you can control how you manage your e-mail when you are at home. Establish a firm policy that either you will not check school-related e-mail at home or you will check it only during a certain time period while at home.

If a parent or guardian has a serious concern, do not attempt to respond via e-mail. Take the time to make a phone call, instead. When you do this, you show that you take their concern seriously and you will prevent the problems caused by the lack of clarity in writing a response.

Finally, take care to organize your e-mail correspondence carefully. Create folders for students whose parents or guardians communicate frequently or who have serious concerns. Make a point of saving communication about discipline or behavior concerns. Be careful to save messages that can serve as documentation that you have cooperated with the parents or guardians of students with special needs, learning disabilities, medical problems, or other serious educational matters.

MAKE PRODUCTIVE PHONE CALLS

One of the essential skills that teachers should acquire is to ensure that every phone call you make to the parents or guardians of your students is positive and productive. Because making phone calls is much more time-consuming than writing a quick e-mail response, it is essential that you develop a procedure to make this task as efficient and meaningful as possible. Here is a five-step procedure for making a successful phone call to request help when a student has misbehaved:

Step 1: When you first call, take these three actions: state that you experienced a problem, ask if they have time to talk with you, and enlist their help in a respectful manner.

"I had a problem with Bob today, and I wonder if you have time to help me with it?"

Step 2: Be very specific and objective about the problem. State exactly what and when it happened. Be prepared to elaborate, but be careful to avoid expressing any negative emotions.

"Bob was ten minutes late to class for the fourth time, and he also did not have his textbook."

Step 3: Explain specifically what you did to solve the problem. Explain that your actions did not solve the problem. Remain calm and objective. Your purpose is to resolve a negative situation, not vent your frustration.

> "I reminded Bob that he needed to provide a note excusing his tardiness before the end of the day, but he did not return with that note. I was able to lend him a textbook so that he would be able to complete his assignment."

Step 4: Ask for help. Listen while parents or guardians explain what they know about the situation. Make sure to listen carefully and clarify any points you do not understand.

> "I wonder if you would please discuss this with Bob. The frequent tardiness is not just detrimental to his success, but it is also disruptive for the rest of the class. And although I was able to lend him a book for today's class, I would like to see him be prepared for class in the future."

Step 5: Finish the call by thanking them for taking the time to talk with you and for working out a solution with you. Affirm your belief that the problem has now been solved.

> "I appreciate you taking the time to work on this with me. With our combined efforts, I feel sure that Bob will be on time and prepared for class from now on."

MAINTAIN A CLASS WEB PAGE

Although your school district may provide the means for you to host a class Web site, many schools do not have this extremely useful way to communicate with your students and their families. A class Web page does more than just serve as another online site for your students to browse.

With a classroom Web page, you can keep students and their parents or guardians informed about what is happening in your classroom; connect students through blogs, wikis, and online discussions; build pride and a sense of community in your class; and set a positive tone when you showcase student achievements.

While there are thousands of teacher pages on the Web for you to search for ideas about what to include on your own page, you can also consider posting information about these items:

▶ Projects

▶ Due dates

▶ Syllabi

▶ Class notes

▶ Handouts

▶ Links to helpful sites

▶ Upcoming events

▶ Information about class activities

▶ Inspirational stories, quotations, and mottoes

▶ Class goals

▶ Useful resources for students

▶ Puzzles and brain teasers

- ▶ Enrichment activities
- ▶ Remediation activities
- ▶ Vocabulary lists
- ▶ Reading lists
- ▶ Study tips
- ▶ Photographs of students
- ▶ Information about you, your experience, and your teaching philosophy

Here are three helpful sites for teachers who want to establish basic classroom Web pages that allow effective communication with students and their parents or guardians. The first two sites below are free of charge at the time of publication. The third site offers more features than the free sites, but does so for a reasonable fee.

- ▶ **Scholastic (http://teacher.scholastic.com/homepagebuilder).** At Scholastic's classroom Web page creation site, you can build a home page in three very easy steps.
- ▶ **School Notes (http://schoolnotes.com).** At School Notes, you can post classroom notes and resources with ease. School Notes offers examples of teacher Web pages to use as examples as well as user-friendly directions and suggestions.
- ▶ **Teacher Web (www.teacherweb.com).** For a reasonable yearly fee, you can create and maintain an extensive Web page with the tools and support offered by Teacher Web.

HOW TO MAINTAIN STUDENT PRIVACY

The Family Educational Rights and Privacy Act (FERPA) is a law that regulates the privacy of a student's educational records. Although the law is far-reaching and complicated, it does provide guidelines for educators with regard to the importance of maintaining the privacy of student information. Maintaining a student's privacy is not only a legal requirement, but is part of your obligation to your students and to their parents or guardians.

The following guidelines will help ensure that you manage student information in a legal and ethical manner:

- ▶ Don't post grades in such a way that students have access to each other's grades. Even if you disguise student names, this practice can lead to unpleasant speculation and a breach of privacy.
- ▶ Although the editing of a peer's work is an acceptable learning activity, actually grading each other's papers has received negative attention in recent years. It is a better practice to grade the papers yourself.
- ▶ If you use an electronic grade program while students are nearby, be careful that they cannot view the screen.
- ▶ Follow your school's policy about photographing students. There are many legitimate reasons why parents or guardians may not want photographs of their children published by a school employee.

▶ Be especially careful about how you manage the confidentiality of medical information that you may have about a student.

▶ Safeguard information you may have about a student's learning disabilities and past experiences in school. Keep this, as well as other confidential information, in a secure area.

▶ Be extremely discreet about what you say about a student when you communicate with colleagues via e-mail or in writing. Use initials or disguise the identity of the student in another way if it is impossible to communicate face to face.

▶ In a conversation with a parent or guardian, be prepared to gracefully and truthfully sidestep intrusive questions about other students by saying, "I can't talk to you about another student."

To learn more about FERPA and its effect on your classroom, search the Federal Department of Education's Web site (www.ed.gov) by using *FERPA* as a search term. You can learn how to make informed decisions about how to legally and ethically handle student information by reading about the history of the act, court cases and rulings, your responsibilities, and student privacy rights.

To learn more about how to build positive relationships with the parents or guardians of your students, see this section's "Making Positive Choices."

Making Positive Choices

Instead of . . .	Try to . . .
▶ Allowing parents and guardians to worry needlessly	▶ Send home frequent notes, e-mails, and other informative messages
▶ Refusing to send home daily or weekly progress reports	▶ Use the "Student Progress Checkup Form"
▶ Giving out your personal contact information	▶ Be prompt in returning phone calls and e-mails at school
▶ Dreading contacts from parents or guardians	▶ Be proactive in establishing a positive working relationship
▶ Allowing visitors to wander around in search of your classroom	▶ Meet them at the office and escort them cordially to your classroom
▶ Beginning a conference with negative concerns	▶ Always focus on the student's strengths before asking for help with problems
▶ Being vague about problems students may be experiencing	▶ Show examples of student work that illustrate your concerns
▶ Trying to recall what was discussed at a conference	▶ Immediately document the specific details of the conference and file the information in a safe place
▶ Allowing students to see their grades on a computer screen	▶ Write their grade on a slip of paper or print a progress report
▶ Posting grades	▶ Protect student privacy by speaking to each one quietly about grades

QUESTIONS FOR REFLECTION

Use the information in this section to guide your thinking as you reflect on these questions. They are designed to encourage you to think more deeply about the issues in the text or to discuss those issues with colleagues.

▶ Why is a positive relationship with the families of secondary students an important component of their success? How do you establish this relationship with the families of your students?

▶ What techniques do you use to make documenting home contacts easier? Why is this important? How can you improve the way that you do this?

▶ What is the biggest problem that you experience when dealing with the parents or guardians of your students? How can you overcome this problem?

SECTION EIGHT

Establish a Cooperative Classroom Climate

In this section you will learn

- How to relate well to your students

- How to help students deal with peer conflicts

- How to build a sense of community in your classroom

- How to help students learn how to relate well to others

- How to establish a positive classroom culture

THE SYNERGY OF A COOPERATIVE CLASSROOM CLIMATE

Classroom discipline is not just about preventing trouble or coping with bad behavior. Rather, it should lead to the establishment of a classroom environment where all students feel a sense of connectedness with each other and with their teacher. With these positive connections, students work together well while supporting and encouraging each other's successes.

In secondary classrooms where the climate is cooperative, synergy occurs when students and teachers work together so well that everyone's success is greater because of their combined efforts. The positive energy generated by a cooperative classroom causes students to try harder to both compete with and support each other. When the atmosphere in your classroom is cooperative, you will find it easy to build on your students' individual strengths as you watch the class shape itself into a true community of learners.

To create this synergistic classroom environment, you will have to manage some important tasks. You will have to get to know your students as well as you can as fast as you can. You will have to help your students become familiar enough with each other that they can work together well. You will have to teach your students the social skills and routine courtesies that smooth the way for a cooperative class atmosphere.

The result of this effort on your part is a classroom where your students feel a sense of belonging; where success builds on success; and where students benefit from a positive self-fulfilling prophecy. In a cooperative classroom, teachers help students view themselves as members of a team. Everyone—teachers and students alike—wins when the synergy of a classroom becomes a positive force.

WHAT TO DO WHEN YOUR SCHOOL'S CLIMATE IS NOT POSITIVE

Despite our best intentions to provide a positive, productive classroom environment for every student, when the schoolwide climate is negative, we struggle to teach and our students struggle to succeed. Contrary to what many people may believe, schools with a negative environment are not confined to the inner city or to impoverished rural areas. Any school can have a negative climate.

Although many influences can have a negative bearing on the climate of a school, some are obvious: an unsafe location, a history of low academic success, a strong gang presence, a physical plant that is in need of cleaning and repair, a lack of effective procedures and policies, and a lack of administrative support for teachers, just to name a few.

Unfortunately, schools with a negative climate are easy to identify. At these schools students tend to

- ► Focus on other activities instead of academics
- ► Report that they do not feel safe
- ► Experience little academic success
- ► Have poor attendance
- ► Experience problems with their peers as well as with their teachers
- ► See very little purpose for an education
- ► Flaunt school rules
- ► Report that their morale or school spirit is low
- ► Experience class disruptions due to violence and threats of violence
- ► Have a high percentage of discipline referrals

If you teach in a school where the environment is not always constructive, you can do a great deal to make a positive difference in the lives of your students. More than other teachers, the effectual educators in a school where the environment is not positive tend to direct their students toward the future. They help students establish goals and develop skills that will lead to a productive and happy life ahead.

In order to manage this, however, your attitude should be one of realistic optimism. Teachers who are effective in schools with negative climates are not unmindful of the daily challenges that they and their students face. Instead, they acknowledge their problems and then find ways to solve or at least manage them so that students can be successful.

Along with a sense of realistic optimism, successful teachers in a school where the climate is not positive tend to acknowledge the big picture of the school and not just focus on the problem areas. This perspective will allow you to acknowledge the problems you encounter at school and then move forward to help students find success.

Finally, these teachers also tend to believe that change is possible and that they are the agents of that change. With this attitude firmly in place, teachers have been known to inspire entire classes to reach unprecedented and unanticipated success.

With this attitude, you will have a much greater chance of successfully managing your daily challenges than if you spend your days bemoaning your school's problems. In addition to these productive attitudes, there are several strategies that you can use to cope with the negative elements of your school's climate:

- ▶ Start small. Keep your classroom clean and organized so that students have an orderly place for learning.

- ▶ Focus on the positive elements in your school and work to strengthen them. Become a band booster, football team fan, or sponsor of a student club.

- ▶ Involve as many people as you can to make positive changes at your school. Enlist support and help from student organizations, community groups, the parents and families of your students, and your colleagues.

- ▶ Go beyond your community to seek support from your faraway colleagues. There are many teacher forums where you can share ideas about how to improve conditions at your school with teachers in other school districts:

    - Teachers.Net (http://teachers.net). This site offers over 150 teacher chat boards organized by grade level, curriculum, region, and special interests.

    - TheApple (http://theapple.monster.com). Here you can join groups, participate in discussions, read and respond to blogs, and much more.

    - SchoolNet (www.schoolnet.com). This site offers many resources for teachers as well a growing online community.

- ▶ Do what you can to strengthen your students' literacy and math skills. In secondary schools, many of the problems that began when students were younger impede their ability to learn independently.

- ▶ Work with your colleagues to support the development and uniform enforcement of school-wide rules.

- ▶ Make sure that all students are aware of school rules, policies, and procedures along with the positive and negative consequences attached to each.

- ▶ Even though bad behavior may be the order of the day in other areas of the school, your classroom should be a place where students are expected to be courteous, respectful, and focused on learning. Don't give in to students who think that bad behavior should be acceptable in your classroom.

- ▶ Be realistic about what you can achieve. While you may not be able to change the total environment of your school quickly, even small changes are worthwhile. Move forward with reasonable, achievable goals.

CONNECT WITH YOUR STUDENTS

Many teachers who have traveled abroad to third-world countries have had the opportunity to observe the schools in those countries. Often these teachers return home appalled at the unendurably primitive conditions in which teachers are expected to teach and students are expected to learn.

They describe classrooms with no equipment, supplies, texts, electricity, or even enough potable water for comfort. Students study at benches or sit on the ground for many hours after walking long distances to school. Teachers and students suffer together from the extremes of weather in schools without any sort of efficient climate control.

Even though they may be appalled at the conditions they observe, teachers also are awed by the superior learning they witness taking place. They recount stories of dedicated students who turn in work that is not only insightful, but beautifully written in a perfect script.

Students and teachers with no books somehow find a way to read the world's greatest literature. Students and teachers with no calculators solve difficult mathematical problems. Students and teachers with no access to the Internet manage to have an astounding grasp of the world's political events.

Somehow those resourceful teachers and their students have achieved what seems impossible to us. They have achieved the truest aim of education: learning that will lift us far above our sometimes uneasy daily lives. The question that faces us is an important one. How can we attempt to duplicate the learning success created by those inspiring teachers in our own classrooms?

Successful learning is not dependent on such modern essentials as computer networks, interactive texts, competitive sports, or even photocopiers. Students everywhere need to enter into an important partnership with their teachers. The personal link between teacher and student is essential for successful learning and for a class climate geared to self-discipline.

The following strategies are designed to foster this necessary link between teacher and student. Many of them seem to be almost instinctive acts by excellent teachers who are mindful of the fact that one of the biggest complaints unsuccessful students have about school is that no one seems to care about them. These teachers reach out to students because they know the secret to a successful class is their personal relationship with each child.

▶ Take the time to get to know your students as people.

▶ Use a kind voice when speaking with them.

▶ Set up your classroom so that you can walk around to every desk easily.

▶ When a student speaks to you, stop what you are doing and listen.

▶ Be clear about your role as a teacher who will enable students to achieve their dreams.

▶ Use humor. Laugh when funny things happen in your class.

▶ Show your appreciation for the good things your students do.

▶ Stress that you won't give up on your students.

▶ Allow your students to get to know you. Often our students are convinced that we sleep in the teachers' lounge all night and eat only lunchroom food. They need to see your human side.

▶ Agree with them as often as you can.

▶ When there is a problem, don't automatically assume a student is at fault. Listen to your students as they explain their version of events before passing judgment.

▶ Move your desk to the back of the classroom if you can. This small action signals a student-centered attitude on your part.

▶ Call parents or guardians when good things happen.

▶ Share your feelings with your students and allow them to share theirs.

▶ Use positive language with them. Be careful not to appear overly negative or critical.

▶ Take notice of the special things that make each student unique.

- Stop and chat with pupils anytime: when you are monitoring their progress, in the hall or cafeteria, or even when you are away from school.
- Create opportunities for success every day.
- Speak to every student each day. Include everyone in class discussions.
- Make pens, paper, and extra books available when students need a loan.
- Set aside an afternoon or morning for "office hours" when you can provide extra help for those students who need it.
- Offer small perks whenever you can.
- Be sincere, generous, and tactful in your praise.
- Keep students busily involved in interesting work.
- Be a well-prepared and well-organized teacher who takes the time to present interesting lessons.
- Contact their parents or guardians when your students are absent more than one day to see what's wrong.
- Set limits for your students. They need a comfortable framework in which to operate.
- Talk with students when you notice a change in their behavior or attitude. For example, if a normally cheerful student seems distracted or upset, there's a good reason for the change.
- When students confide in you, follow up. Ask about how they did on the history test that was troubling them or check to see if their grades have improved in math class.
- Be concerned enough for their futures to help students set long-term goals.
- Involve pupils in projects that will improve the school or community.
- Focus on students' strong points, not on their weaknesses.
- Stress that you and they have much in common: goals, dreams, and beliefs.

THE BASICS OF A GOOD TEACHER-STUDENT RELATIONSHIP

Pamela Smart and Mary Kay Letourneau are former teachers who became instant household names not for their classroom skills, but for the improper relationship that each entered into with a student. While teachers who are involved in inappropriate relationships with their students are certainly not a new facet of education, this type of relationship still has the capacity to create shocking headlines. For each headline revealing the lurid details of an inappropriate relationship between a teacher and student, however, there are hundreds of teachers who carefully build productive and appropriate relationships with their students and who never make headlines for the good that they do.

Even though each relationship that you will build with your students will be different from all the others, you should take the following actions to guarantee that the relationship that you build with your students is one that is both appropriate and productive:

- Take care to always treat your students with respect and teach them to treat you with respect in return.
- Ensure that your students are physically and emotionally safe while they are in your care.

- Be clear in your definition of your role as an educator, a role model, and as a friendly adult. Make sure your students are clear about your role.

- Make certain that your goals for your students are ones that they also believe in and will work toward.

- Assure your students that your primary role is to help them succeed.

- Make certain that your students learn how to cooperate with each other and with you.

- Make a point of listening to your students and teach them how to listen attentively to you.

- Make sure that your students perceive you as a teacher who treats them with fairness.

- Be clear with your students that you value them and regard them with affection.

HOW TO GET TO KNOW YOUR STUDENTS

One of the most important parts of creating a cooperative classroom atmosphere is to get to know your students as quickly as you can. You will find that almost every aspect of a successful discipline climate is dependent on this knowledge. Once you gain an understanding of your students, then you will be better able to connect with each one on a meaningful level. Although there are dozens of different ways to get to know your students, you will only need a few to establish solid relationships. In the list that follows you will find several different strategies to help you become acquainted with your students:

- Ask your students to complete one of the inventories found in the following three student inventory exercises.

Student Worksheet

Name: _____ **Date:** _____

1. My greatest asset is . . .

2. The nicest thing I ever did for anyone was . . .

3. The nicest thing anyone ever did for me was . . .

4. One question I have about life is . . .

5. One thing I've always wondered about is . . .

6. My teachers last year will tell you that I am . . .

7. My friends will tell you that I am . . .

8. People like me because . . .

9. One thing most people don't know about me is . . .

10. I am an expert on . . .

11. I want to know more about . . .

12. When I am twenty-five, I will . . .

13. Five years from now, I will . . .

14. When I want to, I have the ability to . . .

15. A famous person I admire is _____ because . . .

16. The bravest thing I ever did was . . .

17. I have trouble dealing with . . .

18. I appreciate it when teachers . . .

19. I am proud of my . . .

20. I like _____ because . . .

(Continued)

Student Worksheet *(Continued)*

STUDENT INVENTORY: IMPRESSIONS

21. I really need to . . .

22. My favorite class is _____ because . . .

23. My friends make me laugh when they . . .

24. My pet peeve is . . .

25. When I am sad I . . .

26. The most stressful thing in my life is . . .

27. The most influential person in my life is _____ because . . .

28. If I had one hundred dollars I would . . .

29. I am named for . . .

30. It was easy to learn . . .

31. It was difficult to learn . . .

32. I have no regrets about . . .

33. I want to know more about . . .

34. A friend once showed me how to . . .   .

35. I like _____ music because . . .

36. My favorite color is _____ because . . .

37. One dish I can cook well is . . .

38. I show self-respect when I . . .

39. What is a mistake that taught you a lesson? What lesson did you learn?

40. What is an obstacle that you face? How do you plan to get around it?

Student Worksheet

STUDENT INVENTORY: ATTITUDES

The right attitudes are crucial for success in school and in life. This inventory will help you check which ones you already have underway and which ones could use a bit of work. Get your pencils ready!

Study the list below and decide how you stand in relation to each of the positive attitudes that create successful students.

1. Color the space under "1" if the attitude does *not* apply to your school life at all.
2. Color the space under "2" if the attitude applies to your school life *some* of the time.
3. Color the space under "3" if the attitude applies to your school life *most* of the time.

1	2	3	
			Kind
			Patient
			Curious
			Strong-willed
			Able to concentrate
			Flexible
			Respectful of evidence
			Skeptical
			Ambitious
			Open-minded
			Ready for change
			Tolerant of ambiguity
			Confident
			Sincere
			Honest
			Understanding
			Compassionate
			Persistent

(Continued)

Student Worksheet *(Continued)*

STUDENT INVENTORY: ATTITUDES

1	2	3	
			Inventive
			Hardworking
			Thorough
			Willing to be a pioneer
			Brave
			Self-disciplined
			Able to laugh easily
			Able to laugh at self
			Sensitive
			Generous
			Fair-minded
			Respectful of others
			Respectful of self
			Respectful of authority
			Neat
			Able to maintain self-control
			Loyal
			Creative
			Articulate
			Values the importance of an education
			Able to follow through on an idea
			Energetic
			Able to work on a team
			Willing to help others

STUDENT INVENTORY: ATTITUDES

1	2	3	
			Alert
			Able to achieve long-term goals
			Optimistic
			Punctual
			Respectful of social values
			Independent
			Able to request help
			Able to admit mistakes
			Cooperative
			Easy-going
			A deep thinker
			Friendly
			Healthy
			Able to act with common sense
			Hungry for knowledge
			Cheerful
			Trustworthy
			Willing to try
			Imaginative
			Empathetic
			Willing to take a risk
			Appreciative
			Practical
			Given to detail
			Forgiving

Student Worksheet

What others would tell you about me . . .

1. My favorite teacher last year would say . . .

2. My parents would say . . .

3. My grandparents would say . . .

4. My neighbors would say . . .

5. The security guard at the mall would say . . .

6. My future children would say . . .

7. My youngest relative would say . . .

8. My oldest relative would say . . .

9. My pet would say . . .

10. My girlfriend or boyfriend would say . . .

11. My best friend would say . . .

12. The lunchroom staff would say . . .

13. The teacher who taught my hardest class last year would say . . .

14. My future mate would say . . .

15. My coach would say . . .

16. The custodians would say . . .

17. My remote control would say . . .

18. The clerks at the store I go to often would say . . .

19. My parents' neighbors would say . . .

20. My future employer would say . . .

Teacher Worksheet

Please Tell me About Your Child!

Please use the space below to tell me what I need to know to successfully teach your child. Please feel free to include strengths, goals, medical information, learning styles, family information, past experiences, and anything else that you can share about your child that will allow me to better understand his or her needs as a student in my class.

_____

_____

_____

_____

_____

_____

_____

- At the start of a term, send home a form asking for information from the parents or guardians of your students. A sample form is included for you in the "Parent or Guardian Inventory."

- Ask your students to describe themselves to you in one hundred words or fewer.

- End class each day by having your students write reflections. Although these should usually be about the content of the lesson, you can learn a great deal about your students by asking them to write about themselves from time to time.

- Ask the students to make three statements to the class about themselves. Two of the statements must be true and the third one should be false. Have the other students try to guess which one is the false statement.

- Have your students contribute slides for a class slide show. They can include photographs, favorite sayings, interests, and other personal information. You can run this as a continuous loop periodically throughout the term so that students can see how they have changed while in your class.

- Ask the students to list five things they can contribute to the class and then display the list in a prominent place in the classroom.

- Observe your students as they interact with each other informally at the start and end of class. You can learn a great deal by paying attention when your students talk to each other.

HOW TO LET YOUR STUDENTS KNOW THAT YOU CARE

- Post a large calendar and have your students put their birthdays on it. Those students who have birthdays during holidays can mark a day they would like to use instead to celebrate the event. On that day, put a "Happy Birthday!" message on the board. At the beginning of the term you can spend some time at the computer to design a card for your students. Photocopy these cards and have them ready for your students.

- Praise and reward your students often as individuals and as a class.

- Use your very best manners in dealing with your students. Insist that they do likewise.

- Pay attention to your students' health. When a child seems ill, send that student to the nurse. If a child has to miss several days of school, call home to see how he or she is doing. When homebound work is requested, be prompt in sending it out and include a get-well card.

- Speak to your students when you see them in the hall or in the neighborhood.

- Ask about their family members. If you have taught brothers or sisters (or even a parent) of one of your students, ask about them. If you know that a family member is ill, show your concern.

- Use a simple sentence—such as "What can I do to help you?"—to project a caring attitude.

- Send home a note when good things happen to a student in school. Share your pride with the family.

- Write notes to your students. Write on their papers and use plenty of stickers.

- Take photographs of your students and put them on the wall for all to see.

- Be accessible to help your students before or after school. Offer student help sessions on a specific day each week. You don't have to stay for a long time, but you can help those students who may be struggling.

- Tell your students that you like them. Take a few moments after a long week to recount all the good things they have done. This simple action will increase the likelihood of having another good week.

- Seek their opinions. Give your students many opportunities to share their ideas with you.

- Attend school events. If your students are playing in a football game or performing in a band concert, go to show your approval and appreciation for their hard work.

- If a student is featured in the newspaper for something positive, clip out the article and post it for everyone to see.

- Lend materials to those students who have accidentally forgotten theirs.

- Ask your students to tell you about their weekends or holidays. This is easier if you ask them to write an informal response instead of giving a verbal account.

- Allow your students to have a voice in the classroom. Listen to them. It's easy to provide opportunities for this. For example, you could give them a choice of due dates or a choice in types of test questions.

- Notice and compliment changes in personal appearance. Be sincere even if the change is not to your personal taste.

- Set responsible behavior limits and be fair in expecting everyone to abide by them. This "tough love" approach to classroom control will set a positive tone that underlies all other discipline actions that you take.

BOUNDARIES IN TEACHER-STUDENT RELATIONSHIPS

Although one of the first dire warnings given to many new teachers reminds them of the potentially career-ending consequences of becoming friends with students, somehow this warning is not as easy to heed as it would seem. While it is important that we like being with our students, a teacher's role is to be a friendly adult, not an adult friend. For some teachers, having a room full of admiring students is exhilarating enough to make them forget the role they are to fulfill.

There are plenty of reasons why it may be difficult for teachers of secondary students to keep the boundaries of friendship in place. Because our students frequently seem almost grown up, they may appear mature enough in their interests, problems, and attitudes to have a real kinship with us. We are also human enough to want to be liked. It is flattering to have students find what we say interesting. Some teachers in a too-friendly relationship with students may also have overextended the relationship in an attempt to help especially troubled students.

Because every educator's teaching style is different, there can be varying degrees of familiarity with students. Before you make a regrettable mistake in deciding on a course of action in your relationship with your students, ask yourself these questions:

- Would my actions or words be the same if we were in the presence of other educators or the student's parents or guardians?

- Do I manage my classroom in such a way that I am comfortable when administrators drop by?

- Are the actions I am taking with my students quick fixes for problems instead of lasting solutions?

If you are not sure if your demeanor around your students is within acceptable boundaries, these are some warning signs that you should not ignore:

- Your students confide too much personal information in you.
- Your students are too interested in your personal life.
- Your students comment that you are just like they are.
- You notice that some students are uncomfortable with the informal atmosphere in your class.
- You meet with students outside of school for nonschool-related reasons.
- You are in contact with students through social networking sites.
- You advise students not to tell other educators or their parents something.
- Your students call or e-mail you about personal matters.
- Your students want to call you by your first name.
- You e-mail students on nonschool-related business.
- Your students have your cell phone number.
- Your lessons emphasize interesting activities rather than solid content.
- Other teachers comment negatively on your teaching style or relationship with students.

SEEKING FEEDBACK FROM YOUR STUDENTS

Have you ever looked at old photos of times when you thought you looked great—only to be horrified at your appearance? It's funny how stylish we thought we looked, but the old photos show us a very different reality. Usually our reaction is an agonized cry to family members, "Why didn't somebody tell me?!"

The truth is that we often think we present one image to the world but, in reality, the image is not at all what we expect it to be. When we're teaching, it's especially important that we present an image that will help our students succeed—and we often think we do. When we are trying to work as a team with our students, however, we need feedback from them about just how well we're doing.

Often our students are reluctant to speak up in class for a variety of good reasons. Fear of ridicule by peers, shyness, fear of rejection, or the inability to think quickly are just a few of the insecurities that plague students. We can certainly benefit from hearing what our students have to say if we allow them a safe outlet for expressing themselves. There are several effective ways you can get useful feedback about your teaching from your students.

- The most commonly used method is also the least formal: pay attention to their reactions. If a class appears to be bored, the chances are good that they are. If they seem interested and involved, the chances are also good that they are both of those.
- Another way to find out how you're doing is to ask your students to write a reaction to the class. You could offer this as a closing exercise to a class period. Try asking one of these questions:
  - What advice do you have for me when I teach this unit again?
  - If you were the teacher, what would you do differently in teaching this lesson? Explain your reasons.
  - What did you find most interesting and helpful about this lesson?

► A third way to build a team atmosphere in your class and get feedback from your students at the same time is one that many teachers find helpful. Try using a suggestion box. You can benefit from the advantages of having one in your classroom if you use common sense in establishing it for your students. Try the following techniques for setting one up in your room:

- Decorate a box neatly so that your students will take it seriously. Shoe boxes are the ideal size.

- Place the box and a stack of small slips of paper near the door so that students who want to respond to you through the suggestion box can do so in relative privacy.

- Empty the box yourself at least once a day. Don't allow students to do this because the writing inside is directed to you and is not meant to be read by others.

- A good place to begin with teaching your students to use a suggestion box is to get them to write slips at the end of class in which they comment on the activities of the day or ask questions. This will begin to get them in the habit of communicating with you directly.

- Be sure to tell your students when you want them to sign their names to their suggestion box writing. Start with having them sign their writing if you are not comfortable with the maturity of your class and their ability to treat the privilege of a suggestion box responsibly.

- Teach your students to be careful about the content of their suggestions. Stress that there is to be no foul language or other unpleasant writing for you to deal with.

- Suggest some things they might want to write about: the activity in class, the homework assignment, the topic being studied in class, test questions or format, or necessary personal information.

- The suggestion box should be an open issue for discussion in your classroom. Thank those students who make sensible suggestions for you and for the class, but be sensitive enough not to mention names.

TEACH SOCIAL SKILLS

When your students treat each other and you with the common courtesies that make life more pleasant for everyone, you will find it much easier to create a cooperative classroom environment. Although secondary students are certainly old enough to have mastered social skills, many have not. Even though the social skills that are appropriate for a school setting are ones that are remarkably consistent as students progress from grade to grade, it still requires a steady effort on your part to help students learn to treat each other with courtesy.

Fortunately, teaching social skills is neither a time-consuming process nor one that requires a great deal of planning and preparation on your part. Rather, social skills are taught first by conscious modeling on your part, and then by raising student awareness and providing consistent encouragement.

The "Checklist of Social Skills All Secondary Students Should Master" that follows includes some of the social skills that are appropriate for secondary students. Examine each one to determine your class's strengths and weaknesses in this area and begin to plan how you will help your students master all of them.

Teacher Worksheet

CHECKLIST OF SOCIAL SKILLS ALL SECONDARY STUDENTS SHOULD MASTER

Use the checklist below to target the school social skills that you may need to emphasize with your students.

Secondary students should

1. _____ Use "please," "excuse me," and "thank you" when speaking with each other and their teacher.

2. _____ Use an appropriate volume when speaking. This includes the start and end of class.

3. _____ Not interrupt others unnecessarily.

4. _____ Make an effort to control angry outbursts or other unpleasant comments.

5. _____ Ask permission before taking something that belongs to someone else.

6. _____ Refrain from using inappropriate language such as profanity or insults.

7. _____ Drop used tissues in the trash.

8. _____ Stay upright in their seats unless they are ill.

9. _____ Not clutter the aisles with their personal belongings.

10. _____ Slip quietly into class when tardy or when returning from being excused so as not to disturb others.

11. _____ Raise hands as a signal for attention and then wait to be called on.

12. _____ Show that they are attentive by looking at a speaker.

13. _____ Clean up their work area.

14. _____ Respect others' values, outlook, and life experiences.

15. _____ Address each other and their teachers by using appropriate names.

WHAT TO DO WHEN A STUDENT CONFIDES IN YOU

When a student turns to us for help, solace, or advice, we are being trusted with a part of that child's heart. It is one of the reasons we go into education. Although the situation varies from child to child, the educator's responsibility is the same. We have to find out the best way to help the child while remaining emotionally uninvolved enough to be part of the solution—and not part of the problem. This is not an easy task for anyone, but it is a necessary one.

When a student confides in you, you will have to handle the situation in one of two ways. What the student tells you will determine what actions you will need to take. You will either need to involve other professionals or you will be able to provide counsel yourself.

When You Need to Involve Others

▶ As a teacher you are legally obligated to protect the safety and well-being of all your students. When a child confides that he or she is in a situation that threatens either safety or well-being, you must involve other professionals. Begin by taking what the child says seriously. Inform a guidance counselor of what the child has told you. If your school does not have a guidance counselor, then contact an administrator. These fellow professionals should then contact the appropriate social agency to help your student.

▶ What type of confidences warrant the involvement of others? Contact a counselor if the information involves sexual abuse; physical abuse; neglect; pregnancy; threats and intimidation by a family member, neighbor, or peer; substance abuse; illegal activity; depression; and anything else that seems serious enough to indicate that outside support is necessary.

▶ If a child confides to you that he or she is considering suicide, it is critical that you react to this emergency without delay. Even if the child's remarks don't seem particularly sincere to you, react as if they are a shout for help. This is certainly a situation where the saying "Better safe than sorry" should apply.

▶ If a student begins a confidence by trying to make you promise not to tell anyone else, do not agree. Be clear with the child that you cannot promise this, but that you can and will accompany him or her to talk with counselors, parents, or administrators and that you will remain accessible and involved.

When You Can Provide Counsel

▶ If the information the student confides in you is something that is troubling, but does not require outside assistance, still remain cautious in your approach. Keep in mind that you are a professional educator and an adult. Do not let your emotions at the moment influence you to act in any other way. Your student may see you as a friend, but you must remain a professional educator in the way you handle the situation.

▶ Protect yourself with common sense. Talk to the student in a place that cannot be misinterpreted. Keep the door to your classroom open, for example, if you are meeting there. Also be careful at this emotionally charged time about how you touch a student.

▶ Another common-sense strategy is to imagine that your words of advice could be printed in the daily newspaper. Would you sound like a wise counselor in public? Do not open yourself to public humiliation by acting in less than a professional way.

- Many of the problems faced by your students will be caused by troubled peer relationships. Listen to these problems and do your best to give sensible as well as sensitive advice. Encourage your students to be self-confident and tolerant whenever you can.

- Make sure you don't make a situation worse by agreeing with a student's poor assessment of another student. You do not need to engage in gossip with the student. Instead, provide advice that is based on common sense. Encourage your students to take responsibility for themselves and for their emotions.

- Listen sympathetically to your students and to their parents or guardians whenever you can. Make the advice that you give an extension of the principles you promote in your classroom.

- Resist the temptation to reveal details about yourself and your private life to a student who confides in you. Focus on the child's problem, not on your personal situation.

- Remember that the one expression that will turn your students off quickly is, "Well, when I was your age . . . "

- After a child has confided in you, don't mention the secret in the faculty lounge. A student's trust is a precious thing. Don't violate it.

- Be sympathetic, but do not criticize the student's parents or other teachers. This is unprofessional as well as counterproductive.

- You can deal with many student problems by helping students put the troubling events into perspective. Encourage your students to see beyond the problems and emotions they are experiencing at the moment. Help them see that their problems will fade in time. This is good advice for all of us to follow.

THE IMPORTANCE OF MODELING COURTESY

Transforming a classroom full of awkward adolescents into a cooperative community of learners is the dream of secondary teachers. We want our students to be pleasantly cheerful and polite to each other and to us.

In order to have our dream come true, we must teach our students the importance of courtesy, and then we must insist that they treat others with exquisite politeness. Courteous behavior oils the machinery of the classroom: preventing discipline problems, building teams, and making everyone's day easier.

Successful teachers realize that classes are social groups. We often use this to our advantage when we are in the process of creating positive peer pressure. We teach our students that when we expect and encourage them to be courteous at all times, the payoff for everyone is in enhanced learning opportunities. We know that pupils who interact in a positive way take a vital step in creating a more successful classroom environment.

Savvy teachers use all of the tricks of the trade to create polite students. We can reward individuals and classes with little treats and effusive words of praise—especially at the start of the term—when we are trying to instill the importance of polite behavior in our students.

We can shamelessly use the power of peer pressure to steer students in the right direction as we try to be as supportive as possible of our students' needs to express themselves and to just be teenagers. We can allow them plenty of opportunities to express themselves without fear of sarcasm or ridicule from us and from their classmates. We can help our students clarify their goals and values, and we can give our students plenty of responsibility so that they can learn to be polite.

All of the tricks of our profession are useless, however, if we ourselves are rude. The most important technique for the secondary teacher who wants to encourage courtesy is to be a model of courtesy. In a hundred small acts every day we can model the kind of courteous behavior that we want from our students.

When a child slams a book, we can say, "Do I slam a book while you are talking?" "No." "Then please don't slam a book while I am talking." Being able to ask, "Do I treat you with disrespect?" and have the child answer "No" can be a powerful tool for the teacher who wants to foster courtesy in a student who is sometimes disrespectful of authority. It is with small exchanges and actions such as these that we show our students the kinds of behavior that will make their lives more successful.

Our students are far more observant of us and what we do than we can ever imagine. Use this awareness to your advantage to teach one of life's most important lessons: the absolute need for courtesy in a sometimes rude and unfeeling world.

USE CONFLICT RESOLUTION STRATEGIES TO CREATE A PRODUCTIVE CLASSROOM

In even the most peaceful classroom, conflicts can arise naturally and frequently. Teenagers, by their very nature, are volatile and dynamic beings. As a classroom teacher, it's up to you to make sure that those conflicts do not interfere with the cooperative climate that you want to establish. Your students will model themselves on the way that you react to conflict. Your actions, attitudes, and reactions are crucial to establishing harmonious relationships among your students. If they see their teacher working to resolve problems in a cooperative manner, then students will be more likely to adopt a similar stance when they experience conflicts themselves.

Even though our students may be prone to conflict, there are many strategies that you can adopt to help students learn to work together in harmony. When your students are in conflict with each other, these suggestions may help.

Preventative Measures

▶ Pay attention to the interactions of your students. When you see that relations are about to sour among a group of students, a quiet word or two from you will often put things right.

▶ Teach your students that they have control over their moods. They can change an unpleasant attitude. They do not have to act out a negative feeling.

▶ Make sure you fully understand your school's policy on student conflict and the teacher's role in mediation. You will be more comfortable in the role of conflict mediator if you understand what your supervisors expect you to do.

▶ Make your stand of zero tolerance for threats, bullying, and intimidation well known.

▶ It is better for you to teach your students how to settle their own differences rather than have you or other adults settle them.

▶ Be careful about the activities in your classroom that may set up a fierce competition that can then go too far and turn into conflict.

▶ Whenever you can, promote the values that can make it easier for students to avoid conflicts:

- Tolerance of each other's differences
- Respect for each other's views
- Willingness to work together for the mutual good of the class

Dealing with Peer Conflict

▶ Help students understand the issues that may have caused the conflict rather than just focusing on the actions that each took in the course of the conflict.

▶ Do what you can to help students learn to listen attentively to each other. In resolving a conflict, it is imperative that all parties listen carefully to each other and work to understand each other's viewpoint.

▶ Help students understand the concept of a win-win situation instead of just emerging victorious over an opponent. Learning to reach common ground is an important skill that can make resolving conflicts almost a straightforward process.

▶ Teach students that if a peaceful resolution cannot be reached, they may need to involve another party—a counselor, peer mediator, or even an administrator.

▶ If you see that trouble is about to escalate, help students talk things over in a calm manner. Arrange for them to do this. Be the mediator if necessary.

▶ If a conflict seems to be more complex than you feel comfortable handling, involve other adults in the mediation process. A good place to begin to seek help is the guidance department. Ask a counselor to help students who cannot work out their differences.

▶ When you work with students who are in conflict, it is essential for your own peace of mind and for the mediation process that you remain calm. Model the reasonable and open-minded attitude that you want your students to have.

▶ Work to tone down the hurt feelings and anger in a conflict. Be careful not to take sides while you are doing this. Help students try to come together on issues.

▶ When you work with students on ways to solve problems, lead them to understand that they should look for a fair solution. This does not mean they will always be right.

▶ Use the active thinking skills that you teach your students to use in solving any problem to solve their own conflicts. Here is a six-step approach students might take:

- Define the problem from all points of view.
- Generate as many solutions in a brainstorming session as possible.
- After the brainstorming, study and evaluate the solutions generated.
- Decide upon the best solution as a good course of action to follow.
- After deciding what to do, determine how to implement the solution.
- Finally, after trying the solution for a few days, meet again to assess the situation and evaluate how well the differences are being worked out.

A useful online site for more information about conflict resolution in the classroom is

Peace Education Foundation (www.peaceeducation.org). This organization offers various resources that can help secondary educators help students learn to resolve their conflicts in a positive and productive manner.

ARMING OUR STUDENTS: TEACHING THE ART OF THE ALTERNATIVE RESPONSE TO RUDE CLASSMATES

"Did not!" "Did too!" "Did not!" "Did too!" "You wish!" "Don't hold your breath!" "Hey! I'm talking to you!" "Get out of my face!" "I'm gonna get you!" "He makes me sooo mad!"

By the end of the first day of school, almost every secondary teacher, even those who teach seniors, has heard some form of these childish exchanges all too often. In many classes this type of interaction is a daily problem. A few students who have not been taught to be polite or respectful of others can create havoc when they react in an aggressive and angry way in response to what they perceive as slights from other classmates.

This tension at school has serious implications for all of us. News stories regularly report the devastating effects of our violent social climate on our students. Stories about teens having been murdered for such offenses as stepping on someone's shoe by mistake, or looking at a stranger "funny," no longer have the power to shock us that they once held.

We follow legislative debates about the increasingly prevalent practice of trying youthful offenders as adults. Many of us have trouble accepting that the children we see accused of robbery or cold-blooded murder don't appear to be very different from those mischievous youngsters in our classes.

Far too few of our students enter secondary school with more than basic social skills. Many students do not understand how to be tolerant, how to get along well with the majority of their classmates, or even how to cope when people are rude to them. Most of our students are just beginning to learn the business of creating positive relationships with other people.

One of the ways we can help them acquire these social skills and create a pleasant classroom environment at the same time is to give our students some alternative ways to cope with bad-mannered classmates who are insulting, tactless, inconsiderate, and rude.

The list of responses here is not meant for those situations where a student's safety is in jeopardy or when a more serious response is required to stop potential violence. Instead, these alternatives are designed to help students deal with the smaller irritations caused by daily interactions with others. Some of these are simple. Some are simplistic. All are effective in teaching students that they do not have to answer rude behavior with rude behavior.

What to Do When Someone Is Rude to You

- ▶ Smile and say nothing.
- ▶ Treat the remark with good humor and chuckle softly as if you found it amusing.
- ▶ Ignore the person by walking away.
- ▶ Tell a friend, a parent, a teacher, or a counselor.
- ▶ Count from one to ten several times.
- ▶ Take six deep breaths. Exhale slowly.
- ▶ Silently ask yourself what caused the rude person to be cranky today.

- Return rudeness with kindness! Pay the offender a compliment.
- Let five minutes pass before you allow yourself to speak back.
- Go to the water fountain for a drink. Splash a few drops of cool water on your face while you are there. This will help you cool off.
- Quickly write out all the mean and hurtful things that you would like to say to the person who has hurt your feelings. Tear it into tiny pieces when you are finished and carefully throw them into the trash can.
- Make yourself forgive and then make yourself forget.
- Pretend you didn't hear an unkind remark.
- Make a conscious decision not to let it bother you.
- Mentally picture the rude person as a small fluffy mouse wearing a large silly hat.
- Go for a jog around the block.
- Place yourself in the shoes of the person who was unkind. Try to understand what caused it.
- Pat yourself on the back for staying calm.
- Think of the last nice thing that someone said to you.
- Turn to a classmate and pay that person a compliment.
- Repeat "I am in control of my attitude" ten times.
- List your ten best personality traits.
- Think of a hero and ask yourself what that person would do in your situation.
- Picture yourself walking across a beautiful field of fresh snow.
- Ask yourself if this incident is really worth the stress.
- Remind yourself of another time when you acted in a mature and responsible manner.
- Imagine how wonderful it will be when you are attending your graduation.
- Tell yourself, "I can't let this bother me because my goal in life is to . . ."
- Clench your left hand tightly and then relax it. Do this five times and let your troubles be relaxed, too.
- Close your eyes and imagine that you are eating your favorite meal.
- List ten things for which you are thankful.

CREATE A SENSE OF COMMUNITY BY HELPING STUDENTS LEARN ABOUT EACH OTHER

A cooperative classroom cannot be achieved until students are familiar and comfortable with their classmates. While taking the time to help students get to know each other well is important, it can also be time consuming. If you are struggling to make sure that every possible concept in your state standards is covered thoroughly, then you should consider choosing an activity from the list below that takes less time than others.

- You will be surprised at how many of your students don't know their classmates' names, especially their last names. If you spend a few minutes playing a chaining game in which students try to recite each other's names in an unbroken chain, you will eliminate this problem. You can even use this technique later to show your students effective ways to memorize facts.

▶ After you have met with your students for a few days, assign each one to a permanent study team. This group will watch out for each other all year. When you review, this is the group that will work together. They should exchange phone numbers so that absent students know whom to call to get missing notes and assignments. The possible tasks that study teams can perform in your class are limited only by what you choose for them to do based on their maturity and ability. This technique is a positive way for students to support each other while focusing on the study skills needed for success in school.

▶ Take photographs of your students and post them.

▶ Ask those students who claim they already know each other well to write out five facts about each other for you to read.

▶ Try to create a class newsletter. In this activity, your students can share a variety of ideas with each other depending on the discipline you teach and the ability of your students. Include facts they discover about the school, interviews with other students about various topics, interviews with other teachers, cartoons, predictions, and anything else you and they decide would be worthwhile to include. Keep the tone upbeat and stress the value of working together as your students complete their newsletter.

▶ Be sure to spend time at the start of the term assigning the classroom duties and responsibilities that your students can take care of for the good of all.

▶ Make it a point to focus on your students' strengths by asking them to reveal what they do well. You will be pleasantly surprised at the skills your students already possess.

▶ Place a large map on the board and mark each student's birthplace on it.

▶ Spend some time having your classes create a class motto.

▶ Have your students bring in magazine pictures and words that indicate things that are of value to them. Combine these into a giant collage that shows how your students can be different yet still part of the whole.

▶ Put your students into pairs to determine ten things they all have in common. Go beyond the obvious to deal with the mental traits they share, past experiences, future goals, problems, successful attitudes, or whatever traits you want to focus on at the moment.

▶ Ask your students to offer some wise advice that they display on miniposters to inspire them all year. You can also take this same wise advice and publish it in a booklet to be shared with younger students if it's appropriate.

▶ Post a large calendar and have the students record their birthdays on it. Establish a simple ritual that you and your students follow to celebrate each one.

▶ Have your students bring in their baby photos to display. This is not only an excellent icebreaker, but it is also an attractive way to decorate your room as the students get to know each other.

▶ Put your students into small teams and have them illustrate a school-success topic in a cartoon panel that you provide for them. They should generate the story line using the actual members of their team as the characters. Stick figures are acceptable for those teams who are not gifted in drawing. The point of this assignment is to have them focus on school success while working together. Display these for the enjoyment of all.

USE INTERVIEW PROJECTS TO HELP STUDENTS LEARN ABOUT EACH OTHER

A popular way to help students learn about their classmates is to have them interview each other. While this technique usually ends in students introducing each other to the class, it is such a widespread activity that much of its appeal is fading. Revive this excellent idea with some ingenious twists of your own, or you can try some of the following suggestions:

► Instead of having students mumble a series of facts about each other to the class, have your students write descriptive paragraphs about each other that you then photocopy and compile into a booklet for all of your students to read. This will be the most intently read document that you will present all year. Make sure it's successful by giving guidelines about the types of material you want emphasized in each paragraph. You will also need to be specific about the appearance of the work so that it can be photocopied easily.

► Another twist on this topic is to have each student interviewed by two others who then write paragraphs that you publish.

► A successful way to get the students chatting together productively in the interview is to give each one a common object and ask that student to interview the other one in order to determine what the second team member and the object have in common. When your students present their findings to the class, be prepared for the fun that you will have as you watch your students compare each other to egg beaters, tissues, or whatever silly objects you can find.

► Yet another spin on the interview project is to videotape your students making their presentations about each other. Plan this assignment carefully; you should be able to have your students working together productively in no time.

ENJOY THE BENEFITS OF A DIVERSE CLASSROOM

In any secondary school, it's not unusual to see very young and undersized boys walking with classmates who are old enough to shave and drive themselves to school, girls in miniskirts talking with friends whose *hijab* provides modesty, or recent immigrants from developing nations sitting next to students whose ancestors have been in America for centuries.

The differences among students even in the same grade level can be significant. Many factors can contribute to the range of diversity among students in a classroom. Maturity, age, ethnicity, race, gender, sexual orientation, academic aptitude, socioeconomic status, and family background are just a few of the more obvious ones.

As a teacher seeking to create a cooperative classroom, the differences can be daunting until you determine the best ways to help students celebrate their differences. One noteworthy way to do this is to be matter of fact about the differences among your students. Your reaction can greatly determine how your students react to each other. If you are accepting of a student's learning disability, for example, other students will be more likely to be accepting also.

While you should not overlook differences among your students, teaching them to acknowledge and value their commonalities is also important. Team-building activities and icebreakers are useful strategies to help students learn what they have in common and how to work together well. One user-friendly online resource for dozens of icebreaker and team-building activities is managed by entrepreneur Seth

Marbin. His Teampedia (www.teampedia.net) site offers many different types of teen-friendly activities contributed by various site visitors.

While many people define culture solely in racial or ethnic terms, the truth is that culture is far more wide-reaching than this narrow definition would imply. We all belong to many cultural groups based on features such as: economics, geography, age, gender, religion, education level, past experiences, aspirations, or interests. Each one of these cultural groups affects how well we and our students interact with each other.

If we ignore the cultural differences we find in our students, we create the potential for a clash of values. Some of the discipline problems that arise from this result in students who are in conflict with each other, with their teachers, and with the expectations of a school environment.

If, instead of ignoring them, we choose to accept and celebrate those same cultural differences among our students, we will tap into rich resources that will help us create a classroom climate of shared trust, respect, and appreciation. There are three approaches you can take to dealing with cultural diversity. You could follow some general guidelines, explore cultural heritages, and create another culture for your students. These approaches are not exclusive of one another and can be used together successfully. The first of these approaches, following general guidelines, can help you incorporate the many cultures in your classroom into a solidly successful working unit.

General Guidelines

▶ Even if you have lived there all of your life, take time to find out about your community's various cultural groups. Understanding this and how those groups are represented in your school system will help you begin to understand your students better.

▶ Accept the fact that you cannot stop racism or intolerance if that is what students are taught at home. However, you can and should stop it at school. Make your position clear through word and deed.

▶ Allow no remarks or actions from your students that indicate a less-than-respectful and appreciative attitude toward each other's culture.

▶ Any successful school program requires the involvement of parents and guardians. If your students are having trouble relating to each other because of cultural differences, then get parents or guardians involved as quickly and as positively as possible.

▶ Do all that you can to increase the self-esteem of your students. Students who are sure of themselves will be less likely to have to turn on others to feel better about themselves.

▶ Do not ignore cultural differences. To do so is to make your students feel unappreciated and unworthy.

▶ If your students are not behaving in ways that you like, examine the motives behind the actions. For example, if some of your students have trouble making eye contact with you, try to determine if this is a way of showing deference for your role as a teacher before you assume this body language signals defiance or disrespect.

▶ Stress the importance of open-mindedness and acceptance for people whose beliefs or lifestyles are not the same as those of your students. You can do this in your classroom every day by modeling those traits yourself.

▶ Provide plenty of opportunities for discussion about the topic of cultures and the differences among people. These discussions do not have to involve hours of class time, but can be an important part of your closing or opening exercises.

- Recognize that the concerns of a parent or guardian who is not part of your culture may not be the same concerns that you have. If you are sensitive to this when you speak with parents, then you will find yourself asking questions to help determine what their goals for their children are before you impose the beliefs of another culture.

- Do not challenge the cultural beliefs of your students in a mistaken attempt to make them choose between the values they hold and the ones you would like to impose. This heavy-handed strategy will only result in resentment or confusion, not enlightenment. It is better for you to expose your students to as wide a variety of beliefs and cultures as you can while guiding them to make wise choices for themselves.

BUILD A POSITIVE CLASSROOM CULTURE

Time and time again people who have risen from the depths of poverty and adversity have credited their success to the importance that school played in their lives when they needed guidance. School provided them with the hope of a future away from the misery of their daily existence. See this section's "Making Positive Choices" for suggestions on how to create the cooperative classroom culture that promotes student success.

While the circumstances for your students may not be as extreme, there are students in your class who need support and guidance in their lives. One way to provide this for them is to create a classroom culture that supersedes the various other cultures in the room.

In a classroom culture, the teacher and students develop a sense of loyalty to the class and to the group that results in a positive and productive atmosphere. Students in this kind of classroom act as if they are in one large family of mutually supportive friends. The teamwork skills that your students will learn in a classroom culture are ones they will use later in their workplace experiences.

You can create a successful classroom culture in many ways. Pick those strategies from the following list that will best fit your teaching needs:

- When a new student enters the class, have the other students write quick notes of welcome and advice on how to succeed in the class.

- Have all students take part in determining the class rules by encouraging their active participation through class discussions.

- Involve students in the daily tasks of the classroom. They can and should be responsible for a variety of tasks such as cleaning up, passing out papers, taking care of shared materials, running errands, and tutoring each other.

- When there seems to be a conflict between what you want and what the group wants, allow students to speak up to present their side of the story through a spokesperson. This is an activity that would be appropriate only if the situation is one in which you are willing to compromise, such as changing the due date of a major assignment. It is also an activity that makes students feel you value their opinions when they are expressed clearly and logically.

- Encourage students to help each other in understanding their lessons as often as possible. Students who take the time to tutor or assist each other with assignments not only learn the material better themselves, but they also form a helpful bond with the students they are assisting.

▶ Your students could enter into a fund-raising event to help others who are less fortunate than themselves. Students who work together for the good of others will experience a real boost to their own self-esteem.

▶ Instead of raising money, your students could also work together on a project outside of class. There are limitless opportunities for this. They could work at a soup kitchen, clean up a highway on Earth Day, send greeting cards to nursing home residents, or paint playground equipment in a local park.

▶ Keep a chart of the good things you see your students doing and post this chart in a prominent place to remind them of their successes.

▶ Put students in charge of shared materials. They will take better care of equipment and books if they are the ones responsible for them.

▶ Encourage students to form study groups to get together to prepare for big tests and projects.

▶ Use plural possessive pronouns often. Saying "our" room, "our" books, and "our" desks is much more friendly and inclusive than "mine, mine, mine."

▶ Take their help when they offer it. If a student wants to help you carry something or run an errand, accept.

▶ Have students contribute to the shared materials the school system does not provide for them. They can bring in tissues, pens, paper, and old newspapers for everyone to use. They will value this more than if you provide these items for them.

▶ Display their work. Few things increase a student's sense of pride than seeing his or her project displayed for all to see.

▶ Take photographs of your students and display them. Make lists of your students in each class and display them with the photos to show your pride in each one. You can use computer calligraphy or other special effects to make the lists and the photographs as attractive as possible.

▶ Create a "wall of fame" to showcase the good things your students accomplish.

▶ Have a class newsletter that the students themselves compose.

▶ Engage your students in as many real-life problems to solve as possible so that they can not only work together, but they can also see that there is a place for this type of activity throughout their lives.

▶ Have a class goal for your students to work toward. They might all work to improve their behavior so that they could have a class outing or go on a field trip, for example. The emphasis here should be on the things they can do as a group to improve their behavior.

▶ Teach your students the importance of saying kind things to each other. Picking on each other and saying insulting things is something that is too easy for many of our students to do. Steer them toward being as complimentary to each other as possible in an effort to get along with every member of the class.

▶ Play icebreaker games with your students so that they know each other well enough to learn to like each other. Make sure they know each other's names and a little bit about each other at the beginning of the term.

▶ Ask their advice and opinions. Students often have useful insights to problems that perplex adults.

▶ Use your sense of humor and encourage them to use theirs to have shared jokes and other friendly connections.

▶ Celebrate birthdays and silly events as well as every success that you can.

▶ Have students work together to help each other make up missed work. They should be the ones who remind each other of this so that you do not have to nag.

▶ Stress the importance of courtesy as a mark of respect to each other, the class, you, and to themselves.

Making Positive Choices

Instead of . . .	Try to . . .
▶ Complaining about the problems at school	▶ Join with colleagues to solve schoolwide problems
▶ Allowing students to fail your class	▶ Tell students that you will not give up on them
▶ Having a negative attitude about your students	▶ Make a point of taking a positive approach when confronted with classroom challenges
▶ Being too informal in your relationships with students	▶ Remember that you are a teacher and not a friend to your students
▶ Allowing students to just get by in your class with little interaction with their classmates	▶ Make each one feel as if he or she is a valued part of a learning community
▶ Allowing yourself to make a rude remark when a student is rude to you	▶ Remember that you are a role model for the entire class
▶ Allowing students to be rude to you and each other	▶ Teach social skills and the value of courtesy
▶ Ignoring unkind remarks that students may make to each other	▶ Teach them how to show their support of each other's efforts
▶ Tolerating small class conflicts	▶ Use conflict resolution strategies to help students work together well
▶ Complaining about the skills that your students lack	▶ Focus on their strengths

QUESTIONS FOR REFLECTION

Use the information in this section to guide your thinking as you reflect on these questions. They are designed to encourage you to think more deeply about the issues in the text or to discuss those issues with your colleagues.

▶ Why is it particularly important to establish a positive relationship with every student in your class? What techniques in this section did you find helpful? Are there any that you can add?

▶ How diverse is your classroom? How do you make the diversity a positive force?

▶ What do you do to help students create a sense of community in your class?

SECTION NINE

Maintain Order with Effective Instruction

✔ **In this section you will learn**

- How to understand the connection between instruction and discipline

- How to design engaging, relevant instruction

- How to use classroom technology resources effectively

- How to help students collaborate well

- How to improve the way you monitor students

THE RELATIONSHIP BETWEEN INSTRUCTION AND DISCIPLINE

To understand the relationship between instruction and discipline, examine these classroom scenarios. In the first, two students desultorily finish their independent work for the day a few minutes early and have nothing to do. The first student asks to leave the room to retrieve something from a locker, while the second student writes a note to a classmate and tosses it across the room. This activity makes enough noise to catch the teacher's attention. While the irritated teacher interrupts the entire class to investigate the reason for the paper-tossing event, the first student ostentatiously returns from the hall only to playfully knock a book from the desk of a classmate.

In a second, more successful classroom, the same two students finish their work early, and double-check each other's work for accuracy before turning it in. They then immediately begin working on a free-choice project that allows them to work together on an online research project about the material they are currently studying. They work together quietly until the end of class.

In both classrooms students have work to do, but in the successful class, students know what to do and how to do it well. They have a reason for completing their assignment, the opportunity for collaborative work, and options in some of the types of assignments they are offered. Because they are so busily engaged in learning, these students do not have the time or inclination to misbehave. They have something more productive to do other than wander the hall, pass notes, and annoy classmates.

The close relationship between effective instructional practices and a successful discipline climate is key to understanding not only how to design and deliver instruction, but also how to make sure that students behave appropriately enough to master the material that they have been assigned. In short, using effective instructional practices is one of the most important ways that classroom teachers have of creating a discipline climate where teachers and students can work in harmony.

PROVIDE ENGAGING INSTRUCTION

Although we may want to teach so skillfully that we rivet our students' attention from the first day of class until the last, sometimes teachers find it convenient to fall back on the same old handouts and activities that have been at least moderately successful in the past. Often these less-than-fresh activities result in less-than-interested students with all of their attendant discipline problems.

Skillful teaching means lessons that promote interest, discovery, creativity, involvement, and—ultimately—success. If we want to promote a positive discipline climate through skillful teaching practices, then we need to provide our students with activities that are innovative and challenging. Designing engaging lessons is not difficult if you consider a few of the broad criteria that encourage student interest in a classroom assignment.

First, adolescents are interested in making personal connections to the material they study. Use eye-catching references to teen interests such as sports teams, music groups, fashions, or even the names of your students to capture their attention.

Teenagers also want their work to have a practical purpose. They want to know just how and when they can use the theoretical work they may be learning in class. Provide plenty of opportunities for students to apply new knowledge and to build on what they have already learned so that they can see a reason for the effort they expend in learning.

Your students will find it easier to be engaged in an academic task if they have an opportunity not just to collaborate with classmates, but to collaborate on projects that require hands-on activities. Students tend to be engaged fully when they work together to create slide shows, videos, and multimedia presentations or discover the solutions to open-ended problems while working in a laboratory environment.

Finally, teens have an interest in the unusual or attention-grabbing aspects of almost any topic. Quirky video clips, unexpected lesson requirements, and unique assignments are all examples of instruction that appeal to the fascination that many adolescents have with unconventional topics.

Fortunately, the possibilities for creating engaging activities are endless. You will find the two lists that follow helpful in offering instruction that will engage your students. The first is a list of general strategies that can be applied to many different types of instructional activities. The second is a list of specific innovative activities that should appeal to a wide variety of students.

General Strategies

You can make the assignments that you require of your students more interesting if you adopt some of the following general suggestions:

▶ Include opportunities for student movement and activity whenever appropriate.

▶ Offer as many choices and optional assignments or activities as reasonably possible.

▶ Have students work with others when practicing a new skill so that they can support each other's learning.

- Make sure students know how they will benefit from the material you have assigned.
- Arrange for groups to compete with each other.
- Announce that you are going to display student work.
- Time your students as they work on their assignments.
- Create a real-life application for student learning whenever you can.
- Create brief activities that can be assessed before students leave class.
- Design lessons that are about fifteen minutes in length before either offering a brief break or switching to another assignment.
- Give students an outline of a presentation to complete as they listen to a lecture or presentation.
- Occasionally offer small tangible rewards.
- Ask students to use their imaginations or to take a creative approach to a routine assignment.
- Praise and encourage your students as they work on difficult material.
- Offer a checklist of activities so that students know what they need to accomplish during class.
- Appeal to your students' sense of altruism to encourage them not only to study the instructional material, but also to help others at the same time.
- Post a chart of their progress or have students keep a chart of their individual progress.
- Make the work you assign as attractive as possible by using clip art and other appealing text features.
- Have students set personal goals for assignments and then work to achieve those goals.
- Arrange frequent formative assessments or progress checks so students can feel confident that they are on the right track with their work.
- Design assignments so that the work becomes progressively more difficult as students work through a unit of study.
- Provide plenty of models, demonstrations, and examples so that students can feel comfortable that they know how to do their work well.
- Help students understand their learning in the context of the learning that they will accomplish all year by showing them how today's lesson will lead to future lessons.
- Include high-interest and unusual elements in a lesson. Use a dramatic prop or costumes to get their attention.
- Pose a problem for students to solve together.
- Instead of telling them what is wrong with their work, focus on what your students did correctly.

ACTIVITIES TO ENGAGE STUDENTS

The following list of activities can help you design instruction that will keep your students absorbed in learning instead of disrupting class with off-task behavior:

- Create an advertisement that could be used in print or electronic media
- Make up test questions
- Take an interactive quiz online
- Create a puzzle
- Solve a puzzle

- Create a slide show
- Take a virtual tour of an online museum
- Rewrite a story
- Brainstorm
- Analyze a television show, Web site, news article, or radio announcement
- Create a time capsule
- Make a blog post
- Classify words and meanings
- Complete a word sort
- Complete a KLW chart
- Maintain an electronic portfolio
- Take photographs
- Share photographs online
- Create a word wall
- View a movie clip
- Join a wiki discussion
- Write a reflection
- Play a game online
- Fill in the blanks
- Create a scenario and act it out
- Write an autobiographical sketch
- Research using a database
- Annotate a text
- Complete a graphic organizer
- Evaluate two items that are similar
- Translate something into another language
- Create a scrapbook or portfolio
- Create a virtual scrapbook or portfolio
- Make a timeline
- Write a biography
- Create a fictional treasure chest
- Study an online map
- Invent and play a board game
- Use clip art to illustrate the key points of a report
- Write a caption
- Create a Web page
- Hold a treasure hunt or scavenger hunt
- Make a collage
- Make a word cloud
- Host a talk show
- Create a wall of fame
- Draw a comic strip
- Stage a mock trial
- Write an e-mail
- Have a panel discussion
- Enter a contest
- Make a video
- Design a brochure
- Debate an issue
- Produce a children's book
- Be a critic
- Teach the class for the day
- Invent a dialogue
- Draw a diagram
- Write an exposé
- Take a field trip
- Write a firsthand report
- Make flash cards
- Make electronic flash cards
- Create a flip book
- Write a parody
- Make a tabloid newspaper
- Create a flowchart
- Set up your own art gallery
- Conduct a survey
- Create a graffiti wall
- Design a greeting card
- Make a flag or banner
- Send an e-mail to a well-known person
- Use clip art to illustrate a book

- ▶ Invent a better way
- ▶ Create a class newsletter
- ▶ Make a map
- ▶ Stage a play or class skit
- ▶ Observe an unusual holiday
- ▶ Write to a pen pal
- ▶ Make a sketchbook
- ▶ Take photographs
- ▶ Design a postcard and send it
- ▶ Plan a journey
- ▶ Hold a press conference
- ▶ Hold a recognition ceremony
- ▶ Make up a questionnaire
- ▶ Make a flip chart
- ▶ Decorate a bulletin board
- ▶ Create a radio show
- ▶ Read a book aloud
- ▶ Design a T-shirt
- ▶ Reenact an event
- ▶ Take an online survey
- ▶ Pass a note
- ▶ Make a recording
- ▶ Listen to digital recordings online
- ▶ Make a public service announcement
- ▶ Hold an auction

BUILD IN RELEVANCE

Making sure that students understand the relevance of the material that they are expected to learn is important because it will prevent many discipline problems. When students know that their work has a meaning beyond just mastery for a test, they tend to work with more purpose and attention. Their efforts will be more focused when students can not only see a practical purpose for their learning, but also understand how they will benefit from their hard work.

When you design instructional activities, be careful to build in opportunities for students to explore the ways that their learning can be put to use not only in your class, but also in other disciplines and in real-world situations as well. To make this process easier, try asking yourself these questions as you plan instruction:

- ▶ How can students benefit from this material in the present and in the future?
- ▶ When will students need to apply their learning in the future?
- ▶ Can students apply what they are learning in another discipline?
- ▶ Will students be able to use this material to create solutions to real-world problems?
- ▶ How can students use what they are learning to construct a new product?
- ▶ What practical advantages are there in learning the material under study?
- ▶ Will students need to know this information as a building block to new learning?

PACE INSTRUCTION TO KEEP EVERY STUDENT ON TASK

One of the most important ways to prevent discipline problems from disrupting your class is to make sure that you assign just the right amount of meaningful work that will keep students engaged in learning activities for the duration of the class. The pacing of instruction is complicated because it requires that in addition to determining that the activities we offer are appropriate, we also need to pay close attention to the speed at which we expect students to accomplish the work. Even though appropriately pacing instruction may be an important component of any discipline plan, the dramatic variations in students' preferred learning styles, readiness levels, and work habits make it difficult to design instruction that all students can finish at the same time.

Although pacing instruction for maximum learning is a skill that usually requires a great deal of experience to master, the following guidelines can make it easier for you to ensure that the instruction you offer is designed to keep students engaged in learning for the entire class period.

- Always have the next assignment ready for those students who complete their assignments early.

- Allow students who finish their other work early to begin their homework assignments in class; this is a reasonable use of their time if they know how to complete the work.

- Consider providing opportunities for high-interest enrichment and remedial activities for students to complete when they finish their basic assignments. If you provide students with plenty of attractive optional assignments to choose among, they will tend to use their time more constructively than if they have only one extra assignment that they perceive as just additional work to do.

- Use a mixture of whole-group, small-group, and individual instruction to manage the pace of assignments.

- Build in ways for those students who may need help completing assignments to receive that assistance early in the course of an assignment so that they do not fall behind the other students.

- One way to make sure that all students are working productively is to ask them to stop every now and then and share with classmates what they have learned or questions that they may have.

- Arrange a checklist for students to follow as they complete their work so that they know how to pace themselves and to plan for themselves how to accomplish their assignments.

WHAT TO DO WHEN WASTED TIME CAUSES PROBLEMS

Problem

The lesson is not appropriate for the ability of every pupil.

Possible Solutions

- Assess students to make sure that lack of ability or basic skills is the problem and not just a lack of motivation.

- Check the reading levels of the students and provide extra help with reading assignments if students are poor readers.

- Allow flexible deadlines so that students who need longer to complete the assignment can take more time.

- Provide interesting enrichment assignments for those students who have mastered the material quickly.

- Provide a variety of assignments to appeal to everyone's strengths. Pay attention to the importance of learning styles in reaching as many of your students as possible.

- Encourage students to work together in groups so that they can help each other.

- Provide as many hands-on and real-life experiences for your students as your subject matter allows.

- Offer study sessions after school and encourage other teachers in your building to join you in after-school tutoring.

- Don't lower your expectations for students who are struggling. Encourage and support their efforts, but don't give up or allow them to.

Problem

The students are distracted by an upcoming event such as a holiday, the prom, or a pep rally.

Possible Solutions

- Prepare yourself mentally for the change in your students so that you can remain in control of the situation.

- Channel that energy into productive activity. If the students have engaging lessons, then they will be more likely to stay focused. Design your most productive lessons for the times of the school term when you anticipate distractions.

- Now would be a good time to pull out those puzzles that students enjoy solving if you want them to work quietly.

- If you don't mind noise, engage your students in some of the low-tech games described in this section.

- Try to design a lesson around the theme of the upcoming event so that your students can be excited and productive at the same time.

- If students are normally well behaved, tell them they can have a set amount of time to chat and be excited. Set a time limit with them and tell them that when the limit is up, you expect them to settle down to work. Often just a small amount of time—two or three minutes—is all that they need to clear their minds to settle to work. Students will also appreciate your understanding.

Problem

The students lose interest in a lesson because it seems to take too long to do.

Possible Solutions

- Break long-term assignments into manageable blocks of work so that students can see that each small step leads to a finished product.

- Try to divide your class time into short blocks so that students can have a change of pace.

- Use graphic organizers to help students see where an assignment is leading. Some students just need to see a visual representation of what you expect them to do before it makes sense to them.

- Use a checklist so that students can feel they are accomplishing something and moving ahead with purpose.

- If students are working in teams, assign one student to be in charge of keeping everyone working productively.

- When possible, allow students a choice of activities. You don't have to change or eliminate activities, but if you allow students to choose which of three activities they want to do first, for example, then they are likely to stay on task.

- Set time limits for completing tasks within a class period. This encourages students to work toward a goal.

- Sometimes a tangible, extrinsic reward will motivate students who might stray from an assignment to stay busy to complete it.

Problem

The students are disruptive while they are waiting for further instructions or for a classmate to finish an assignment.

Possible Solutions

- Design your instruction so that students have a series of tasks rather than just one thing at a time.

- Designate a spot on the board or some other place in the room where students are to check for further instructions.

- Give students a long-term project, such as reading a library book or completing a series of puzzles to complete when they have finished their work.

- Make it a part of the culture of your classroom that students work from the beginning until the end of class instead of just until they have completed an assignment.

- Put students in study teams to work together; they tend to work more efficiently.

- Always provide an enrichment assignment for those students who complete work early. Make this a habit when you are writing lesson plans.

- Encourage those students who find an assignment easy to help those who don't.

- Be careful to place the homework assignment on the board before class starts so that students who want to get started on it early may do so. Be clear with them that it is okay to start homework in class only if they have finished their other work.

- Give your students a checklist of assignments so that they can work on a series of assignments rather than having to consult you after each step.

DIFFERENTIATE INSTRUCTION TO ENGAGE YOUR STUDENTS

As classrooms expand to accommodate the increasing diversity of our students, so has the spread of a very successful teaching practice, differentiated instruction. In twenty-first-century classrooms, it is not unusual for advanced learners to be seated next to students whose readiness levels, background experiences, or preferred learning styles vary widely. Other differences in today's classrooms can include factors such as learning disabilities, physical disabilities, culture, and levels of home support.

Although a diverse classroom can be an exciting place where students grow socially and academically as they learn to cooperate with others, the potentially negative impact of this varied student population can be profound also. It is disheartening to design rigorous instruction only to have students begin an assignment, work on it for a few moments, and then lose interest as the activities don't engage their attention. The resultant off-task behavior can turn a carefully planned lesson into an unpleasant experience for teachers and students alike.

Differentiated instruction works well as a pedagogical strategy because it meets students at their various readiness levels and then offers instruction geared to meet their needs. It also works well as a part of a classroom discipline plan because the focus on allowing students to work on appealing assignments that encourage self-efficacy and academic success engages students so fully that they have something better to do than misbehave. Although differentiated instruction strategies vary from teacher to teacher, they share these common elements:

▶ The three main elements of classroom instruction—content, process, and product—can all be adjusted to promote student growth and achievement.

▶ The focus is on the needs of the learners as they learn the content and skills mandated by a district's curriculum rather than just on the material to be covered.

▶ Many different approaches to the delivery of instruction are necessary to reach all students.

▶ Teachers take a proactive stance toward dealing with student learning differences. For example, instead of waiting until the students miss answers on a test and then offering remediation, teachers in a differentiated classroom design various types and levels of instruction to appeal to many learning styles, interests, and readiness levels.

▶ Formative assessments are a key element to designing and adjusting instructional activities.

One of the most appealing aspects of differentiated instruction is its adaptability to any subject and type of student. While the activities and strategies of teachers who use differentiated instruction are limitless, each one is designed to meet the needs of individual students rather than the traditional approach in a one-size-fits-all classroom. In the list that follows you will find some of strategies that you can offer using differentiated instruction to reach all of the students in your class:

▶ **Flexible grouping:** Teachers offer whole-group, small-group, and paired-partner groups to assist students as they collaborate. Groups vary according to the activities and needs of students.

▶ **Tiered activities:** Because student readiness levels vary widely, assigning work according to those levels is a powerful way to engage students. The tiers of activities are usually arranged according to these three groups: students who need a great deal of supportive activities to begin to understand the material, students who have a reasonable grasp of the material and only need some support, and students who have already mastered the material and are ready to advance to the next unit of study.

▶ **Anchor activities:** This strategy allows students to work independently on an ongoing assignment directly related to the curriculum throughout a unit or a semester. For example, a student in a world studies class may choose to conduct extended research on the impact of trade routes on ancient civilizations. This research would be accomplished when the students have free time in class or are between assignments.

▶ **Task cards.** Because of the various ongoing activities in a differentiated classroom, giving whole-group directions can be confusing to many students. Instead, teachers offer explicit written directions and examples on task cards that students may refer to as needed.

▶ **Alternative texts.** Because not all students read at the same level, offering alternative texts is a logical response to help students improve their literacy skills.

▶ **Electronic collaboration.** Students can use blogs, microblogs, and wikis to communicate and collaborate with each other on classroom projects.

▶ **Jigsaws.** Teachers divide a common text into manageable sections and assign groups to become experts on various sections. They then teach the material in their section to the other groups.

▶ **Choice boards.** Teachers offer a menu of possible tasks related to a unit. The menu can be arranged according to various differentiation areas such as tasks that appeal to various learning styles or tasks that appeal to various levels of Bloom's Taxonomy.

▶ **Learning contracts.** Students enter into an agreement with their teacher to complete a certain type and number of tasks related to the material being studied. (See Section Five for more information on learning contracts.)

▶ **Metacognition journals.** Students reflect on their learning and make self-assessments about their progress by writing about how they master the material. Here are some question stems that can guide your students' thinking in their journals:

- What if . . .
- Who seemed . . .
- Where do you see . . .
- Can you list . . .
- Where do you find . . .
- What facts . . .
- How would . . .
- Where in the text . . .
- Can you explain . . .
- Can you describe . . .

▶ **Learning partners.** The student works closely with another student to produce a common product or to study difficult material together.

▶ **Small-group instruction.** Long a staple of elementary classrooms, small-group instruction can be effective at the secondary level. It is especially appropriate to use this strategy in conjunction with tiered instruction.

▶ **Interactive bookmarks.** These versatile bookmarks, readily adapted to any discipline, allow students to stop while engaged in reading a passage. Usually interactive bookmarks are teacher-generated and geared to specific course objectives.

Although these are just a few of the many strategies that can be used to differentiate instruction, many more activities and strategies can make including differentiated instruction a productive way to teach as well as manage your class. To learn more about differentiated instruction, consult these resources:

Amy Benjamin. *Differentiated Instruction Using Technology: A Guide for Middle and High School Teachers.* Larchmont, N.Y.: Eye on Education, 2005.

Judith Dodge. *Differentiation in Action.* New York: Scholastic, 2005.

Sheryn Spencer Northey. *Handbook on Differentiated Instruction for Middle and High Schools.* Larchmont, N.Y.: Eye on Education, 2004.

Carol Ann Tomlinson. *How to Differentiate Instruction in Mixed Ability Classrooms.* (2nd ed.) Alexandria, Va.: Association for Supervision and Curriculum Development, 2004.

HOW TO HAVE SUCCESSFUL HOMEWORK ASSIGNMENTS

One of the most troublesome parts of any teacher's day begins just as soon as the school day itself ends. Students who do not do their homework create huge frustrations for themselves, their parents, and their teachers. Through very careful planning on your part, by creating an awareness of the importance of the assignment and by instilling a sense of confidence in your students, you can eliminate most of the problems associated with homework.

Work to find ways to make homework successful for students, their parents, and yourself as often as possible. Think of homework assignments in three steps: what you do before you make the assignment, what you do while making the assignment, and what you should do when the assignment effective is due.

Prior to the Assignment

▶ Never make homework a punishment. To do this is not only unfair to your students, but they will not take the assignment seriously.

▶ Make sure the homework you assign is relevant to the needs of your students and will further mastery of the objectives for the material under study.

▶ Homework should be independent practice of a skill covered in class, a review of old material, in-depth enrichment, or a preview of new material.

▶ Follow your district's policy on the amount and types of recommended homework assignments. If your district does not have a formal policy, then check with the other members of your department to find out what the informal policy is.

▶ Spend some time thinking back to your own school days. What made homework enjoyable or miserable for you? How can you incorporate your own experience into your assignments?

▶ Aim for assignments that students can do independently, can be accomplished in a reasonable length of time, are interesting enough to engage their attention, are relevant, are useful, are based on an objective, and that provide practice or a deepening of understanding.

▶ Expect that your students will help each other on homework assignments, even the ones you would prefer they do individually. Either allow them to consult with each other or create assignments that can only be completed by individual students working independently.

▶ Have a very structured homework pattern for less-organized students. Students should have a clear idea of when they need to schedule time for homework.

▶ Parents and guardians can be very powerful allies in avoiding homework hassles. Make sure you are all on the same side by keeping parents informed, providing them with copies of your syllabus, alerting them quickly if a problem arises, and being very structured and organized about homework.

- ▶ Be willing to change due dates if your students seem genuinely distressed or overwhelmed by the workload.

- ▶ Don't allow students to do homework for other classes in your class. Be careful not to snatch the papers and books from students who are caught doing this. Simply make sure they are put away and the student is back on task.

- ▶ Take other teachers' assignments into account and be reasonable with the length of time your assignments will take.

- ▶ When you can, include your students in planning when particular assignments will be due, what material they need to practice, when major tests are given, and which types of review work they need whenever you can. While you do this you still remain the master planner, but your students will have a much-appreciated voice in their homework decisions.

- ▶ Create an informal and brief questionnaire at the start of the term to get your students thinking about homework: its importance and their attitudes about it (see the "Homework Questionnaire for Students" that follows).

- ▶ Give your students the tools they need to get their work done easily. Stress the importance of a quiet place to study at home, a storage place for papers and materials, setting aside time, getting organized, and planning how to accomplish the work. It's also important to discuss with your students how to handle study breaks and the phone calls that interrupt their study schedule. Students need help in handling their responsibilities.

Student Worksheet

1. Why is homework an important component for classes at the secondary level?

2. Why is homework important for this class?

3. What types of homework assignments have you been given in the past few years? Please list as many as you can recall. Use the back of this sheet if you need more space.

4. What kinds of homework assignments helped you learn the material better than the others?

5. What kinds of assignments do you prefer?

6. On which nights of the week do you find it difficult to do your homework?

7. What kinds of assignments do you find difficult to do?

8. What do you think is a fair policy about late assignments?

9. On average, about how long do you spend on your homework each night?

10. What advice do you have for other students to help them complete homework assignments well and on time?

▶ The minutes that you spend each day on making students aware of their homework responsibilities will be more than paid off in increased student success.

▶ Make sure students know why they have to do each assignment so that they won't feel martyred to busywork. Your students should have a clear idea of what they should learn from each assignment.

▶ Avoid confusion by making sure the directions are clear and your students know exactly what they have to do in order to succeed on each assignment. Take time to go over each set of directions so that they know exactly what to do.

▶ One of the most effective ways to get students to pay attention to their homework responsibilities is to include the homework on their syllabus. Each student should have a copy to keep in their notebooks. Arrange a checklist space for homework assignments so that your students can keep track of what they have accomplished. Write the homework objective on the board and have students copy it onto the syllabus.

▶ Enlarge a copy of the syllabus and post it beside the door so that students can see it on the way out of your room. Highlight the homework assignment for the day to catch their attention.

▶ Write the assignment for that particular night in the same place on the board each day. Near the end of class make a quick check to see if all students know what the night's work will be.

▶ Ask students to explain to you what the homework assignment is, how to do it, and what they can gain from doing it.

▶ You can end class by asking students to plan how much time the homework will take and what hours they intend to set aside to accomplish it. They should share this with each other. Ask a different student each day to explain the assignment to the class.

▶ Many teachers now post their homework electronically. Post homework assignments online as far in advance as you can. Although it is not always easy to maintain an online syllabus, your students will benefit enormously if you make the effort to keep their online homework schedule up-to-date.

Teacher Worksheet

SAMPLE SYLLABUS

Date	Objective	Classroom Activity	Homework	Grade

▶ Engage your students in discussions throughout the year in which you ask them to evaluate various assignments as to relevance, information learned, skills sharpened, or difficulty.

▶ Have your students jot down how they studied: the time they began and ended, when breaks happened, in what order they did their homework, which assignments they found more successful than others, and other topics that will shed insight on the homework situation in your classroom.

▶ Check homework at the start of class on the day that it is due. Most students are upset when they do homework that is never graded. While you do not have to grade every assignment, taking the time to review it with students is a productive learning activity.

▶ If you do not want to give a grade on the actual assignment, then you can give a quick quiz after you and your students have discussed the homework.

▶ One way to avoid homework hassles while involving parents is to allow any student who does not have the homework completed to bring in the assignment without penalty if the child has a note from home stating that the parent is aware that the assignment is not yet complete. This note should be brought in on the day the assignment is *due*—not the next day or later. This act of understanding on your part will put the responsibility for the homework on the child while treating the parent and the child with respect.

▶ A note or phone call home after the second missed or late assignment will often correct the problem. If it doesn't, at least you have contacted the parents and alerted students to the seriousness of their actions.

▶ Be reasonable when the unforeseen happens. A power outage that lasts for hours is good reason for not completing an assignment; a regularly scheduled soccer game is not.

▶ Be aware that many students justifiably resent teachers who allow students to turn in late homework assignments without penalty. Determine a fair policy for late work in your classroom and make parents and students aware of your policy.

▶ One way to increase the number of completed homework assignments that many teachers have found to be successful is to ask students to explain why they did not do their work. They then need to have the form signed by a parent or guardian and returned to class. A sample form that you can adapt for your class is the "Parent-Teacher-Student Homework Notification Form" that follows.

▶ Hold students accountable for their work in a variety of ways. The loss of a grade is not enough to deter a determined student from not doing an assignment. Contact parents, create a fair late policy, and find other ways to make your students see the importance of completing their homework promptly.

Student Worksheet

PARENT-TEACHER-STUDENT
HOMEWORK NOTIFICATION FORM

Date	Homework	Teacher	Parent

Student Worksheet

MISSING HOMEWORK EXPLANATION FORM

Student name: _____ Class: _____

I do not have my homework today because:

_____ I did the assigned homework but I did not bring it to class.

_____ I forgot my homework.

_____ I did not have materials at home.

_____ I chose not to do my homework.

_____ Please explain any other reason below.

_____

_____

_____

Student Signature_____

This information may be shared with a parent or guardian.

TEACH THE PROCESS OF LONG-TERM PROJECTS

In recent years even very young children in many schools have been assigned a wide variety of long-term projects to complete outside of class. These projects in the early school years can take a wide range of forms such as history booklets, science experiments, or even more creative topics such as dramatic presentations and poetry collections.

As students grow older, their assignments become more complex and time-consuming, but the frustration involved in long-term projects for students, parents, and teachers does not diminish. Often these projects involve a bewildering amount of research, extracurricular resources, organizational skills, creativity, and controversial parental involvement—all of which can overwhelm even the best students.

Few experienced teachers have been spared the misery of seeing an innovative project that seemed promising on the day that it was assigned degenerate into a muddle of poor work turned in by discouraged students who are obviously relieved to get the assignment over with at last.

Long-term projects can be successful for everyone concerned when you teach your students how to achieve each step involved in completing these projects. With careful planning and by teaching the skills necessary for success, these assignments can fulfill their promise and become the enjoyable learning experiences they were designed to be.

- ▶ Choose a topic and a format that are intrinsically interesting and appropriate for your students.

- ▶ If you select topics and formats that are as close to real-life situations as possible, you will motivate your students to succeed more easily than if you assign work that has little relevance to their present or future lives.

- ▶ Allow as many choices as you can for your students when you design the project. If students choose their own topics, they are more likely to enjoy the project and will be more successful.

- ▶ Skills as well as knowledge are necessary to complete out-of-class projects. Give your students both of these vital components.

- ▶ It is important to teach the process of working on a long-term project if you want students to do well on it. Recall the techniques *you* used when you did well on projects and use these to assist your students.

- ▶ Be sure to allow enough time for your students to do a good job on their projects. In the daily press of work, it's tempting to hurry students so that we can move on to the next item on the curriculum that we are supposed to cover. Be careful that your students have the time they need to do excellent work.

- ▶ Make certain all students have equal access to the resources necessary to complete the work. Transportation to a public library or finding money to buy art supplies may be problems for some. Be sensitive to the needs of your students, and offer assistance and intervention at the onset of the assignment.

- ▶ When you make the assignment, be sure to include flowcharts, checklists, and other visual aids to make the interim steps of the assignment clear to your students. Your students not only need to see the big picture of what it is you are asking them to accomplish, but they also need to see the smaller steps they need to take in order to achieve the final result.

- ▶ Be sure to include a final criteria list for evaluating the final project. Students should have a clear idea of exactly what they need to do in order to succeed before they begin the assignment.

▶ Between the time you make the assignment and when your students begin working on it, encourage them to plan what they need to do to achieve success. Have students write out a project proposal in which they describe what they want to do, what materials and outside resources they need, how they are going to accomplish each step, and any other information you think is necessary to demonstrate that they have thought through each step of the work they are about to begin. Hold conferences with your students to discuss each proposal and resolve any potential problems before they can become serious.

▶ Teach your students about plagiarism each time you assign a long-term project. All students should be taught the importance of crediting the source for any work that is not their own.

▶ Break a large project into smaller parts with separate deadlines and grades for each part.

▶ Teach your students the skills necessary to successfully complete each smaller part of the whole assignment.

▶ Time-management skills are vital to the success of any project. Work with your students to show them the error of procrastination and any other bad habits they need to eliminate in order to use their time efficiently.

▶ Don't hesitate to show your students the shortcuts that will make the project easier. Work done quickly and easily is much more fun than work that is a struggle to slog through. Be careful to spell out what parts of the project are okay to complete with the help of others and what parts you expect your students to complete by themselves.

▶ Take your students' artistic talents into account when you assign a creative project. Many students are intimidated by projects that demand drawing or other artwork. While you certainly should discourage students from cutting pictures from books or magazines, there is nothing wrong with photocopying work or generating computer graphics for most projects if credit is given for the source.

▶ Computer skills are wonderful timesavers for those students who can use computers to research or finish a project. Encourage your students to use the technology that is available to them in your school or community by allowing time for this and arranging for someone to teach them the specific computer skills needed for your project if you are not able to do so yourself.

▶ Include as many models of each step in the project as you can so that your students know exactly what they should do. Don't just show them the final project; show them models of the steps in the process.

▶ Be very specific when you explain what your students need to do at each point of the project process. Don't assume they know what to do to achieve the results you want from them.

▶ Arrange time for frequent peer reviews of the steps in the assignment. Students benefit when they share ideas with each other. Also arrange your schedule so that you are available to students who need to consult with you.

▶ Have your students explain the process and comment on their progress at each step in the project. They need to assess their own progress and plan what they need to do next in order to achieve the quality of work you expect.

▶ Stress the importance of 100 percent accuracy and excellent work in the final product. Have high standards for the assignment and help your students achieve them throughout the project process.

▶ Avoid an unpleasant experience by grading each part of the project as the steps are completed. One final grade is not as effective or as fair as several grades for the various skills and knowledge that students learn along the way to the final product. This will also alert students and their parents to the problems that arise early in the process so that these problems can be solved before they snowball into failure.

▶ Students can become so bogged down that they fall behind and never get caught up. Design a long-term project so that your students must complete all of the steps. Avoid the inevitable result of this by helping your students accomplish each part of the assignment to the best of their ability before moving on to the next part.

▶ Have students assess themselves at the end of a project. Ask them to reflect on the project and the parts of the process that they did well or that were troublesome for them. This will provide meaningful closure to the entire project process.

STUDENT NOTEBOOKS: ORGANIZING FOR SUCCESS

Teaching students how to organize their paperwork is an important responsibility for all teachers. Don't assume your students know how to keep their notebooks and other papers in order. Many of them have never been taught the skills necessary to keep themselves organized.

Make teaching organizational skills and notebook keeping part of your plan to prevent discipline problems. Not only will you teach your students important organizational skills, but you will also create competent learners. Students with good note-taking and organizational skills are much more likely to do well than those whose idea of keeping up with papers is to stuff them into their backpacks or gym bags. Another benefit of teaching notebook keeping is that it is a constructive activity that will keep your students engaged and on-task in class.

Spend a few minutes on this topic each week and you will be more than rewarded in the improved performance of your students. The following strategies are designed to help your students become more organized.

▶ Keep your requirements for a notebook logical, sensible, and simple if you want your students to remain consistently well-organized.

▶ Teach your students why they need to keep their papers in order. They need to see that this is an important lifetime skill, not just another hoop they need to jump through in order to pass your class.

▶ Spend time each day at the beginning of the term to make sure students are getting off to a good start with organization. Make frequent periodic checks of their notebooks to make sure your students understand that keeping them organized should be a priority.

▶ Encourage your students to purchase three-ring binders. These are durable and can be used for years, while paper binders or folders often self-destruct in a matter of weeks.

▶ After your students have purchased their binders, focus on the ways you want them to keep their papers and notes orderly. The easiest way to do this is to have students file each paper they have by its date. If you do this, your students will find it easy to review for tests by checking their work against the course syllabus.

▶ Your students should color-code their notebooks for quick identification.

▶ Taping the edges of binders will often extend the life of each notebook. So will encouraging your students to value their investment in their notebooks.

- Teach your students to be businesslike in labeling the covers of their notebooks. They should neatly label their notebooks with their names, the subjects in their notebooks, and any other appropriate information that would enable anyone who finds a lost notebook to return it promptly to its owner.

- Discourage student doodling, stickers, or other marks on the covers of notebooks only if you feel that they seriously distract your students from the task of keeping work in an orderly fashion.

- Your students will also benefit from a recloseable pouch in their notebooks. In this pouch they can keep pens, pencils, and flash cards. You can show them how to make these pouches for themselves from small food storage bags if they are unable to purchase them.

- Encourage your students to use pens. Pen is much easier to read than pencil after a few weeks of being filed in a notebook.

- Have your students label every page in their notebooks so that they can immediately tell what it is. This labeling should include the date, since papers should be filed by date.

- You may want to have your students separate papers into various categories such as test papers, homework assignments, or class notes. While this is one way to keep a notebook, students who file papers by date will find it easier not only to keep up with their papers, but also to see a logical progression in the development of what they have studied.

- Encourage your students to use different colored inks or highlighters when they study their notes. "Looking over" their notes is not an efficient method of learning the material they have so neatly organized. Taking time to highlight or even rewrite material in their own words ensures greater retention.

- Purchase a hole puncher for the papers you return to your students. Students can't file them in order unless you have provided this service for them.

- At the end of each grading period, have your students clear out their notebooks and transfer their papers to a set of files they have set up for this at home. This will keep their notebooks in better order, while the material they will need for big tests and exams is still safely well organized.

ASK PRODUCTIVE QUESTIONS

The art of asking questions well is one that takes time to develop. The right questions asked at just the right time can turn an ordinary class discussion into a memorable experience for students and teachers alike. This skill is one that all teachers can develop no matter what the age or ability level of their students. While it is a skill that takes planning and practice, it pays off in increased student enthusiasm and success.

Enthusiastic and successful students will create a positive learning climate with few disruptions. When you capture and hold the attention of all your students, a questioning session turns into a learning session for the entire class.

Happily, learning the art of asking questions well is not difficult. First, you must plan questions that are going to generate good answers. Develop ones that build on each other logically.

There are two types of questions that you will want to ask your students. *Recall questions* require a factual response based on previous learning. *Thought questions* require a more in-depth answer and can also be open-ended. Both kinds of questions, when handled with delicacy, help establish an atmosphere of trust in your classroom.

After you have decided on the questions you want to ask your students, teach your students the routine you want followed for questioning sessions before you ever hold the first one. When your students know what you expect from them, you will all benefit.

With practice you can set the stage for academic and social success in your classroom. Use as many of the following strategies as you can in each questioning session when you want to involve every student in your class in productive learning:

▶ When you ask a question, it is crucial that you wait for a response. You must allow everyone enough time to think of an answer. After you have waited, call on a student to respond. This technique not only takes practice on your part, but also requires you to train your students to wait for you to call on them and not to blurt out answers.

▶ After you have asked a question and waited, call on a student by name. Remember that if you call a student's name before you ask the question, the rest of the class is automatically uninvolved in the questioning.

▶ If you are in a questioning situation where all of your students are expected to give a response and one student refuses, still hold that student accountable by saying, "I'll come back to you." Be pleasantly firm if you want a response from every student.

▶ Avoid responses from an entire group. You can't hear from everyone when your students shout out answers at once. Too many students successfully tune out when the group is expected to answer, and individuals are not held accountable.

▶ Don't follow a pattern when you call on students. A good way around this bad habit is to photocopy your roll book at the start of the term and use it to mark off your students' names as you call on them at random. You will find this much more effective than following alphabetical order or calling on students in rows.

▶ You and your students should devise simple signals for yes-or-no questions. You could use thumbs up or thumbs down, one finger held up or two fingers held up, or any other signal that will help you engage each student's full attention.

▶ When answer choices are limited to several categories, such as in a classification, make up response cards in advance.

▶ Another excellent way to get all of your students fully involved is to ask them to write their answers before you call on anyone. You could have them put their pencils down as a signal that they are through writing. This technique also forces your students to think for themselves.

▶ Never be sarcastic about a wrong response. Your students must be allowed to make mistakes.

▶ Encourage your students to be responsive and to answer without fear of ridicule from you or from their classmates. Don't allow students to laugh at a classmate's incorrect answer. Instead, direct them to be helpful. Say, "Who can help _____with this answer?"

▶ Try not to repeat a question. Your students need to listen and stay focused. If your students don't seem to understand one of your questions, ask a student to rephrase it for you.

▶ Teach your students to speak loudly enough for all to hear. Avoid repeating their answers for them. Instead, ask them to repeat.

▶ Respond to every answer. If it's correct, say so. When it's an incorrect response, react calmly. If part of an answer is correct, then you must respond to that part. Continue until you have an answer that is entirely correct.

- In order to keep your students engaged, it is necessary for you to move around the room as you question them. Standing near daydreamers often forces them to pay attention to you.

- An effective way to end class is with a three-minute drill session. End the drill session by asking for a recap of the information covered in the drill.

- When conducting rapid-fire drills, don't be predictable. Ask a student a question, go to another student for the next question, and then return to the first one for the third question. This way no one is let off the hook because of a correct answer.

- Make sure you ask one question at a time. A shower of questions will only confuse your students.

- An effective questioning technique is to poll your students on the issues you have just taught them. Forcing everyone to take a stand or to express an opinion will engage them more readily than if they are allowed to sit passively.

- Design questions that will allow students to go beyond simple yes-or-no answers if you want to promote thinking and student involvement.

- Consciously promote student interaction by asking some students to comment on the answers given by others. Setting up a crossfire situation will force them to think. It keeps everyone interested and the class lively.

PLAY GAMES WITH YOUR STUDENTS

Playing games with your students creates a positive class atmosphere at the same time that it makes learning enjoyable for those students who like to interact with their classmates.

Playing team games with your students allows them to compete successfully in a controlled environment.

If it has been a while since you have played many team games yourself or if you do not feel comfortable adapting the games you already know for your classroom, don't be daunted. Your students have a wealth of knowledge about the types of games that they enjoy playing and are usually more than willing to share that knowledge with a teacher who offers an opportunity for the class to have fun and learn at the same time.

There are also many sites online for teachers who would like to integrate online educational games into their classrooms. Two helpful sites to begin exploring are

- **High School Ace (http://highschoolace.com).** Dyann K. Schmidel and Wanda G. Wojcik have created this site, which features a wonderful Web directory with many games, references, and puzzles for high school students.

- **The Problem Site (www.theproblemsite.com/games.asp).** This site offers dozens of worksheets, references, puzzles, and links to educational games.

In addition to online games, there is still a place for the low-tech games that teachers and students have played for decades. Some of the more popular old-fashioned team games are described as follows:

Ball Toss. Line up your students in two teams facing each other. As soon as a student correctly answers a question, that student tosses a soft foam ball to a student on the opposite team. Now that student must answer the next question.

Board Games. Design your own board game to fit your topic. You can either make smaller boards and photocopy them for several students to play in a group or you can make a giant one for your entire class to play. Keep the rules simple, but have lots of color and excitement built into the game and the questions that you ask. The tasks you assign your students in a board game range from simply answering questions correctly to solving just about any sort of problem. You can also ask students to create their own board games.

Capture the Block. In this review game, begin by having each student create twenty questions with answers about the material. Place the students into groups of three. Next, use the "Table" feature of a word-processing program to create a table that has six columns and ten rows. Print out a table for each group. Create markers numbered one through sixty and place them in a bag for each group of three players. Your students will combine their questions and answers. They should number each question so that they have a bank of sixty questions with answers. Students begin play with one student drawing a numbered marker. The student has to correctly answer that question. If that happens, the student gets to color in the block. The student with the highest number of captured blocks wins.

Chain Making. To help students improve their memorization skills or to use some free time productively, play a chaining game. This is simply a sophisticated version of the old alphabet game where one player thinks of an object beginning with the letter *a* and the next player recalls that object and another beginning with the letter *b*. Your students don't need to be restricted to letters of the alphabet, but can recall as many facts or dates as your lesson involves.

Charades. This age-old acting game is probably already one of your students' favorites. Use it to teach information about people, events, discoveries, literature, and any other topic that seems to lend itself to this format.

Flash Cards. One of the most useful study techniques to teach your students is to use flash cards to learn new information and to review previously learned material. Either make flash cards large enough for the entire class to use all at once or have your students make up their own and use them in groups. Award points to the individuals or teams who guess accurately.

Game Shows. Popular trivia game-show formats can usually be adapted to your classroom with a minimum of modification. Game-show formats are especially useful to review or introduce new material.

Hangman. This perennial favorite can be played in any classroom with a chalkboard and by students of almost any age. Students will often entertain themselves in free-time situations in a classroom by playing a version of this childhood amusement. It is especially useful for fact recall and vocabulary review.

Name That Time, Battle, and so on. This game is similar to "Twenty Questions" in that students try to guess the answers with as few clues as possible. You should make up the clues in advance. On game day, you will call them out one at a time. Be sure to mix up the difficulty level of the clues in order to keep your students engaged as long as possible.

Olympics. Periodically you may want to review various concepts or material by holding an Olympics. You can let your imagination roam while creating the events, or you can put some of your students in charge of creating and staging the learning events. In either case, your goal is to review information while having fun. Divide your students into various teams and keep a total team score. Recall as much as you can about the actual Olympics when creating your own events.

Quiz Bowl. Set up a tournament of quick questions and answers involving as many of your students as possible. Make the Bowl as elaborate as you can with various levels of difficulty, several different rounds, varying scores, and other incentives designed to keep student interest piqued.

Races. Arrange all sorts of events around the concept of racing. You encourage your students to be the first to solve problems, look up words, learn information, or do any other competition you devise.

Shopping. Here is a useful way to use some of the junk mail that most of us receive. Plan a shopping trip for your students. Give each one a certain amount of "money" and a group of people to shop for. Hand them the junk mail catalogs and stand back. Your students will surprise you with the choices they make for their fictional recipients and probably with their own shopping skills. The benefits of this lesson include improved mathematical skills, clarification of values, and even increased vocabulary.

Simulations. Although most simulation games are often sophisticated computer ones, you and your students can enjoy low-tech ones, which are simple to construct. Plan the scenario you want your students to enact, then involve them in it with a written description or by role-playing. A very popular version of this game is to have your students imagine that they are shipwrecked on a deserted island and have to plan ways to survive. Simulation games can be used to help your students think creatively, learn to work cooperatively, examine their values, solve problems, or satisfy just about any purpose you have in mind when you create the game for them.

Spelling Bee. This game can be used for almost any lesson; it's certainly not restricted to just spelling. Place your students in two rows facing each other. Ask questions in sequence along the rows. Students who answer correctly stay in the game; those who answer incorrectly sit down. This is a good way to review quick facts or to reinforce recall of vocabulary terms.

Sporting Events. Divide your students into teams and use the board to wage fierce games of football, baseball, soccer, or whatever sport is the current favorite in your classroom. Students advance play in the game by answering questions correctly or by completing assigned tasks.

Storytellers. Even sophisticated older students can excel at this game if it is geared to their level. To play, one student begins a story, stops after a few sentences, and points to another student to continue the plot. You can use this activity to teach or review vocabulary, facts, the order of events, or other similar material.

Talk Show. Have your students stage a talk show to interview characters in literature or history or in any other discipline. Choose your most outgoing and trustworthy student to be the host and let that student interview the guests about their problems or contributions. The audience of interested students will get as involved as if they were at an actual television talk show. Plan ahead to make sure that all of the participants have the information they need to succeed at this activity.

Telephone. This child's game can be played to teach facts or introduce new information. Even older students will enjoy playing this game if it is played at top speed with the emphasis on accuracy. To play telephone, have a student read a fact or series of facts from a paper that you have created. That student has to repeat the information to another and that student, in turn, tells another one. In the old version, the fun comes from the scrambling of the message. In the version you want to use, keep the information short and the number of repetitions limited to no more than five before checking to see that it is still accurate. You could have rows or small groups compete against each other.

Tic-Tac-Toe. In this game, your students earn the right to play by answering questions or by solving problems.

Trashketball. In almost any novelty store or catalog geared for games, you should be able to find and purchase a basketball hoop designed for a trash can. You can use this to keep your classroom clean, or you can use it as part of the games you use for learning. Be sure to explain the rules for throwing paper into the hoop carefully and to communicate those rules clearly to your students to make sure that the play is both safe and fun.

Treasure Hunt. Stage a treasure hunt to have students figure out new information and get moving in a productive way at the same time. You can involve areas outside your classroom for extra interest and to get your students really up and moving. There are endless variations of this game that you can play with your students to get them interested and engaged in a topic. If you are not clever at creating clues, assign a team of students who would do a good job at this task and to direct the hunt. The real treasure is the enjoyment and learning that your students will experience with this activity.

Twenty Questions. To play this game in your classroom, write the correct answer on a slip of paper and have students guess it with a series of questions. Keep count of the number of questions that they have to ask in order to figure out the answer. In this game, the lowest score wins.

Unscramblers. This is a fun way to improve retention of facts, improve your students' vocabularies, or teach correct spelling. When your students play this game, they fill in missing letters and unscramble mixed-up words in messages that you send them. This is a creative way to improve all sorts of skills and have fun at the same time. An alternative would be to have your students create their own messages to unscramble.

Classroom-Management Advice for Game Days

▶ Make sure that each activity has a sound educational purpose and isn't only functioning to kill time in a pleasant way.

▶ Modulate the intensity of the competition in your classroom by having teams play against teams. You should determine the team members so that no one gets chosen last.

▶ Try to structure your activities so that as many students as possible are involved at one time. Students sitting around watching other students play a game is not what you should aim for when creating a situation for maximum learning for everyone.

▶ Teach good sportsmanship in advance of the game day. Be very explicit about how you expect your students to play.

▶ Be concerned about safety. Stop any game as soon as it starts to become unsafe. Teach your students why safety is important and consistently enforce your safety rules.

▶ Accept the fact that some games are much noisier than others.

▶ Keep a running total of the various teams or individuals if you wish to keep the scoring even.

▶ Allow students to be scorekeepers and timers so that you can be free for monitoring.

▶ Make your games as realistic as possible with music and other props where necessary. Your students will find it easier to get into the spirit of the game if you make this extra effort.

- Consider making ribbons that your students can use for bookmarks or buying stickers or other inexpensive trinkets for prizes.

- To determine who goes first, have your students draw numbers from a container that you keep on hand for this purpose.

- Have your students work together to set rules and to plan scoring procedures. The more decisions they make and the more involved they become, the better the activity will be.

A helpful site for those teachers who would like to purchase educational games for their classroom is maintained by Next Generation Training (www.EducationalLearningGames.com). Here you will find over four thousand games that cover a variety of ages, subjects, and difficulty levels.

HOW TO USE TECHNOLOGY TO ENHANCE INSTRUCTION

Using the technological resources available in any school only makes sense when educators consider that they are preparing students for the future. Using technology to enhance instruction will also serve to help you create a positive discipline climate in your classroom. Students who are engaged in work that is intrinsically interesting will spend more time on task than those students who are bored with the same old assignments day after day.

General Technology Integration Sites for Teachers

- Although there are many helpful sites for teachers interested in integrating technology into their classrooms, one of the most user-friendly is Eduscapes (http://eduscapes.com). Eduscapes is a portal with links to many other excellent technology sites. One of the best of these sites for teachers is Teacher Tap (http://eduscapes.com/tap/index.htm). Click on the home page link at Eduscapes to access this site where you will find a great deal of helpful support information geared for teachers in a hurry.

- At Education World (www.educationworld.com), teachers can find dozens of strategies and techniques for integrating technology into the classroom by clicking on the "Technology Integration" icon.

- Discovery School's technology expert, Kathy Schrock, publishes Kathy Schrock's Guide for Educators (http://school.discovery.com/schrockguide), where you can learn valuable tips and ideas for using technology to capture and sustain your student's attention.

- Although Kelly Tenkely is an instructional specialist at an elementary school, many of the sites and suggestions she writes about on her blog, *iLearn Technology* (http://ilearntechnology.com), are appropriate for secondary-level students.

- Developed by the Department of Education, Teacher's Guide to International Collaboration on the Internet (www.ed.gov/teachers/how/tech/international/guide) is designed to help teachers reach out globally using the Internet.

Learning Circles

In brief: Students join students in other countries to participate in collaborative learning projects covering a wide variety of topics.

To learn more: Visit the International Education and Resource Network (http://iearn.org/circles) to learn more about how your students can join students from across the world in learning projects. iEARN is a nonprofit organization made up of almost thirty thousand schools and youth organizations in more than one hundred countries.

Problem-Based Learning Projects

In brief: Project-based learning (PBL) is an instructional method requiring students to consider a real-life problem in collaborative groups with the goal of generating solutions or information about the issue. It is student-centered, practical, and engaging.

To learn more: While there are many sites online that offer information about how to get started with PBL, the most comprehensive and useful site at the time of publication is offered by the Illinois Mathematics and Science Academy (http://pbln.imsa.edu). IMSA offers professional development and training in addition to links, resources, and other useful information about PBL on its Web site.

Computer-Based Research

In brief: Students choose and narrow a topic. They then use the Internet to compile information about the topic.

To learn more: Although the topics and projects for computer-based research are limitless, one helpful site that offers solid suggestions on how to successfully manage computer-based research in your classroom is offered by HotChalk. You'll find dozens of useful ideas, links, resources, and lesson plans to help your students learn research skills at their lesson plans page (www.lessonplanspage.com).

Collaboration

In brief: Students work with other students online to collaborate on various projects and assignments.
To learn more:

CreateDebate (http://createdebate.com) is a site where students share their ideas by engaging in online debates. Participants can select topics on the site or submit their own ideas.

Edmodo (http://www.edmodo.com) offers students and teachers a secure platform for microblogging, and sharing files. It is similar to Twitter.com, but is not open to the general public and so protects students' privacy.

Voice Thread (http://voicethread.com) is an exciting way for students to share their comments about documents, images, presentations, and videos. Students can use Voice Thread in a variety of engaging ways from digital storytelling to online collaboration as they participate in conversations about the media they are seeing.

Electronic Visualization

In brief: These sites help students comprehend what they are learning by providing images that help them make those connections.

GlogsterEDU (www.glogster.com) is a user-friendly site that allows students to make online presentations with video, music, graphics, and other media.

At Tag Galaxy (www.taggalaxy.com) students can browse through the thousands of photographs on Flickr, a photo-sharing site.

The New York Public Library's digital database contains over a quarter million images in various collections for public access (http://digitalgallery.nypl.org/nypldigital/index.cfm).

The National Archives and Records Administration has partnered with Google (http://video .google.com/nara.html) to offer a collection of newsreels from the World War II era, NASA documentaries, and other American history documentaries.

Electronic Portfolios

In brief: Students can create online binders or notebooks with electronic documents that they can then share.

To learn more:

At Zoho (https://writer.zoho.com) students can create and upload documents using some of the templates at this site as well as store and share them.

Live Binders (http://livebinders.com) is a site where students can collaborate or work individually to create portfolios of various types.

Practice and Review Opportunities

In brief: Students can use online sites either to review the information they are studying or to practice skills.

To learn more:

At Class Marker (www.classmarker.com) teachers can create free online quizzes for students to take online.

Quizlet (http://quizlet.com) is a site that offers students an opportunity to create and share online flash cards.

Your students will find hundreds of study guides and other support materials at Shmoop (www .shmoop.com).

Another useful site for students to preview, gather information about, and review hundreds of assigned texts is the popular Sparknotes (www.sparknotes.com). Students can also find practice material and suggestions for various standardized tests.

Alternative Texts

In brief: In addition to the texts you offer your students, they can take advantage of the many electronic texts offered online.

Book Glutton (www.bookglutton.com) is a site that offers students an opportunity to read e-texts with other students. While many of the texts are free at the time of publication, not all of them are.

At Foot Note (www.footnote.com), thousands of historical documents are available for students to browse. Documents are in easy-to-find classifications to make it very useful for students and teachers.

Scribd (www.scribd.com) offers thousands of alternative texts for students as well as the opportunity for students and teachers to upload and share documents.

Publishing

In brief: Students can create and then share their work in visual or audio form at these sites.

To learn more:

Apple's GarageBand feature on Macintosh computers is a feature that allows students to create and share a podcast.

Audacity (http://audacity.sourceforge.net) is another free, open-source software that allows students to produce and broadcast podcasts.

At Teen Ink (http://teenink.com), students can share their original work with thousands of other teens.

You can learn practical advice from experts and other educators that will enable you to help your students publish their writing at Publishing Students (www.publishingstudents.com).

At Make Beliefs Comix (www.makebeliefscomix.com), students can create and then share comics online.

Electronic Field Trips

In brief: Instead of an expensive and time-consuming actual field trip, students can journey far in time and space without leaving the classroom with electronic field trips. Although there are countless virtual field trips offered online, the site below offers additional support for those teachers who want to create their own e-field trip experience for their students.

To learn more:

EFieldtrips (www.efieldtrips.org) offers many different field trips as well as support for those educators who want to create their own.

Organization

In brief: Student organization aids are rapidly gaining in popularity as students learn to use online sources to keep their school work on track.

With Wipeelist (www.wipeelist.com), students can maintain a free organized electronic "to-do" list.

Similar to Wipeelist, Ta-Da List (http://tadalist.com) offers students the flexibility of sharing their lists in an online community or with friends as well as maintaining it privately.

Deadline (http://deadlineapp.com) is a site that sends students e-mail reminders of upcoming deadlines. Very easy to use, it can help students remember due dates for long-term assignments as well as daily work.

HELP STUDENTS STAY ON TASK WHEN WORKING WITH COMPUTERS

Although classrooms and computers can be a successful combination, when secondary students use computers without carefully planned procedures in place, the result can be less than successful. Off-task behavior, illegal or inappropriate downloads, cyberbullying, and loss of valuable instructional time are just a few of the problems that can plague a class when students are not using classroom computers suitably.

Because of the widespread use of computers as an aid to instruction, it is more important than ever for teachers to make sure that their students use them productively. In the lists below, you will find suggestions for ways to help students who are using computers in a classroom with only a few computers and ways to help students who are in a one-to-one laptop classroom.

A Classroom with Only a Few Computers

▶ At the beginning of the term, go over the rules for acceptable computer use so that students are aware of what is expected of them.

▶ Be careful that you have checked all the pages and links on any site that you use with students to make sure that they are safe and appropriate for classroom use.

▶ Give explicit directions as students begin work so that they have a clear idea of what is expected of them and can avoid confusion and off-task behavior.

▶ Have students work in pairs or triads to complete assignments. Assign specific roles so that all students participate. One student can record observations, one use the keyboard, one use the mouse, and so on. To encourage equitable use of computer time, set a timer and rotate tasks at intervals.

▶ Consider offering a pencil-and-paper activity at the same time that some students are at the computer so that everyone is actively learning for the duration of the class.

▶ When students have finished the assignment, they can serve as experts who can offer advice to others who may be struggling.

A One-to-One Laptop Classroom

▶ Care of student laptops can become an issue when students can't complete their work because of improper maintenance of their equipment. Spend time periodically reviewing your school's procedures for caring for computers and managing chargers.

- ▶ Teach laptop etiquette. A rule that many teachers find useful is that all lids should be down while the instructor is talking.

- ▶ Not every school Internet filter is 100 percent effective. Be aware of the sites your students are visiting.

- ▶ Be careful to monitor students while they are using their laptops. Set up your classroom so that you can see their screens easily. Walk around frequently to monitor their activity.

- ▶ If your school district has Internet logging software available for teachers, consider using it to show students a record of the sites they have visited while in class. This often serves as a useful deterrent for students who may be tempted to visit sites that are not appropriate for school.

- ▶ Establish a negative consequence for those students who do not follow class rules about computer use. Often denying the privilege of using a computer for a specified period is enough of a deterrent to keep many students working on the assigned work instead of just browsing their own pick of Internet sites.

TEACHING STUDENTS TO WORK WELL TOGETHER

One of the most successful techniques to gain popularity in classrooms in recent years is collaborative learning. Those teachers who have spent long hours perfecting this teaching strategy claim that it has revolutionized the learning process in their classrooms. On the other hand, those teachers who have not mastered this technique shudder at the thought of noisy, out-of-control students busily engaged in learning nothing. Collaborative learning can be an effective technique for preventing many discipline problems if students are taught how to work well together.

Using collaborative learning activities effectively in your classroom requires a great deal of planning, patience, and persistence on your part, but the rewards are worth the struggle. Students who work well together enjoy the experience and benefit from it. The following suggestions will help you master this teaching technique.

Group Monitoring Form

Use this form when you need to monitor group work systematically and to focus on specific areas of concern (see the "Group Monitoring Form" that follows). Although you can use this form to monitor any behavior that you want, some of the areas you might want to monitor are on- or off-task behavior, noise level, progress, and specific assignment completion.

Teacher Worksheet

GROUP MONITORING FORM

Group	Behaviors Monitored	Comments
1		
2		
3		
4		
5		
6		

▶ Start with pairs or triads. Putting too many students in a group is a common mistake.

▶ Have a very clear objective for the activity and make sure every student in the group understands this objective. A good way to guarantee this understanding is to have one person in the group take the responsibility of explaining it to the rest of the group.

▶ Not every assignment will be successful when it's done by a group. Be careful to design activities that require that students work together.

▶ Design activities that force your students to work together successfully. You could try these:

- Give only the necessary materials to one student so that all of them have to work together to get the job done.

- Divide the task into various parts to complete a larger whole.

- Give a reward for group success.

- Give different members parts of the information that they must share in order to grasp the big picture.

▶ If the project is one that is fairly lengthy or involves several different parts, provide your students with checklists and deadlines so that they can stay organized.

▶ Figure out your personal areas of concern about student collaboration and begin to deal with them. Some areas that have caused other teachers problems are excessive noise, time off-task, group evaluation, and the lack of student responsibility.

▶ Make sure every group member has a specific task and understands how to do it well.

▶ Teach your students the interpersonal skills necessary to work together well. For each activity you have students do, teach them a specific skill to practice. Some of these skills are listening well, developing an open mind about the opinions of others, asking questions, staying on-task, and taking responsibility for the work. An opening icebreaker is a good idea for each new group configuration even in a classroom where students know and like each other, but have not worked together as a team before.

▶ Closely monitor your students while they are in groups. You might even have a checklist so that you can work to promote desirable behaviors or eliminate unproductive ones. Observe how students work together and make sure your students are doing so as productively as possible by offering assistance and suggestions when needed.

▶ Teach students how to deal with their concerns, questions, or side issues that might be off-task behaviors by taking these to a designated area of the room. In this area, you should provide paper and markers or pens so that students can list their concerns as topics with which they need help. This will allow group members to temporarily put these on hold to come back to later.

▶ Have students begin working together by developing a few ground rules for their own group. Give one or two rules as models and then ask students to create others.

▶ You can actively intervene and direct the process if students work in class. You will also find it easier to assign grades if you observe your students working together.

▶ In a long or complex project, it is best to begin with brief activities that encourage group members to work together successfully.

▶ Build in checkpoints for lengthy projects. Make sure all students have met these minideadlines before going further. Students will be responsible at these points for keeping the teacher up-to-date about their progress.

▶ Make sure you create a classroom that is conducive to collaboration. Have chairs arranged in groups and materials handy to avoid traffic-flow problems.

▶ After a group has worked together on an assignment, have the members discuss how well they worked together as a group. What were their strengths and weaknesses? What would they do differently the next time they worked together?

▶ With the increased popularity of collaboration, some students can be confused about when it's okay to work together on an assignment and when it's not. Make sure you continue to be very clear about this with your students.

Group Selection

Although you can do brief teamwork sessions with random grouping or by having students "count off" for larger or more complicated projects, often you will find that if you spend time creating group configurations, your students will be more successful. The least effective way to put students into groups to work together is to have them choose their teammates. Avoid this if you want to have your students fully engaged.

The size of a group can depend on several factors: the maturity of your students, the length of time they will be working together, the resources they will need, the type of task they will have to do, and the interpersonal skills they already possess.

A mixed group based on low, medium, and high ability levels is often the most productive, especially if you work with your students on the ways that you want them to interact with each other. With less-capable groups, use smaller groups where everyone can have an important part.

In the following list, you will find some quick ways to arrange temporary groups where students will work together only briefly. In these situations, a random grouping of your students is appropriate.

▶ Have the students arrange themselves according to their birthday months and dates.

▶ Have the students count off according to the name of the group.

▶ Ask the students to arrange themselves according to the first letter of their last names.

▶ Assign each group a name and have the students draw slips of paper with the name of their group on each slip.

▶ Assign each group a color. Create slips corresponding to the group colors and ask the students to draw slips.

▶ Ask the students to move around the room at random while you count down from twenty. When you reach zero, the two people they are standing nearest to become their group members.

▶ Assign a different quotation about the lesson to each group. Type the quotation and then cut it into parts. Mix up the parts and have the students draw them. Students then move around the room finding the people with the other parts of their quotation who then become their group members.

▶ Write the names of one half of a famous pair from literature (Romeo and Juliet, for example), history, science, or math on a slip of paper. Mix up the slips and have students draw the names. They then find their corresponding partners.

▶ Place each student's name on a note card and shuffle the cards thoroughly. Deal the cards into individual groups.

▶ Photocopy pictures of objects related to the lesson and glue them on note cards. You should have as many of the same pictures as you want students in a group. For example, if you want four students in a group, have four photocopies of the same object. Have the students match their note cards.

▶ Write vocabulary words and their meanings on separate slips of paper. Mix up the slips and have the students draw them. Students find their partners by matching the word and its meaning. This also works well with math facts.

▶ Cut photographs into pieces and mix them up. Have the students draw the pieces and then match them up to determine their groups.

The Teacher's Role in Collaborative Learning

▶ Set clear, measurable objectives for each activity.

▶ Keep students on the right track by giving immediate feedback through constant monitoring. You will be most effective if you stay on your feet while your students are working in teams.

▶ You should spend more time coaching and monitoring than delivering a lecture.

▶ Solve problems or help your students figure out ways to solve problems.

▶ Make sure resources are available to students.

▶ Teach the skills students need to work together.

▶ Organize students' work for maximum efficiency.

▶ Provide deadlines so that you can fairly evaluate your students.

▶ Deal with students who are reluctant to participate fully in the team. Some ways to do this are
  ● Remove the offending students and have them complete the work by themselves.
  ● Be very specific about the tasks they need to do.
  ● Break the tasks into more manageable assignments for students who may be overwhelmed.
  ● Contact parents if necessary.
  ● Be very fair when grading others in the group when one student has problems and the others don't.

▶ Give your students many examples to use as models.

▶ Be a sounding board for ideas and problems.

▶ Provide resources and materials as well as guidance.

▶ Remember that collaboration doesn't become successful only on the days that students are working together. Its success begins on the first day of the term with the atmosphere that you establish for your classroom.

▶ Be aware that this is probably the area of biggest concern for parents and students.

▶ Don't just give a group grade; be sure to give individual grades as well.

▶ You will find it easier to evaluate your students fairly if the objective for the activity is measurable.

▶ Keep a log of your students' progress as they work on each day's activity during the course of a long project. This way you won't have to try to recall the various contributions that each student made to the group's progress.

▶ Make sure you divide the workload evenly among your students in a group and grade them evenly also.

▶ Give generous feedback as the group works on its project. Students need to be clear about their progress if they are to achieve success.

▶ Give individual grades on tests on material that the group was supposed to master during the project. This will encourage individual accountability.

▶ Avoid trouble by making the group grade only a portion of the entire grade.

▶ Be careful not to reward students who do not put forth an appropriate amount of effort.

▶ If a project is going to take several days to complete, give daily grades for working together. Base this on objective and measurable criteria that your students are made aware of in advance so that they understand what they need to do to achieve success.

SOME QUICK COLLABORATIVE ACTIVITIES WITHOUT TECHNOLOGY SUPPORT

▶ Ask the entire class a question. Allow them to think about their responses. Have your students discuss their responses in a group and reach a consensus to share with the larger class.

▶ Have a group list as many items as it can in a category that is under discussion. The group can do this easily if there is only one pen and one piece of paper that needs to be passed from student to student in the group.

▶ At the end of an assignment or a unit of study, ask students to write a group reflection about their work.

▶ Ask students to work together to create graphic organizers about the information in a unit of study.

▶ Have students work together to answer guided questions and then explain their teammates' answers to the rest of the class.

▶ Students can work together to complete a worksheet or drill exercise. Be sure to provide structure for this by assigning specific questions to various team members.

▶ Have groups brainstorm master lists of information that they know about a topic either before you begin studying the material or as a review after your class has covered it.

▶ Have the students review for a test by drilling each other, comparing notes, or writing study guides together.

- Have the students outline the main points of a lesson and share their outlines with the group to check for accuracy.

- Editing papers and checking for proofreading errors is a group task that makes a teacher's job of evaluating papers easier.

- Assign a large topic to a group and have the members report on it through various methods. Make sure each member understands the part he or she will play in presenting the final report.

- Have the students work together to preview a reading passage and write questions or predictions about it.

SOME QUICK COLLABORATIVE ACTIVITIES WITH TECHNOLOGY SUPPORT

- Viewing multimedia presentations
- Creating multimedia presentations
- Writing peer reviews of work
- Creating or viewing visual essays
- Interviewing experts in other schools or communities
- Adding graphics to a text
- Creating a class or group Web page
- Contributing to the maintenance of a class Web page
- Researching information for a group project
- Creating team newsletters
- Contributing to a discussion about the material under study
- Posting questions about the day's lesson
- Creating slide shows

MONITORING STUDENTS' BEHAVIOR

One of the most important skills teachers need to develop when successfully managing student collaboration and all classroom behavior in general is learning how to monitor students' behavior. Monitoring means getting up from behind your desk and staying on your feet all day to oversee your students. It means you are acutely aware of what each student is doing every minute of the class. It requires the hyperalertness of a combat veteran, the patience of Job, and the stamina of an Olympic athlete.

Monitoring students is one of the most important skills that successful teachers can master. At its worst, monitoring happens when a lecturing teacher pauses for breath and says, "Does everybody understand?" while obviously hoping that everybody does.

At its best, monitoring is giving door-to-door attention to your students. It is the famous "eyes in the back of the head" that is the hallmark of excellent teachers who can write on the chalkboard and tell a student in the back of the room to stop passing notes at the same time. It is one of the most important ways we can connect with our students. Monitoring enables us to reach each student because it helps every one of them to feel important.

There are several good reasons for mastering the techniques involved in successful monitoring. Here are several of the advantages to being a good classroom monitor:

▶ Problems can't get out of control.

▶ You build rapport and a positive climate.

▶ Students assume responsibility for behavior.

▶ Everyone stays on task.

▶ It reinforces good behavior.

▶ You appear to be a good classroom leader.

▶ Students take you seriously.

▶ Your personal stress levels decrease.

▶ Learning moves forward.

▶ You can show you care.

▶ You deal with difficulties in a positive way.

If you are not sure you are monitoring as effectively as you can be, it's not hard to get started right away. Here are some strategies for you to use:

▶ Unless you and your students are working together in a circle, stand up. Move around. This body language will make you seem accessible and relaxed.

▶ Make sure you arrange the furniture so that you can monitor everyone. Students in the back of the room count on the fact that you will not notice what they are up to. Try to avoid long rows of neatly placed desks or groups of desks crammed so closely together that you have trouble getting to them.

▶ The simplest request that teachers who are monitoring overlook is to ask their students to put their book bags and other materials underneath their desks. If you remember this, you can move around without having to worry about tripping.

▶ Pay attention to the eye contact you have with your students. Eye contact keeps them alert as well as involved in the classroom activity. You also send the nonverbal message that you find your students important when you look at them as individuals.

▶ Stay relaxed and positive. A good monitor enables, facilitates, and helps—not prowls around irritably trying to catch a naughty child in the act.

▶ Spread out your attention. Do you tend to focus on only a few students? Most teachers tend to do this. A good way to determine if you are guilty of this is to carry a photocopy of your class roll. When you speak with a student, place a check next to the name. After doing this for a couple of classes, you should be more aware of the unconscious patterns in the way you attend to your class.

▶ Be alert, also, to how much time you spend with each student. A student who spends fifteen minutes in a conference with you has received considerably more attention and support than the students who only have your attention for less than a minute.

▶ Be very careful that you don't ignore students who need help. It's easy to get bogged down in a crowd of students who need attention and overlook a student. If there are several who are waiting to speak with you, reassure them that you will get to them.

- Don't allow long lines of students waiting to see you. A better solution is for students to put their names on the board so that you can then see them in order. You could also take a deli-counter approach and have students take a number. See them in the order of the numbers. You could also have those students who know how to help with a particular problem assist the others.

- If you use monitoring to keep students on task, be sure to stand near them. A quick nod of the head, a light touch, a glance, or even a few quiet cautionary words are all it takes most of the time.

QUICK MONITORING TECHNIQUES

- Encourage students to work together to monitor their own group for noise, on-task behavior, and progress (see the "Group Monitoring Form").

- When students work collaboratively, assign the role of monitor to one student in the group.

- Give students silly stickers, tags, or badges to wear when they have reached a certain point in the assignment.

- When you are walking around the room, ask students to tell you five things they have just learned from the assignment.

- If the work for the day involves several smaller assignments, create a checklist of work for students to use and to show you their progress when you come by.

- Project friendliness. Sometimes just a smile will get a daydreamer back on the job.

- Consider offering a small reward to the students who reach a certain point in an assignment.

- Put students' names on the board and have them check off their names as they prove to you they have met the assignment requirements.

- Divide an assignment into small steps. Monitor by asking students to show you each step.

- Have the students who are successful at an assignment put their names on the board as potential helpers.

- Write a fact from the lesson on the board and have students add a different fact to it as they finish working. This is also a great way to review.

- Say, "When I come by your desk, please show me the correct answer to_____."

- Set a time limit for an assignment and walk around the room with the timer ticking or a stopwatch running. This usually helps students stay on task.

- Ask, "At this moment, what are you doing that's right?"

- Tell students that you intend to record the name of every student you see off-task when you make a check at random times. You can also record the names of all students who are on-task at the same time.

- Tell students that if they have a question about the work that other students might have also, they should write it on the board. You can address it when you get a chance.

- If students tend to play while waiting for you to check their work or answer a question, teach them that they are wasting time. They need to understand the difference between a delay and an abrupt halt.

▶ Arrange signals for your students. If they have asked three other people for the answer to a question and still need help, then they can signal you by holding up a sign with a giant "?" on it. You could ask them to let you know their progress by a thumbs up or thumbs down when you make a check.

USE A SYLLABUS TO PREVENT PROBLEMS

Most of us can recall from our own college days the advantages of using a syllabus. We used a syllabus to plan projects and papers, keep track of daily assignments, anticipate the more interesting lecture topics, check due dates, schedule extra study time for tests, and just stay organized in general (see page 210). Too few of us, however, pass these advantages on to our students for a variety of reasons, most of which deal with a lack of confidence in our ability to plan in such a structured fashion.

▶ A syllabus not only helps students stay organized, but it also promotes self-discipline. Students who know what to do and when they are supposed to do it are much more likely to be better behaved than those who are confused or who don't know what they are supposed to do in order to succeed in your class. A syllabus allows students to take responsibility for their learning by letting them see the big picture of what they are supposed to learn. The benefits of a syllabus to you and your students far outweigh any reluctance you might feel for not giving it a try.

▶ When designing your own syllabus, don't just list study topics and dates. There are many things you can add to a syllabus to help your students become more organized and self-disciplined. Try adding some or all of these items to yours:

- Simple drawings or cartoons
- Space for students to record their grades
- Space for classroom activities
- Space for homework assignments
- Space for class objectives
- Inspirational messages

▶ In addition to these items, you will also need to teach your students how to use a syllabus. You will have to work hard at first to get them in the habit of checking it instead of just asking you what the homework is, but the effort will soon be rewarded when you see your students begin to take responsibility for their work.

▶ A syllabus can serve as a planner/organizer for your students if you show them how to use it for a personal planner also. They can circle the dates on which they are absent from class, underline any make-up work that's due, and keep track of their goals in the class.

▶ If you are not confident about using a syllabus, start small. Put a week's worth of work on your first syllabus and then expand it when you and your students are comfortably using it regularly.

▶ One way to handle the problem of schedule changes is to build in flexible time. Allow an unscheduled day every two weeks or so to compensate for the time that is often lost to the numerous interruptions that seem to plague our school days. Be sure to use that day in productive activity, however, not just as free time simply because it was initially unscheduled.

- Don't be afraid to change your syllabus. It's tempting sometimes to schedule more work than can be realistically accomplished in the allotted time. Don't hesitate to work with your students to drop, add, or shift items on the syllabus. In fact, your students will appreciate it if you check with them about their other class schedules and try to arrange user-friendly deadlines whenever possible.

- Keep in mind that a syllabus can be much more than a listing of topics. It can be an effective tool for teaching your students time management, developing organizational skills, and preventing discipline problems.

WHEN YOU NEED A SUBSTITUTE

What do you want to think about while you are at home feverish with flu? Do you wonder if your students are working quietly, or do you convince yourself that they are gleefully tormenting the hapless substitute? Have you created the kind of classroom environment where students are self-directed in your absence?

It's not easy to miss school if you are a responsible teacher. So much could go wrong that many of us go to work even when we are not well rather than have to deal with a substitute and the problems that missing a day of school can cause. However, you *can* maintain a climate of positive discipline when there is a substitute teacher in your place.

Instead of hoping that you will never be absent, take an hour or so to get organized, and you will be able to trust your students to continue as if you were with them. While a large part of the discipline problems that occur when you are out can be attributed to the inability of the substitute teacher to maintain your standards and contain the high spirits of your students, the solution to these problems lies with you. There are many steps you can take to see that your class runs smoothly even though you are not in the room.

- Make it a point to use your leave sparingly. You will set a good example for your students; they need you in the classroom. You also need to have plenty of accumulated leave time in case you are in an accident or some other serious misfortune befalls you.

- As soon as you know that you are going to be absent, secure a substitute. The competent ones are usually booked weeks in advance.

- Be kind to your sub. Don't leave material to be photocopied or written on the board. If you don't have time to do it, chances are that your sub won't either. The most frequent substitute complaints are no lesson plans, plans that are impossible to follow, no seating chart, missing materials or equipment, and not enough for the students to do.

- Whenever possible, communicate directly with your students before or during your absence. They will appreciate this show of respect that you have for their maturity, and you will appreciate the lack of confusion and trouble that this simple act will save all of you.

- Very early in the year, set up a folder with the routine information any substitute would need to run your class smoothly. Include these items in it:
  - An up-to-date seating chart
  - A photocopy of your roster
  - A daily schedule

- A copy of the school rules
- A copy of your class rules and procedures
- Fire drill and emergency information
- The names of student helpers
- The names of students with special needs (in case you have a sub who does not believe in sending sick children to the school nurse)
- The names and room numbers of helpful colleagues
- Hall passes
- A copy of your daily schedule
- Where you would like for the sub to leave your plans
- A scratch pad so the sub can leave notes

▶ You should also make a folder of emergency plans to be used in case you cannot get your plans to school. These can be high-interest worksheets or activities that require very little instruction. If you are really cautious, you will leave enough plans for five days. Save time by using the same emergency plans every year. The time you spend early in the year on organizing materials for possible use by a substitute will save you stress when you are ill or rushed for time later.

▶ If you have time, consider taking photographs of your students while they are seated in their assigned seats. Print these photographs and label them so that the sub can easily identify those students who may not be in their assigned seats or who may be misbehaving. When students are aware that you have done this, they tend to behave better.

▶ Don't leave a film for a substitute to show while you are out. Students won't take it as seriously as when you are there, and technical difficulties could cause problems. Don't assign a trip to the library, either. Students tend to be disruptive whenever there's a break in the routine. Use your common sense instead. Plan a quiet lesson of independent work that is easy for your sub and your students to follow.

▶ Make the lesson you leave for your students meaningful. Drills and review exercises are good. Be sure your substitute knows to collect the papers for the day's work so that you can see who was on-task and who wasn't. You should also ask for a grade on the assignments your students do while you are out. Be sure you have the sub tell them that this will happen so that they will be encouraged to stay on-task.

▶ Teach your students what to do when you are out. Hold them to the same standards of behavior and performance as when you are there with them. You might even want to role-play some scenarios of possible substitute problems with them. Select a few students to be substitute assistants early in the term. Discuss their duties so that they can help the substitute keep the instruction running smoothly.

▶ Be sure to specify in your plans whether you want students to work together during an activity. Many substitutes are not comfortable with the noise level associated with group activities.

▶ Put yourself in your sub's place. Would you be able to walk into an unfamiliar classroom filled with unfamiliar adolescents and immediately follow your plans?

▶ If you need to be on an extended leave, stay in contact with your principal. Parents and other staff members will ask about you, and your supervisor needs to be able to answer their questions. Work as closely as you can with your substitute to maintain the direction you want the instruction to take. This is the only time you should leave your grade book with a substitute. Do everything you can to minimize the disruption in learning as well as to protect your professional reputation.

To learn more about how you can make positive choices that will enhance your ability to use effective instructional practices to maintain an orderly classroom, see this section's "Making Positive Choices."

Making Positive Choices

Instead of . . .	Try to . . .
▶ Offering instruction to bored students	▶ Help students make a personal connection to the material
▶ Presenting overused activities that no longer interest your students	▶ Use media, online sites, competition, rewards, or other interest builders throughout a lesson
▶ Offering whole-group instruction	▶ Differentiate instruction to meet the needs of all of your students
▶ Doing most of the talking during a class period	▶ Encourage students to collaborate and discuss the material
▶ Having the students sit and wait for others to finish their assignments	▶ Pace instruction so that another assignment is ready each time the students finish their work
▶ Assigning homework as a punishment	▶ Remember that the purpose of homework should be to extend learning, not punish
▶ Wasting time during a class discussion	▶ Have the students organize their thoughts by writing their ideas before sharing with the class
▶ Repeating students' oral responses so that the entire class can hear	▶ Encourage students to speak loudly enough for others to hear and for the rest of the class to listen carefully
▶ Offering class review games that have grown stale	▶ Shake things up by having the students play online games to review
▶ Having the students browse inappropriate sites	▶ Be clear about the expectations and procedures for using a computer in school

QUESTIONS FOR REFLECTION

Use the information in this section to guide your thinking as you reflect on these questions. They are designed to encourage you to think more deeply about the issues in the text or to discuss those issues with colleagues.

▶ How important is effective instruction to a positive discipline climate? How have you seen evidence of this in your own school experiences?

▶ Which of the instructional techniques in this section are ones that you would like to explore? How will you go about this?

▶ How important is technology in your daily instruction? How do you keep up with this rapidly changing field?

SECTION TEN

Promote Achievement and Learning

In this section you will learn

- How to employ motivational techniques
- How to offer assistance with study skills
- How to provide critical-thinking skill activities
- How to help students benefit from formative assessments
- How to establish a culture of excellence

THE ROLE MOTIVATION PLAYS IN A POSITIVE DISCIPLINE PLAN

In classrooms where the discipline climate is positive, teachers motivate, encourage, and challenge their students not just to grudgingly comply with the class requirements, but also to move on to be self-determined about their academic work. When students are motivated to perform well, then school is not just successful but fun for everyone.

The lack of motivation that you may see in your students is not a new phenomenon nor is it limited to your classroom. The reasons that students are not interested in doing their work are ones that teachers everywhere grapple with. Here are just a few of the more common ones:

▶ The work is too difficult, too easy, not relevant, or boring.

▶ Students are distracted by a classmate or an event that happened outside of school.

▶ Their home culture may have different values from the values of their school.

▶ Students may have undiagnosed learning problems.

- Many students have trouble working quietly for extended periods.
- The assignments do not appeal to their preferred learning styles.
- Students may have life goals that are unrealistic.
- Some students may have little or no curiosity about the lesson.
- They perceive their teacher or classmates as uncaring.
- Students may lack the necessary prerequisite skills or background knowledge to be able to do the work.
- Their peers mock them for academic success.
- Students believe that the work is not relevant to their immediate or future needs.
- They cannot read or write well enough to do the work.
- No one at home stresses that they need to do well in school.

In the face of these daunting reasons for our students' lack of motivation, it is not always easy to find the right approach that will encourage our students to be interested enough in what our class offers to stay focused on their work. Savvy teachers use many techniques, strategies, tips, and activities to appeal to as many of our students as often as we can. A multifaceted approach to the complex and challenging problem of reaching and teaching our students is a tactic that works for many of us.

You can also encourage your students by using the online site BoostUp (www.boostup.org). At Boost-Up you can help students sign up for an encouraging motivational message delivered in various ways. The premise of this inspiring campaign is to encourage at-risk students to stay in school long enough to graduate and be successful citizens.

MAKE SURE STUDENTS KNOW HOW TO DO THEIR WORK

One of the most obvious ways to motivate students to stay on-task and perform well in your class is to make sure that they know how to do their work. When students are not sure of what they are supposed to do to after you have given either verbal or written directions, then it is only natural that they will be not interested in trying to complete an incomprehensible assignment.

Fortunately, learning to give clear and coherent instructions is a skill that is easy to master (see "How Well Do You Give Instructions?" that follows). Begin by making sure that the instructions you give are in line with the objectives for your course and that your students are aware of this. When students know how their instruction fits into the standards or objectives of a course, then they have a context for their work that makes it easier for them to understand the purpose of the assignment.

Teach your students to stop what they are doing and listen to you as you explain what they are supposed to do. Commanding your students' attention is important if you want to ensure that they know how they are supposed to accomplish their work.

As you give either written or verbal directions, make sure that you do not flood your students with too much information at once. Break the instructions into small, manageable steps that students can follow independently if necessary.

Be brief, logical, and focused when giving directions. Don't throw in extraneous information that may confuse students. Be specific and direct instead.

If you see that students are not clear about what to do, don't hesitate to offer examples and more explanation. Sometimes asking students to restate the directions themselves will be sufficient to allow everyone to have the same understanding of the requirements of an assignment.

Teacher Self-Assessment

HOW WELL DO YOU GIVE INSTRUCTIONS?

In the list below, you will find seven statements about the way that you give instructions to your students. In the blank beside each one, estimate how often you meet these expectations for successfully giving instructions.

1. *Always*   *Sometimes*   *Never*   I command their attention.

2. *Always*   *Sometimes*   *Never*   I allow enough wait time for students to have a chance to focus.

3. *Always*   *Sometimes*   *Never*   I break down assignments into manageable steps.

4. *Always*   *Sometimes*   *Never*   I state my directions in a positive way.

5. *Always*   *Sometimes*   *Never*   I reinforce verbal directions with a written example.

6. *Always*   *Sometimes*   *Never*   My students feel as if they can ask me to repeat the directions.

7. *Always*   *Sometimes*   *Never*   I seek clarification from my students.

STUDY SKILLS APPROPRIATE FOR SECONDARY STUDENTS

One of the most effective ways to motivate students to succeed is to make sure that they know how to do their work quickly and accurately. Many secondary teachers assume that their students were taught how to study during their earlier school years, but this is seldom what happens. It is also important for you to teach the specific study skills necessary for success in your particular discipline.

Incorporating study skills into your class will not be difficult if you choose one or two useful skills to focus on in each lesson. For example, if you are going to lecture, begin by teaching students how to take notes while listening. Teachers who take the time to show students study skills such as how to keep an organized binder or take good notes provide valuable assistance in helping students learn to be independent learners.

Another technique that many teachers have found helpful is to teach a new study skill each day. In the list below you will find study tips appropriate for daily use.

In General

- Do your work correctly the first time so that you do not have to redo it.
- Make a study schedule and stick to it.
- Use your strengths. For example, if you learn best by doing, then be an active student. If you are able to memorize facts quickly, develop and use that skill.
- Use small blocks of time.
- Pay attention to your syllabus or course outline so that you can anticipate the material you will be expected to learn.
- Use color to keep your supplies and materials organized.
- Get in the habit of trying to learn material the first time you see it instead of delaying your learning.
- Have an organized space set aside as a study area.
- Talk with your classmates about the successful study techniques that they use.
- Assemble materials for projects in advance of the time that you will need them.
- Use the record feature of your cell phone to record important information and notes.
- Prioritize your responsibilities so that you can accomplish the work you need to do.

Writing Assignments

- Make your work as neat and legible as possible.
- Type your work whenever you can. Use a spellchecker and a grammar checker to make sure your work is free from careless errors.
- Look over your paper one last time before turning it in.
- Reread the assignment directions to make sure that you know exactly what the requirements are.
- Take the time to carefully label all the parts of your assignments.

Reading Assignments

▶ Begin a reading assignment with a preview of the text.

▶ Try the SQ3R method when you have unfamiliar text to read: Survey, Question, Read, Recite, and Review.

▶ Maintain a personal dictionary of words that you learn as you read. Don't hesitate to check definitions as you read.

▶ Make a point of learning a new word each day. A good source for this is the word of the day feature at www.dictionary.com.

▶ Use self-sticking notes as you read to keep track of key ideas, information, vocabulary terms, or questions you may have as you read.

▶ Use a highlighter whenever possible to identify important information and areas that you would like to explore further.

▶ Look for key ideas as you read. Use text features to help you with this.

▶ Look for supporting details that can help you understand the key ideas in a passage.

▶ Be an active reader who highlights, asks questions, outlines, and takes notes as you involve yourself in the text.

Homework

▶ When you record homework assignments, be sure to write them down correctly.

▶ Before you begin, estimate the time that you will need to complete your assignments so that you can plan how to accomplish your work well.

▶ Use your daylight hours to do homework whenever possible.

▶ Do your hardest or most boring assignments first.

▶ Practice until you understand the material.

▶ Make a schedule of how you plan to do your homework and stick to your schedule.

▶ Take minibreaks at intervals.

▶ Avoid distractions such as the phone or the Internet.

▶ Set minigoals and reward yourself when you accomplish each one.

▶ Pace yourself so that you will be able to accomplish your work without stress.

▶ Plan to finish all of your homework.

▶ Put your assignments in your binder at the end of a work session so that you will remember to take them to school.

Listening

▶ When you are in class, listen actively so that you can ask meaningful questions if necessary.

▶ Take notes as your teacher delivers instruction.

▶ Be careful to pay attention and take notes when a teacher repeats information for emphasis.

- Arrange with a classmate to share notes after class in case either of you misses information.
- If your computer is open in class when an instructor is talking, don't be distracted. Pay attention to the teacher instead of your computer.
- Create an outline of the information you hear so that you can organize your thoughts.

Note Taking

- Use your own abbreviation system for commonly used words.
- Review your notes within twenty-four hours to make sure that you have mastered the information.
- Use graphic organizers instead of paragraphs as you take notes.
- Space your notes out on a page so that you have room to add to them or annotate as you study.
- Use the two-column method of note taking. This method allows you to write information as you read or listen and then review it later using key words or summaries to learn the material.
- Make sure that your notes are legible enough that you can read them later.
- It is better to have too many notes than not to have recorded information that you need to study.
- Be logical and orderly in the way that you organize your notes. You must be able to refer to them later.
- When you are taking notes on a reading assignment, use the glossaries and the table of contents to help you understand the material and take thorough notes.
- Writing a summary of your notes in your own words is an excellent way to learn the material.
- Put your notes on flash cards whenever you can. If you color code your flash cards, it will be even easier for you to recall information.

Class Time

- Use your time in class wisely. Focus on learning instead of the activities of your classmates.
- Settle down to work quickly.
- Have your materials ready so that you do not have to waste time looking for supplies.
- Sit near the teacher if possible so that you can avoid distractions.
- Be prepared for class by reading or previewing the material in advance. Much of the work that students do in secondary classes requires independent preparation.
- If you have a few minutes between activities or at the end of class, review notes, preview material, or study. Try not to waste time.

Test Preparation

- Use a combination of different methods to prepare for a test. Listen to an audio tape, rewrite your notes, and study with a friend instead of just "looking over" your notes.
- Explain difficult concepts to a classmate or study buddy as you try to learn them.

- Don't try to cram right before a test.
- Study in brief, intense bursts of concentration.
- As you learn material, try to anticipate potential test questions.
- Spend enough time studying so that you can learn all of the material.
- Only study the material that you do not know.
- Make sure that you know what the test will cover.
- Get enough rest so that you can think clearly.

Test Taking

- Survey a test before you begin answering questions.
- Pay attention to the verbal directions that your teacher gives at the start of a test.
- Read the directions several times to make sure that you understand exactly what you are supposed to do.
- When you have matching or multiple-choice questions, scan all possible answers.
- Don't leave any questions unanswered if you possibly can avoid doing so. Attempt to earn at least partial credit.
- Use the process of elimination when you have multiple-choice questions. This will increase your chances of being able to guess correctly if you are not sure of an answer.

POSITIVE REINFORCEMENT MAKES THE DIFFERENCE

One of the most successful tools secondary teachers have in dealing with misbehavior in the classroom is the use of positive reinforcement—a far stronger motivational tool than negative reinforcement. In other words, rewards, encouragement, praise, and intrinsic motivation are far more effective than punishment in helping students learn to control themselves. Positive reinforcement is a powerful tool because it allows us to reach students who are so used to negativity that they are no longer strongly affected by it. Positive reinforcement allows us to give valuable support to the student behavior, improvement, and effort that we want to see again.

What reinforcement theory gives the classroom teacher is a useful way to help students see that they have choices to make in every action they take. Students can be encouraged to see the benefits of choices that will result in a positive consequence. By immediately reinforcing behaviors that we want students to continue, we show them the connection between their behavior and a positive consequence.

When we set a supportive tone in our relationships with students through positive reinforcement, we tend to encourage their good behavior and discourage the bad. Finally, we also benefit because this type of reinforcement will move students away from a competitive atmosphere and toward the intrinsic motivation that is so necessary for self-discipline.

USE ENCOURAGEMENT AND PRAISE

While there are many different ways to motivate students to succeed, both encouragement and praise are important aspects of the positive reinforcement that is a necessary part of a productive discipline environment. Those teachers who want their students to perform well should praise and encourage their students every day.

While they are similar in that both are examples of positive reinforcement, praise and encouragement differ in significant ways. Praise tends to be general and to focus on the student. When teachers tell their students that they are "superstars," for example, they are offering praise.

Encouragement draws specific attention to the student's work and effort. For example, when a teacher writes, "The way that you've explained this process is logical and well thought-out," the comment is directed to a student's work and not to the student. Both can serve as formative assessments whose purpose is to offer sincere and constructive feedback. Both should be an integral part of your classroom discipline plan.

HOW TO USE ENCOURAGEMENT AND PRAISE EFFECTIVELY

▶ Be careful not to overdo it. Being gushy or overdramatic will render your words ineffective because students will regard them as insincere.

▶ Be straightforward in what you say. Vary the words you use so that students will know you are paying attention to them as individuals.

▶ Be sure that your approval is for the actions of your students, not for the worth of the students themselves if you want to encourage good behavior.

▶ Make a point of saying something positive to every student every day. Many of us unconsciously tend to favor one gender over another or some students over others. Be careful to reach everyone.

▶ Make your approval specific. Students who have a clear idea of what they did right can continue that behavior. Don't say, "Nice job!" Instead give specific comments that will indicate what was "nice" so that students will have a clear sense of what they need to do to continue the good behavior.

▶ Be aware of the connection between your body language and the words you say. Let your facial expression and tone express your approval and interest as well as your words do.

▶ Be sensitive to whether students would prefer public or private recognition. Some students, shy or simply self-conscious, would prefer not to be in the limelight for any reason. Others thrive on public recognition. Be very careful to respect their preferences.

▶ Don't compare students with their classmates. Let them see that you appreciate their behavior for its own worth.

▶ Phone home or send an e-mail whenever students have reached a major goal. Parents or guardians should be part of the reinforcement whenever possible.

EMPLOY EXTRINSIC MOTIVATION

Extrinsic motivation is a type of positive reinforcement that deals with tangible rewards serving as behavior motivators for students. While it can be tempting to use extrinsic motivation too often, one of the dangers of tangible rewards is that students may become so interested in the reward itself that they lose sight of the intrinsic motivation you want them to develop.

Be careful not to overstress the rewards you offer students. If rewards are to be valued by students, they must be contingent upon good behavior, not just on the personality of a student. You should also make certain to pair a reward with praise. If you don't help students make this connection, they may not fully understand that they earn rewards through their own efforts and good behavior.

Rewards that you can use to reinforce positive student behavior usually fall into two categories: items that students receive and activities that students enjoy. Use this list of both types of rewards to spice up your motivational techniques.

Items That Students Receive

- An honor such as being voted "Most Improved Student"
- Badges or buttons
- Certificates
- Bookmarks
- Extra time to complete an assignment
- Having their photographs appear on the class Web page
- Peer recognition
- Being included in the class honor roll
- Having their names displayed on a classroom wall of fame
- A thank-you note from their teacher
- Having you send a positive e-mail or note home
- Having you call home with a positive message
- Stickers

Activities That Students Enjoy

- Tutoring other students
- Attending a banquet
- Creating a bulletin board
- Videotaping an activity
- Completing an alternative assignment
- Doing homework for another class
- Participating in a special project
- Watching a film
- Being team captain
- Displaying work for others to see
- Going on a field trip
- Solving puzzles
- Writing notes to a classmate
- Being selected as a discussion moderator

- ▶ Having a free reading period
- ▶ Using the library during free time
- ▶ Being elected as class representative
- ▶ Being included in a class lottery for prizes

TECHNIQUES FOR INCREASING INTRINSIC MOTIVATION

Some of the greatest joys in a teacher's life are those happy moments when we realize all of our students want to do the work that we have assigned. We revel in the happy hum of their chatter as they settle down to tackle the problems posed in their assignments. The sense of satisfaction we feel when our students are excited about their work is one of the chief reasons that so many of us look forward to school each morning year after year.

Students who are busy doing their work just don't have time to misbehave. The challenge for all secondary teachers, of course, is how to create that desire to work in every student every day—day after day, week after week.

The most effective way to promote excellent behavior, however, is intrinsic motivation. Intrinsic motivation is the incentive to work that is an essential part of the lesson plan or presentation. It is not a separate component, but rather, is built into the lesson itself.

Intrinsic motivation is the most effective stimulus to student achievement because its effect lasts much longer. Tangible rewards tend to be short-lived and not very useful once the student has or has not won a prize. For a long-term, fundamental change in students, intrinsic motivation has been proven to be successful over and over again.

There are many ways to include intrinsic motivation techniques in a lesson. Many effective teachers seem to do this instinctively by using a variety of strategies to sustain their students' interest in each assignment. All of us who want to motivate our students to achieve more or to perform at higher levels of success will follow their example and include more strategies for intrinsic motivation in our own lessons.

To boost your students' interest and desire to work productively, experiment with the following techniques that will help you build intrinsic motivation into your assignments. Try to include more than one in each lesson to reach as many students as possible.

- ▶ Stimulate your students' curiosity by making your lessons suspenseful and novel. Most teens are interested in the new and different. Use this inclination to make a mystery out of old material.

- ▶ Teach students to evaluate their own progress throughout a unit of study. Begin or end class by asking them to tell you what they have learned, what skill they have mastered, or what they have accomplished. You can even say to them, "You'll know you're on the right track when . . . " and have them finish the statement.

- ▶ Don't work against the nature of your students. Instead, adapt their interests, hobbies, concerns, experiences, dreams, and cultural backgrounds into lessons as often as you can in order to make the material compelling for them.

- ▶ Use your students' competitive instincts to your advantage. Instead of pitting one student against another, try putting students in teams to oppose other teams of students. However, the best sort of competition to foster is the effort that a student can make to improve his or her own performance. Get students into the habit of asking themselves how they can improve each assignment so that it is better than the previous one.

▶ Help students make a personal connection to the lesson. They should be able to identify with the people in the material under study. One simple way to do this is to use their names when creating worksheets or questions. Another is to have students involve themselves in the material through a written response. An example of this strategy in a history class, for instance, would be to have students describe how they would find food, shelter, and clothing if they were to find themselves suddenly transported to ancient Greece. In written responses such as these students are forced to deal with compelling concerns rather than dry facts.

▶ Include assignments that require higher-level thinking skills. When students are asked to evaluate or judge material, they are doing much more interesting work than those students whose teachers only ask them to comprehend information. Open-ended questions are inherently interesting because they do not risk a student's self-esteem. Students who are afraid of failure will be able to complete these questions successfully.

▶ Expand on your students' previous learning. Once you have done this, it shouldn't be too hard to help them move on to the new learning you want them to master.

▶ Use a variety of media when you want to galvanize your students into paying close attention. Adapt these to the needs of your students: newspapers, advertisements, music, T-shirt slogans, cartoons, 3-D material, movies, art, computers, television, magazines, radio, and videos.

▶ Play games with your students. There are many different kinds of games your students will enjoy playing in class. You could use sophisticated computer games or the low-tech ones that have been popular with students for years. (See Section Nine for more information on classroom games.)

▶ Put students who are in teams in charge of the successful learning of their teammates. A successful team project involves giving each student part of the information that they will all need to know. After each person has presented his or her part to the rest of the group, the entire group will benefit from the successful teaching by their teammates.

▶ Make one assignment dependent on the successful completion of another. Tell students they won't be able to move on to the next project until they have acquired the learning they will need from the first assignment.

▶ Be enthusiastic and project that enthusiasm to your students. Never admit that you find an assignment dull or that you fear they will find it less than intriguing or exciting themselves. Do all that you can to get students excited about what they have to learn. Hold a pep rally before a quiz if that is what it takes to generate enthusiasm.

▶ Remember the old saying, "Nothing succeeds like success." Design lessons that are easier at the beginning of the term so that your students can experience immediate success in your class. This will be much more effective than if they do poorly at first.

▶ Include opportunities for your students to use their imaginations and to indulge in fantasy in your class. The enormous success of computer simulation games should show educators the power of our students' imaginations. Even in classes that don't appear to lend themselves to this type of work, a creative teacher will find a way. For example, in math class, teachers could ask students to imagine holding a conversation with Archimedes, Pascal, or Euclid and then write about it.

▶ Have older students serve as mentors to younger ones. Either older students could mentor your students or yours could mentor younger students or, hopefully, both. What mentors do that is successful is to show students what they need to know in order to succeed in school. In order to make good life choices for themselves, students need to see that others have done it and that they can, too.

- ▶ Keep parents or guardians involved in class activities. Make sure you inform them of due dates for big projects and other information that will help them encourage their children to do well in your class.

- ▶ Make sure the appreciation you show your students is focused on the positive qualities you observe about their work habits or their assignments. If they know exactly what they have been doing right, students will be encouraged to keep trying to do well.

- ▶ Encourage open-mindedness and tolerance in your students so that they won't be afraid to take intellectual risks. Many students are so afraid of failure and rejection that they are not willing to share their ideas and expertise with others.

- ▶ Pace your lesson delivery so that time doesn't drag for your students. Move quickly from one point to the next in a smooth flow of assignments so that students don't waste time.

- ▶ Involve your students in projects of all types—simple and complicated, long-term and short-term.

- ▶ Project an air of confidence to your students. They should feel you have unshakable faith in their ability to succeed at every assignment.

- ▶ Too often students are kept in the dark about the "big picture." They don't understand how one assignment will lead to others. They don't see why they should learn certain skills or material. Combat this fragmented approach to their education by giving each one a course outline and by using a syllabus.

- ▶ Be explicit about the criteria for success on each assignment so that students know what it is they have to do to be successful.

- ▶ Break larger assignments into manageable amounts of work with clear deadlines. Provide checklists or other graphic organizers to help students stay focused. When students see each assignment as part of a progression of work, they will be more inclined to complete each assignment.

- ▶ Include a variety of learning styles and modalities in each assignment. Students who are encouraged to learn in a variety of ways will be more successful than those who aren't.

- ▶ Use a variety of assessment techniques so that if a student fails at one evaluation, he or she won't quit trying because of one low grade.

- ▶ Give daily feedback to students. Return papers promptly. Monitor progress by staying on your feet and interacting with your students. Teach students to give each other feedback by proofreading or double-checking each other's work.

- ▶ Reward effort. Not every pupil will master every lesson to your satisfaction, but you should recognize those who try their best.

- ▶ Provide many opportunities for students to display their work and to be recognized for their accomplishments. This will keep them focused on the important things in class, not on misbehaving. This technique is especially effective for the troublemakers in your class who have grown accustomed to attention for the wrong reasons.

- ▶ Hold your students accountable for their work. Use graphic organizers such as checklists, charts, and calendars. Have them assess their own progress and determine what they need to do to stay successful.

- Inspiring messages, banners, posters, and "thoughts of the day" mean more to most students than we can ever imagine. You never know when the right words will help a struggling student.

- Listen to your students and remain flexible. Students should have a strong voice in the classroom. Teachers who are able to successfully respond to student concerns will create the class climate where students are motivated to do their best.

- Use technology. Computers are inherently interesting to most students who may quickly grow bored with applying pen to paper. Using technology can make even mundane tasks easier and more interesting.

AROUSE STUDENT CURIOSITY

One of the surest ways to motivate students to do their work is to stimulate their inquisitive natures when confronted with unfamiliar material. Even though no two classes are alike, you can still find many different ways to capture and hold your students' attention by arousing their curiosity about the subject under study. The following list provides some simple and quick ideas you can adopt to motivate your students to stay on task by heightening their eagerness to learn more about the material in a lesson:

- Do the unexpected: sing, pass out crayons, wear a silly hat, draw cartoons on the board, and so on.

- Start dropping hints about the interesting information they will learn in an upcoming unit. Refuse to do more than just drop mysterious hints.

- Ask your students questions about the material that they are about to learn.

- Hang twinkling lights to spotlight an important part of the lesson.

- Download some of the royalty-free sound effects from Partners in Rhyme (www.partnersinrhyme .com) to create a sound montage related to an upcoming topic of study.

- Hold up a box filled with objects relevant to the lesson and ask students to guess what's in it. You can also ask students to connect the objects to the lesson.

- Move desks around or ask students to trade places with each other in preparation for an exciting class.

- Write several seemingly unrelated words on the board and ask students to predict how they could be related to the day's lesson.

- Hand out blindfolds and have students put them on. Give them objects from the lesson for them to identify without peeking.

- Wear a costume or have costumes for your students to wear.

- Have students fill in a partially completed graphic organizer before the lesson begins and then check it afterward to see how well they knew the material.

- Show a video of you introducing the lesson.

- Have groups of students create brief videotapes about upcoming lessons and show them to their classmates as a preview.

- Ask students to make a post on a classroom wiki page.

- Write a famous saying on the board and ask students to predict how it will fit into the day's lesson.

- Tell students, "Once you finish this assignment, you will be able to . . ."

- Put the topic on a sheet of paper and pass it around the room asking students to write what they already know about it.

- Decorate your classroom to match the topic of the lesson.

- Display a word wall with the unusual words from upcoming lessons.

- Write words that are relevant to the lesson on construction paper. Hand them out and have the students unscramble them to re-create a sentence.

- Give the students a list of key words and phrases to watch for when you introduce new material. Pass out simple rewards for the first students to notice them.

- Have the students try to complete a handout with statements about upcoming material.

- Ask the students to solve an online jigsaw puzzle at Jig Zone (www.jigzone.com) or Jig Saw Planet (www.jigsawplanet.com). At both sites you can upload your own images to create a puzzle related to the day's topic.

- Count off the students into teams without first telling them why they will be working in groups.

- Ask the students to view a slide-show presentation of teaser slides about the topic.

- Show the class a montage of photographs and graphic images to preview the material.

- Have the students guess the answers to riddles that relate to the lesson.

- Turn off the lights in preparation for an especially dramatic part of the lesson.

BUILD CRITICAL-THINKING SKILLS

One of the strongest movements in education in recent years is the emphasis on critical-thinking skills. Unlike some educational fads that have had a deservedly short shelf life because they can only be used for a few students, the new emphasis on critical-thinking skills applies to all students. Older teens as well as younger ones can benefit from activities that are designed to help them develop their thinking skills.

Critical-thinking and creative-thinking activities can enhance the learning in any classroom because, while they are enjoyable, they are also effective skills for increasing retention and successful performance. Those students whose teachers help them develop their critical-thinking skills are much more likely to be productive and on-task than those students who slog through rote memorization exercises. They are also far less likely to dream up ways to disrupt class than those frustrated students who liven up the lesson by acting out.

In order to expand their thinking skills, pupils need to have a knowledge of the subject matter, a knowledge of the various types of thinking skills you expect them to use, and plenty of opportunities for practice.

Be careful to avoid a common mistake made by many well-intended but misguided teachers. Don't teach critical-thinking skills in isolation from the other work your students do. Setting aside one day every month to focus on critical-thinking skills is not a good idea. Your students simply won't benefit from this. They need to practice critical thinking often in order to develop their skills. It is better to make critical thinking part of the everyday work in your class.

One of the easiest ways to begin to include critical-thinking activities in your classroom is to start slowly and then raise the awareness level of your students so that they begin to recognize the various levels of thinking they are expected to do in school and in life.

Here are some strategies for incorporating critical thinking into your class. Many of these ideas should help you prevent discipline problems from beginning because students are engaged in their work.

How to Raise Awareness

▶ Your students need a copy of Bloom's Taxonomy to keep in their notebooks. You should also enlarge a copy and post it in your classroom. You will need the common vocabulary if you are to teach your students to think.

▶ Have students get into the habit of labeling the question types in assignments to raise their awareness of the types of thinking they could be doing.

▶ Another way to have students increase their levels of awareness about critical thinking is to have them make posters illustrating each type.

Some Pointers for Success

▶ Encourage your students to be open-minded and tolerant when they listen to each other's ideas. Strive to build a community of trust in your classroom so that hesitant students will not be afraid to take risks.

▶ In addition to being open-minded about each other's responses, your students should also work to be open-minded about ideas of their own that seem odd or far-fetched. All great inventions and discoveries begin with a fresh idea.

▶ Put students in groups to brainstorm, solve problems, form a consensus, or do any of the countless other activities that a group situation inspires in students who are working on their thinking skills.

▶ Use critical thinking to help students unlock what they already know about a subject and then help them discover more on their own. Ask them to make connections between new material and previously learned information. It's especially effective if students can make these connections between subjects that do not seem to be related at all.

▶ Teach your students to look beyond the surface. Have them study an object, such as a small piece of gravel, and collect ideas about it until they have exhausted every possibility. Students will be surprised at what their classmates noticed when they share ideas.

▶ Give your students enough time to think when you ask them a question that is not just a recalling of facts. Allowing students to jot down possible responses will ensure this.

▶ Small details are important when students are practicing their critical-thinking skills. Teach your students to key in on these as well as on the "big picture."

▶ Homework will be more effective if it involves critical thinking rather than rote exercises. Give meaningful homework assignments to spare you and your students from discipline problems.

▶ Games, puzzles, riddles, time-management sponges, logic quizzes, and other lively exercises are perfect ways to stimulate your students' thinking skills.

▶ Use time that might be wasted. Opening and closing exercises are good times to practice these skills with your students. Since this time is often wasted, you have nothing to lose in trying a brief critical-thinking exercise with your class.

▶ Be sure to model the skill you are trying to teach so that your students understand the criteria for success. Many examples will reassure your students that they are on the right track.

▶ Have your students deal with real-world issues as often as you can so that they can connect their textbook learning to their futures. Use advertisements and clippings from magazines and newspapers as well as audio-visual support whenever you can to stimulate your students' thinking.

▶ Teach your students the research techniques that are appropriate for your subject matter and for the age level of your students. Students need to be able to retrieve and manipulate information quickly. Technology can also speed up this process if your students are computer literate.

▶ Students who get to interact with each other learn more successfully than students who are in classrooms where they are encouraged to sit still and be quiet.

▶ Organize material around big ideas and concepts if you want students to connect it to other learning and retain it.

▶ Students need to take responsibility for their learning. Encourage them to become involved in how they learn, how they approach the material, and even in gathering the additional material that they would like to study for enrichment.

▶ If you want students to learn from their mistakes, don't write corrections. Show them how to revise and edit instead.

▶ Encourage students to ask questions. Those students who bug you with questions are probably more motivated than those polite students who are sitting passively watching you work.

▶ It is crucial that you make your students aware of their thinking processes and how to use reasoning skills effectively.

▶ It is better to teach a small amount of information in depth than to cover a huge range of material as fast as you can.

▶ If you want students to do their work, they have to see a valuable reason for doing that work.

▶ Students need knowledge as well as skills in order to think critically and approach their work with enthusiasm.

QUESTIONS THAT SPARK CRITICAL THINKING

One of the easiest ways to involve your students in higher-level thinking skills is by asking open-ended questions designed to stimulate and direct thought. Open-ended questions provide a nonthreatening opportunity for your students to shine. Questions that require students to think, but at the same time have no real incorrect answers, will give your students confidence as well as practice in decision making.

In the list below you will find some general questions grouped according to Bloom's Taxonomy. These can be adapted to almost any classroom or to almost any group of students. Of course, there are thousands more that you can use, but these questions should help you focus on the vital critical-thinking skills necessary for student success.

Comprehension

▶ What advice does your group have for my future students about this project?

▶ Write a summary of today's class notes in fewer than one hundred words.

▶ What are some things we can learn from this experience?

▶ What have your previous teachers done to help you review for an important test that we could try here?

Application

▶ What steps did your group take to arrive at that answer?

▶ What did you learn in another class today that you can use in this class right now?

▶ What did you learn in this class today that you can apply to another class?

▶ How can you apply what you have learned today in class to your own life right away?

▶ How will you use what you learned today in the future?

▶ How could you modify today's lesson to make it easier to remember all of the key issues in it?

▶ What organizational skills do you have that you can teach to the class?

▶ What are some logical ways to set up your notebooks for maximum efficiency?

Analysis

▶ What is the quickest way to learn the facts in today's lesson?

▶ What are the underlying principles that govern the lives of most of your classmates?

▶ What are the reasons for the behavior we studied today?

▶ Why should all students be treated fairly regardless of previous behavior?

▶ What are some of the things you could say to someone else who wants to cheat by copying your homework that won't make you feel awkward?

▶ Since I really wasn't clear in the way that I phrased that test question, what suggestions do you have for me?

▶ If I change the date of the test, we will be off schedule. What do you suggest we do about that?

▶ How do you think I should signal you to be quiet when you are working in your groups?

Synthesis

▶ Choose ten facts from today's lesson to create a puzzle to help a classmate review.

▶ Demonstrate the main point of today's lesson to a classmate.

▶ List the events that you just read about in the order that they happened. Now change the order of just one event and explain what the new outcome would be.

▶ Group the items on the board according to a criteria that you devise.

- If you were a newspaper reporter writing about the events in this class this week, what would the headline of your article be?
- Create relationships among these items.
- List as many ways as you can that you are like your classmates.

Evaluation

- Rate this class against the other classes that you have attended this week.
- What qualities caused the people in today's lesson to succeed?
- How do you know when you have done a job to the best of your ability?
- What are the errors in logic in the passage that you just read?
- Defend a classroom rule to a classmate whose opinion is very different from yours.

TASK STEMS TO MOTIVATE STUDENTS THROUGH CRITICAL-THINKING ACTIVITIES

To involve your students in critical-thinking activities at various levels of thinking, try some of these stems when you design instruction.

- It is not important because . . .
- It is important because . . .
- By contrast . . .
- How can you justify . . .
- Do you disagree because . . .
- On the positive side . . .
- What is the relationship between . . .
- Similarly . . .
- Would it be better if . . .
- An interesting part is . . .
- How could you determine . . .
- What is your opinion of . . .
- Imagine if . . .
- What evidence can you find to . . .
- How do you think this applies to . . .
- How would you prioritize . . .
- What can you conclude . . .
- Do you agree with the outcome of . . .
- Which statements support . . .

- ▶ What facts prove . . .
- ▶ If you had to choose . . .
- ▶ How is ___ related to ___ . . .
- ▶ How could you determine . . .
- ▶ What other way would you plan to . . .
- ▶ Can you use these facts to . . .
- ▶ What do you think about . . .
- ▶ What inference can you make about . . .
- ▶ What is the main idea of . . .

ACTIVE LEARNING STRATEGIES FOR ACTIVE STUDENTS

Students who are engaged in active learning are far more likely to stay focused on their assignments instead of disrupting a positive classroom environment. If you want to motivate students to perform well during class, consider adding some interesting, high-energy activities to your daily lessons to encourage them to interact with each other in lively discussions and other appealing classwork.

- ▶ Have the students lead conferences with each other and with you. When students take the lead, their interest and confidence soar. Prepare a set of guidelines that encourage them to take the lead in designing effective conferences and then allow them to assume responsibility for their role as conference facilitators.

- ▶ Stage a confrontation. Have another adult come in and fake a high-stress situation that relates to the material the class is preparing to study.

- ▶ Announce that you have made deliberate errors on the board or on their handouts and ask the students to find them.

- ▶ Get out the colors and ask your students to use them to highlight or do another activity that brightens a lesson.

- ▶ Put a humorous drawing on the board or have students sketch some of the facts of the lesson. Ask the right-handers to use their left hands and vice versa.

- ▶ When you are delivering instruction, pause frequently and have the students write a summary of what you have said in the previous three to five minutes.

- ▶ When students have a passage, chapter, or other text to read, guide them through it with active learning strategies such as these:
  - A scrambled list of events to put in order
  - A list of statements for students to agree or disagree with
  - A list of people and places to match with information about them
  - A cause-and-effect chart
  - Give students a set of questions that they will answer as they read the text. Discuss the questions before they read in order to see what information they already have. Help them see how the questions are aligned with the text and how they should answer them.

▷ Give the students a checklist of the key points to watch for so that they can check them off as they find them while reading.

▷ As soon as you have discussed a general question as a whole group, have the students then jot down what they heard that they agree with, disagree with, or that gave them a new idea.

▷ Have the students participate in small-group round-robin activities. Have students form groups of threes or fours. While there are many different ways to manage a round-robin, one way that many teachers have found effective is to have students pass around a sheet of paper with each student writing a fact or opinion or other bit of information on the sheet until either time is called or they have reached a certain number of entries. This allows students to share their knowledge in a nonthreatening way as well as see what their classmates know about the topic.

▷ When you have students work together in pairs, time them. Students who know that they have only a short time to work together will focus better than those students who think that they and their partners have the entire class period to work.

▷ Ask students to involve themselves in their learning by using review strategies such as these:

- Associate body motions with the material
- Quiz themselves
- Use colored pens to rewrite the main ideas
- Recite or sing the information
- Create mnemonic devices
- Teach the information to a classmate
- Create a vivid image of the topic
- Restate information in their own words
- Create a quiz and give it to a classmate

▷ Have the students make flash cards and use them to study together. Flash cards with sketches or drawings are more effective than those on which the words are just written out in haste.

▷ Do a Whip Around. Have students stand and quickly recite a fact or other item from the lesson before sitting down.

▷ Hold a Hot Potato Review. Write review questions on note cards so that there is one question per card. Have the students stand with their cards in a circle. Toss a soft rubber ball to a student and have that student read a question to the group. That student tosses the ball to a student who has to answer the question and then ask another student. Repeat until all the questions are asked and answered.

▷ Set up a quiz bowl tournament of quick questions and answers involving as many of your students as possible. To add interest, vary the level of difficulty, rules of play, way of scoring, and incentives.

▷ Line up your students in two teams facing each other. As soon as a student correctly answers a question you ask, that student tosses a soft foam ball to a student on the other team. That student has to answer the next question.

▷ Put students in triads. Each triad needs a large sheet of paper and markers. Ask the students to draw lines to divide the paper into thirds. Call out a topic and have each student write as much as he or she knows about the topic in one of the spaces. All three students should write at the same time for two minutes. When time is called, the students should discuss their responses.

- Stage a fishbowl question-and-discussion group. Select a few students to sit in the center of a discussion group and have the rest of the class sit around them. Have the discussion group answer the questions posed by the larger group. Rotate the students in and out of the fishbowl discussion group.

- Divide the class into two groups. Have one group read the day's text lesson independently while you teach the others crucial information from the lesson. Have the groups then pair up with each other and exchange the information they have learned.

- Give students a brief passage and have them read it silently. Then ask them to comment on the passage or answer questions about it. After this, have them mingle until they have found three other students who can concur with their comments or answers.

- Post signs around the room for the various stages of the day's lesson if it involves independent work or practice. Students will stay focused on learning longer if they are allowed to move around from spot to spot, completing a set number of activities at each area. This would be particularly effective for a drill of mixed or cumulative information such as the skills needed to perform various types of math calculations or practice in sentence writing or even the various parts of a history unit.

- Print questions from the lesson on small strips of paper and dump them into a box. Start counting backwards from twenty and hand the box to a nearby student. As you continue counting, that student then passes the box to a classmate who continues to pass it on until you hit zero. At that point the student with the box has to pull out one of the questions and answer it correctly. Continue until all the questions are answered.

USE INDUCTIVE LEARNING TO ENGAGE STUDENTS

In deductive teaching, which is currently the most common way we teach almost any subject, teachers present a broad concept, conclusion, or result and ask students to determine the evidence that proves that concept, conclusion, or result. In deductive learning, students move from broad or general concepts to specific ones. When we ask students to explain the causes of a war or the effects of a social movement, for example, we are using deductive teaching strategies. Deductive teaching is popular because it is time-tested, effective, and logical.

Inductive teaching strategies are intrinsically engaging partly because they demand that students look at the world just a bit differently than they are used to doing. Teachers who use inductive teaching strategies present facts, examples, and other evidence and then ask the students to draw generalizations and conclusions. Inductive thinking requires students to move from specifics to broad or general ideas. For example, students are taught the various causes of a specific war and then are expected to figure out that other wars may have been started because of similar reasons.

Inductive teaching, because of its novelty, has a wide appeal to those students who are easily bored or distracted or who are detail-oriented. In this list you will find some examples of inductive teaching activities that you can adapt to make your lessons as engaging as possible.

- Read two versions of an event to your students and ask them to analyze them for a specific cause, effect, or other criteria.

- Ask the students to examine artifacts related to the lesson and predict how they will relate to the information they are learning.

- Show different photographs and ask the students to tell you what they observe about how they may be related.

- Show the students various photographs of two creatures common in most neighborhoods: a ladybug and a spider. After examining photographs of these two creatures, ask the students to chart their observations about how these animals can survive when winter comes.

- Show video clips of various objects in motion and ask the students to determine the properties of the physical laws that govern objects in motion. What laws are the same in all of them?

- Ask the students to compare two very different objects such as a file cabinet and a shoe.

- Ask the students to contrast two very similar objects such as a cup and a mug.

- Write three quotations on the board that do not seem to be related to the lesson and ask the students to relate them to the lesson.

- Show examples of three different types of leaves and ask the students to tell you what they can learn about leaves from looking at the three that are before them.

ANOTHER USEFUL METHOD OF USING INDUCTIVE TEACHING: CASE STUDIES

The term *case study* when applied to teaching techniques is a method by which students investigate a real-life situation to draw conclusions and information from it. Potential case studies can be found just about anywhere; news reports are a good place to begin. For example, a teacher shows students in a biology class an article about a recent local rare bird sighting. After reading the article, the students examine photographs, a map of the area, and data about the bird. The students then work with the data and the local newspaper accounts about the sighting to determine the causes and the possibility of another visit from the bird in the future.

Here is the step-by-step procedure that teachers can use to successfully incorporate case studies in deductive teaching (see Figure 10.1).

APPEAL TO YOUR STUDENTS' ALTRUISM

One of the most powerful motivational tools we teachers can readily access is free and easy to find: it lies within our students—their idealistic natures. When students can be made aware of the plight of others less fortunate and encouraged to use their own inner resources to help, everyone benefits from their actions. One of the most significant reactions is that students feel connected to their classmates and valued for their contributions to the class. As a motivational tool, appealing to your students' altruistic natures can be a powerful force in the classroom as students work together for the good of others.

Service projects do not have to be time-consuming or distracting to be effective. Begin simply by examining the subject you teach for opportunities for service projects. For example, if you teach science, consider planting a garden at your school or clearing a path or determining how to recycle or save energy. Next, use your ideas for a project to create a lesson plan to promote the activity. Be sure to design activities that meet your course objectives. Finally, be sure to discuss your plans with a supervisor or a

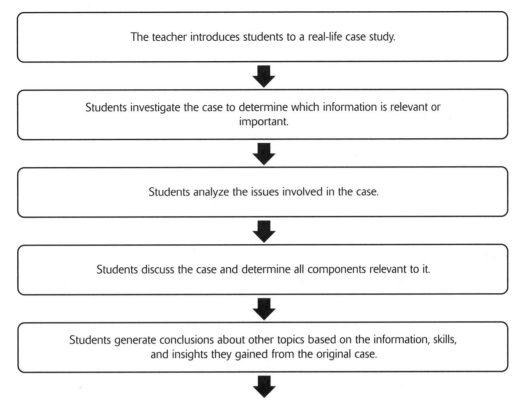

Figure 10.1. How to Use Case Studies in Inductive Learning Instruction

trusted colleague to make sure that your ideas are sound, in line with school policies, and don't compromise the safety of your students.

Some of the easiest ways to begin include projects such as these:

▶ Practice Random Acts of Kindness

▶ Visit a local nursing home

▶ Contribute food to an animal shelter

▶ Assist Meals on Wheels volunteers

▶ Clean the school grounds

▶ Collect canned foods, toys, or clothing

▶ Complete classroom good deeds

▶ Help a shelter for pets

▶ Work for Habitat for Humanity

Even though service projects have been a staple of school life for decades, the difference now is that the Internet makes it easier for students to reach out to others. Try some of the sites below to encourage your students to work together for the good of many.

INTERNET RESOURCES FOR SERVICE PROJECTS IN YOUR CLASSROOM

http://servicelearning.org

This University of Colorado Web site has extensive links to helpful information about service learning, a list of topics for students to explore, and contact information for agencies that are involved in service projects.

www.Freerice.com

At this addictive game site, every correct answer contributes rice to the UN World Food Program.

www.freepoverty.com

Free Poverty is a world geography game in which students test their knowledge of the world. For each correct answer, students donate ten cups of clean water to third world countries.

http://aidtochildren.com

Aid to Children is a vocabulary game like Free Rice. For every correct answer, $0.25 cents will be donated to children in need through World Vision.

www.clickforachange.com

Click for a Change is a site where students can play different types of online games in several different categories. Every game contributes money to a charity. The Click for a Change group selects various charities to support instead of supporting one particular cause.

http://charitii.com

At Charitii students can play word puzzles to donate water and food, protect the rain forest, or provide education to people in developing nations.

www.helpthirst.com

Help Thirst is a site where students donate water to those in need. It asks players to play memory games instead of answering specific trivia questions as some other sites do.

SHOW STUDENTS HOW TO BENEFIT FROM FORMATIVE ASSESSMENTS

As teachers and students are well aware, assessments are a ubiquitous aspect of their educational lives. While summative assessments serve to assess how well students have mastered material, formative assessments are designed to help students improve their knowledge or skills as they work through a unit of study. In fact, frequent formative assessments are one of the most valuable tools teachers can use when offering either whole -group or differentiated instruction.

The range of formative assessments is limitless. In this list you will find some of the many formative assessment activities that you can use to determine how well your students have mastered the material under study.

- Labeling maps
- Labeling diagrams
- Oral questions
- Questions to be answered in complete sentences
- Essay questions
- Multiple-choice questions
- True-or-false questions
- Matching questions
- Putting items in order of importance
- Placing items in chronological order
- Research projects
- Research papers
- Self-evaluation
- Students evaluating each other's work
- Completion of checklists
- Analogies
- Teaching material to someone else
- Posters
- Booklets
- Portfolios
- Book reports
- Questions designed to facilitate comprehension
- The number of correct responses in a class discussion
- Completion of a project based on previous knowledge
- Recognition of names in the news
- Class newsletter
- Organized notebooks
- Restatement of material in the students' own words
- Reading more on their own about a particular topic

- Worksheets
- Contracts for work to be completed
- Oral reports
- Formal speeches
- Problem solving
- Models
- Project progress reports
- Letters to the media
- Restating definitions
- Creating definitions
- Word games
- Puzzles
- Sentence completions
- Questions generated independently
- Identification of main points
- Original writings
- Classification of material into categories
- Evaluating material for themselves
- Combining various elements in a lesson
- Recognizing characteristics
- Recalling facts
- Using context clues
- Applying knowledge from one unit of study to another
- Completing an experiment
- Summarizing
- Expressing opinions
- Making comparisons
- Drawing contrasts
- Analyzing information
- Debating issues
- Constructing models
- Paraphrasing

- Illustrating ideas with words
- Writing samples
- Drawing maps

- Drawing diagrams
- Applying book knowledge to real-life situations

As valuable as formative assessments are, however, one of the most difficult challenges for teachers of secondary students involves helping them learn to use formative assessments as encouragement to stay on task and work hard to achieve their potential. The problem that many secondary teachers experience with this type of assessment stems from the reaction that their students can have to a poor performance; often they can become so discouraged that they quit trying to do their assignments well. Other negative reactions can include defiance, angry outbursts, and other unpleasant class disruptions.

Teachers who are prepared for this potential reaction, however, can help their students overcome their initial negativity and learn how to use the information they gain from formative assessments to improve their academic performance. In this list you will find a variety of ways that you can help students overcome their negative reactions and benefit from formative assessments:

- Many students only want to complete assignments that will be graded by a teacher. To overcome this reluctance without having to assign a grade for every paper that your students complete, consider grading only part of an assignment, giving a quiz on the material instead of a grade, or allowing the students to select their best work from a group of assignments.

- Other ways to use formative assessments to encourage students to improve their performance can include these quick methods:

  - Help students correct their papers for a return of partial credit or for a chance to retest.

  - Ask students to complete a brief self-reflection sheet about the assignment (see "What Did You Learn from This Assignment?").

  - Allow students to write an explanation of their thinking process on various questions. They can include an explanation of what they should have been thinking as well as what guided them to answer the way that they did.

  - Have students explain to partners what they will do differently on the next assignment, how they prepared for this one, and what they learned from their work.

  - If the assignment has included a checklist (steps to complete, mistakes to avoid, final reminders, and so on) for students to use before submission, ask the students to use the information they have gained from the formative assessment to personalize their own checklist before they submit a final version of the assignment.

  - Ask students to assess their readiness to move on to new material. If they are not ready, ask them what their next steps should be.

  - Often students are more willing to take more time and care assessing another student's paper than they are their own. Use this tendency to have students help each other determine their weaknesses and strengths. Have students complete a reflection sheet (see the "Reflection Sheet for Formative Assessments").

Student Worksheet

WHAT DID YOU LEARN FROM THIS ASSIGNMENT?

I know this thoroughly:	I almost know this:	I need to review this:

Student Worksheet

REFLECTION SHEET
FOR FORMATIVE ASSESSMENTS

Your name:_____ Your partner's name:_____

How would you rate the assignment?   Self: A B C D F   Partner: A B C D F

What are the strengths of the assignment?

Self: _____

_____

_____

What are the weaknesses of the assignment?

Partner: _____

_____

_____

Suggestions from your partner: _____

_____

_____

_____

ENLARGE THE LEARNING ENVIRONMENT

One of our most important tasks as educators is to help our students enlarge their lives. No matter where they live—in rural areas, suburbs, or cities—our students need our help to see that the world is a much larger place than the four walls of a classroom can ever contain. When we move our students into the larger world beyond their textbooks, we offer them benefits they cannot learn by just sitting quietly at their desks.

First of all, when we help our students see that they are part of a large community, those students see that they can have more interesting lives than those of their classmates who either drop out or who do not succeed in school. Their lives can be enriched by possibilities rather than restricted by problems when they learn to see beyond their day-by-day concerns.

Students who are encouraged to explore a variety of interesting places and ideas have an opportunity to interact with many kinds of people. They then develop skills that will help them learn to get along well with others. Often students learn to appreciate their communities better just by learning about the many things other people do to make all of our lives easier.

However, the most welcome benefit that comes to those students whose teachers take them beyond the classroom is an increased sense of self-confidence and an openness to new experiences. We know that our attempts to enlarge their worlds have been successful when we see that our students have become more self-confident and comfortable in the ways they relate to each other and to new situations.

There are many ways we can enlarge the learning environment for our students. Here is a list of some of the ways you can help your students begin to view themselves as citizens of a larger community. Pick a few that you think your students will enjoy and experiment to find the ones that will work best for you.

▶ Your students can tutor younger students in their neighborhood. Working with primary or elementary children will increase their own knowledge of what they are teaching as well as their sense of self-esteem.

▶ Help your students feel they belong to a school community by promoting school spirit. Show pride in your school and help your students see that it is important for them to become involved in school events also.

▶ Take your students to both the school library and the public library. Libraries open the door to the world. Teach your students how to be responsible patrons so that they can benefit from these resources.

▶ Use the Internet. Your students can enjoy exploring cyberspace and learning about the advantages of our information age. See Section Nine for more ways to use the Internet to help students reach out globally.

▶ Encourage students to join school clubs and organizations.

▶ Students can also join community civic organizations. Many organizations will welcome the energy offered by secondary students.

▶ Have older students mentor your students. Even college students with busy schedules will be willing to help out younger students who need the advice and guidance of more experienced friends.

▶ Arrange for guest speakers to share their expertise and experiences with your students.

▶ Expose your students to art. Inexpensive prints of well-known paintings can add a great deal to your students' knowledge of the world of the arts.

- Take your students on field trips to points of interest near and far. Certainly no students should graduate from high school without visiting their state capitol.

- Play music that students don't normally listen to. Classical music is something that even the most unsophisticated students grow to appreciate if they are exposed to it often enough.

- Have your students find out about their communities by surveying community members about a variety of topics or issues.

- Encourage students to visit a college campus even while they are still in middle school so that they can have an idea of what college is like for those students who work to earn a place there. For those who cannot visit a campus, writing for information is a good idea. Students should not wait until their senior year to begin to explore their college options.

- Encourage your students to serve as unofficial "big brothers" or "big sisters" to students who need someone to help them.

- Help your students establish peer-tutoring sessions outside of class to help each other study.

- Encourage your students to read for pleasure or to listen to books on tape to broaden their horizons.

- Stress the importance of watching television sensibly. Educational television programs will help your students understand the worlds of nature, politics, the arts, history, and similar topics.

- Publish your students' writing in as many different ways as possible. Encourage your students to enter contests.

- Some ways of enlarging the classroom are much simpler than others. Put up a large map and have the students talk about where they are from or places they have visited.

- Involve your students in a research project that they would enjoy. Learning about an event in the past or a group of people in an area of the world very different from their own will open their minds.

- Have your students write letters to well-known people. Authors, entertainers, government officials, and sports figures are often generous in their willingness to write back to students to share the secrets of their success.

- Have your students become involved in local, state, and national government issues. Even something as simple as encouraging them to join your school's PTA will be a good way to get students started on becoming involved in issues that can have a direct effect on them.

- Your local chamber of commerce office has information about your community that your students probably don't know. Have students contact this organization to become aware of the many resources available to them in their communities.

- Enlarge your classroom by team teaching with a colleague or by combining your classes for a project. Art students and English students can work together, for example, to produce a booklet or another project that combines the talents and skills of the two groups.

CREATE A CULTURE OF EXCELLENCE IN YOUR CLASSROOM

It is ironic that we have such different expectations for the various people we encounter in our daily lives. We expect that our daily newspapers will be delivered on time every day. We demand that other drivers stay on their side of the road. We require that doctors be accurate in diagnosing our ailments, and we certainly want the pharmacist to fill our prescriptions correctly.

We have the same expectations for the other adults we encounter: postal workers, repair personnel, telephone operators, technicians, bankers, lawyers, nurses, clerks, custodians, inspectors, manufacturers . . . in fact, we expect excellent service from everyone.

When it comes to our students, however, our expectations for academic and behavioral success drop drastically. Many of us are just glad to have made it through yet another long day at school.

Why are we willing to settle for so little from our students? Why can't we have the same performance expectations for these very important people in our lives that we have for the others we meet?

We can. In fact, it is up to us to show students how to achieve their best. An important part of a teacher's responsibility is to help students cultivate the habit of mind that will encourage them always to put forth their best efforts—even on the smallest tasks.

There are several techniques we can incorporate into the culture of our classrooms that will help us encourage this fundamental change in our students' thinking. Here are some methods that will help you create a classroom with a culture of excellence.

Technique 1

Teach your students that it is not enough for them just to complete their assignments. Too often students seem to sleepwalk through their assignments while not learning the information they are supposed to master. Just doing the work is not enough.

Technique 2

Promote the desire to learn more about a subject in your students when you plan your lessons. Ask questions that are designed to arouse their curiosity. Comment on the appearance of their papers, the depth of thought evident in excellent work, and the importance of paying attention to details. If you incorporate these ideas into every lesson, you and your students will soon be striving to achieve more than they thought they could.

Technique 3

Promote the concept of 100 percent plus. When you teach your students to aim for 100 percent plus on every assignment, you are encouraging them to strive for excellence. Some of the ways you can indoctrinate your students into accepting this standard include

 ▶ Placing posters and banners around the room to encourage students to do their work and then do a little extra.

 ▶ Creating a display area for papers that are extremely neat, accurately done, or go beyond the expectations for the assignment.

 ▶ When you make an assignment, asking students to suggest some of the ways they can exceed the requirements.

 ▶ Rewarding students' efforts at doing their best.

 ▶ Encouraging students to be self-confident about what they achieve with just a bit more effort. Get them in the habit of asking themselves the question, "What is just one more thing I can do to make this assignment better?"

▶ Teaching your students the importance of focusing attention and concentrating their efforts, particularly at the end of an assignment when they may be tempted to rush to finish.

▶ Sharing excellent papers with the class. Show them the reasons that some papers exceed the requirements for an assignment.

▶ Discussing the standards your students will have to meet in the workplace. They should understand that taking a 100 percent-plus attitude to their work now is something that will give them a competitive edge later.

Please see this section's "Making Positive Choices" for more positive choices that can help you motivate your students to succeed.

Making Positive Choices

Instead of . . .	Try to . . .
▶ Being vague in your directions for various assignments	▶ Offer task cards, models, examples, and demonstrations so that students know how to do their work well
▶ Being too general in the way you offer praise	▶ Use specific and detailed encouragement about the student's work
▶ Offering a pizza party or other treat as a reward	▶ Use a variety of tangible and intrinsic rewards
▶ Allowing students to be bored and unproductive	▶ Increase intrinsic motivation by deliberately planning appealing lessons
▶ Impressing students with the difficulty of the material	▶ Begin each unit of study with lessons that are student friendly and then become progressively more difficult
▶ Emphasizing comprehension-level thinking	▶ Use Bloom's Taxonomy to create dynamic lessons that encourage higher-level thinking skills
▶ Allowing students to be passive learners	▶ Add high-energy activities to encourage active learning
▶ Directing students to read a passage	▶ Guide their reading with interactive questions to answer
▶ Telling students to study by "looking over their notes"	▶ Use activities that encourage active review strategies
▶ Providing ho-hum lessons	▶ Give students a case study to solve together

QUESTIONS FOR REFLECTION

Use the information in this section to guide your thinking as you reflect on these questions. They are designed to encourage you to think more deeply about the issues in the text or to discuss those issues with colleagues.

▶ How important is motivation in your instruction? What techniques work well for your students? Which of the techniques in this section surprised you?

▶ How do you help your students improve their critical-thinking skills? Which activities work well for you? Are there any technology-based activities that would help you with this?

▶ How altruistic are your students? How can you incorporate this inclination into your teaching practices?

SECTION ELEVEN

Prevent Discipline Problems

In this section you will learn

- How to prevent various discipline problems

- How to understand the role that teachers have in discipline problems

- How to use conferences and detentions effectively

- How to cope well with difficult classes and students

- How to increase positive and decrease negative behaviors

CREATE A POSITIVE CLASSROOM WHEN YOU PREVENT DISCIPLINE PROBLEMS

Preventing problems from getting started is only common sense. Discipline problems rarely happen in isolation. Once students start disruptive behaviors, their classmates may be tempted to join in. Crowd control is more difficult and less likely to succeed than planning ways to keep students engaged and interested in their work and in behaving well.

Even small disruptions such as having to nag students to stop talking can snowball into hours and hours of lost instruction time for the other students in the class as well as for the misbehaving ones. These disruptions can be stopped early and easily with just a bit of effort and planning.

It is also much easier to plan ways to prevent, or at least to minimize, discipline problems than it is to have to deal with their aftermath. Serious discipline problems are dangerous. No teacher wants to deal with threats, intimidation, or the terrifying consequences of violent students who may or may not be armed.

The toll that constant disruptions can take on even the most dedicated teachers is heavy. Many teachers leave our profession to look for other careers rather than have to continue to face an unruly mob. It is hard to find satisfaction in a workplace where rude and uncontrollable adolescents make a mockery of our ideals for a peaceful classroom. We can—with some planning, organization, practice, and skillful teaching—prevent almost all of the discipline problems that could plague us.

WHEN YOU ARE THE CAUSE OF THE PROBLEM

Sometimes teachers create their own discipline problems. We cause them because we inaccurately assess our students' needs, fail to plan adequately for emergencies and daily activities, misread our students' reactions, or unknowingly commit any number of mistakes.

The good news about the mistakes we make in our classrooms is that we have control over them. We can prevent them. Discipline problems that we do *not* cause ourselves are not as easy to manage.

In the following list of common teacher-made mistakes, you will find some of the reasons that you may have experienced discipline problems. With each mistake listed here you will also find a way to avoid making it into a discipline problem.

Mistake 1

You refuse to answer or give a poor answer when students question you about why they should learn the material you want them to master.

Solution: At the start of a unit of study we need to be careful to provide students with the reasons that they need to learn the material in the unit. Start each class with a review of the purpose for learning the information in the day's lesson. Also make sure students are aware of the real-life applications for the learning you require of them.

Mistake 2

You present yourself in too tentative a fashion—too easily sidetracked, too tentative, too permissive.

Solution: Approach your students with sincere courtesy and confidence. Set limits and take a positive approach to your students by preparing interesting lessons and attending to the classroom-management concerns that will make your students more successful in school.

Mistake 3

You are too vague in giving directions to your students.

Solution: Be specific when telling students what they need to do. Instead of saying "Don't be annoying," a better choice is to say "Please stop tapping your pencil."

Mistake 4

You are unclear in the limits you set for your students, resulting in a constant testing of the boundaries and of your patience.

Solution: Be as specific as possible in setting limits when you establish your class rules and procedures. Students need to know and understand just what they should do and what will happen if they choose not to follow the directions you have for them.

Mistake 5

You present yourself as less than professional by making mistakes on handouts or on the chalkboard.

Solution: Be careful to write as correctly as possible and to have someone proofread your work if you are not as skilled at writing as you would like to be. When you make a mistake, graciously admit it when a student calls it to your attention and immediately correct it.

Mistake 6

You use inappropriate language with your students.

Solution: Present yourself as professionally in your speech as you do in your dress. You are a role model. Be careful to avoid using profanity. Don't overuse street language or slang in an effort to be friendly.

Mistake 7

You give too many negative directions. This sets an unpleasant tone for your students.

Solution: Make an effort to replace your negatives with positives. Instead of saying "Don't play around," you will be more positive if you say "Get started on your assignment now."

Mistake 8

You try to solve discipline problems without trying to determine the underlying causes.

Solution: Spend time trying to figure out what caused the problem to begin with. If you don't determine the root of the matter, you won't be successful in preventing it from reoccurring. You may also misread the situation and make a serious mistake in trying to solve it.

Mistake 9

You overreact to a discipline problem by becoming angry and upset.

Solution: Instead of spending your energy in anger, take time to examine the problem objectively before acting. Take a problem-solving approach to really deal with it.

Mistake 10

You refuse to listen to your students when they are trying to express their feelings about a problem.

Solution: Encourage students to express themselves in an appropriate manner and give them the opportunity to do this. Not allowing discussion or an airing of feelings is a serious mistake that will only cause the problem to become more serious as students grow increasingly frustrated.

Mistake 11

You neglect to command attention. Teachers who talk even though students aren't listening are not productive.

Solution: Refuse to give directions until you have your students' attention. There are many techniques you can follow for commanding attention: setting a timer, asking a leading question, holding up something unusual, and standing in the front of the room are just a few.

Mistake 12

You create problems by having lessons that are not interesting.

Solution: Take the time to plan stimulating lessons that have many varied activities. Well-planned lessons that engage students in meaningful activities from the time they enter your classroom until the time they are dismissed are an excellent defense against discipline problems.

Mistake 13

You have lessons that are poorly paced. Students either have too much work to do and give up or they don't have enough work. You also make this mistake when you have lectures that are so long that you can't keep your students' attention throughout.

Solution: Think of your class time in fifteen-minute blocks and schedule activities that can be completed in that time (or in a longer block with a brief break or change of pace) to keep students at their peak of learning.

Mistake 14

You make mistakes in assigning punishment by doing so without proof or by blaming the wrong student.

Solution: Determine what happened before you act. Punishing unfairly will create long-lasting bad feelings among your students. Although it will take longer than rushing to act, taking your time to assign blame is always a good idea.

Mistake 15

You are inconsistent in enforcing consequences. This will lead students to a steady testing of the limits of good and bad behaviors.

Solution: Establish the consequences of rule breaking at the start of the term and then be as consistent as possible in enforcing the rules. Make sure the consequences are ones that you will be comfortable enforcing throughout the term if you want to be consistent.

Mistake 16

You assign punishment that is not appropriate for the offense.

Solution: When you establish consequences for the rules of your class, make sure they match the seriousness of the offense if you want your students to learn from their mistakes.

Mistake 17

You neglect to create class rules or have ones that are not workable.

Solution: Before the term begins, plan the rules that you would like to govern your classroom. Make sure these rules are ones with which you are comfortable and that you know you can consistently enforce.

Mistake 18

You punish students for something while overlooking another, more serious situation. For example, you reprimand a student for leaving a book bag in the aisle during a test, but neglect to notice that others in the room are cheating on the test.

Solution: Take care to assess a situation as completely as you can before acting. Never punish anyone unless you are absolutely sure of what the problem is and who is to blame. Be aware that it is easy to overlook misbehavior if you are distracted.

Mistake 19

You teach lessons where students are passive learners and therefore likely to become disruptive.

Solution: Plan assignments in which your students are up and doing activities. There should be a lot of movement and noise and excitement in your class.

Mistake 20

You go to school each day without the belief you must have in order to help your students succeed: that students can learn and achieve the things you want for them.

Solution: There is no substitute for high expectations. If your students are to achieve success in your class, you must first demand it from them. Expect great things from your students and then help them achieve your expectations.

WHEN WHAT YOU SAY CAUSES PROBLEMS

Although each region of the country may have its own dialect, there seems to be a common language that teachers from all regions have picked up as if by osmosis from our years in school, from our education classes, and from our teaching experiences. We know we can calm students and win them over to our side of a dispute by choosing our words carefully.

We also need to be aware of the power that our words can have to upset students. In the midst of a discipline problem, we need to be careful to use language that will help our students calm down and make the choice to behave better instead of worse.

In this list you will find some comments or questions that many teachers tend to use when exasperated with their students. These comments and questions will not make any discipline situation better. Instead, they have the power to frustrate students and result in an even worse disruption.

Examine this list in view of your own experience. If you know that these comments are unproductive, then you can choose words that will encourage rather than discourage your students.

▶ You don't want me to call your mom, do you?

▶ I'll send you to the principal . . .

- If you don't get to work this instant, you will fail!
- Whom do you think you're talking to?
- How many times do I have to tell you . . . ?
- What am I going to do with you?
- You know better than that!
- Why would you do such a stupid thing?

CONDUCTING USEFUL STUDENT CONFERENCES

Ours is a society that values its mentors. Even very young children are familiar with many images of wise elders counseling young people. Literature, art, and the media provide us with traditional portraits: grandfathers teaching youngsters to fish, grandmothers passing along family recipes, and parents teaching their children to ride a bike or drive a car. Along with these traditional, family-oriented images are the less traditional ones where someone who is not a family member is the trusted counselor—police officer, minister, doctor, and teacher.

Our students need us to provide them with mentorship. They need us to work with them on a one-to-one basis even though most of the work we do with our students is done with groups of various sizes. One of the best ways to do this kind of mentoring in a school setting is by holding a conference with a student.

There are many times in the course of the term when you will need to confer with a student or with groups of students. Some of these times may be when you are helping them plan long-term projects or improve their performance by completing other academic assignments.

Conferences can also be very useful in establishing a positive working relationship with a student who has misbehaved. When the two of you can sit down together without the rest of the class as a distraction and can work out a solution to the problems that the student has been experiencing, then conferences are powerful tools for positive discipline. You can begin to provide the mentorship that your students need.

STRATEGIES FOR SUCCESSFUL STUDENT CONFERENCES

Holding a conference with a student is not difficult, but it can be more successful if you plan ahead to take some positive actions to guarantee success. The following strategies will be most effective if you are working with a student who has already misbehaved and who you think is mature enough to respond well to a conference.

- Arrange a time for the conference that is agreeable for you both. Be sure to show respect for your student's schedule by being as cooperative as possible about the time. It is also a good policy to set in advance an ending time for the conference. Fifteen minutes should be a reasonable amount of time for most conferences.

- When you arrange a place for meeting, remove as many distractions as possible. Other students should not be in the room waiting and listening; however, it is not a good idea to meet one-on-one with a student behind closed doors.

- Make the meeting place comfortable for you both. Offer pen and paper for taking notes. Sit side by side in student desks or at a table. Avoid unpleasant situations where the student sits slumped while you are free to pace.

- When the student arrives for the conference, be courteous in your greeting. If you are relaxed and calm, then it is likely the student will also be relaxed and calm.

- Begin your meeting by stating that the purpose of the conference is to decide on a solution to the problem. Avoid blaming and rehashing your disapproval if you want to solve the problem.

- Take the initiative by stating the problem as you see it. Take time not only to discuss the negative aspects of your student's behavior, but also to stress the positive attributes that you see in your student as well.

- Focus on the behavior itself, not on the personality traits of the student. Avoid name calling or labeling.

- Let the student then state his or her side of the story. Listen attentively. Take notes.

- Restate the problem in your own words to make sure you understand the problem and to show your sincere interest in solving it.

- Be positive but firm in conveying that the responsibility for change is the student's. Offer help and support to encourage a resolution.

- Together with your student work out a plan that will help solve the problem. Brainstorm together if needed. Ask questions that lead to a solution: What could you do instead? How could you handle the situation better?

- Agree on a plan that satisfies both of you. Restate it so that you both have a clear understanding. Make sure the plan is easy to carry out.

- Once again affirm that you are willing to offer help in solving the problem.

- In calm, matter-of-fact terms, explain the negative consequences that the student will have to deal with if he or she does not carry out the plan.

- Be very clear that you have put past misbehavior behind you and that you do not hold a grudge.

- At the end of the conference, ask the student if there is anything else that needs to be said. Offer a chance to listen once again.

- Be courteous in thanking the student for deciding to work with you. Express your optimism that better days lie ahead for you both.

MAKING DETENTIONS BENEFICIAL FOR YOUR STUDENTS

Although it seems at times as if violent and disruptive behavior occurs too often in schools, there are still many measures that we can take to control student behavior in our classes. Because the best discipline plan is one that prevents problems from beginning, some situations will inevitably arise that will need to be handled privately by teachers and students so that problems are either prevented or kept manageable. One way to do this is by detaining students after school.

Plan to make the time when you keep students after school productive. The purpose is to resolve problems that the detained student is having in your class. Many teachers make the mistake of using detentions only to punish students. If it is your goal to help students improve their behavior, then you should plan detention activities that will help you reach that goal and that are not merely punishment.

Although there are dozens of approaches to take when detaining students, the following methods and suggestions should make the process easy to manage and effective in preventing more misbehavior.

How to Issue a Detention Notice

▶ Find out what your district's policy on student detentions entails. If your district encourages you to use this method of disciplining students, educate yourself about the correct procedures to follow. Be meticulous in following them.

▶ Decide what to do if a student does not serve the detention. What should happen next? What should you do? Determine what the policy is on this issue before you need to implement it.

▶ Many students take detentions lightly, but most parents do not. Use this to your advantage. Getting parents or guardians to cooperate with you in having a child serve a detention is a sensible course of action. Call home to let them know a detention notice has been issued to their child. Ask for their cooperation in helping the student serve it.

▶ If your district allows it and it's convenient for you, consider holding morning detentions.

▶ Before you write out the detention notice, try to prevent the misbehavior. Privately warn the student of the rule he or she is breaking and that a detention is a consequence for breaking that rule. Students should not be surprised when you issue a detention for misbehavior.

▶ Be very clear with your students that a parent or guardian must sign the notice and that they must return it before they can serve the detention. You should never cause a parent worry because a child was late coming home from school and the parent was not informed of the detention.

▶ Avoid writing out the notice when you are upset, angry, or in a hurry. You will appear less than professional. Use a dark pen and write neatly. Correctly spell the names of the child and of the parents and guardians. Be specific so that parents will know what went wrong and what steps you have taken to correct the problem.

▶ Issue the detention quietly and privately at the end of class. Do not embarrass the student.

▶ Detentions do not have to be long in order to be effective. Thirty minutes set aside to solve a problem with a student should be sufficient.

What to Do During the Detention

▶ Detention time should never be play time. Plan what you want to accomplish with your detained student and work to attain that goal.

▶ You will accomplish more if you detain only one student at a time.

▶ During a detention you should establish a very businesslike atmosphere. Do not tolerate less than acceptable behavior.

▶ During the detention hold a conference with your student. Follow these steps:

- Begin by asking the student to explain his or her point of view.
- Discuss the situation to clarify any misunderstandings that either of you might have.

- The student should generate a list of possible solutions to the problem.

- Both of you should then discuss the possible solutions and agree on a course of action.

- Have the student write out a brief explanation of the problem and the solution that you both have agreed upon.

- After you have read the student's report, both of you should sign the agreement as a closure to the detention.

▷ Make a phone call or send a letter home to notify parents or guardians of what you and the student have agreed upon as a resolution.

Mistakes Many Teachers Make

▷ Do not give a student a ride home. If a parent has signed the detention notice, then transportation is not your responsibility.

▷ Do not leave a student alone in an empty school. Wait with the student until his or her ride home arrives.

▷ Keep a record of the conference on your personal calendar or on the back of the detention notice.

▷ When you give students detention notices, have them write a brief sentence stating that they were given the notice and then sign it. Keep this in your records.

▷ Never issue a detention to an entire class or to a large group of students. You will look ridiculous and the detention will be a waste of time for all concerned.

▷ If a student loses control and crumples or tears the notice, continue to act in a very calm manner. If the student does not come back for the note and apologize before the end of the school day, contact his or her parents or guardians by phone at once. You should also lengthen the time of the detention since additional misbehavior now has to be resolved.

▷ Be careful to protect yourself. Do not remain in your classroom with a student after school with your door closed. Keep the door open at all times to avoid being unfairly accused of misconduct.

Other Uses for Detention Time

Students do not have to misbehave to be detained after school. There are many reasons for you to work with students outside of class. Some academic reasons for detaining students are to make up work, to tutor or be tutored, and to get extra help on study habits.

ESSAY QUESTIONS THAT WILL HELP SOLVE DISCIPLINE PROBLEMS

Sometimes you will need to talk with your students about a particular problem they are having in class. One of the best ways to get students to think about what they have done and what they need to do to correct the situation is to have them write out their thoughts in a fairly organized manner before they try to talk with you about the problem. Such an essay is not busywork; rather, it is a useful tool in which to begin a dialogue with students.

Have students write these responses at an after-school detention or during a conference. They could even write them at home and bring them to the conference or detention if it seems appropriate to you and your students. This should be used as a prelude to a conference, not just as punishment.

▶ What steps can I take to make sure I get to class on time?

▶ How can I improve the way I tackle the homework assignments I have each night so that I can benefit from them?

▶ What other choices can I make rather than continue to hit or insult my classmates?

▶ What steps should I take when I am having trouble with an assignment?

▶ What are the reasons that I should turn in all work on time?

▶ What are my goals for this class and how can I achieve them?

▶ What methods can I use to help stay focused in class?

▶ What are some of the ways I can show that I respect the rights of my classmates?

▶ What are some of the ways I can show that I respect myself?

▶ What are some of the appropriate behaviors I have used in this class in the past?

HOW TO HANDLE THE DIFFICULT CLASS

We all have one at some point in our careers—the class that is so difficult to manage that we daydream about a change in our profession on the way home from school. A difficult class turns our determination to help students succeed into a desire just to make it through one more class period. Fortunately for you and for your difficult students, there are many ways to turn a class like this into a successful one.

What causes a class to be difficult? There can be many reasons. Sometimes the class is too large for the room so that the seating arrangement cannot be modified adequately. Sometimes there is an unpleasant chemistry among students and between students and teacher. There can be an unequal distribution in the ability levels of students so that the more capable ones are frustrated by the less motivated or less successful ones.

Many students in a difficult class lack goals for their lives or even for the successful completion of the course. Sometimes the time of day can have a negative effect on students. Many teachers will agree that classes that meet after lunch tend to be harder to settle than morning classes.

Peer conflicts can also disrupt a class. Students who are busy disagreeing with each other have little time for the successful completion of their class work. Sometimes, too, a class is given a negative label by teachers in earlier grades and that label becomes a harmful self-fulfilling prophecy.

Perhaps the most serious reason that classes are difficult lies in the way the students in the class regard themselves and their ability to succeed academically. Students who do not believe they will succeed have no reason to try. Successful teachers with difficult classes have found that they can turn the negative energy in the room into a positive force through patience and by persistently communicating their faith in their students' ability to succeed.

There are many ways to begin to overcome the problems posed by a difficult class. The specific strategies you choose will depend on your particular students and their needs. The ideas listed here are strategies that can start you on your way to turning a difficult class into a successful one.

▶ Attack the problem on as many fronts as possible as quickly as you can in order to gain control of the situation. Examine such factors as the physical arrangement of the room, your relationship with troublemakers, the type of lessons you deliver, how your students handle transition times, and how consistently you enforce the rules and consequences you have established for your students.

▶ Get help from a variety of sources. Even the smallest schools have many different resources that can help you cope with a difficult class. Some of these include other teachers, coaches, counselors, administrators, nonfaculty staff members, parents or guardians, siblings, other students, and community members.

▶ Use data to inform your decisions. Make observations, conduct surveys, collect exit slips, and go though student transcripts. Do whatever you can to gather the data you need to make wise decisions about how to manage a difficult class.

▶ Keep the expectations for all of your classes high. Lowering your expectations is the easiest and most painful mistake to make.

▶ Establish from the first class meeting onward that you are the person who controls the class. Demonstrate that you will regulate the behavior climate in your classroom for the benefit of everyone with the help of all students.

▶ Work on the noise level every day until your students are willing to modulate their voices for the good of everyone. Teach students the volume that is acceptable and productive and the noise levels that are not. Establish signals for helping them stay quietly on track.

▶ If your class is boisterous, regulate the kinds of activities that you give them. These students need lots of quiet, well-structured work, but this should be interspersed with activities that allow them to move about and interact with each other in positive ways.

▶ Make sure your students know positive things about each other. It's easier to build trust and respect when students know their classmates.

▶ Call parents or guardians as soon as you can when a problem arises. At best they will work with you in a teamwork approach to help their child. At worst you will have notified them of the problem. You will have also protected yourself from an administrative reprimand if the problem escalates.

▶ Teach ethical behavior. Don't preach, but encourage your students to make good choices in deciding how to live their lives.

▶ Be prepared. Staying organized is an essential element in dealing with a class of students who can be unruly.

▶ You must be able to call everyone by name if you want to gain control of the class early in the term.

▶ Help your students get organized and stay that way. Make sure everyone has the materials needed to succeed in your class. Show them how to work quickly and efficiently.

▶ If you are having trouble motivating your difficult class, consider giving them their work in the form of contracts where they are allowed a certain measure of freedom in how they accomplish their assignments. Students will regard a work contract as evidence of your trust in their maturity.

▶ Smile at your class. Share a good laugh together. If you were videotaped while teaching them, would your body language reveal your positive feelings or would it express your distrust and other negative emotions?

▶ Be friendly, but firm. You are the adult in the room who is responsible for setting the successful tone that is appropriate to encourage your students.

▶ Never lose your cool. Even in the face of serious student rudeness, never even consider raising your voice in anger. You won't make your point. Even if you succeed in cowing your students temporarily, your victory will be short-lived.

▶ Don't allow any free time where your students just sit around waiting for the class to end. Keep them productively engaged every moment of class.

▶ Be unpredictable. Sometimes students misbehave in order to entertain themselves. Provide a safety net of routines and procedures, but spice up your lessons so that students will be interested in doing their work.

▶ Play a lot of games with your difficult students. Because they enjoy the variety and activity of games, these are successful learning tools. Be sure to establish and enforce the rules of fair play in order to avoid trouble that might mar an otherwise productive experience.

▶ Offer incentives other than grades. Some students who have never made a good grade are not really interested in them. Keep the rewards small, frequent, desirable, and tangible.

▶ Plan activities around the short attention spans of many of your students. Be sure these activities include plenty of opportunities for practice and review.

▶ Teach students how to be respectful to you, their classmates, and themselves. Stress the importance of a pleasant tone of voice and a tolerance for others as ways to show respect.

▶ Provide relevant work for your students. If adolescents can see a need for doing an assignment, they will engage themselves in it quickly.

▶ Praise good behavior as often as you can. Difficult students need to know when they do well. If you praise an entire class for good behavior, that will help create a positive class image. Some of the positive labels you can give your class could include

• Hard working	• Sensible
• Confident	• Enthusiastic
• Cooperative	• Diligent
• Independent	• Flexible
• Trustworthy	• Mature
• Caring	• Sympathetic
• Supportive	• Altruistic
• Dependable	• Dedicated
• Peacemaking	• Tolerant
• Resourceful	• Inspiring
• Friendly	• Responsible
• Honorable	• Organized
• Good sports	

- Make sure the work you assign is appropriate for the ability level of your students. No one wants to do work that is too hard or too easy.

- Consider alternative methods of assessment for a difficult class. Portfolios and projects are among the many types of evaluation that will help build confidence. Also give frequent short quizzes and tests.

- Celebrate your triumphs. Focus on the positive changes in your students.

- Make a list of the troublemakers in your class. Chances are, you won't have more than five. When you stop to consider the situation, you don't have a difficult class. You have a class with a few difficult students in it.

- Use media to grab and sustain attention. Art, music, cartoons, and films are all things that will help you manage difficult students more easily.

- Make sure your students can read well. School becomes more manageable for those students who are skillful readers. Teach, reteach, and reinforce reading skills no matter what your subject matter.

- Create a persona for your class where they see themselves as helpful members of a team. Teach them what synergy (the whole is greater than its parts) is and show them the ways they can create this for themselves.

- Arrange a time-out room with another teacher. Gently remove the offending student to that other teacher's classroom when the misbehavior becomes intolerable.

- Stop frequently to review and to assess progress. Make sure everyone knows what to do.

- Enable students to become competent. Work toward this goal and you will see a change in their behavior if they have been unsuccessful in the past.

- Stay on your feet and monitor everyone. Students who know that you are vigilant in watching over them will behave better than those students whose teacher is busy with paperwork.

- Make sure you go over the rules and procedures of your class as often as you need to in order to have everyone understand them.

- Model courtesy and the other qualities you want from your students.

- Be straightforward with difficult students. This does not mean you have to be unkind, but tell them as specifically as possible what you want them to do and what they should not do.

- Acknowledge the rights of individuals in your class. Showing students that you are fair in enforcing rules is a good way to begin.

- Have your students set goals for themselves at the start of the term and work toward those goals from then on. This will help them direct their learning and will give them the reason to keep trying when things become difficult for them.

- Create a businesslike atmosphere in your class. Get off to a good start and make it evident to everyone that learning is the priority in your room.

- Plan how to manage for the periods in your class when students are likely to be disruptive. Three of these are usually the beginning of class, transitions between activities, and the end of class.

- Turn the ringleaders into your allies and the rest of the class will usually follow along. Create a sincere relationship with every student in the class so that they all feel valued. This is especially important for the class leaders who can influence other students in a positive way.

- Don't threaten. Students should be aware that you mean what you say, but they should not be frightened into compliance.

- Teach students to use a pleasant tone of voice when speaking with each other and with you. This will help reduce the number of angry outbursts you will have to mediate.

- Get them involved in helping each other. Students who share their expertise with a classmate in a productive way will not disrupt the class while they are engaged in this activity.

- Have your difficult students be the ones who run your errands and manage the daily business of the classroom. Giving troublemakers a sense of responsibility and of your trust will often encourage them to behave better.

- Give difficult students who are seeking attention an opportunity to earn it for positive rather than negative reasons.

- Be clear with your students that you expect them to do their work and that you will help them learn to do it well. Make this a priority in your classroom so that they understand there is no time for disruption because they have bigger and better things to do.

- Don't give up. Try to reach out in as many ways as you can. A difficult class calls for a creative and fearless teacher.

WIN OVER YOUR DIFFICULT STUDENTS

Difficult students come in all varieties. Their disruptive behaviors can run the gamut from openly hostile defiance to quietly passive aggression. Unless they are managed with care, difficult students can destroy the positive environment that you want for all of your students, including the troublesome ones.

Experienced educators know that the best way to help difficult students learn how to manage their behavior is not through direct confrontation or anger, but by convincing them that cooperation with their teacher and classmates is far more advantageous than negative behavior. Even though it is not always easy to maintain a calm demeanor when students repeatedly misbehave, making the effort to win them over is far more likely to create long-term success than if you react in anger. To convince your difficult students to work with you instead of against you, consider adapting some of the suggestions in the list that follows:

- Avoid angry confrontations. Because you are an adult and an authority figure confronting a younger person whom you supervise, a confrontation may intimidate, anger, or otherwise alienate students.

- Choose to view difficult students as challenging students instead of problem students. With this shift in attitude, you are more likely to work to solve problems rather than simply react to incidents of bad behavior.

- Look past the behavior to try to understand the whole student. This will help you offer the acceptance and respect many misbehaving students crave.

- Be clear with students that while you may not like their behavior, you still have affection for them.

- Many students have such a strong need for attention that they will seek even negative attention. Try to satisfy this need by providing as much positive attention as possible.

- Try to define the problem as exactly as you can. Being able to work on a specific issue will make it easier to have a successful outcome than if you just have a vague idea of the problem.

- Work to understand why difficult students act the way they do. When you understand their needs and motivations, then you will find it easier to work with them productively.

- Be patient and persistent. Creating a positive relationship with difficult students may take more time than you can anticipate, but your determination will be rewarded.

- Make sure that your difficult students perceive you as not only a firm teacher, but also a fair one.

- If you find that nothing you do seems to be working to help a difficult student, seek help from colleagues and other involved adults. Sometimes it takes a concerted effort to help students improve their negative behaviors.

- Don't take the negative behavior of difficult students personally. Your students do not really know you as a person—just as a teacher who sets limits that they may not find comfortable.

- Remember that while the misbehavior may be the responsibility of the difficult student, teaching that student how to work well with you is your responsibility. Together you and your difficult students can work out solutions that will benefit all of the students in the class.

HOW TO INCREASE THE POSITIVE BEHAVIOR IN YOUR CLASS

- When you write lesson plans, make sure to include motivating activities that are designed to inspire students to want to do their work well.

- Make a positive home contact early in the school year to establish a strong working relationship.

- Praise your students when they do things that you would like to have them repeat.

- Design instruction that is flexible enough to meet the various learning styles in your class.

- When teachers are firm but fair, students will be aware of what's acceptable and what is not. Hold students accountable for their behavior.

- Be careful that your body language reflects positive and caring messages.

- Use encouragement to make students aware of how to succeed. Encouragement offers advice in the formative stages of assignments so that students can proceed with a clear sense of what they are doing well.

- Use competitive activities. Asking students to beat their own personal best scores on a test or other assignment is a positive way to encourage competition.

- Help your students establish and achieve short- and long-range goals so that they have a reason to complete their assignments.

- Center instruction around clearly defined objectives so that students can see why they are studying a particular topic.

- Listen to your students. This is especially important when there has been a problem.

- Provide plenty of models and examples so that students can be confident that they know how to succeed.

- Design instruction that is challenging but attainable.

► Activate your students' prior knowledge before beginning a new unit of study or even as a review of previous material so that students will be interested and engaged.

► Build on your students' interests. Students who have the opportunity to work on problems related to issues that they are already familiar with and interested in tend to be more engaged and on-task than those who are not.

► Invite community leaders into your classroom so that students can see connections between the topics that they study in class and their applications in the real world.

► Recognize effort. Although teachers can't grade something as intangible as effort, helping students see the correlation between effort and success is a useful tool in encouraging students to keep working until they achieve success.

► Check frequently for understanding.

► Praise only the good behavior and ignore as much of the bad as you can.

► Involve students in appropriate decision-making opportunities.

► Be friendly, firm, and fair.

► Offer assistance when you see that a student is struggling by asking, "How may I help you?"

► Protect the dignity of your students.

► Stand in the same spot when making announcements as a signal that students are to pay attention to you.

► Select a behavior that you would like to increase and chart student progress.

- Figure 11.1 gives an example of a simple chart that can be displayed on a chalkboard or as a poster. In this chart, the number of complete daily assignments is compared with the number of incomplete ones. When students see their efforts displayed in this way, they

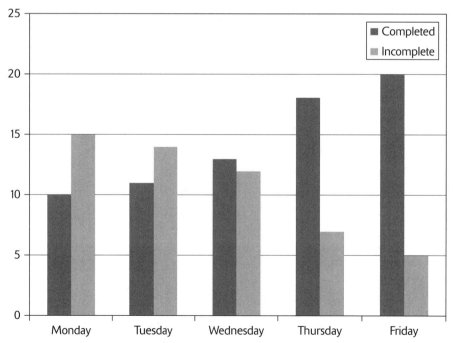

Figure 11.1. Chart Behaviors You Would Like to Increase

not only have a better grasp of the specific problems and successes they are experiencing, but also can work together to improve their success rate.

▶ Be clear about your expectations for behavior.

▶ Some students, especially those who are struggling, may have very limited exposure to successful adults. Provide examples of role models for them.

▶ Have an alternative plan ready in case a lesson is not working well.

▶ Have a predictable routine so that students know what to do and how to accomplish it.

▶ Use a variety of media to attract your students' attention and engage their interests.

▶ Include different learning modalities in every lesson.

▶ Keep a file of short activities to use as transitions or enrichment. (See Section Four for activities.)

▶ Stand at the door and greet students as they enter the room. This will give you a quick idea of the emotional weather for the day.

▶ Make frequent checks for understanding. This will keep problems manageable.

▶ Announce tests, quizzes, and major projects well in advance of the due date.

▶ Have students estimate how long their homework will take so that they can plan to achieve it.

▶ Smile at your students.

▶ Be careful to praise appropriately. Too much gushy praise can have a negative effect.

▶ Communicate your high expectations and your belief that your students can achieve them.

▶ Offer frequent quick challenges to your students. Try activities such as timing them as they set up for class, counting the number of correct responses to a question and then asking for just one more, or challenging your students to beat their personal best on assignments.

▶ Design lesson elements that are of high interest interspersed with more rigorous ones.

▶ Design lessons in fifteen-minute increments.

▶ Post encouraging mottoes and sayings.

▶ Make a plan with students about how they can pull up a low grade.

▶ Encourage students to set their own rules for their class.

▶ Create an inclusive class atmosphere.

▶ Make sure students who are absent know what they need to do to make up their work.

▶ Make a student feel worthy of trust in order to prevent misbehavior.

▶ Keep your students busy from the moment they step into your room until they leave.

▶ Discuss the class rules, policies, and procedures periodically—daily at first and then less frequently thereafter.

▶ Smile at a student who is getting ready to misbehave.

▶ Consider giving a potentially troublesome student a position of leadership in the class.

- Put friends close together so that the more able ones can help those less capable.

- If an exciting school event is causing your class to be out of control, go with the flow and plan assignments that will channel that high energy into productive outlets.

- Make sure the lesson is exciting. Students who are interested in a lesson will usually not misbehave.

- Create a reasonable policy about students who need to leave the room and enforce it.

- Set behaviors for the entire group and reward them when the goals are met.

- Offer tangible rewards for good behavior at unpredictable times.

- If you see a student successfully struggling with temptation in class, be sure to say a quiet word of praise afterward.

- Be emotionally accessible for your students. Warm and friendly teachers have more productive classes than grouchy ones.

- Give a student a second chance. Sometimes a warning can be very effective.

- Hold class award ceremonies at appropriate times to recognize the good deeds of your students.

- If a group is having trouble settling down, say, "I'll give you exactly two more minutes to finish getting to work" and then time them.

- Laugh. You have a sense of humor. Use it.

- Be so soft-spoken, kind, and polite that your students would be ashamed to raise their voices around you.

- Give students as many options about their work as you can without sacrificing your standards. Students who can choose wisely learn to be self-disciplined.

- Control the pace of a lesson carefully. If it is too long or is too rushed, then problems are likely.

- Post conspicuous notices to remind students to stay on-task.

- Reexamine your classroom rules. Are they working? What do you need to change?

- Make sure the consequences for good and bad behaviors are clearly spelled out.

HOW TO DECREASE THE NEGATIVE BEHAVIOR IN YOUR CLASS

- When a student misbehaves, make an effort to repair the damage in trust caused by the infraction. It's up to you to show your students how to correct their behavior and then go forward.

- Observe schoolwide rules, policies, and procedures.

- Make sure your class policies are clearly defined. When there is confusion about a class policy, some students will try to take advantage of the situation. For example, if you are not clear about the deadlines for missing work, some students will procrastinate as long as possible.

- Be consistent. Although it is not easy, consistently enforcing rules, policies, and procedures makes it easy for your students to succeed.

- ▶ Give verbal and written directions that are easy for students to follow.
- ▶ Design class activities so that the pace is brisk and businesslike.
- ▶ Be prepared for class yourself.
- ▶ Attend to the traffic-flow issues that may create student congestion or confusion.
- ▶ Get in the habit of anticipating problems whenever you create student activities.
- ▶ Contact a student's home the third time a homework assignment is not done.
- ▶ Seek help from other adults involved with a student who may be struggling with academic or social issues.
- ▶ Avoid distractions such an open door to a noisy hallway.
- ▶ If a student misbehaves, redirect and move forward.
- ▶ Use proximity to prevent or minimize problems.
- ▶ Perfect the "teacher stare" to discourage misbehavior.
- ▶ Call a parent or guardian and get help for a problem.
- ▶ Hold a conference with a student who misbehaves to work out a solution.
- ▶ Determine on a course of planned ignoring to extinguish misbehavior.
- ▶ Listen to the student's version of a negative incident before taking any action.
- ▶ Ask an offending student what consequences he or she should have to pay.
- ▶ Ask an offending student to list for you some alternative actions that he or she could have taken to prevent misbehavior.
- ▶ Move a misbehaving student to a time-out area in another classroom in order to cool off and prevent further trouble.
- ▶ If a perennially fidgety student is getting restless, send that student on an errand to channel energy productively.
- ▶ If the infraction is minor and a true slip in judgment on a student's part, offer reassurance that you know it won't happen again.
- ▶ If students do not bring the necessary materials to class, arrange a system for lending materials with collateral.
- ▶ Glance in mild puzzlement at a student who appears off-task and shake your head slightly. The signal should be clear that you expect the student to focus on the lesson.
- ▶ Ask an offender to explain the class rule that was broken.
- ▶ After an incident has occurred, examine your own actions. Did you do something to cause the misbehavior?
- ▶ Unobtrusively move a misbehaving student to another seat.
- ▶ Ask a misbehaving pupil to help another student with an assignment. Both should benefit.

See this section's "Making Positive Choices" for more ideas about how to make positive choices that will allow you to prevent many potential discipline problems.

Instead of . . .	Try to . . .
▶ Wondering if you may be too vague, tentative, or permissive	▶ Set limits and plan engaging lessons that will engage students in productive activities for the duration of the class
▶ Having a narrow view of the discipline issues in your class	▶ Determine the underlying causes of the misbehavior to create a long-lasting solution
▶ Delivering lessons that seem to drag until students are bored and off-task	▶ Consider designing lessons in fifteen-minute increments so that students can take brief breaks
▶ Resorting to threats or sarcasm	▶ Remember the power your words have to harm or benefit your students
▶ Setting yourself up for unfair accusations	▶ Confer with students with the door open and in a calm manner
▶ Complaining about how bad one of your classes is	▶ Use as many different ideas, resources, and approaches as possible to solve specific problems
▶ Allowing students to have free time when they have finished their work for the day	▶ Offer exciting review activities to keep them on-task until the end of class
▶ Confronting students who repeatedly misbehave	▶ Win them over by taking the attitude that misbehaving students are challenges, not problems
▶ Having to answer "Why do we have to learn this?"	▶ Center lessons around clear objectives and make sure students know the value of learning the material
▶ Being vague in your behavior expectations	▶ Chart the positive behaviors you would like students to continue and display their progress each day

QUESTIONS FOR REFLECTION

Use the information in this section to guide your thinking as you reflect on these questions. They are designed to encourage you to think more deeply about the issues in the text or to discuss those issues with colleagues.

▶ What do you currently do that is a successful way to prevent discipline problems in your classroom?

▶ How useful do you find student conferences? How can you improve the way you confer with your students when there is a problem?

▶ Which of your students do you find most difficult? Why? How can you help them learn to be more cooperative and successful?

SECTION TWELVE

Cope Successfully with Discipline Problems Once They Occur

In this section you will learn

- How to respond appropriately to discipline problems

- How to investigate and solve discipline problems

- How to intervene successfully and early

- How to make the correct choices to manage discipline issues

- How to cope well when students are violent

THE DIFFICULT TASK OF RESPONDING TO DISCIPLINE PROBLEMS

Without a doubt the most stressful part of our profession is not the long faculty meetings, the hours of grading papers, or yet another revision to the curriculum. Instead, the most stressful part of the day for secondary teachers involves dealing with discipline problems once they occur in our classes. Since a discipline problem can run the gamut from a missing ink pen to a student with a weapon, discipline problems play a large part in our professional lives.

Another reason that discipline problems cause us so much distress is that each one is unique—and difficult. We constantly have to balance the needs of the individual who has misbehaved against the needs of the rest of the students in the class.

Our determination to prevent the problem from being repeated is one of our unexpected strengths in dealing with problems. Another is the ability that successful secondary teachers have to repress our own human feelings of dismay, sorrow, or anger in order to deal calmly and professionally with a student who has misbehaved. We quickly develop our creativity, knowledge of human nature, and ability to make fast decisions under pressure.

Any discipline problem presents three big issues for teachers. First of all, we need to keep the disruption to a minimum. The fewer people who are disturbed by a student's misbehavior, the better.

The next issue we cope with is how to keep students from repeating their mistakes. Most of us spend a great deal of emotional energy trying to determine what we can do to help students solve their problems once and for all.

Finally, we have to help students learn that they have choices in their actions. Students who realize this are closer to becoming self-disciplined than those students who blame their friends, their enemies, mean teachers, unkind parents, and the dog that ate their homework last night. When students learn that the choices they make have a direct connection to their success or failure in our class, then we know that this part of our job is complete.

There are many resources concerning how to cope with discipline problems. Two very useful books for all secondary teachers include *Teacher's Pocket Guide to School Law* by Nathan L. Essex (Prentice Hall, 2010) and *School Law: What Every Educator Should Know, A User-Friendly Guide* by David Schimmel, Louis Fischer, and Leslie R. Stellman (Allyn & Bacon, 2007).

To learn more about safety issues, your rights, and your responsibilities as a classroom teacher, visit these sites:

▶ National School Boards Association (www.nsba.org) maintains a site with a great deal of useful information on a variety of educational topics. To access links to their information on school safety, use *school safety* as a search term on the home page.

▶ The site maintained for school leaders by the Drummond Wilson law firm (www.schoollaw .com) has many resources related to discipline issues.

HOW TO SUCCESSFULLY INVESTIGATE A BEHAVIOR PROBLEM

Fortunately, teachers do not have the special forensics science training or scientific equipment to become skilled at investigating classroom discipline problems. In almost every instance, when a negative behavior incident occurs, determining what happened is a pretty straightforward process if you take a commonsense approach.

First of all, be very low key. If you are clearly distressed or excited, students who may be afraid of getting into trouble are not going to volunteer useful information. You will only make the situation worse if you overact.

Don't be surprised if your students are reluctant to tell on each other. In some areas where there is a strong gang presence, this could even be dangerous for some students. Reprisals of various kinds are something that many secondary students fear. If you demand that an entire class tell you what happened, then it is very unlikely that you will learn anything useful. A better technique is to ask students to jot down their version of what happened and turn it in anonymously. Having every student do this and then drop it into a container as they exit ensures that their responses will be confidential. This technique makes it easier for students to cooperate with you without being regarded as a "snitch" by classmates.

Finally, even though a behavior incident may have disrupted your class, you should not keep the students from attending their other classes. If an administrator is involved in the incident, then that person may choose to hold students, but you should not impose on your colleagues by detaining students.

EMPLOY THE STEPS OF THE PROBLEM-SOLVING APPROACH

Instead of merely reacting when a problem arises, successful teachers create a positive outcome by using a problem-solving approach. Although a successful teacher may really want to indulge negatively in anger or sarcasm or petty revenge, he or she knows that none of these will fix the problem and so opts for a productive response instead.

When teachers take a problem-solving approach to discipline dilemmas, they create an opportunity to resolve problems. When you can sit down with a misbehaving student and work through a problem in a calm and logical manner in an effort to solve the issues that cause it, then you are on your way to a positive discipline climate in your classroom.

Here is a quick review of a common problem-solving approach that many teachers find helpful when dealing with discipline problems:

Step 1: Define the problem. Work with students to determine the causes of the problem.

Step 2: Generate as many solutions as you can. Student input is crucial at this point to elicit their cooperation.

Step 3: Work together to evaluate each solution.

Step 4: Choose the best solution.

Step 5: Decide with your students how you plan to implement the solution.

Step 6: After you have put the solution to work, evaluate its effectiveness. Revise it if necessary.

THE IMPORTANCE OF EARLY INTERVENTION

One of the most important responsibilities that teachers have is to help students who are in trouble get out of trouble as quickly as possible. We should strive to keep the time that our students are off-task to a minimum. Our goal is to do this without disrupting the other students in the class.

How do you begin? When you see a student misbehaving, you have three choices to make about how you want to deal with that problem.

Ignore the Problem

This is an appropriate course to take if the problem is minor and fleeting.

Briefly Delay Acting on the Problem

This is an appropriate course to take when your intervention will cause more disruption than the misbehavior itself.

Intervene to Stop the Problem

This should be the course of action you take if the problem is interfering with the learning of the student who is off-task or the learning of the other students in the room.

If you do choose to intervene, there are many reasons to do so promptly when you see that a student is misbehaving. Here is a list of some of the good reasons that should help you decide to intervene to stop disruptive behavior as quickly as you can:

▶ You will avoid problems that can become more serious. An example of this type of problem is two students who begin with mild horseplay, then become angry, and finally engage in a fistfight.

▶ You will contain the problem to one or two students. If students observe a classmate being reprimanded for a particular type of misbehavior, then they will be less likely to engage in that misbehavior. Misbehavior that is dealt with by early intervention rarely spreads to other students.

▶ You make it clear that you are in control of the class. You are the classroom leader, not the unruly students in the room. This show of leadership and confidence will stop many problems from beginning.

▶ You will maintain a well-managed discipline climate. Your students will stay focused on learning rather than on disruptive behavior.

Effective Intervention Strategies

If you are brief and positive in your intervention, you will accomplish more than if you engage the student in a lengthy discussion. If you follow your intervention with a brief reminder of the rule that your student should be following, then you are also putting that student in control of his or her own behavior.

The following strategies can improve the effectiveness of your interventions. Experiment with the ones you feel most comfortable with and continue to use the ones that you find valuable.

▶ Use nonverbal language to get your point across. Move closer to a student. Make eye contact.

▶ Move to the misbehaving student and quietly remind him or her of the rule that is being broken. Ask why the rule should be followed. You can also quietly ask if you can help. This will alert students to the fact that you are aware they are off-task.

▶ Make sure students know the next step in the sequence of their lesson so that they know what they should do next. This will give them a reason to work efficiently.

▶ Change the seating arrangement if students are distracted from their work. It is best to do this at the start of class after giving the student who is being moved a warning the day before.

▶ Send students who may need a break on an errand or to get a drink of water.

▶ Pay attention to body language and other clues to your students' emotional states. If you can see at the start of class that a student is upset, then you should take action to prevent the problem from being more serious.

▶ Call home to discuss a problem with the student's parents or guardians. Often the important adults in a student's life complain that teachers allow a problem to become serious before they call for help. Calling when you first notice that a student is beginning to have persistent problems is a sound management technique to follow.

▶ Speak frankly with a student who is experiencing problems in your class. Offer help and encouragement. Stress that you will help, but that the student needs to take responsibility for behaving well.

The "Behaviors and Interventions Checklist" that follows will guide you in deciding which intervention is appropriate for a misbehavior that you may be experiencing in your class.

Teacher Worksheet

BEHAVIORS AND INTERVENTIONS CHECKLIST

In this checklist you will find some common behaviors and a suggested level of intervention for each one. Although different schools have different interventions for various behaviors, it is best to use the most unobtrusive intervention possible. In this list, the suggested level of intervention applies to the first few incidents of the behavior only. Any small misbehavior can become a serious disruption if it occurs often, and you should increase the level of intervention to meet the seriousness of the disruption.

Behavior	Ignore the Problem	Briefly Delay Acting on the Problem	Intervene to Stop the Problem	Involve an Administrator and Other Adults
Daydreaming	X			
Lack of materials		X		
Chronic lack of materials			X	
Talking while the teacher is talking			X	
Off-task and excessive talking			X	
Missing homework assignment		X		
Chronic missing homework assignments			X	
Lying to the teacher			X	

(Continued)

Teacher Worksheet (Continued)

Behavior	Ignore the Problem	Briefly Delay Acting on the Problem	Intervene to Stop the Problem	Involve an Administrator and Other Adults
Stealing				X
Cheating on a test				X
Cheating on homework				X
Tardy to class			X	
Chronic tardiness			X	
Cell phone use in class				X
Forged note				X
Lingering in the hallway		X		
Chronic requests to leave class			X	
Name calling			X	
Intentional profanity directed at the teacher				X

Behavior	Ignore the Problem	Briefly Delay Acting on the Problem	Intervene to Stop the Problem	Involve an Administrator and Other Adults
Unintentional profanity			X	
Messy work		X		
Getting ready for dismissal early		X		
Sleeping in class			X	
Talking back to the teacher			X	
Rolling eyes		X		
Horseplay			X	
Slow to settle to work		X		
Weapon possession				X
Inappropriate remark			X	
Inappropriate touching				X
Refusal to work			X	

(Continued)

Teacher Worksheet *(Continued)*

BEHAVIORS AND INTERVENTIONS CHECKLIST

Behavior	Ignore the Problem	Briefly Delay Acting on the Problem	Intervene to Stop the Problem	Involve an Administrator and Other Adults
Refusal to cooperate with the group			X	
Off-task while online			X	
Substance abuse				X
Insignificant vandalism			X	
Serious vandalism				X
Refusing to clean the work area			X	
Brief inattention	X			
Chronic inattention			X	
Ostentatiously acting bored		X		
Eating in class without permission			X	
Out of seat frequently			X	

Behavior	Ignore the Problem	Briefly Delay Acting on the Problem	Intervene to Stop the Problem	Involve an Administrator and Other Adults
Unusually loud comment	X			
Challenges or confronts teacher			X	
Challenges or confronts classmate			X	
Rushing though assignments		X		
Negative nonverbal reaction	X			
Talking, but shushed by classmates	X			
Insulting to classmates			X	

THE CHOICES TEACHERS HAVE WHEN DEALING WITH DISCIPLINE PROBLEMS

When a student misbehaves there are many effective actions we can take that replace the harmful and outdated punishment practices of the past. We do not have to be abusive in order to make our students aware of their mistakes and the steps they need to take to correct them.

The creative secondary teacher practices many techniques during the school term in order to help students who have trouble behaving well. Sometimes what works for one student will not be effective for another. To complicate the issue further, sometimes what is effective for one student at one point may no longer work as well soon afterward.

The complexity of the discipline process is one of the exciting challenges of teaching. Today's teachers have a wide range of options to take when misbehavior happens in a classroom. Some of the most commonly used strategies are listed here in order to guide you to make effective choices when you have to find successful ways to manage discipline problems.

Ignore the Misbehavior

This is an effective option if you plan it, if the misbehavior is fleeting, and if other students are not seriously affected by it. Give some thought to what kinds of behavior you find tolerable, what you find disruptive, and what you anticipate the result of ignoring will be before you decide to ignore misbehavior.

Delay Taking Action

It is appropriate to delay taking action when the action you would take will cause further disruption. As an example, if it is the rule in your class that no one has permission to chew gum and you see a student with gum, you might choose to delay speaking to that student until you can do so quietly so that other students are not disturbed by your correction.

Use Nonverbal Actions

Nonverbal actions such as physically moving closer, making eye contact, giving hand signals, or making positive facial expressions are nonintrusive ways to deal with student misbehavior. A more complete list of some nonverbal signals used by teachers can be found in Section Nine.

Praise the Entire Class for Its Good Behavior

When students who are misbehaving hear a teacher say to the room in general, "It is encouraging to see so many of you working hard to complete this assignment. I am sure you will all be finished by the end of the period," the off-task students will usually realize that far more students are doing what they are supposed to do than not. Praising the entire group for its positive behaviors will not only encourage those who are doing well to stay on track, but also remind those who are not behaving well of what they should be doing.

Give a Gentle Reprimand

Giving a mild verbal reprimand when a student misbehaves will usually end the trouble. When you do this, you need to move closer to the student if you can and be businesslike and firm. Try to be positive instead of negative. "Open your book and begin working" will be more effective than a more negative command such as "Stop playing around this instant." Don't allow the student to argue with you or to engage you further in an attempt to seek inappropriate attention. Be firm and friendly when reprimanding students.

Confer Briefly with Students

There are many ways to hold a conference with a student. You could schedule time outside of class hours or you could meet briefly with the student while others are engaged in an independent activity. In a brief conference you can remind the student of the rule that was broken, establish a signal to remind the student to stay on task, redefine acceptable limits of behavior, encourage positive actions, and discuss the consequences of student misbehavior.

Hold a Longer Conference with Students

Schedule a longer and more formal conference with students when there are several issues to be resolved or when the misbehavior is serious. At this type of conference the emphasis should be on determining the causes of misbehavior and deciding what needs to be done in order to remediate them. Ask the student to write out a report of the incident from his or her point of view. Having a student write a report is effective because it forces students to consider their actions and the effects of those actions on others and on their own futures.

Have Students Sign a Behavior Contract

There are several examples of behavior contracts in Section Five that you could use or adapt for your students. A behavior contract will encourage students to learn to control their own behavior. It is an effective discipline option because it forces the student to acknowledge the problem and the steps that he or she must take to solve it.

Move a Student's Seat

When students misbehave several times in a class period, often where they sit in the room is one of the causes. For example, if a student with attention deficit disorder sits in the back of the room, it will be harder for that student to stay focused. Immature students who sit with friends often distract each other with horseplay and talking. These problems and others can be improved by moving the pupils. If you are going to move a student, try to do so as discreetly as possible; moving several students at the same time is one way to accomplish this. Warning students at the end of class one day that they will be moved the next day also gives them time to adjust.

Chart the Behavior of the Entire Class

One of the quickest ways to make a class aware of its positive and negative behaviors is to post a modeling chart and graph them so that everyone can see what they are doing right or wrong. There are many different ways to do this. If you want to be as discreet as possible, use a graph to note the negative behaviors you want to eliminate or the positive ones you want to encourage.

Contact a Parent or Guardian with an E-Mail, Phone Call, or a Note

Helping students learn to behave well is a task that requires teamwork among all of the people involved: student, teacher, and parents or guardians. When the adults in a student's life work together to reinforce each other's expectations and beliefs, then everyone benefits. If you are having trouble helping a student learn self-control, involve the parents or guardians with an e-mail, note, or a phone call. Too often teachers hesitate to do this or wait until the behavior has become serious. Early intervention with a request for help in solving the problem so that the child will benefit is always a good idea.

Arrange for a Conference with Parents or Guardians

Sometimes, in spite of our best efforts, a student continues to misbehave. After we have tried several times to remediate the situation, then spending more time with a parent than is possible in a brief contact is called for. Meeting with parents or guardians face to face is often a very useful technique for students who persist in misbehavior.

Refer a Student to an Administrator

When you have exhausted all other possibilities or in the face of severe misbehavior, it is time to refer a student to an administrator. Students should know that you will do this, but that you will do it only if the situation is severe enough. Be careful not to abuse this discipline option by referring students for relatively minor offenses that you can handle with an organized discipline plan. (See "How You Can Determine If a Discipline Action Is Appropriate.")

Teacher Self-Assessment

HOW YOU CAN DETERMINE IF A DISCIPLINE ACTION IS APPROPRIATE

Use this checklist to determine if an action you are considering taking to help students improve their behavior is one that is appropriate and will produce the results you want. You should be able to answer "yes" to all of these questions.

1. _____ Is the action I want to take based on sound educational practices?

2. _____ Is it consistent with school policy?

3. _____ Is it part of the rules I have established in my classroom?

4. _____ Can my students anticipate that this will be a consequence of their actions?

5. _____ Is the discipline action I plan to take part of a hierarchy of consequences?

6. _____ Is the action related to the offense?

7. _____ Will my students regard this as a fair action?

8. _____ Is this action geared to preventing or minimizing disruptions?

9. _____ Are other adults involved if the situation warrants?

10. _____ Does this action help students deal with the reasons for their misbehavior?

11. _____ Will students understand that this action will provide closure to their misbehavior?

12. _____ Is this part of a long-term solution to the problem?

HOW TO REFER A STUDENT TO THE OFFICE

At some point in your career, you will probably have to refer a student to an administrator for behavior that is either severely or persistently in violation of school or classroom rules. While no teacher likes to refer a student to an administrator, there are ways to make the process easier for everyone involved. Some of these ways involve steps to take before the infraction occurs and some involve actions you can take after the student has misbehaved. If you are not sure whether a misbehavior should be referred to an administrator, here are some guidelines that can help you decide what to do about a specific misbehavior. Some behaviors that should be referred to an administrator are

- Habitual tardiness
- Persistent disruptions
- Cheating
- Truancy
- Violent behavior
- Threats
- Substance abuse
- Weapons
- Deliberate profanity
- Vandalism

Some behaviors that you should handle yourself before involving an administrator are

- Excessive talking
- Not working
- Chewing gum or eating candy
- Poor work habits
- Rude comments
- Scribbling on desks
- Inattention

Before the Infraction Occurs

- Make sure you are familiar with the school rules and procedures that apply to your students. Become aware of the ways the school board and your other supervisors expect you to handle student misconduct.
- Prevent misbehaviors through sound educational practices and the consistent enforcement of rules.
- Handle routine misbehaviors yourself. If a phone call to parents or guardians would be effective, there is no need in most cases to involve an administrator. Establish your rules, policies, and

consequences early in the term and follow through when necessary. Document the methods you use to handle these routine misbehaviors. Apply the questions in the "Behavior Analysis Log" that follows to make this process easier.

▶ There are usually preliminary measures you should take before you refer a student to an administrator. Talking with the student, contacting parents or guardians, and asking a student to sign a behavior contract are three of the most important early interventions you should try.

▶ Make sure you have the necessary referral forms on hand so that you don't appear foolish or disorganized if a time comes when you have to refer a student to an administrator.

After the Infraction Has Occurred

▶ Once a student has misbehaved to the point that you will refer him or her to an administrator, make sure you prevent a bad situation from becoming worse by maintaining the student's dignity and privacy in front of classmates.

▶ When you talk with a student about an infraction, don't threaten or bully the student even if you are angry. Calmly state your policy and the consequences for misbehavior.

▶ Calm down before you write the referral. Your language should be as professional and objective as possible. Many different people will see the referral. Use language that is behavior-oriented and factual. Do not state your opinion of the student's behavior or sink to name calling.

▶ Call the student's parents or guardians before the end of the day to inform them of the incident and of your action in referring their child to an administrator.

▶ Make sure you also tell the student when you refer him or her to an administrator. The best way to do this is privately at the end of class.

▶ Once you have referred a student to the office, let go of it emotionally. By completing and turning in a referral form, you have put the matter into someone else's hands. Some administrators may take a different approach to solving the problem from yours. Don't try to second-guess administrators when they need to make decisions about the best course of action to take.

▶ Go back and examine the actions that led to the final referral. Was there anything you could have done early in your relationship with this student to have prevented this misbehavior from reaching the final point?

THE IMPORTANCE OF ANECDOTAL BEHAVIOR RECORDS

Here you will find two forms that are designed to help you make better decisions about how you deal with behavior problems in your class.

Use the "Behavior Record Form" that follows to keep a running account of the disruptive behaviors of each of your students. When you need to make a referral for persistent misbehavior, you will have the necessary information for an administrator to make a fair evaluation of the student. You can also refer to it when you contact parents or guardians so that you can be specific about the problems their child is experiencing.

The "Behavior Analysis Log" that also follows will help you focus on the way you handle each behavior problem in class. Use it to record the important information about an incident and the steps taken to improve the situation.

Teacher Worksheet

BEHAVIOR RECORD FORM

Behavior Record for:

Date	Time	Place	Disruption	Teacher Response

Teacher Worksheet

BEHAVIOR ANALYSIS LOG

Student's name:

Date of the incident:

Description of the incident:

What actions did I take?

What was happening just before the disruption?

What could I have done to prevent the incident?

What steps should I take in the future to make sure this does not happen again?

HOW TO PRESERVE YOUR STUDENTS' DIGNITY

Adolescents are particularly sensitive people. They spend their lives in a push-me-pull-you world longing to be independent and part of the crowd at the same time. Whatever sets them apart from their peers in a negative way can be exquisitely painful.

With this extraordinary sensitivity in mind, it is easy to see how quickly an unintentionally demeaning word or deed can wound our students' fragile pride. The dilemma for educators is that we have to correct our students' behavior while protecting their self-image at the same time. While this is not always an easy task, it is one that is vital to the cooperative relationship that should exist between teacher and student. In the two lists that follow you will find advice on what you should be careful to do and what you should be careful not to do to help preserve your students' dignity.

To preserve a student's dignity, be careful to

▶ Take the student's concerns seriously

▶ Use a kind voice when talking with the student

▶ Be as patient and understanding as possible

▶ Listen carefully to your student

▶ Try to be as fair as possible when delivering a reprimand

▶ Ask sufficient questions to be sure that you have an understanding of the incident

▶ Work to resolve problems and not just punish the student

▶ Assure the student that you believe that the misbehavior will not happen again

▶ Make every effort to see the entire child and not be affected by a brief moment of bad judgment

To preserve a student's dignity, be careful not to

▶ Call a student a name, even in jest

▶ Compare one student to another

▶ Reprimand a student in front of the class if at all avoidable

▶ Allow a confrontation to build in front of others

▶ Ignore a student who needs your attention

▶ Raise your voice

▶ Be sarcastic or insulting in an attempt to have the student learn from a mistake

HOW TO HANDLE CHRONIC MISBEHAVIOR

We all teach at least one—the student who misbehaves with unrelenting intensity day after day. Dealing with the demands of this student's constant energy-sapping misbehavior can be exhausting and frustrating for teachers and classmates alike.

Although the misery caused by a student with chronic misbehavior issues is rarely restricted to just one teacher and rarely develops overnight, it is possible to help this student learn to develop the self-control and productive attitudes necessary to become a positive part of any class. Allow the principles that follow to guide your decisions as you work to help this student assume responsibility for behaving appropriately.

Principle 1: Attend to safety issues first. If your students' chronic misbehavior can result in injury to themselves or others, then it is your responsibility to act decisively and quickly to protect everyone involved. Never allow behavior that jeopardizes student health, safety, or welfare.

Principle 2: Keep disturbances as inconspicuous as possible. When you can limit the amount of damage from chronic misbehavior, you send a strong message to everyone in the room that the focus in your class is not on misbehavior but on learning instead.

Principle 3: Adopt an attitude of support, encouragement, and cooperation. With this combination of affirmative attitudes, you will be far more likely to create a positive change in your students than if you just seek to punish.

Principle 4: Expect slow and steady progress rather than overnight success. There is no quick fix for chronic misbehavior that has taken years to develop. Help your students who struggle with a tendency toward chronic misbehavior by using a behavior contract or setting a clearly established goal for improvement.

Principle 5: Replace a bad behavior with a positive one. Often students who misbehave do not know how to behave appropriately. Use plenty of models, examples, and concrete details to allow your misbehaving students to have a clear idea of just how they are supposed to behave.

Principle 6: Celebrate your successes. For the students who improve their behavior, recognition of effort and persistence can make a real difference in their desire to continue to improve. Small tangible rewards can serve as reinforcements and reminders of successful behavior.

HOW TO MANAGE STUDENTS WHO WANT TO SLEEP INSTEAD OF PARTICIPATE IN CLASS

It is a damning indictment of a school when it is possible to walk through the hallways and see classroom after classroom where teachers allow some students to sleep through class day after day. The reason given by most teachers who allow students to sleep is simple: "At least they're not bothering anyone when they're asleep!"

What a tragic waste of student time and energy. There are two categories of students who sleep—one is acceptable and one is not. The acceptable one is illness. Sometimes a student comes to school and is too ill to participate in class, but cannot go home for whatever reason. At this point classroom teachers should use their best judgment about what is good for these students and may allow them to put their heads down.

On the other hand, chronic sleeping in class is a discipline problem that can be successfully managed with patience, persistence, and a step-by-step approach. Follow these steps if you want to have all of your students awake and participating every day.

Step 1

Talk to the students who want to sleep in class to determine the cause. Many students will cite one of these as a reason for sleepiness: family problems, long hours at an after-school job, a late party, late television shows, or a late date. Counsel your students about better ways to manage time so that sleeping in class will not continue.

Step 2

Hold a goal-setting conference with the student who still has trouble staying awake in class. Show that student the importance of staying awake in order to meet the long-term goals that he or she may have.

At this conference you should also help the student set short-term goals to help reach the longer one. Both types of goals should be put in writing and a behavior contract drawn up in which the student can see the steps he or she must take in order to solve this problem.

Step 3

Pay more positive attention to these students so that they will have a good reason to stay awake. Increase the number of positive interactions you have with them so that they know you care enough to take an active interest in their lives and well-being. When a student starts feeling successful and capable in a class, the problem of sleepiness will cure itself in most cases.

Step 4

If you have tried to work with a sleepy student and nothing has helped, then it is time to contact the parents or guardians. There may be an underlying cause you know nothing about and the student is not willing to share. Parents of students who are chronically sleepy can do much to modify the home environment so that the child will get the rest at home that he or she needs.

WHAT TO DO WHEN STUDENTS LACK MATERIALS

When students occasionally forget their textbooks or other materials, this really is not a problem that can't be solved by a quick trip to a locker, the loan of a book from the extras in the classroom, or sharing with a friend.

The problem with forgetting materials comes when students repeatedly "forget." This causes discipline problems in time off-task and in distractions. Students who regularly don't bring their materials to class have determined that there is no real reason to bring them.

There are several tactics you can use to deal with this problem. Look over the list that follows and pick the ones you think would be most helpful to you and your students:

> ▶ Prevent problems with materials by reminding students what they will need to bring to class on the following day. You can do this by telling students what they will need at the beginning of class and then at the end asking them to tell you what they should bring. Make it part of their homework assignment, post it on the class Web page, and display reminder signs.

> ▶ Try to have extra textbooks in the classroom so that you will be able to lend one to almost any student who slips and forgets. Three are not too many to keep track of if you are busy, especially if you have the students who borrow books from you write their names on the board to remind you that they have done so.

> ▶ If forgotten materials continue to be a problem even after all that you do to prevent it, then you will need to call home to speak to parents or guardians about your concern. Perhaps you and the parents could work together on a behavior contract to help the student become responsible.

> ▶ If missing ink pens or pencils are a problem in your classroom, set up a system where students can borrow from a shared bank of supplies. Ask every student to donate a new pen or pencil and put two or three students in charge of these. Wrap a strip of tape around the top and number each one. When students borrow these pens or pencils, the students who are in charge of distributing them should record the name of the borrower and the number on the board to remind

them to return them at the end of class. This system promotes self-discipline because students run it themselves and are responsible for contributing to it.

▶ If you have students who are unable to afford school supplies, lend them the materials that they need with collateral until they can purchase their own. You can do this discreetly if you see that a student is having trouble and would appreciate the help. You could also ask students who take materials from you to work in the classroom before or after school to defray the cost.

HOW TO HELP STUDENTS WHO DAYDREAM

Of all the discipline problems teachers have to face in the course of a school year, daydreaming is the most gentle. This thought crime does not involve other students or noise or weapons or even intentional discourtesy.

A daydreamer is simply a student who has more interesting things to think about than your class and the work you have assigned. Daydreamers only cause problems when their inattention is prolonged enough that they are off-task long enough to attract your attention.

There are several simple techniques to help daydreamers stay focused on learning while they are in your class. Use or adapt these to help your students be as productive in real life as they are in their dreams.

▶ Close monitoring will keep many daydreamers focused on the task at hand. If the room is quiet, the lesson dull, and the teacher sitting at a desk, daydreamers will be encouraged to drift away. Stay on your feet and closely supervise everyone to keep all dreamers working. Call on daydreamers by name when the class is involved in a discussion.

▶ If monitoring and moving around does not work as well as you would like, focus all of your students on the work at hand, and then move close to the student who is daydreaming and stay there until he or she is on-task again. Offer assistance or ask a question to help daydreamers stay focused on the assignment.

▶ Examine the lesson you have planned. Is it interesting? Are the activities varied, challenging, and engaging so that students will want to do the work? If the assignment requires that a student write or work in a team with other students, then daydreaming will be reduced. Reading silently and listening to lectures are prime times for daydreaming.

▶ If an upcoming event such as the prom, a championship game, or a holiday seems to cause more off-task behavior and daydreaming than usual, try to incorporate the event into the day's lesson in an attempt to redirect your students' thinking into productive work instead of daydreams.

▶ Examine your seating chart. Is the daydreamer facing away from you? At the back? Near a window? Move dreamers to a spot in the room where it will be difficult for them to lose the focus of the lesson.

▶ If daydreaming is a chronic problem for a student, then you must schedule a conference with that student to discuss the problem and its solutions. You may be satisfied after talking with the student that the problem is solved. However, if you are not confident that the problem can be solved just by talking about it, then you and the daydreaming student should enter into a behavior contract designed to help the student stay focused on school work.

HOW TO MANAGE STUDENT CELL PHONE USE IN CLASS

One recent and very rapid change in education is evident in the policies that govern student cell phone use. Just a few short years ago, student cell phones were banned in almost every school district in all fifty states. Today, however, millions of students of all ages carry their cell phones to school every day.

Cell phones at school invoke both strong positive and negative reactions because the policies governing their use have not caught up with their technical capabilities. While almost everyone agrees that students are safer because they have cell phones, the issues associated with the discipline problems that accompany phones at school are not easily solved.

The problems caused by cell phones at school are significant. Cell phones can create distractions that disrupt the learning environment in various ways. Students can misuse their phones by texting each other in class, bullying other students, taking unflattering photographs or recordings of teachers, or using phones to instigate fights that they then post online. Phones also are attractive targets for thieves. Perhaps the most significant negative impact that cell phones can have in a twenty-first-century classroom, however, occurs when students use them to cheat on tests and other assignments.

Although there are disadvantages to having cell phones in school, there are also many emerging classroom uses of this ubiquitous tool such as audio and video recording, creating and sharing mobile Web pages, or conducting student surveys. Just a few other classroom uses could include such activities as

- ▶ Photographing class notes to share with absent classmates
- ▶ Accessing the Internet
- ▶ Texting classmates about missed assignments
- ▶ Making and listening to podcasts
- ▶ Responding to questions via the text feature
- ▶ Listening to audio recordings of assigned texts
- ▶ Using calculators

It seems obvious that the cell phones themselves are no more of a problem than pencil and paper; student misuse of the devices creates problems. As a teacher, you will find it easier to cope successfully with cell phone issues in class by taking a commonsense approach. First, follow the guidelines set forth by your school district concerning cell phones. If you are not comfortable with those guidelines, then work with your administrators and other colleagues to make positive changes. Next, make sure all students are aware of the school's policies so that they have an understanding of the times when they can use their phones and the consequences for not following school policies. Be consistent in your enforcement and students should soon learn to be self-disciplined about their cell phone use.

One useful resource to help you learn more about how cell phones can be used productively in class is *Toys to Tools: Connecting Student Cell Phones to Education* by Liz Kolb. Published by the International Society for Technology in Education (October 15, 2008), this book offers strategies and advice about how cell phones can be a positive presence in a classroom.

HOW TO MANAGE HALLWAY MISBEHAVIOR

Many secondary teachers who visit elementary or primary schools are amazed at how quiet it is when students are in the halls. We grin at all of the cute youngsters as they whisper "shush" at each other as they move through the halls on their way to lunch or to the library. In the lower grades, it seems that the worst misbehavior in the halls is talking above a whisper or being in a crooked single-file line.

Our grins quickly fade, however, when we return to our schools and face the chaos of the halls. Our problems are much more serious. Common hallway misbehaviors in secondary schools include cursing, sexual harassment, bullying, fighting, shouting, running, knocking down other students, cutting classes, selling drugs, brandishing weapons, and vandalizing school property.

Many of us are reluctant to deal with these problems in the hallways because we don't know the students who are misbehaving. We are far more comfortable when we correct the behavior of our own students. We have a relationship with them and can anticipate a positive response from them.

What happens between the lower grades and secondary grades to cause this drastic breakdown in behavior? Part of the problem, of course, lies in the fact that our students are older and larger and coping with the many pangs of adolescence. But the real answer is in the fact that in the lower grades, students are not allowed in the public areas of the building without adult supervision. In secondary schools, for the most part, students are expected to behave well without adults marching them from place to place.

The Importance of Adult Supervision

While we should not be expected to put our students in orderly single-file lines in the hallways, if misbehavior in the hallway is a problem, more adult supervision is necessary. There are several good reasons for increasing the number of adult supervisors in the public areas of a secondary school:

▷ Areas with adult supervision are more orderly and quiet than those without an adult presence. Students know that in the presence of an adult they will be held accountable for their actions. They act more responsibly because of this.

▷ Students know that an adult will help if another student is tormenting them. Supervised areas are safer for students than the unsupervised places in a school.

▷ Behaviors that could grow into serious ones can be contained while they are still minor. Cross words between students are easier to deal with than the fistfight that could result from those cross words.

▷ Students welcome the stress relief that comes from an orderly environment. Coping with the hallways and other public areas in a school can be very hard on students who are smaller or less aggressive than others. Adults in the hallways make life easier for everyone.

Importance of Students' Self-Discipline

In addition to increasing the number of adults who supervise the hallways in your school, there are several actions you can take to help your own students learn to be self-disciplined about their behavior while in the public areas of the school.

▷ Students may not be aware of what constitutes good behavior and what constitutes bad behavior while they are in the hallway. Make sure they are aware of any school policy they are expected to follow. You can do this early in the term in a positive and pleasant class discussion.

▷ When you stand in the doorway to greet your students as they enter class, you are also supervising the hallway. Make sure your own students go to their desks to begin their opening assignments and do not lounge around in the doorway blocking traffic and causing hallway problems.

- Make the behavior of all students in the hallways an open issue for your students. Brainstorm with them about some of the good behaviors and bad behaviors that should and should not happen in the public areas of a school.

- Since what happens in the hallway may have a negative effect on the behavior in your class during the first few minutes, make those first few minutes as meaningful and interesting to your students as you can. You want your students to feel they are missing out on something wonderful if they are late or not immediately on-task.

- Make sure your students know they can count on your support if they experience trouble from other students in the hallway. Some students are the targets of repeated attacks by bullies and need your help in dealing with this problem.

- Recognize that the hallways may be stressful for your students. Ask them how they cope successfully with the problem. You could do this as a quick closing exercise and as a positive way to interact with students to help them solve their problems.

HOW TO HANDLE REQUESTS TO SEE THE SCHOOL NURSE

The school nurse is a valuable ally for those teachers who want to create a positive climate in their classrooms. The school nurse can help in a variety of ways: by helping keep the lines of communication between school and home open, by keeping you informed about the health of your students, and by working with you to learn what you can do to help every child be healthy enough to function well.

Many teachers do not see that the role of the school nurse is as important for the welfare of their students as they perceive their own role to be. These are the teachers who ignore health information from the nurse and who then treat every student alike regardless of the serious health issues that some students face. Use the following suggestions to help you deal with requests to see the school nurse in a sensible way:

- Pay attention to the information you receive from the school nurse about your students. Keep it on file for quick reference when you need to deal with any problems that might arise.

- Make yourself aware of the chronic diseases your students might have such as asthma, sickle-cell anemia, allergies, or diabetes. While these diseases are not always visible, they profoundly affect the well-being of the students who have them. You should also contact the school nurse about the best way to help any pregnant students you might teach. You might think a student is misbehaving when that student is actually ill.

- Ask the school nurse for a supply of adhesive bandages and safety pins to reduce the number of times students have to leave your room for minor problems.

- If a student requests to see the nurse, respond at once. Let that student go with a properly filled-out pass. Be very sensitive to the embarrassment that a student might feel in asking your permission.

- If you doubt that a student's request is legitimate, consult the school nurse after the visit to make sure. When students see that you and the other adults in the building are working well together, they are less apt to try to fool you. If the student is using a visit to the nurse as an excuse to leave the room, examine the cause of this behavior. Work to increase that student's self-esteem through improved work habits and an increased sense of cooperation with you and with the other students in your class.

HOW TO HANDLE VANDALISM

Vandalism takes many forms. Spray paint on walls, broken windows, smashed lights, cigarette burns in the restrooms, damaged library books, damaged bulletin boards, broken equipment, and scribbles on desktops are just a few examples of this problem.

Vandalism stems from a lack of respect for the school, from boredom, from insufficient adult supervision, and from a lack of accountability. Vandalism is an easy problem to stop—unlike so many of the other problems we face in education. Use the following techniques to prevent vandalism from beginning and to cope with it once it happens.

Prevention

▶ Monitor! At the end of class let students know that you will check their desktops and other areas of the room for stray marks or other signs of destruction. Students who know that you are alert will not be as disposed to destroy school property as those students who know that they can get away with it. Holding students accountable for their actions is the best defense you have against future incidents of vandalism.

▶ Discuss the problem of vandalism with your students and ask for their suggestions on how to prevent it. Those students who might not care will take notice when they hear their classmates express disgust at vandalism.

▶ If your classroom is neat and clean, then students are going to respect this and keep it clean. Vandalism is not a crime to a student who writes with markers all over a bulletin board that has already been defaced by other students. A coat of fresh paint and a few small repairs will prevent a great deal of future vandalism.

▶ Keep cleaning supplies on hand to clean off stray marks right away.

▶ Don't encourage your students to use illustrations in their reports and papers that they could have cut from books.

▶ Pay attention to the length of time that students are out of your class when they ask for a hall pass. Teach your students that they are expected to return promptly. Students who linger in the restrooms or halls will be more tempted to vandalize property than those who are aware that their teacher is waiting for them to return.

▶ When you decide on the furniture arrangement in your classroom, don't allow your students to shove their desks too near the walls or bulletin boards where acts of vandalism are easy to commit.

▶ Cover textbooks and encourage students to treat them well. Make informal checks as you walk around the room to see that students are taking care of them. You can teach your students to take notes on self-sticking notes that they can keep on each page of the book. You can also show them how to make blank bookmarks from notebook paper as another way to take notes on the text without writing in their books.

▶ Cover bulletin boards with background paper so that the damage students may do is just to the paper, not to the surface of the bulletin board itself.

What to Do When a Student Has Vandalized School Property

▶ When you notice that a student has vandalized property, confront the student about it. Send a note home to let parents or guardians know that the incident has happened.

▶ Use the technique of overcorrection to handle vandalism. If a student has marked on a desk, for example, that student should clean all of the desks in the room. If a student has defaced a bulletin board, then that student should not only re-cover that bulletin board, but the others in the room as well.

HOW TO MANAGE PROFANITY

Profanity is a fairly common problem in many secondary schools. Our society's standards about what is appropriate language to use at school have relaxed considerably in the last few years. Not too long ago, the expression "School sucks!" was considered indecent language. Now most people regard it as rude, but not necessarily indecent.

Profanity may seem to be a perplexing problem at first, but it really isn't. While it is not considered an educational best practice to wash a student's mouth out with soap, there are still many effective ways to deal with this problem.

Although there are dozens of ways to effectively deal with the problem of profanity in your classroom, most of the incidents of inappropriate language fall into one of the two most common categories described next. Use the guidelines for dealing with each type to get this problem under control in your classroom.

Category 1: Unintentional Profanity

In this category students simply make a slip of the tongue while they are chatting with one another. In this category students do not mean for you to overhear them. Sometimes this type of profanity happens in the hallways where students don't think they can be overheard by adults.

▶ Discuss the problem of swearing at the start of the term. Have students brainstorm reasons why this type of language is not acceptable everywhere. Explain that everyone has various levels of language and that students need to practice a more formal one at school so that they will be able to speak correctly in situations where it is expected. Have students discuss the ways they can break this habit.

▶ Establish a hierarchy of consequences to help students remember not to swear. Here is a possible sequence:

- **First offense:** Warning
- **Second offense:** Ten-minute detention
- **Third offense:** Ten-minute detention and phone call to parent or guardian
- **Fourth offense:** Referral to administrator

▶ Be careful when you overhear cursing not to turn to a student and say "What did you just say?" unless you want to hear the curse word again. You can usually tell by the shocked looks on the faces of the students near the guilty one that the word was inappropriate.

▶ Be aware of those times in your class period when your students are prone to swear. Some potential trouble spots are at the start of class, at the end of class, between activities when students are switching mental gears and have time to chat, and when there is a loosely structured activity with a lot of student movement and conversation.

▶ Many times students who have cursed accidentally will try to convince you that they really said something else. Don't accept this.

- ▶ Pay attention, however, if a student is genuinely remorseful and immediately apologizes. At that point the negative consequences should not have to be enacted because the student has enough self-discipline to realize that the mistake should not have happened and has tried to undo the error. If the student continues to forget, then you should enact the consequences.

- ▶ Even though cursing is more common now than it used to be, you should not allow even mild words to just slip by without acting unless you want your students to believe that you think swearing in class is acceptable.

- ▶ No matter how tempted or angry you may be, never swear in class yourself. Your students need you to be a role model.

Category 2: Intentional Profanity

Some words are bombs. As soon as students say them, they know they have gone over the line of what is and what is not acceptable behavior. These are the hateful words that students throw at you or at other students when they are out of control with anger. This is a very different situation from the first category where a student does not mean to curse in front of you. In this type of incident, students deliberately use language to try to hurt the object of their anger. Most of the time these incidents also involve other problems: racial slurs or insults. Usually these incidents involve the "major" curse words . . . not just *hell* or *damn*.

You should not deal with this situation by yourself. This is a serious matter and should be taken seriously. You have two choices to make, depending on the severity of the offense:

- ▶ If you are convinced the student is really out of control with anger, send for help and have the student removed from the classroom at once. You should then follow through with a written referral to an administrator and by contacting the student's parents.

- ▶ If you think the student will not further disturb the class, you may allow him or her to remain, but you should refer the student to the attention of an administrator before the school day is over. The situation should be dealt with before the student returns to your class. You should also phone the parents or guardians to let them know what happened and that you have referred the child to an administrator.

HOW TO INTERVENE WHEN STUDENTS ARE TARDY

For many teachers one of the most persistent discipline problems does not concern violent misbehavior or loud challenges of authority; instead, it involves students who are tardy to class. Although this problem is not as immediately urgent as an out-of-control student who is in the midst of a tantrum, a tardy student can disrupt a class almost as effectively. Alert teachers must be aware of the negative influence inherent in tardy students and work to minimize the troublesome potential in their disruptive behavior.

Strategies for coping with tardy students must include ways to prevent the problem from becoming a serious one in your class, some general guidelines for dealing with tardy students, and techniques for coping with the two types of tardy students. The following techniques can improve the effectiveness of how you treat this problem in your class.

Prevention Strategies

▶ The first few class meetings are crucial in establishing the expectations you have concerning the prompt arrival of all students. Make tardiness control a strong priority on those five days and you will avoid many problems later in the term.

▶ The most obvious way to promote promptness is to be on time yourself. Your students will follow your example.

▶ You must make it important for your students to be on time to your class. Begin class the second the bell rings with an interesting and worthwhile assignment. When students rush to be on time, you know the tardiness problem is on its way to being solved.

▶ Reward those students who are in their seats and already working when the bell rings to begin class. You don't have to do this every day. You could reward students early in the term until they are in the habit of being on time to class and less frequently later. Some quick little rewards you could offer are stickers, bonus points on a test or quiz, a treat, a grade on their warm-up assignments, reduced homework, or a chance to enter a class lottery for rewards.

▶ Don't allow your students to lounge around the doorway between classes. They often slow down the arrival of other students and disrupt the smooth start of class with horseplay.

▶ Post your procedures and go over them as often as necessary in order to educate your students about the importance of being on time to class and the consequences of being late to class.

General Guidelines

▶ What do you mean by tardiness? Define it for your students. Most educators will agree that a student who is inside the room but not in a seat is not tardy; others are sticklers who insist that a student who is not sitting down is tardy. They have trouble justifying this interpretation to students and their parents. Be reasonable.

▶ Encourage your students to help each other be on time to class. For example, if students are late because they have forgotten their books, other students could remind them earlier in the day to bring their books to class. When you encourage your students to work together as a team, many of the problems you have with tardy students will disappear.

▶ Praise your classes as often as you can for their promptness. This is a pleasant way to reinforce their good behavior.

▶ Praise those individuals who overcome their tardiness problems. Express your appreciation for their maturing behavior.

▶ Whenever you discuss the problems of tardiness with students, put the responsibility for their behavior where it belongs. Ask your tardy students what steps they intend to take to eliminate the problem. Offer support and encouragement, but don't accept the blame for their errors.

▶ You must ask students why they are late. Do this privately later in the class period to minimize disruptions. When tardy students arrive in class, look at them and acknowledge their presence, but do not make all of the other students stop to watch as you interrogate the offending student.

▶ Don't accept shabby excuses. Set your established procedures into motion if you hear excuses that are not legitimate.

- Don't hesitate to ask parents or guardians for help with tardy students. These caring adults can often offer insights as well as some solutions to the problem.

- Never embarrass your students with sarcastic remarks such as, "We're glad you could finally make it!" or "It's about time you got here!" These will not earn you respect nor will they solve the problem.

Specific Types of Tardiness

Tardy students usually fall into two categories: the occasionally late student and the student who is habitually tardy. Both can be remedied.

- For the occasionally late student, allow one tardy to class per semester. Anyone could have a legitimate reason for being late to class one time. Forgiveness the first time shows a humanity and understanding that your students will appreciate and respect.

- After students have used their allotment of one late arrival without penalty, you should then regard them as habitually tardy students. Enact a system of increasingly punitive steps aimed at eliminating the problem. You will need to devise a step procedure with which you are comfortable. Here is a suggested one:
  - First tardy: Warning
  - Second tardy: Ten-minute detention and home contact
  - Third tardy: Fifteen-minute detention and home contact
  - Fourth tardy: Thirty-minute detention and home contact

- You and your habitually tardy students need to work together to understand the underlying reasons for their behavior. After you have done this, continue to hold them accountable for their actions.

HOW TO INTERVENE WHEN STUDENTS ARE TRUANT

A child's attendance record is one of the most reliable indicators we have of the social and financial pressures that take a toll on stressed families. When a family is in turmoil, the children have difficulty attending school regularly.

Of course, family problems are not the only reason that a child is chronically absent from school. Illness is a frequent cause, especially during the times of the year when respiratory illnesses seem to affect every student in our classes.

There are many other reasons for a student to miss too much school. In some families an education is not valued, and children are not expected to attend with regularity. In some others, older students are needed to help at home to take care of the younger ones when a parent works. Students who are also parents find it very difficult to continue their own schooling with the additional responsibilities of being parents themselves.

Some students miss several days in a row because of a legitimate reason and become so discouraged at the amount of work they have missed that they choose to sit out the rest of the term. We all know of students whose educational needs are not being met in the school setting where they are assigned and who unofficially drop out by refusing to attend.

Regardless of the causes, it is important that we encourage students to attend school regularly. Indeed, attendance is one of our most important responsibilities as educators and as adults who are concerned about the welfare of the young people in our care. Here are some suggestions that can help you cope with this serious discipline problem:

▶ Talk to the students to find out the reasons for their absence. Unless you do this you don't know whether to offer support or to involve other staff members in an effort to help the student.

▶ Contact the students' parents or guardians to make sure you are working together on the truancy problem. Some parents will request a phone call whenever their child is absent. Although this is time-consuming, it is worth it if the student realizes that he or she cannot cut class without getting caught.

▶ Make sure all of your students feel successful and involved in class so that they will have a reason to attend regularly.

▶ Create a policy for make-up work that will be useful in helping students stay caught up when they are out. This will prevent them from being too overwhelmed when they come back after an extended absence.

▶ Make sure your records are accurate. It's not easy to keep accurate attendance records, but this must be done if you want to be as fair as possible to students.

▶ Encourage students and their parents to keep a calendar of the days when they are out of school. Sometimes parents don't realize just how many days their children are out of school until they see such a reminder.

▶ Follow your school district's policy for attendance procedures. If you are the only teacher in the building who is not doing this, you will open yourself to accusations of unfairness.

▶ Send a letter home when students have missed the third day in your class. Keep a record of the letter as documentation that you contacted parents or guardians about a problem before it became serious.

▶ Make sure students who are not doing well in school understand their options. Some students believe they can drop out and pick up a GED certificate. They do not realize just how lengthy and rigorous the exam for this certificate is. Some students may be interested in attending classes at night to get ahead or to catch up if your district offers them. Have counselors speak to your students who are having trouble with attendance so that they understand the options that are available to them.

▶ If you have students who are in trouble at home and who are missing school because of family or social problems, seek help for them. Start with the counselors at your school to help your students find the kinds of social support that will help them be able to attend school.

HOW TO REDUCE EXCESSIVE TALKING

Every teacher is unique. We each have our own teaching methods, classroom management style, and learning philosophy. In spite of these individual differences, however, there is one problem that we all have in common. None of us—from the most skilled veteran to the recent graduate struggling with that difficult first semester—escapes this discipline problem. We all have to find ways to successfully manage the problem of excessive talking.

While the days of silent students have passed, the noise level in a class must still be appropriate for the activity that is under way. When students are off-task, they seldom amuse themselves quietly. The noise level in an unproductive class can be deafening. The students and the teacher suffer when this happens.

Although there are dozens of approaches to take when your students talk excessively, using just a few effective strategies will help you begin to solve this problem for yourself and for your students. Examine the following approaches in view of your own experience and use the ones you find helpful:

- Be emphatic with your students when you speak with them about this problem. You should make it very clear when it is okay for them to talk and when you want them to work silently. If you are clear in communicating your expectations to your students, they will not repeatedly test the limits of your tolerance for noise.

- Avoid the sound-wave effect of a loud class time followed by a quiet one followed by a loud one again. Be consistent in the way you enforce the rules in your class about excessive talking. Teachers who are not consistent spend their time getting the class quiet, allowing the noise level to build up to an intolerable level, and then getting the class quiet again in an endless and ineffective cycle.

- Make your students feel they can succeed in your class. Students who feel they are part of a worthwhile experience have a reason to stay on-task and to cooperate with you. They show respect for themselves and for their classmates when they have a reason to work. Students who do not care about their work, your expectations, and their classmates have no reason to respect the class rules about talking.

- Sometimes *you* are the problem. When your students are working quietly and productively on an assignment, don't keep talking to the class in general. When you repeatedly interrupt their work by distracting them with your own conversation, you make it harder for your students to work quietly.

- Begin every class with an activity that will focus your students' attention on the work they will be doing. This focusing activity will help them make a transition from the casual chatting they may have done in the hall on the way to your class to the purposeful work that you want them to begin.

- Teach your students that they must be responsible for their talking if you do not want to spend all class period "shushing" them. Use positive peer pressure to help them monitor each other's behavior so that your own monitoring efforts will be more effective.

- Direct their conversation if you have a group that likes to talk. Get them talking productively about the lesson. If you are successful at doing this, their need to interact with each other and your need to have them master the material will both be satisfied.

- Spend time observing your students to figure out why they are talking excessively so that you can turn this problem into an advantage. They may be talkative because they are excited, friendly, in need of more challenging work, unsure of the limits that you've set, or dozens of other reasons.

- If your students tend to talk when they have finished an assignment and are waiting for others to finish, sequence your instruction so that there is always an overlapping activity for your students to begin right away. This could be another in a series of assignments, a homework exercise, or even an optional assignment for enrichment.

▶ Sometimes when students are very excited, allow them to spend a minute or two talking to clear the air so that they can focus on their work. Be clear in setting time limits when you do this.

▶ Stay on your feet when your class has a problem with talking. Eye contact, proximity, and other nonverbal cues will help. Persistent and careful monitoring will encourage students to stay focused on their work rather than on conversation.

▶ During a movie or oral presentation when students may talk instead of listen, prevent this by giving them an activity to do. Students who are taking notes or filling out a worksheet will not have time for chatter.

▶ If the noise level is too loud, give students quiet activities that require them to write or read independently. These assignments should be designed to interest them, not just keep the class busy.

▶ Shifting gears from one activity to another is difficult for many students. Make transition times as efficient as possible in your class to avoid this problem.

▶ If the entire class persists in having a problem with excessive talking, chart their behavior for them to see tangible evidence of it. Create a bar graph each day where you rank their success at managing their problem with talking on a scale of one to ten. Sometimes students are not aware of the severity of a problem until they can see it in a format such as this.

▶ Move students who talk too much away from each other. Placing one of them near where you spend most of your time will help your monitoring efforts.

▶ Use good-natured, but firm signals to indicate that students should stop talking. Some signals that are appropriate for secondary-level students include writing a reminder on the chalkboard, holding up a silly sign on a poster, saying a code word that your students recognize, counting backward from ten, flicking the lights, ringing a bell, turning music on or off, putting your finger to your lips, holding your hands over your ears, writing a time-limit countdown on the board, holding your hand up and counting by folding your fingers, standing in the front of the room obviously waiting, having them put their pens down when you call for attention, or timing an activity and obviously watching the clock.

HOW TO AVOID POWER STRUGGLES

Do you recognize any of these students and their behaviors? Although students who want to engage in power struggles with the adults in their lives can appear in different guises, teachers can unfortunately find some guises easier to recognize than others:

▶ The student who complies with your directions—but at a deliberately and maddeningly slow pace

▶ The class clown who disrupts the flow of instruction with attention-grabbing comments

▶ The defiant student who is openly confrontational, oppositional, and rude

▶ The disrespectful student who somehow manages to be just rude enough not to be referred to the office

▶ The passively aggressive student who consistently does not have materials or completed work

▶ The student who can do well in school, but who chooses not to

▶ The student who has perfected the fine art of eye rolling when you give directions

Sometimes the frustration, stress, and misery caused by a student who wants to engage you in a power struggle may make intervention appear not worth the trouble. After all, unlike some discipline problems, often power struggles build slowly and require long-term solutions. Many teachers find it easy to adopt defensive attitudes:

▶ I can't change her anyway. Why even try?

▶ Only five more minutes of class left . . .

▶ It's May. Soon this will be another teacher's problem.

▶ If the parents can't do anything, why should I even try?

The long-term, heavy toll of a power struggle on students and their teachers makes action imperative. If teachers don't choose to act to resolve a power struggle, the results can be disastrous: a loss of instructional time, distracted students, the escalation of misbehavior, and unhappy and unproductive students.

To avoid a power struggle with students, it is important to know when to intercede to keep a student's misbehavior as nondisruptive as possible. It is far easier to prevent a student from misbehaving than to have to deal with a full-blown power struggle. One important component of this is to know when you should act. Try these guidelines:

▶ If a behavior is limited to one student, try to ignore it as much as you can.

▶ If a behavior is brief in duration, try to ignore it.

▶ If a behavior is distracting other students, it's time to act.

One of the unique features of a power struggle is that it is often easy for teachers to make mistakes in managing the issue. Our judgment can become so clouded with negative emotions that we have trouble coping successfully. To prevent this, remember to avoid these mistakes:

▶ Losing sight of the student behind the behavior

▶ Not adopting a problem-solving approach

▶ Not dealing with the stressful effect a defiant student can have on your day

▶ Ignoring the problem until it becomes difficult to manage

▶ Not involving parents and other concerned adults early on

▶ Losing your cool and otherwise showing your anger

▶ Using an office referral as a solution instead of as short-term relief

You can take several steps to cope successfully with students who want to engage in a power struggle. The first step you should take is to identify the positive and negative leaders among your students. Do this by observing their actions and the reaction of the rest of the class to them.

Next, turn negative leaders into positive ones with a delicate touch. What they want to do and are already pretty good at doing is simple: leaders want to lead. A wise teacher will give them plenty of constructive opportunities to do so—luckily there are plenty of those opportunities in every class period. Here are just some of the small actions you can take that will allow leaders to be productive instead of destructive influences in your classroom. Class leaders can

- ▶ Be the person who makes sure everyone knows what the homework assignment is
- ▶ Serve as the moderator in role-play situations
- ▶ Lead a class discussion
- ▶ Be the reporter for small-group discussions
- ▶ Speak for their classmates at assemblies and other meetings
- ▶ Serve as a liaison between you and the class
- ▶ Monitor groups working on class assignments
- ▶ Take class votes, collect money, and assume responsibility for issuing texts and passing out papers
- ▶ Manage debates or panel discussions
- ▶ Run errands and pick up supplies
- ▶ Consult with other students about choices in due dates, projects, and materials and report to you
- ▶ Greet guests and be the helper when there is a substitute

Be as overwhelmingly positive with your class leaders as you can. Never belittle them. You will only appear foolish, as the rest of the class immediately takes sides sympathetically with their classmates. Praise class leaders as often as you sincerely can.

Reinforcing their positive behaviors is the best strategy you can take with students who want to engage you in a power struggle. You will gain their cooperation as well as the approval of the entire class when you make it clear that you want everyone in the class to succeed.

As a final suggestion for avoiding a power struggle, it's important to maintain a level-headed approach to the problem. You won't be able to win over every student despite your obvious sincerity and very best efforts. It is unrealistic to expect otherwise of yourself and of your students.

HOW TO INTERVENE WHEN STUDENTS CHEAT

It's no secret to teachers, students, or parents that cheating is a widespread practice in classrooms. This plague affects all of us involved in education in one way or another. You do not have to stand by and let your students cheat. Honesty should be part of the culture of your classroom and, indeed, of all classrooms. You can prevent much of the cheating that could occur and lessen the negative impact of cheating once it does occur when you begin early to discuss this issue openly in your class.

You can take many positive actions to control this situation in the classroom. When you help your students feel confident about their mastery of the material and about their chances for success, you will decrease the pressures on them to cheat. In addition to this, you can make sure your students know just how you stand and what you will do if they cheat.

There also are many unsuccessful ways to try to control cheating. The worst action you can take is to ignore an incident of cheating. This makes you an accomplice. Another negative approach would be for you to "talk things over" with the child and not put any sort of consequence into effect. This sends a clear message to the student that you are willing to allow cheating under certain circumstances.

When you deal successfully and consistently with cheating incidents as they arise, you make your students aware that cheating is not going to be tolerated in your classroom. Dealing with cheating should be something you do consistently every day in your class, not just when you nab an offending student.

The most effective way to handle this issue is to use a two-step approach. The first step is to do everything you can to prevent cheating from happening at all. In the list that follows you should find some effective ways to do this. The second step involves the actions you can take once you discover a student has cheated. These tactics can improve the way you handle this serious discipline issue in your class.

Step 1: Prevention

▶ Know your school's policy on student cheating and follow it. If all teachers in a school consistently enforce a schoolwide policy on cheating, then the battle is almost won because students will know they are not supposed to cheat and what the consequences will be if they do.

▶ Make sure your students know exactly how you stand on this issue. State your position early and often throughout the term.

▶ Encourage students to talk about cheating during class discussions. They will surprise you with the insights and experiences they are willing to share with a concerned adult. There is tremendous negative peer pressure at work in classrooms concerning cheating. Class discussions will give your students guidance on how to handle it.

▶ One positive way to help your students become self-disciplined on this issue is to make a poster of their ideas on how to handle cheating. Ask your students to brainstorm some effective ways to prevent cheating.

▶ Another tactic to help your students see that they have options on this topic is to arrange for them to role-play sensible ways to handle cheating in various situations.

▶ Be a positive role model: don't be guilty of cheating yourself. Model honest behavior by annotating photocopied material and by respecting copyright laws for films, software, books, and other material. Be sure to tell your students why you do this.

▶ Discuss the need for honest behavior in all walks of life. Help your students see cheating as part of the big picture of life choices. Listen and advise. Don't lecture.

▶ When students are engaged in any sort of research, they should credit their sources. Even very young children can be made aware of the breadth of plagiarism and the importance of avoiding it. Show students how simple it is to credit sources and reward them when they do so.

▶ Tell your students whether it's okay to work together on an assignment or not. Don't assume that they know. State your expectations in advance of each assignment.

▶ Keep desktops and work areas clean so that you will notice if answers are written on them or if a stray cheat note is visible. Make it a habit to do a quick survey several times a day. Keep paper towels and cleaner on hand to wipe away any notes or answers.

▶ Before a test, ask students to neatly stow away their books, papers, and other materials as part of preparing for the test. Make it obvious that you are checking. If you do this, you can then monitor to make sure no tempting cheat notes are available.

▶ Don't allow students to talk during a test or quiz.

▶ Students should not turn sideways in their seats during a test. Talk to your students about taking a commonsense approach to avoiding the appearance of wrongdoing.

▶ Don't leave tests or quizzes on your desk where anxious students might be tempted to peek at them.

- If your students need a cover sheet for tests, provide it. Use recycled handouts or scrap paper.

- Don't allow students to have extra paper on their desks as a writing pad. Allow them to fold the test paper or issue an extra sheet of recycled paper to create a softer writing surface instead. Extra paper is an obvious hiding place for disguising cheat notes.

- Any questions your students may have during a test should be directed only to you. Walk over to the student who has a question. Students should remain seated during tests in order to avoid inadvertently seeing another's paper.

- Monitor your students very closely during a quiz or test. You can't do this by sitting at your desk. Move around the room frequently.

- Give several different versions of a test—even during the same class period. Do this often at the start of a term and at unpredictable intervals later.

- Don't use the same worksheets or tests year after year. Older students will frequently share these with younger ones.

- For a test where you expect lots of detailed memorization, consider allowing your students to bring in a small legal cheat sheet. Determine the limits of the size and the information on it in advance. This will lessen their anxiety and reduce the temptation to cheat.

- When students finish a test early, either have them keep their papers until you collect them all at once or have them turn them in and begin another assignment immediately. Bored students are far more likely to get into trouble than busy ones.

- Ask your students to tell you about all of the ways they have seen or heard of people cheating. Even the most experienced teachers are surprised at some of the sophisticated lengths to which many students will go to cheat.

Step 2: Dealing with Cheating Once It Has Occurred

- If you have caught a student cheating, the first thing you should do is arrange a private conference with the student to determine the reasons why he or she cheated. Sometimes students cheat because they have copied other students' work for so long that they really don't understand that doing so is not just cooperating with a classmate, but cheating. Others cheat because they have a very real fear of failure and are not prepared for class. Still others cheat because they do not see the relevance of the learning and of the tasks they are asked to perform. Whatever the reason, talk with the student in a calm manner to determine what went wrong and to help the student see other options that could prevent future cheating.

- When you catch one of your students cheating, contact his or her parents or guardians at once. Cheating is, without question, an issue that involves parents, teacher, and child.

- Put the school's policy on cheating incidents into action. Sometimes this means involving counselors and administrators. Make sure when you speak to parents or guardians that they understand what actions you will take.

- Unless your school's policy prohibits it, you may want to allow the student to make up the missing assignment. This would be an effective action if the offense was a first one and if you determined that this would be beneficial to the student after talking with the student and with the parents or guardians.

- If you suspect that a student is cheating on another teacher's assignment while under your supervision, don't accuse the child outright. Collect the work if you can and discuss it with the other teacher. If the child has cheated, you should work together to handle the problem.

- If you do catch a child cheating, protect the child's privacy. Never publicly accuse a student of cheating. Don't chat about a cheating incident with other students. Cheating should be treated with confidentiality.

- Don't ask a student to confide in you about another student's cheating. This is awkward and unfair to both students.

- Never accuse a student unless you are absolutely sure that cheating has occurred. You must have proof before you act.

- If a student confides in you that another is cheating, counsel that student about the best way to cope with this additional pressure. Make sure you take such confidences seriously and act with discretion to take the necessary steps to solve the problem.

- Once you have settled an incident with a student, forgive and forget. Convey this attitude to all guilty students and you will provide them with an incentive to start fresh and put their mistakes behind them.

Cybercheating

Although technology has greatly enhanced education for millions, it can also be used for a less positive purpose: cheating. Students who cybercheat do so in a variety of ways. Just a few of the ways students cybercheat include

- Purchasing essays
- Photographing tests and sending the digital image to classmates
- Texting answers to classmates
- Plagiarizing parts of essays
- Accessing notes stored on phones

Although the problem of cybercheating is widespread and growing rapidly with new developments in technology, there are several things that savvy teachers can do to manage the issue:

- Educate your students about what constitutes cheating. Many students are so accustomed to cutting and pasting information into essays and reports or sharing information with class-mates that they may not always understand what constitutes cheating.

- Make sure your students know that you are aware of the issue and that you will be checking their work for evidence of cheating.

- Browse some of the many online cheating advice sites maintained by less-than-ethical students. To access dozens of the most current sites, use a search term such as *how to cheat in school*. When you browse these sites, you will learn some of the many ways that students cheat while in class as well as tips for how to recognize that students are cheating electronically.

- Pay attention to your intuition. If a student's work seems to be too good to be true, it may be work that is copied.

- Don't recycle tests and essay topics year after year.

- Try to design instruction that is creative and fresh and that cannot easily be copied.

- Ask students to show all of their work on projects and essays. They should submit notes and drafts as well as final copies.

- Hold conferences with students where you discuss the methods they used to complete their work or ask them to summarize the main points of their essays or test answers.

HOW TO COPE WHEN STUDENTS STEAL

In most secondary classrooms an act of theft will put to a halt even the most interesting lessons you have planned. The unpleasant consequences of stealing go beyond the thief and the victim as the rest of the class is involved in trying to figure out who is to blame and what the victim should do when the guilty person is discovered. All of your efforts to establish an atmosphere of trust vanish as your students stare suspiciously at each other.

The strategies for coping with the discipline problems caused by stealing can be divided into two categories: prevention and techniques for coping with theft once it has occurred.

Prevention

- Be careful to remove temptation. Don't leave your personal belongings out in the open or on your desk. If you carry credit cards, be careful with them at school. Many street-smart teachers do not carry very much cash or take their credit cards to school.

- If you have school money, be extra careful to deposit it if it is meant to be deposited or to keep it in a safe place until you can. If you have school equipment that would be attractive to thieves, be extra careful to lock it away safely and to establish an accounting system for when you check it out for student use.

- Teach your students to be street smart also. Attractive school items that are often stolen are calculators, books, notebooks with notes, yearbooks, watches, jewelry, tapes, and electronic games.

- Discourage your students from bringing large amounts of cash to school and then letting others know about it. Your school should already have a policy that bans headphones, games, and other electronic toys that are easy to steal. Be sure to enforce it if one is already in place.

- Leave your classroom locked when you are not in it. Don't give your keys to students.

- Don't allow students to take things from your desk, closet, file cabinet, or other personal space without your permission.

What to Do Once Stealing Has Happened

- If your teacher's edition of the textbook or something else important to you is taken, offer a small reward for its return. State that you will ask no questions. Honor the "no question" rule even though you would like to know who took the item. What is important is that your belongings are returned to you.

- When you catch a student stealing, keep this information as private as possible. If your school's policy is that you should report theft to an administrator, then you should do so. Certainly the student's parents or guardians should be involved. You should, however, try to help that student maintain a sense of dignity in front of his or her peers.

▶ Try to find out why the student has stolen. Is there something you can do to help the student?

▶ The best thing you can do after a student has been caught is to help the student learn from the mistake and then go forward. Improve your personal relationship with students who are caught stealing so that they can begin to improve their sense of self. Improved self-esteem will help many teens—who might be tempted to go along with the crowd—to resist temptation.

▶ The most common mistake teachers who have an incident of stealing happen in their classrooms make is to keep all of the students in the room until either the item is found, someone tells on a classmate, or a student confesses. The lost class time involved in this procedure for an entire roomful of students is not usually worth the slim possibility of the item being returned.

WHAT TO DO WHEN STUDENTS ARE DEFIANT

The discipline problem many secondary teachers dread most is students who lose control and become defiant—or even violent. These angry students can be loud, abusive, and confrontational or they may resort to muttering, showing disrespect, and refusing to work.

In some ways, the more aggressive and confrontational student is easier to deal with because the intensity of the outburst demands immediate action. Because they often pose a danger to others with threats of violence, teachers don't ignore them. They significantly disrupt a class, but if they are handled quickly and productively, the incident is over. Teachers of these students are also quick to involve parents or guardians, counselors, security personnel, and administrators—all adults who can help.

The less-violent confrontational student poses another type of problem for many secondary teachers. It's not easy to correct students who may only be mumbling under their breath or rolling their eyes. Attempts to correct this behavior can result in vehement denials and accusations of unfairness. Because of the difficult nature of this problem, it is more common in secondary classrooms where many defiant students have had years of practice at being successfully disrespectful.

Defiant students of either type have a serious impact on the positive discipline climate we want to promote in our classrooms. Not only do they cause trouble for themselves, but they can perplex even the most caring teacher. The worst damage they do, however, is to the other students who watch the out-of-control behavior of their defiant classmates and wait to see what steps the teacher will take to deal with it.

To hone your classroom skills in dealing with defiant students, there are many things you can do to prepare yourself to successfully manage these students before they lose control and then to help them once an outburst has occurred. Use the following strategies to prevent defiant students from taking control of your class.

Strategy 1: Anticipate and Prevent as Many Problems as You Can

Many problems with confrontational students can be prevented or minimized with early action. Monitor the emotional weather of your classroom as students enter the room and continue to do so throughout class. If you see that a student is frustrated or upset, offer help and support as quickly as you can.

Too often we are so intent on the lesson we have to deliver that we ignore the unmistakable signs of stress in our students until it is too late. Some of these signs of trouble we need to attend to are

- Refusing to work
- Inattention
- Muttering under the breath
- Angry or exaggerated movements of the hands
- Loud voice
- Facial expressions that signal distress
- Imminent tears
- Work done poorly or not at all
- Note passing
- Slamming books or materials

Strategy 2: Plan What You Will Do If An Outburst Occurs

Even though it is unpleasant to contemplate, if you are a secondary teacher, you will have to deal with defiant students from time to time. Prepare yourself by planning what steps you will take to keep the disruption minimal. Some questions you should consider before a disruption occurs are

- How can I tell when I should act?
- Where will I send an angry student to ensure the safety of others?
- What signs should I pay attention to that will let me know a problem is brewing?
- Which of my students is already heading in this direction?
- What can I do in class tomorrow that will ease some of the stress that my defiant students may be feeling?

Strategy 3: Stay Calm When a Student Is Defiant

Although you should take an angry outburst or other sign of defiance seriously, you should not lose control of your own emotions and of the classroom situation. Keep your voice low. Do not give in to the temptation to threaten the student. Wait a moment or two to gather your thoughts. Often this brief delay will allow the student to calm down.

Strategy 4: Act Decisively

You must act calmly and quickly because the student has forced a showdown with you in front of the rest of the class. Those other students are now involved in that they are waiting to see what steps you will take to deal with the student and to protect them. Often defiant students will go to great lengths to engage in a power struggle. Be aware of this and keep it from happening. It will only make the situation worse. You should show you are serious, concerned, and in control.

Strategy 5: Remove the Defiant Student from the Room

As quietly and calmly as possible, remove the defiant student from the room. This will not only keep the disruption under control, but it will also save more embarrassment for the student who has misbehaved. You cannot begin to help a defiant student in front of an audience. Keep in mind that many school districts have policies that discourage teachers from simply removing a student. Be sure to have a specific destination for any student you send out of class. Arrange for students to have a time-out with another teacher, send them to a counselor, or refer them to an administrator.

Strategy 6: Take a Problem-Solving Approach, Not a Punitive One

When you begin to work with defiant students, acknowledge their feelings of anger and frustration as quickly as you can. While these are not an excuse for bad behavior, the student needs for you to pay attention to the reasons that the outburst happened. Students appreciate it, as we all do, when someone important to them takes them seriously, especially after they have been defiant. After this important first step, deal with the outburst and its causes.

Strategy 7: Make Sure the Work Is Appropriate for the Ability Level of the Students

Students can be frustrated if the work is too difficult or if it does not provide an interesting challenge. Having appropriate and meaningful work with a clear purpose will eliminate many problems. Establish a signal with a defiant student to let you know that the student's frustration is building. Once a student has said or shown the signal to you, take action to help that student.

Strategy 8: Raise Student Awareness of the Problem

If you have a student who persistently speaks to you and to others in a rude or inappropriate tone, tape-record that student so that he or she can hear how it sounds. A tape will also allow you to focus on what actions you do that may trigger the rudeness.

Strategy 9: Work on Your Relationship with Defiant Students

It is up to you as the adult in the classroom to make sure you have a positive relationship with all of the students in your class, even those who are confrontational or defiant. One of the best discipline tools that any secondary teacher can have is a positive relationship with students. Because all students need to be treated fairly, the same standards should apply to every student in your class—regardless of whether a student is frustrated or not.

SUBSTANCE ABUSE

Our social messages about drugs, alcohol, and tobacco are mixed. Teens are bombarded with messages that describe how grown-up these are while being told in an equal barrage that they can be lethal. Being flooded with optimism, many adolescents simply can't believe that the negative messages about these seductive symbols of adulthood really apply to them. They may apply to some other teens, perhaps, but not to them.

By the time teenagers are in secondary-level classes, they have had plenty of time to become thoroughly confused about substances that are illegal for them to use. Many teachers do not know how to help teens with this issue. We are, however, familiar with the negative consequences of teen substance abuse in our classrooms: failing grades, apathy, degraded self-esteem, failure to complete assignments, defiance, and the rejection of social values, to name just a few.

Many of us don't know how to respond when students come to class reeking of smoke or bragging about the fun time they had at a party over the weekend. Many of us are just not sure how far we should go in dealing with this issue. We don't want to overreact and make it impossible for students to come to us for help.

We want to think that educating students about drugs, alcohol, and tobacco is someone else's job: parents and family members. And it is, of course. But in many families the parents and other caregivers are just not aware of the problem or are not able to cope with it.

Educating students about substance abuse is one of our most important responsibilities. If teachers don't take a stand to help students understand all of their options about substance abuse and if family members can't, then who will?

If you want to help your students, but really aren't sure where to start, here is a list of ideas that could help you begin. After the list of suggestions for educating your students, you will find some procedures to follow if you suspect that one of your students is having trouble with illegal substances.

Preventing Substance Abuse

▶ Make students aware of the problems of substance abuse so that they will be able to make choices that are based on facts and the opinions of experts rather than merely on the opinions of their friends. A great deal of what many teens know about illegal substances involves information about the glamorous effects of drugs, tobacco, and alcohol and not the grim reality of addiction. Hold discussions on the issues related to all three substances. Invite students to share their opinions as well as the information and misinformation they already have.

▶ Inviting guest speakers who are older students is an excellent idea even if your own students are seniors. College students can be wonderful sources of information about this topic. Students will listen to older students who speak honestly to them while they will tune out teachers quickly.

▶ Make sure your students are aware of the health risks and social consequences of substance abuse as well as the legal penalties. Many students are unsure of the laws governing illegal substances and of the penalties if they are caught. Local law enforcement officials are often willing to talk with students about their legal rights and responsibilities.

▶ Your school district probably already has programs and policies in place to help students who struggle with this issue. The guidance office at your school is a good place to begin to find out about the community resources available to you and your students.

▶ Make sure all of your students are aware of the school policies concerning all three substances. Students need to know what the consequences will be if they break the rules concerning alcohol, tobacco, and drugs.

▶ The strongest defenses against teen substance abuse are education and a healthy self-esteem. Students who are confident in their ability to successfully manage their academic and social lives are well equipped to make sensible choices for themselves. Work with your students, their parents, and with the other professionals in your school to help students develop a strong positive self-image.

What to Do If You Suspect a Student Is Under the Influence

▶ Don't be tempted to overlook the problem the first time you notice that a student is in trouble in class. Immediately and calmly put your school's policy into effect.

▶ Remove the student from class at once as discreetly as you can. Speak to the student privately and in a nonaccusatory way in order to determine if a problem does exist.

▶ Contact an administrator, security guard, or the school nurse—whoever the person is at your school designated to handle this problem—and explain the situation as you see it. That person will conduct a search if one needs to be done and will then involve the parents and other appropriate school and community personnel.

▶ You should not blame the student or project anything but a supportive attitude. Offer to help the student with this problem and to work together to solve it. Students who have problems with substance abuse need support and encouragement from their teachers, not blame or unpleasant labels.

▶ Throughout your dealings with a student who is having problems because of substance abuse, keep in mind that this is a serious problem that needs to be handled with support from all of the adults in a student's life. You should not attempt to handle this situation without involving other adults.

Here are some resources that may make it easier for you to cope successfully with substance abuse issues in your class.

▶ Perhaps the best-known of all the organizations that help adults and teens deal with substance abuse issues, Mothers Against Drunk Driving (www.madd.org) offers resources, articles, activities, and other information to help stop underage drinking.

▶ The National Institute for Drug Abuse (http://teens.drugabuse.gov) offers a wide variety of tools, resources, games, and other helpful information geared for teachers, teens, and families.

▶ At the site maintained by Teen Help LLC (www.teendrugabuse.us), you can learn about specific drugs that students may be abusing as well as what you can do to help.

WHAT TO DO WHEN STUDENTS ARE VIOLENT

Every teacher's nightmare is that harm could come to our students while they are in our care. Our careers are based on the opposite idea. We want to help our students. Many of the rules and procedures we have established in our classes and in our schools are designed to help us protect our students from harm. A school fight is one of the most harmful events that our students can face.

Experienced teachers dread the first signs of a fight. If it is outside of our classroom, it usually begins with an increase in the noise level followed by students running and pushing each other to get to the fight scene. By the time teachers arrive, a large crowd usually is already gathered, blocking all attempts to stop the violence. At this point the noise and confusion become deafening as the crowd cheers on the students who are fighting.

When the fight is finally broken up, the energy level it generates affects the climate of the school and of our classes for the rest of the day. Our students do not want to settle down to work, preferring to discuss the fight blow-by-blow. An even worse effect is that often fights trigger a series of other conflicts as adrenaline and anger run high throughout the building.

In recent years the numbers of school fights have grown as more and more students bring their conflicts with others to school. As an educator, there are several things you can do to prevent fights from becoming an everyday occurrence and to lessen their adverse effect on the discipline climate of your classroom. An aware teacher can do a great deal to prevent a fight from ever beginning.

Fight Prevention

▶ Watch for the signs of trouble building up among your students. Use your teacher's intuition to determine if violence is likely. Counsel students whom you suspect might be at-risk for fighting. Contact parents and administrators to get assistance.

▶ Bullies often provoke violence. Refuse to allow any student to bully another in your presence. If you hear of an incident where one student teases or torments another, act at once to stop it. Sexual harassment is another form of bullying that can provoke a physical altercation. Make your students aware of the limits they should observe in how they treat members of the opposite sex.

▶ Teach your students that angry words and "playing around" can lead to violence very quickly. Teach this at the same time you teach them the importance of tolerance and courtesy. Encourage good behavior as often as you can. Refer to "Arming Our Students: Teaching the Art of the Alternative Response to Rude Classmates" in Section Eight to help you do this.

▶ Make sure your students are aware of the schoolwide policies your school district has in place to deal with students who fight at school. Most schools have a zero tolerance for fighting and impose severe penalties in many instances. Make sure your students are well-informed so that they can make sensible judgments for themselves before they choose to fight.

▶ Many schools also have programs in place that are designed to help students settle conflicts without violence. If your school does not have a conflict-resolution program, work with guidance counselors, other teachers, students, and administrators to establish one.

▶ Teach your students how you want them to behave during a fight. Make sure they know they are not supposed to block the area so that adults can't get through to stop it. Less-mature students who taunt and cheer on the participants in violence should be discouraged from inciting other students to fight.

▶ A strong adult presence in the cafeteria, restrooms, hallways, bus ramps, and other less-supervised areas of the school will help deter fighting.

▶ Be alert to the possibility of gangs in your school. Often abusive and violent, the widespread presence of gangs in schools has had a detrimental effect on school learning climates in every state. For more information and for ways that you can help your school deal with a gang presence, visit this site:

  ● At the site maintained by a division of the National Bureau of Justice (www.iir.com/ nygc), educators can find links, resources, statistics, and helpful information.

Once the Fight Has Begun

In addition to preventing school fights from beginning, you will probably be called on at some point in your career to break up a fight once angry students have lost control. This is one of the most stressful situations any teacher will have to face. The situation can be made even worse if there are injuries or weapons involved. Here are some suggestions to help you cope with this sad part of school life:

▶ Make sure you are aware of the procedures your school district expects you to follow to protect the fighting students, the crowd, and yourself from harm.

▶ If you are not physically able to stop the students who are fighting, immediately get help from nearby teachers or from the office. Do not leave the area to get help. Send a student if you cannot get help any other way.

▶ Once a fight begins, your first concern should be for the safety of all of the students involved either in the fight or who are in the area. Keep this safety issue in mind when you have to make crucial decisions quickly. You should also be careful in how you attempt to restrain violent students so that no one, including you, is injured.

▶ Be firm and clear with students who are watching the fight that you expect them to report back to class or to go to their seats if the fight takes place in your classroom.

▶ You may be asked to appear in court as a result of witnessing a fight. As soon as you can after an incident, jot down notes that will help you recall important details you may need in court months later. Pay attention to what led to the fight. Get the names of any witnesses.

▶ After a fight is over, model the calm, mature response that you want your students to have. Immediately resume teaching. Do not encourage a discussion of the fight in class: stick to your plans for the day's lesson if you possibly can.

▶ If the fight took place while the participants were under your supervision, contact their parents or guardians to make sure they know how concerned you are about the situation, and so that you can work together to keep it from happening again.

A Fight with Injuries

▶ Deal first with the injured student or students and then with the other students in the area. Send for the school nurse. Do not leave the scene. Send a student if necessary.

▶ If more than one student is injured, help the more seriously wounded student first. Unless you are a trained emergency medical technician, be very careful that the aid you provide does not make the situation worse.

▶ Protect yourself and others from contact with blood or other body fluids.

▶ If you are injured, be sure to seek medical attention for yourself.

A Fight with Weapons

▶ Be aware that there are more weapons stored in students' cars than there are in lockers or book bags. Contact a security guard or an administrator for help if you think an angry student is looking for a weapon.

▶ Before there is any violence, talk with your students about the danger of weapons at school. Make sure they know why they need to report a weapon at once and just how to go about doing so.

▶ If you suspect a student is armed, contact a security guard or an administrator immediately. This is definitely not a situation you should try to handle by yourself.

► If a weapon is used during a fight, make sure other students don't take it afterward. It will be used as evidence. If you are able, confiscate it until you can turn it over to an administrator.

WARNING SIGNS YOU SHOULD NOT IGNORE

One of the saddest aftermaths of school violence is the realization that some teachers have had that they may have been able to prevent a dangerous situation had they only recognized earlier that a student was severely troubled. Given the turbulent nature of the teen years where horseplay, moodiness, and exaggerated emotions are commonplace, educators may observe behaviors that may be outrageous but still age-appropriate.

While it may not always be easy to identify seriously troubled students, it is important to get to know your students well so that you can be alert for the signs of potential problems. One significant way to make this task easier is to forge a bond with the parents or guardians of your students so that you can be aware of any problems as quickly as possible. Although the warning signs of potentially violent students can include the following list, if you observe two or more of these in combination, you should be alert to the potential for serious problems:

► A lack of adult supervision

► Cruelty to animals

► A fascination with gangs and gang activity

► Increased conflicts with peers

► Evidence of being bullied

► Membership in a gang

► An increase in the frequency of discipline issues

► Evident of bullying others

► Incidents of abusive language and threats

► Lack of school-related motivation

► Incidents of misplaced or inappropriate anger

► Increased truancy

► A fascination with violence

► Repeated blaming of others

► Poor academic progress in general

► Evidence of substance abuse

► A sudden drop in academic performance

► Persistent isolation from others

For more information about the signs that all teachers should be alert to in their students, try these resources:

► The **National School Safety Center** offers many free resources to help educators learn how to prevent school violence at their Web site **(www.schoolsafety.us)**.

- A useful blog covering a wide variety of school violence issues can be found at **Keep Schools Safe (www.keepschoolssafe.org)**, an organization devoted to school safety, security, and the prevention of violence.

- At the site maintained by the **National Crime Prevention Council (www.ncpc.org/topics/school-safety)**, educators can access tips and resources geared to keeping schools safe.

To learn more about the positive choices you can make as your work to manage the potentially negative effects of misbehavior in your class, see this section's "Making Positive Choices."

Making Positive Choices

Instead of . . .	Try to . . .
▶ Waiting until a problem becomes serious and disruptive	▶ Intervene early to keep students safe and productive
▶ Allowing easily distracted students to be off-task	▶ Be proactive in planning strategies to help students who struggle with attention disorders
▶ Reprimanding an entire class that is having difficulty settling down to work	▶ Praise individuals who are ready for their good behavior so that the others know what is expected
▶ Engaging in a power struggle	▶ Work out ways that those students who seek power can be a positive force in your class
▶ Allowing tardy students to disrupt your class	▶ Work with latecomers to solve the problem that causes them to be late to class
▶ Allowing a student to misbehave day after day	▶ Set aside time to plan a strategy to prevent further misbehavior, rather than just reacting to each incident
▶ Writing an angry referral notice to send a student to the office	▶ Make an effort to regain your calm and professionalism before writing. Many different people will read the notice.
▶ Sending students to the office for minor infractions	▶ Ask yourself if you have tried every possible intervention
▶ Leaving a fight scene to get help	▶ Send reliable students for help
▶ Letting school problems build up until you are burned out	▶ Make a point of coping with the daily stresses of your professional life

QUESTIONS FOR REFLECTION

Use the information in this section to guide your thinking as you reflect on these questions. They are designed to encourage you to think more deeply about the issues in the text or to discuss those issues with colleagues.

- What type of discipline problems occur most frequently in your class? What techniques have you found helpful in coping successfully with them?

- How often do your students engage in serious misbehaviors such as defiance, fighting, or cheating? How do you cope when an incident happens? How can you help students once they have engaged in serious misbehaviors?

- How can you tell if a discipline action is appropriate? What interventions have worked well in the past for your students? What strategies in this section are ones that you believe would work well for your students?

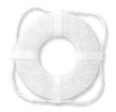

Index

Leaving room: procedure for, 142–144; to see school nurse, 319

Lesson planning, 13, 21

Letourneau, Mary Kay, 171

Limits: at beginning of school term, 9–10; desired by students, 7–8; setting and abiding by, 133–134. *See also* Boundaries

Listening: to parents, 151, 153, 156, 158, 159, 163; to students, 9, 19, 94, 170, 172, 186, 255, 289, 313; study skills for, 247–248; teaching students skills for, 51–52, 79

Literacy skills, 20, 169. *See also* Reading assignments

Lockdowns, 147

Long-term projects, 215–217

Losing your temper, 20, 52

M

Make-up work, 106–107, 145–146

Materials: shared, 142; students lacking, 315–316

Misbehaviors: behavior contracts to diminish, 123–127, 305; checklist of interventions for, 299–303; contacting parents about, 21, 306; detentions following, 281–283; in hallways, 317–319; ignoring, 297, 304; importance of early intervention with, 297–298; investigating, 296; keeping records of, 310–311; nonverbal language to stop, 59, 304; not to be tolerated in classroom, 16; preventing or minimizing, 22; student conferences following, 280–281, 305; students with chronic, 313–314. *See also* Behaviors; Discipline problems

Missed work, 106–107, 145–146

Missing homework, 213–214

Mistakes by students: inexperience as reason for, 8; reducing negative effects of, 9. *See also* Misbehaviors

Mistakes by teachers: causing discipline problems, 18–21, 276–280; with detentions, 283; trying to get students' attention, 51–52

Modeling, 118–119, 186–187

Modeling behaviors, 8, 21, 92

Monitoring students' behavior: importance of, 21, 235–236; strategies and techniques for, 236–238; by students themselves, 94–101

Mothers Against Drunk Driving (Web site), 338

Motivation, 243–274; active learning strategies for, 261–263; by arousing students' curiosity, 255–256; by creating classroom culture of excellence, 272–274; encouragement and praise for, 250; by enlarging learning environment, 271–272; extrinsic, 250–252; formative assessments for, 266–270; by giving instructions well, 244–245; inductive teaching strategies for, 263–264, 265; intrinsic, 252–255; positive choices for, 274; promoting self-discipline with, 92–93; reasons for students' lack of, 243–244; service projects for, 264–266; by stimulating critical thinking by students, 256–261; by teaching study skills, 246–249; Web site for, 244

N

National Crime Prevention Council (Web site), 65, 342

National Education Association (NEA) (Web site), 13

National Institute for Drug Abuse (Web site), 338

National School Boards Association (Web site), 296

National School Safety Center (Web site), 65, 341

Next Generation Training (Web site), 224

Noise levels, 77, 78–79

Nonverbal language, 58–59, 304

Note taking, 248

O

Online activities. *See* Computers

Online resources. *See* Web sites

Organizational skills, 217–218

P

Parents or guardians, 149–166; attitudes to help work with, 150–151; conferences with, 157–159, 306; contacting, about refusal to say "Pledge of Allegiance," 147; contacting, about student misbehavior, 21, 306; documenting contacts with, 160–161; e-mail correspondence with, 162; establishing positive relationship with, 151–156; expectations of, of teachers, 156–157; homework assignments and, 151, 207, 211, 212; maintaining relationship with, 151; maintaining student privacy as obligation to, 164–165; need for positive relationship with, 149–150; phone calls with, 162–163; positive choices for building relationship with, 165; what to expect from, 156

Participation: in classroom decisions, 21; in creation of classroom rules, 5; ensuring, of all students, 8

Passing out papers, 142. *See also* Collecting papers

Peace Education Foundation (Web site), 189

Peer conflicts: avoiding, due to rudeness, 189–190; preventing, 187–188; resolving, 188–189; violent, 338–342

Peer pressure, 5, 22

Performance: assessing, 35, 38; factors negatively impacting, 3; factors positively impacting, 3–4. *See also* Teacher self-assessments

Permissiveness, 54–56

Phone calls, with parents or guardians, 162–163

Physical environment, 71–80; arrangement of student desks in, 74–75; challenges limiting arrangement of, 71–72; ensuring safety of, 64; as important for positive discipline climate, 22; overcrowded classrooms as, 76–78; seating charts and, 75; shared classrooms as, 75–76; successful learning not dependent upon, 169–170; teacher's space in, 73; traffic flow in, 72–73; in well-disciplined classroom, 17. *See also* Classrooms

"Pledge of Allegiance," refusal to say, 147

Policies: classroom, 131–132, 133, 140–141; school, 20

Positive choices: to accept responsibility for creating discipline climate, 14; to adopt comprehensive approach to discipline, 30–31; to build cooperative classroom climate, 196; to build relationship with parents or guardians, 165; to cope with discipline problems, 342; to develop as classroom leader, 61–62; for effective instruction, 241; to establish classroom management system, 147–148; to establish positive classroom environment, 88; to motivate students, 274; to prevent discipline problems, 294; to promote self-discipline, 130

Positive classroom environment: classroom safety for, 64–71; created by preventing discipline problems, 275–276; importance of teacher's expectations to, 28–30; key elements of, 63; managing time for, 80–88; physical environment for, 71–80; positive choices to establish, 88; punishment as ineffective for creating, 4; resources on how to create, 12–13; steps for establishing, 18

Positive interactions with students, 102

Power struggles, how to avoid, 327–329

Praise: in difficult classes, 286; for entire class, 304; tips on using, 250

Preparation for class, 19, 50–51

Preventing discipline problems, 275–294; by avoiding unproductive comments, 279–280; benefits of, 275–276; caused by teachers, 276–280; by decreasing negative behaviors, 292–293; with detentions, 281–283; in difficult classes, 284–288; essay questions for, 283–284; by increasing positive behaviors, 289–292; positive choices for, 294; with student conferences, 280–281; by winning over difficult students, 288–289. *See also specific problems*

Privacy, student: necessity to maintain, 164–165; when students confide in teachers, 185–186

The Problem Site (Web site), 220

Problem solving: as approach to discipline problems, 297; to promote self-discipline, 116–117

Productive classroom environment. *See* Positive classroom environment

Profanity, how to manage, 321–322

Professionalism: behaviors for conducting yourself with, 47–49; to establish productive classroom environment, 18; importance of, for classroom management and discipline, 21; teacher's behaviors exhibiting, 13

Progress reports, 153–154

Punishment: avoided in productive classroom environment, 18; homework assigned as, 207, 241; ineffectiveness of, 4; mistakes made in assigning, 278

Q

Questions: asking productive, 218–220; to encourage self-discipline, 99; essay, to solve discipline problems, 283–284; to stimulate critical thinking, 258–260

R

Reading assignments. *See also* Literacy skills

Reading assignments, study skills for, 247

Reasons for learning, helping students understand, 7, 20, 201

Referring students to office, 306, 308–310

Relationships, peer, 22. *See also* Teacher-student relationship

Relevance, built into instruction, 7, 20, 201

Respect: how to gain, from students, 52–53; mutual, in well-disciplined classroom, 17; showing, for students, 9, 52–53; when handling discipline problems, 313; when saying "no," 134–135

Responding to discipline problems. *See* Coping with discipline problems

Responsibility: for discipline climate, 2–3; students taking, for learning, 17; for teacher's attitude about discipline problems, 14, 18

Role models, teachers as, 8, 21, 92, 118–119, 186–187

Rudeness, alternative responses to, 189–190

Rules, school, 20, 71. *See also* Classroom rules

S

Safety. *See* Classroom safety

Saying "no," 134–135

Schimmel, David, 296

Scholastic (Web site), 75, 164

School climate, negative, difficulty of establishing positive classroom environment in, 168–169

School Law (Schimmel, Fischer, and Stellman), 296

School Notes (Web site), 164

School nurse, requests to see, 319

School rules, 20, 71

SchoolNet (Web site), 169

Seating charts, 75

Self-discipline, promoting, 91–130; by assisting students with ADD, 104–105; behavior contracts for, 120–127, 305; of behavior in hallways, 318–319; behavior modeling for, 92, 118–119; by being consistent, 93–94; by being encouraging and positive, 93; with classroom procedures, 132–133; by encouraging struggling students, 102–104; by focusing on students' strengths, 101–102; by helping impulsive students, 104; by helping students make up missed work, 106–107; by holding students accountable, 93, 128–130; by improving students' self-image and -esteem, 107–109; by increasing positive interactions with students, 102; by linking success to effort, 92; by maintaining high standards, 92; by motivating students, 92–93; positive choices for, 130; problem-solving activities for, 116–117; by supporting underachieving students, 105–106; by teaching good decision making, 115–116; by teaching self-monitoring, 94–101; by teaching setting and achieving goals, 109–114

Self-esteem, of students, 109

Self-evaluation, of self-discipline, 99

Self-image, of students, 107–109

Service projects, 264–266

Skills: literacy, 20, 169, 206; social, 183–184, 189–190. *See also* Study skills

Sleeping students, 19, 314–315

Smart, Pamela, 171

Social skills: for responding to rudeness, 189–190; teaching, 183–184

Standards. *See* Expectations

Stealing, 333–334

Stellman, Leslie R., 296

Strengths, focusing on, 101–102

Stress: vs. challenge for students, 66–67; changing perception of, 46–47; preventing, 45–46

Strict teachers, 4

Student conferences, 280–281, 305

Student notebooks, 217–218, 257

Student worksheets: Assignment Checklist, 97; to help students remember rules, procedures, and policies, 133; Homework Questionnaire for Students, 209; How Stressed Are You? 67; Missing Homework Explanation Form, 213–214; Missing Work Reminder List, 146; My

Goals for Today, 98; Parent-Teacher-Student Homework Notification Form, 212; The Progress of My Grades, 99; Reflection Sheet for Formative Assessments, 270; Sample Group Contract, 127; Self-Evaluation Form, 100; Setting Long-Term Goals, 111; Setting Mid-Term Goals, 113; Setting Short-Term Goals, 114; Student Inventory: Attitudes, 175–177; Student Inventory: Impressions, 173–174; Student Inventory: Reactions of Others, 178; Student Progress Checkup Form, 154; Student Sign-Out Sheet, 144; What Did You Learn from This Assignment? 269; Your Class Goals, 96

Students: with ADD, 104–105; assessing what you want said about you by, 57; character traits of, 5–9; confiding in teachers, 185–186; distractions preventing focus on, 34; general behaviors of, 10–12; helping, learn about each other, 190–192; impulsive, 104; obtaining data on your performance from, 38; paying attention to needs of, 59–60; struggling academically, 102–104; techniques for getting to know, 172–180; underachieving, 105–106; winning over difficult, 288–289

Study skills: assuming students have, 20, 246; list of, for secondary students, 246–248; teaching, 9, 217–18, 246

Substance abuse, 336–338

Substitute teachers, 239–241

Success: high expectations and, 29; holding students accountable for their, 128–130; linking effort to, 92

Suggestion box, 38, 183

Supplies: shared, 142; students lacking, 315–316

Survey Monkey (Web site), 38

Syllabus: homework assignments on, 207, 210; missed work and, 106, 107; parents and, 151, 207; to prevent discipline problems, 238–239; as time management aid, 7, 30, 95

T

Talking: reducing excessive, by students, 325–327; students paying attention to, by teacher, 51–52. *See also* Language

Tardiness, 322–324

Teacher self-assessments: Are You Too Permissive? 54–56; Classroom Leadership Self-Assessment, 37; Determine What You Want Your Students to Say About You, 57; How Well Do You Convey Your Enthusiasm? 36; How Well Do You Give Instructions? 245; How Well-Disciplined Is Your Class? 23; How You Can Determine If a Discipline Action is Appropriate, 307; Sample Self-Rating Rubric, 39; Think It Through: How Would You Rate Your New Discipline Plan? 27

Teacher Tools (Web site), 156

Teacher Web (Web site), 164

Teacher worksheets: Behavior Analysis Log, 312; Behavior Modeling Chart, 119; Behavior Record Form, 311; Behaviors and Interventions Checklist, 299–303; Checklist of Social Skills All Secondary Students Should Master, 184; Contact Documentation Form, 161; Develop Your Classroom Discipline Plan, 24–26; Group Monitoring Form, 230; Parent or Guardian Inventory, 179; Sample Assignment Contract, 121–122; Sample Behavior Contract One, 124; Sample Behavior Contract Two, 125; Sample Introductory Letter, 152; Setting Goals for Improving Your Classroom Leadership, 40–44

Teachers: adolescent character traits challenging, 5–9; as classroom leaders, 33, 37–44, 61–62; as coaches, 34–35; discipline climate as responsibility of, 2–3; discipline problems experienced by all, 1, 3; distractions preventing focus on students by, 34; as most important factor in creating positive discipline climate, 33; placement of desk for, 73; as role models, 8, 21, 92, 118–119, 186–187; Web sites for networking by, 169

Teacher's Pocket Guide to School Law (Essex), 296

Teachers.Net (Web site), 169

Teacher-student relationship: acquiring knowledge about students for, 172–180; actions to foster personal, 170–171; basics of good, 171–172; boundaries in, 181–182; caring, 22, 180–181

Technology. *See* Computers

Teen Help LLC (Web site), 338

Teenagers, character traits of, 5–9. *See also* Students

Tests, study skills for, 248–249

TheApple (Web site), 169

Time management. *See* Class time

Toys to Tools (Kolb), 317

Transitions: ensuring student engagement during, 84–86; reducing disruptions during, 83–84

Transparent classroom, 20, 151

Truancy, 324–325

V

Values, discussing, 5

Vandalism, 320–321

Violent students, 338–342

Virtual classrooms, 76

Visitors in classroom, 147

W

Weapons: classroom safety and, 64, 65; fights with, 340–341; referrals for, 308

Web pages: for communicating with parents or guardians, 163–164; creating, 76

Web sites: on classroom layouts, 75; on classroom safety, 65; on conflict resolution, 189; on coping with discipline problems, 296; for creating and maintaining class Web pages, 164; for creating surveys, 38; on cyberbullying, 71; for educational games, 220, 224; on gangs, 339; for information on creating positive discipline climate, 13; for motivating students, 244; for networking with colleagues, 169; for planning calendars, 50; on school violence and safety, 341–342; for service projects, 266; on substance-abusing students, 338; for templates for communicating with parents, 155–156; on using technology for instruction, 224–229

Well-disciplined classroom: characteristics of, 16–17; self-assessment of, 23

Wired Kids, 71

Worksheets. *See* Student worksheets; Teacher worksheets

Writing assignments, study skills for, 246

Y

You Can Handle Them All (Web site), 13